Contents

Swami Vivekananda
Philosoper, Litterateur, Visionary 9

I INTERACTIONS 15

Annie Besant 17
Bal Gangadha Tilak 18
Bipin Chandra Pal 19
Mohandas Karamchand Gandhi 24
C.F. Andrews 24
Chakravarti Rajagopalachari 25
Rajendra Prasad 25
Arcot Ramaswami Mudaliar 26
Benoy Kumar Sarkar 27
Sarvepalli Radhakrishnan 30
Jawaharlal Nehru 31
Subhash Chandra Bose 33
Jayaprakash Narayan 33
Lal Bahadur Shastri 34
Indira Gandhi 35
First Meeting With John D. Rockefeller 36

First Meeting With Madame Emma Calve 37
Jagadish Chandra Bose 39
Munshi Premchand 39

II LECTURES AND DISCOURSES 41

The Great Teachers Of The World 43
The Sages Of India 58
The Ramayana 77
The Mahabharata 91
The *Gita* I 114
The *Gita* II 126
The *Gita* III 133
Christ, The Messenger 145
Mohammed's Message To The World 160
On Lord Buddha 163
Religion Is Self-Abnegation 166
Religion Is Realisation 167
Response To Welcome At The
World's Parliament Of Religions 168
Why We Disagree 170
My Life And Mission 172

III VEDANTA, BHAKTI AND CULTURE 191

Practical Vedanta 193
The Vedanta In All Its Phases 210
The Forms Of Love Manifestation 237
The God Of Love Is His Own Proof 239
Narada Bhakti Sutras 242
On Art 247

On Music 248
On Food 249

IV Philosophy 251

On Professor Max Muller 253
On Dr. Paul Deussen 258
Hinduism And Sri Ramakrishna 264
Sri Ramakrishna: The Significance Of His Life And Teachings 270
On Sri Ramakrishna And His Views 272
Sri Ramakrishna: The Nation's Ideal 274
Sri Ramakrishna's Disciple 275
The Soul And God 276
Steps To Realisation 289
On Sannyasa And Family Life 301
On Mantra And Mantra Chaitanya 302
Sadhanas Or Preparations For Higher Life 303
Reincarnation 309

V Shiva And Krishna 325

The Dance Of Shiva 327
Shiva In Ecstasy 328
To Shri Krishna 329
The Story Of The Boy Gopala 330

VI On India 333

Historical Evolution Of India 335
The Story Of Jada Bharata 346

India's Message To The World 351
The Education That India Needs 360
Struggle For Expansion 367
The Problem Of Modern India
And Its Solution 370

VII Man and Freedom 381

Nature And Man 383
The Reality And Shadow 387
The Power Of The Mind 388
The Importance Of Psychology 391
Freedom Of The Self 396
Law And Freedom 397
Man The Maker Of His Destiny 402
On Doing Good To The World 407
The Goal 409
Work Is Worship 410
On Charity 412
On Fanaticism 413
Worldwide Unity 416
The Free Soul 417

VIII Yoga 431

Four Paths Of Yoga 433
Karma In Its Effect On Character 437
The Ideal Of Karma Yoga 445
Bhakti Yoga 455
The Chosen Ideal 462
The Method And The Means 465
The Mantra: Om: Word And Wisdom 471

Worship Of Substitutes And Images 475
Preface To Raja Yoga 478
Prana 481
The Psychic Prana 494
Pratyahara And Dharana 500
Dhyana And Samadhi 508
Introduction To Jnana Yoga 518
Maya And Illusion 523
The Cosmos 540
Immortality 549

IX CITIES AND PLACES 561

The Advaita Ashrama, Himalayas 563
The Shrine Of Amarnath 565
The Vale Of Kashmir 570
At Nainital And Almora 573
The House On The Ganga 577
Walks And Talks Beside The Jhelum 582
The Belur Math: An Appeal 589
Swami Vivekananda On Education At Belur 591
The Ramakrishna Home Of Service, Varanasi: An Appeal 593
The Temple Of Pandrenthan 596
On The Way To Kathgodam 604

X HYMNS 607

The Hymn Of Creation 609
To The Awakened India 611
Peace 613
Requiescat In Pace 615

A Hymn To The Divinity Of
Sri Ramakrishna 617
A Hymn To Shiva 620
And Let Shyama Dance There 623
The Hymn Of Samadhi 628

XI FOREIGN PRESS 629

Religious Harmony 631
Vedantism, And What It Is And
What It Is Not 634
On The Brahmo Samaj 636
Child Widows Of India 637
The Women Of India 639
Hindu Widows 644
Philosophy Of Freedom 645
India's Gift To The World 647
Swami Vivekananda On Love 651
An Indian Ascetic 654

Swami Vivekananda

Philosoper, Litterateur, Visionary

Born on 12 January 1863 into an affluent Bengali family in Calcutta, Narendranath Dutta, was one of eight children of Vishwanath Dutta, a successful attorney with interests in a wide range of subjects and considerable influence in society, and Bhuvaneshwari Devi, a woman with a strong, God-fearing mind, who would have a great impact on her son.

As a young boy, Narendranath stood out for his intellect. His mischievous nature notwithstanding, he had a keen interest in both instrumental and vocal music. He was an excellent student, first at the Metropolitan Institution, and later at the Presidency College in Calcutta. By the time he graduated from college, he was well-versed in several subjects. Active in sports, gymnastics, wrestling and body-building, Narendranath, a voracious reader, studied the Hindu scriptures like the *Bhagavad Gita* and the Upanishads with as much interest and fervour as Western philosophy, history and spirituality by David Hume, Johann Gottlieb Fichte and Herbert Spence, among others.

Despite growing up in a religious atmosphere, on the threshold of youth, Narendranath battled a spiritual crisis. Armed with vast knowledge, he questioned the existence of

God, leaning towards Agnosticism for a while. Yet it was difficult for him to completely ignore the existence of a Supreme Being. He even associated with the Brahmo Samaj movement led by Keshab Chandra Sen, for some time. Unlike various sects of Hinduism, the Bramho Samaj recognised one God. Nonetheless, the philosophical questions on young Narendranath's mind on the existence of God remained largely unanswered. It was during this phase of his life that Narendranath first heard about Sri Ramakrishna from William Hastie, the Principal of Scottish Church College.

Narendranath had already sought answers from prominent spiritual leaders of all religions to a single question, "Have you seen God?" None were able to satisfy the seeker in him. One day, in November 1881, he asked the same question to Sri Ramakrishna at the latter's residence in Dakshineshwar Kali Temple compounds. An unhesitant Sri Ramakrishna replied simply: "Yes, I have. I see God as clearly as I see you, only in a much deeper sense." Narendranath was astonished at Sri Ramakrishna's reply. Over time, with patience and pure, unselfish love, Sri Ramakrishna won over the young and argumentative Narendranath, marking the beginning of a unique guru-disciple relationship. Narendranath frequented Dakshineshwar and, under the guidance of the Master, made rapid strides on the path to spirituality. At Dakshineshwar, he also met other young men devoted to Sri Ramakrishna, and they all became close friends.

In 1884, Narendranath's father passed away. His mother and younger siblings turned to him to bail them out of penury. When Narendranath asked Sri Ramakrishna to pray to the Goddess for the financial welfare of his family, he was advised to pray to the Goddess himself. Narendranath did go to the temple to pray but asked the Goddess for 'vivek' (conscience) and 'bairagya' (reclusion) instead of money and wealth. That marked the complete spiritual awakening of Narendranath already drawn to an ascetic way of life.

In mid-1885, Sri Ramakrishna, afflicted with throat cancer, took gravely ill. In September 1885, he was moved to Shyampukur in Calcutta. A few months later he was moved to a villa at Cossipore. Here, a group of young ardent followers of Sri Ramakrishna nursed their Master. Despite poverty at home and inability to find himself a job, Narendranath joined the group as its leader.

Sri Ramakrishna instilled in these followers the spirit of renunciation and brotherly love for each other. One day he gave them ochre robes and sent them out to beg for food, thereby laying the foundation for a new monastic order. He gave specific instructions to Narendranath about the new order. On 16 August 1886, Sri Ramakrishna gave up his mortal body.

Thereafter, fifteen of his young disciples (one more joined them later) began living together in a dilapidated building at Baranagar—Baranagar Math—in North Calcutta. Under the leadership of Narendranath, they formed a new monastic order. In 1887, they formally renounced all ties with the world, took the vows of sannyasa, and assumed new names. Narendranath became Swami Vivekananda or "the bliss of discerning wisdom" (although he assumed this name much later).

The brotherhood lived off on alms donated by patrons, performed yoga and meditation. While most followers perceived Sri Ramakrishna in relation to their own lives, Swami Vivekananda perceived him and his message in relation to India and the world. Additionally, the awareness of his own powers urged Swami Vivekananda to go out into the world. In mid-1890, after being blessed by Sri Sarada Devi, the divine consort of Sri Ramakrishna, known as the Holy Mother, who was then staying in Calcutta, Swami Vivekananda left the Baranagar Math for a tour of India on foot, absorbing the social, cultural and religious aspects of the people he came in contact with. He also witnessed the hardships of the poor masses and vowed to dedicate his life to alleviating their suffering.

Centuries of oppression had robbed the masses of the faith in their capacity to improve their lot. That faith needed to be restored. They needed a life-affirming message that Swami Vivekananda found in the principle of the Atman, the doctrine of the potential divinity of the soul, taught in Vedanta, the ancient system of religious philosophy of India. He understood that despite their poverty, the masses clung to religion, without ever been taught the life-giving principles of Vedanta and their practical applicability. Thus, the masses needed two kinds of knowledge: secular knowledge to improve their economic condition, and spiritual knowledge to restore their faith in themselves and strengthen their moral sense. The only way to disseminate these two kinds of knowledge was through education.

To spread education and work for the uplift of the poor masses and women, an efficient organisation dedicated to bringing the "noblest ideas to the doorstep of even the poorest and the meanest to the people was needed". That motivated Swami Vivekananda to found the Ramakrishna Mission a few years later.

In the course of his wanderings, Swami Vivekananda heard about the World's Parliament of Religions to be held in Chicago in 1893. His friends and admirers in India were keen for him to attend the Parliament. He too felt that the Parliament would provide the right platform to present his Master's message to the world. Swami Vivekananda was also keen to visit America to seek financial help for the uplift of the poor masses in India.

His inner certitude about his mission and his divine calling were both reaffirmed while he sat in deep meditation at Kanyakumari, a coastal town in Tamil Nadu. With the funds collected partly by his Madras disciples and partly provided by the Raja of Khetri, Swami Vivekananda left Bombay on 31 May 1893 for America.

On 11 September 1893, at the World's Parliament of Religion in Chicago, he stunned everyone with his opening line: "Sisters and brothers of America..." The audience responded with a standing ovation. He went on to describe the principles of Vedanta and their spiritual significance, putting Hinduism on the map of World Religions.

For his speeches at the World's Parliament of Religions, he came to be known as an 'orator by divine right' and a 'Messenger of Indian wisdom to the Western world'. After the Parliament, Swami Vivekananda spent nearly three and a half years mostly in the eastern parts of America and also in London spreading Vedanta as lived and taught by Sri Ramakrishna. He founded the Vedanta Society of New York in 1894.

In 1897, Swami Vivekananda returned to India to a rousing welcome. After a series of lectures across the country, he founded the Ramakrishna Mission on 1 May 1897 at Belur Math near Calcutta. The goals of the Mission were based on the ideals of Karma Yoga, with its primary objective being to serve the poor masses in India. Amongst its many initiatives, the Mission established and ran schools, colleges, hostels, hospitals, rural development centres, conducted massive relief and rehabilitation work for victims of earthquakes, cyclones and other calamities, in different parts of India and other countries, and propagated Practical Vedanta through conference, seminars and workshops.

Swami Vivekananda's message was an amalgamation of Sri Ramakrishna's teachings and his own understanding of Advaita Vedanta. He urged people to achieve divinity of the soul through selfless work, worship and mental discipline.

In early 1898, Swami Vivekananda acquired a large plot of land on the western bank of the Ganga at Belur; he wanted a permanent abode for the monastery and monastic order started at Baranagar. A couple of years later, he had it registered as Ramakrishna Math. At Belur Math, he established a new, universal pattern of monastic life, adapting ancient monastic ideals to the conditions of modern life, giving equal importance to personal illumination and social service. The Math was open to all men without any distinction of religion, race or caste.

In June 1899, Swami Vivekananda travelled to the West coast of America. After delivering many lectures there, he returned to Belur Math in December 1900. He spent the rest of his life in India, inspiring and guiding people, both monastic and lay.

A prominent nationalist, Swami Vivekananda had the welfare of his countrymen topmost on his mind: "Arise, awake and stop not till the goal is reached."

Swami Vivekananda had predicted that he would not live till the age of forty. The hectic pace of his work, especially giving lectures and inspiring people, took a toll on his health. On 4 July 1902, he went about a usual day's work at Belur Math, teaching Sanskrit grammar to the pupils. He retired to his room in the evening and the end came quietly during meditation at around 9. He was cremated on the banks of the Ganga.

Before his Mahasamadhi, he had written to a Western follower: "It may be that I shall find it good to get outside my body, to cast it off like a worn-out garment. But I shall not cease to work. I shall inspire men everywhere until the whole world shall know that it is one with God."

I

INTERACTIONS

Annie Besant

A striking figure, clad in yellow and orange, shining like the sun of India in the midst of the heavy atmosphere of Chicago, a lion head, piercing eyes, mobile lips, movements swift and abrupt—such was my first impression of Swami Vivekananda, as I met him in one of the rooms set apart for the use of the delegates to the Parliament of Religions. Off the platform, his figure was instinct with pride of country, pride of race—the representative of the oldest of living religions, surrounded by curious gazers of nearly the youngest religion. India was not to be shamed before the hurrying arrogant West by this her envoy and her son. He brought her message, he spoke in her name, and the herald remembered the dignity of the royal land whence he came. Purposeful, virile, strong, he stood out, a man among men, able to hold his own. On the platform another side came out. The dignity and the inborn sense of worth and power still were there, but all was subdued to the exquisite beauty of the spiritual message which he had brought, to the sublimity of that matchless truth of the East which is the heart and the life of India, the wondrous teaching of the Self. Enraptured, the huge multitude hung upon his words; not a syllable must be lost, not a cadence missed! 'That man, a heathen!' said one, as he came out of the great hall, 'Great Thinkers Ramakrishna-Vivekananda and we send missionaries to his people! It would be more fitting that they should send missionaries to us!'

Bal Gangadhar Tilak

It is doubtful if there is any Hindu who does not know the name of Shri Vivekananda Swami. There has been extraordinary advancement of material science in the nineteenth century. Under the circumstances, to present the spiritual science prevailing in India for thousands of years by wonderful Great Thinkers on Vivekananda exposition and then to kindle admiration and respect among the Western scholars, and, at the same time, to create a sympathetic attitude for India, the mother of spiritual science, can only be an achievement of superhuman power. With English education, the flood of material science spread so fast that it required extraordinary courage and extraordinary genius to stand against that phenomenon and change its direction. Before Swami Vivekananda the Theosophical Society began this work. But it is an undisputed fact that it was Swami Vivekananda who first held aloft the banner of Hinduism as a challenge against the material science of the West. It was Swami Vivekananda who took on his shoulders this stupendous task of establishing the glory of Hinduism in different countries across the borders. And he, with his erudition, oratorical power, enthusiasm and inner force, laid that work upon a solid foundation. Twelve centuries ago Shankaracharya was the only great personality, who not only spoke of the purity of our religion, not only uttered in words that this religion was our strength and wealth, not only said that it was our sacred duty to preach this religion in the length and breadth of the world—but also brought all this into action. Swami Vivekananda is a person of that stature—who appeared towards the last half of the nineteenth century.

Bipin Chandra Pal

I

Vivekananda, however, does not stand alone. He is indissolubly bound up with his Master, Paramahansa Ramakrishna. The two stand almost organically bound up, so far as the modern man, not only in India but in the larger world of our day, is concerned. The modern man can only understand Paramahansa in and through Vivekananda, even as Vivekananda can be understood only in the light of the life of his Master. The Master was a great spiritual force. He was, therefore, inevitably a mystery to a generation possessed by the un-understood slogans of what is called rationalism, which really means lack of that imagination which is the soul of all spiritual life. Imagination is not fancy. It is really the power to cognise, if not to visualise, that which stands above not only the sensuous but also the intellectual plane. The generation to which Ramakrishna belonged, lacked this imagination. He was, therefore, a mystery to it. It was given to Vivekananda to interpret and present the soul of Paramahansa Ramakrishna and the message of his life to this generation in such terms as would be comprehended by them.

Ramakrishna Paramahansa belonged to no sect or denomination or to put it in another way, he belonged to all sects and denominations both Indian and non-Indian. He was a true Universalist, but his Universalism was not the Universalism of Abstraction. He did not subtract the particularities of different religions to realise his universal religion. With him the Universal and the particular always went together like the sun and shadow. He realised, therefore, the Reality of the Universal in and through the infinite particularities of life and thought. Vivekananda clothed this realisation of his Master in the language of modern Humanism.

Ramakrishna Paramahansa's God was not the God of logic or philosophy, but the God of direct, personal, inner experience. Ramakrishna believed in his God not on the authority of ancient scriptures or traditions, nor on the authority of any guru, but on the testimony of his own direct, personal experiences. He was a Vedantist; because, his direct allegiance and early training was in the cult of Bhakti. The Bhakti cult in Bengal has been built upon Vedantism. But the Vedantism of Ramakrishna Paramahansa could hardly be labelled as Shankara Vedantism, nor could it be labelled either as any of the different schools of Vaishnava Vedanta. These labels are for those who borrow their theology from speculations of great thinkers. But Ramakrishna Paramahansa did not belong to this class. He was not a philosopher; he was not a Pundit, whether modern or ancient; he was not a logician; he was a simple seer. He believed in what he saw. The seer is always a mystic. So was Paramahansa Ramakrishna: so was Jesus; so were all the great spiritual leaders of men. The crowd cannot understand them; least of all are they understood by the learned and the philosophers of their age. Yet they reveal that which all philosophies grope after. Paramahansa Ramakrishna, like Jesus Christ, needed an interpreter to explain him and deliver his message to his age. Jesus found such an interpreter in St. Paul; Ramakrishna found him in Vivekananda. Vivekananda, therefore, must be understood in the light of the realisations of Paramahansa Ramakrishna.

II

The story of Vivekananda's conversion has not as yet been told. I do not know if anybody knows how this miracle happened. Vivekananda had been a rationalist and a deist, though he fancied that he was a theist. His early religious associations were with the Brahmo Samaj. They were not very congenial to the development of faith in saints and seers. Ramakrishna Paramahansa attracted, however, many members of the Brahmo Samaj by his great psychic powers and more particularly by his passionate love of God. But they never were able to open the secret springs of the life and realisations of the Paramahansa. They saw him through the prism of the intellect. The Paramahansa never really opened to most of them the secret chambers of his piety. Vivekananda was favoured by the Paramahansa in this matter.

Paramahansa Ramakrishna saw into the innermost composition of Vivekananda's nature and spirit and recognised in him a fit instrument for delivering the message of his own life. This is the real story of Vivekananda's conversion. It is the story of the conversion also of Soul, though it was set in a different psychological setting. Vivekananda felt drawn to his Master by what he hardly knew. It was the operation of what is now called soul-force. When one soul touches another on this deep spiritual plane, the two are united forever by unbreakable spiritual bonds. The two henceforth become practically one; the Master working in and through the disciple, the disciple not even knowing that he is dancing to the tune of the Master. People call it inspiration. Vivekananda worked after his conversion under the inspiration of his Master.

III

The message of Vivekananda, though delivered in the term of the popular Vedantic speculation, was really the message of his Master to the modern man. Vivekananda's message was really the message of modern humanity. His appeal to his own people was, 'Be men.' The man of religion in India had been a mediaeval man. His religion was generally a religion of the other world. It was a religion that enjoined renunciation of the world and all the obligations of the physical and the social life. But this was not the real message of Paramahansa Ramakrishna. He was as much a Vedantin as a Vaishnava. His ideal of piety was a synthesis between these two rival schools of Hindu religion. His cult of the Mother was really the cult of Bhakti, or love of God, realised in the terms of the human motherhood. As with the Bengal Vaishnavas, so with the Paramahansa, the Ultimate Reality was not an abstraction. It was not carnal, but, therefore, it was not without form. And the real form of the Ultimate Reality is the Human Form—not the sensuous form of Man which we see with our eyes, but the spiritual form which stands behind it, invisible to mortal eye. Man and God are generically one.

To help Man to realise his essential divinity is the object of all religious culture. This is what Vivekananda really meant when he appealed to his people to be men. In the ritual of divine worship of the Brahmin, is used the following text which says: 'I am Divine. I am none other. I am not subject to grief and bereavement. I am of the form of the True, the Self-conscious and the Eternally Present. I am by nature eternally free.' This was the message really of his Master as delivered to the modern world by Vivekananda.

It is the message of freedom, not in a negative sense, but in its positive and most comprehensive implications. Freedom means removal of all outside restraint. But constituted as we are, we cannot cut ourselves off from all outside relations, whether with our natural environments or our social environments. Such isolation spells death both physically and spiritually. The law of life is, therefore, not isolation, but association, not non-cooperation but co-operation. And real freedom is achieved not through war, but through peace only. War or renunciation or isolation has a place no doubt in the scheme of life, but only a temporary place as a means to the attainment of the ultimate end which is not perpetuation of the inevitable conflict of evolution, but the settlement and cancellation of these conflicts in a closer and permanent union. Freedom again is one. Freedom from the domination of our passions and appetites is the first step in the realisation of the ideal. Freedom from the fear of brother-man is the next step. Freedom from the domination of any external authority must follow next. In this way from personal freedom, through social freedom including political freedom, Man must attain his real freedom. And when he attains it, he realises finally that he and his God are one. This is the message of the Vedanta as interpreted by Vivekananda. This is really the message of his Master to the modern world.

Some people in India think that very little fruit has come of the lectures that Swami Vivekananda delivered in England, and that his friends and admirers exaggerate his work. But on coming here I see that he has exerted a marked influence everywhere. In many parts of England I have met with men who deeply regard and venerate Vivekananda. Though I do not belong to his sect, and though it is true that I have differences of opinion with him, I must say that Vivekananda has opened the eyes of a great many here and broadened their hearts. Owing to his teaching, most people here now believe firmly that wonderful spiritual truths lie hidden in the ancient Hindu scriptures. Not only has he brought about this feeling, but he succeeded in establishing a golden relation between England and India. From what I quoted on 'Vivekanandism from The Dead Pulpit' by Mr Haweis, you have already understood that owing to the spread of Vivekananda's doctrines, many hundreds of people have seceded from Christianity. And how deep and extensive his work has been in this country will readily appear from the following incident.

Yesterday evening I was going to visit a friend in the Southern part of London. I lost my way and was looking from the corner of a street thinking in which direction I should go, when a lady accompanied by a boy came to me, with the intention, it seemed, of showing me the way. She said to me, 'Sir, perhaps you are looking to find your way. May I help you?' She showed me my way and said, 'From certain papers I learned that you are coming to London. At the very first sight of you I was telling my son, Look there is "Swami Vivekananda." ' As I had to catch the train in a hurry, I had no time to tell her that I was not Vivekananda, and compelled to go off speedily. However, I was really surprised to see that the lady possessed such great veneration for Vivekananda even before she knew him personally. I felt highly gratified at the agreeable incident, and thanked my gerua turban which had given me so much honour. Besides the incident, I have seen here many educated English gentlemen, who have come to revere India and who listened eagerly to any religious or spiritual truths, if they belong to India.

Mohandas Karamchand Gandhi

I have come here [Belur Math] to pay my homage and respect to the revered memory of Swami Vivekananda, whose birthday is being celebrated today [6 February 1921]. I have gone through his works very thoroughly, and after having gone through them, the love that I had for my country became a thousandfold. I ask you, young men, not to go away empty-handed without imbibing something of the spirit of the place where Swami Vivekananda lived and died.

C.F. Andrews

I would refer in the first place to that greater word Advaitam. The word "Advaitam" really means, the occasions of all spiritual life to see as the Upanishads tells us. The Universal self in all things and all things in the Universal self. I feel that the greatest of all debts the youths of modern India owe to Swami Vivekananda is the renewal in practical life of this faith in the Advaitam.

Chakravarti Rajagopalachari

Swami Vivekananda saved Hinduism and saved India. But for him we would have lost our religion and would not have gained our freedom. We, therefore, owe everything to Swami Vivekananda. May his faith, his courage and his wisdom ever inspire us so that we may keep safe the treasure we have received from him!

Rajendra Prasad

Men who lead their fellow beings in any sphere of life are rare and those that lead their leaders are rarer still. These super-guides come not very often upon this earth to uplift the sinking section of humanity. Swami Vivekananda was one of these super souls. It was he who could set the sceptic mind of the West at the rest in the spiritual arena. Ambassadors of spiritual missions had risen before him in the East, but none could speak to the West as he did with that voice of conviction, keeping audiences spellbound and enthralled. The worthy disciple of the worthy Master rose to the pinnacle of spiritual eminence, preaching the gospel of the innate oneness of the human race, and preaching universal love and the affinity of all human souls. Not only Indians but Westerners too stand indebted to Swami Vivekananda for the bequest of viveka (wisdom) to posterity.

The ideal he stood for made universal brotherhood of Man an understandable proposition to a world which was wedded to colour prejudice, having its route in the slavery of man. His spiritual approach roused the conscience of the thinking section of the human community all over the world and he succeeded in bringing home to the West the greatness of the Vedic civilisation. The great disciple of the great Master immortalised the fame and prestige of the land of his birth in a way which remains unrivalled even in the annals of Indian spiritualism in modern times. The sceptical youth with the intrepid spirit rose to be the ablest and wisest heir to the legacy of spiritual wealth of the great enlightened one.

Arcot Ramaswami Mudaliar

I have come under no greater influence than the influence of the life and teachings of Swami Vivekananda. I have spoken of that life and have testified to the great influence that that life has had on the generation which immediately succeeded the premature departure of the Swamiji from this world.

After I began to study in the college, there were friends and elders of mine who used to tell us stories of the days in 1893 when Narendra Datta (Swami Vivekananda)—as he then was—often sat on the pials of the houses of Triplicane and began to discuss with learned pandits in Sanskrit—and some of them in Madras were very learned indeed—the great truths of our religious teaching. The exposition, the dialectic skill he showed, and the masterly way in which he analysed what even to those well-educated and learned pandits were unfathomable depths of Sanskrit literature and law, greatly attracted attention from all and sundry.

Swami Vivekananda was a fighter himself. He was one who knew not any kind of physical cowardice or moral cowardice. He is a citizen of the world. His contribution will stay on forever. His immortal soul pervades the whole universe.

Benoy Kumar Sarkar

If we look upon Ramakrishna as the Buddha of our time, Vivekananda may pass for one or other of the great apostles of yore, say, the scholar Rahula, the constitutional authority Upali, the devoted lieutenant Ananda, the sage Sariputta, or that master of discourses, Mahakachchayana. One can almost say that Vivekananda was all these great Buddhist preacher organisers boiled down into one personality.

He was much more than a mere exponent of Vedanta, or Ramakrishna, or Hinduism, or Indian Culture. In all his thoughts and activities he was expressing only himself. He always preached his own experiences. It is the truths discovered by him in his own life that he propagated through his literature and institutions. As a modern philosopher he can be properly evaluated solely if one places him by the side of Dewey, Russell, Croce, Spranger, and Bergson. It would be doing Vivekananda injustice and misinterpreting him hopelessly if he were placed in the perspective of scholars whose chief or sole merit consists in editing, translating, paraphrasing or popularising the teachings of Plato, Ashvaghosha, Plotinus, Nagarjuna, Aquinas, Shankaracharya and others.

~

With five words he conquered the world when he addressed men and women as 'Ye divinities on earth—Sinners?' The first four words thundered into being the gospel of joy, hope, virility, energy and freedom for the races of men, and yet with the last word, embodying as it did a sarcastic question, he demolished the whole structure of soul-degenerating, cowardice-promoting, negative, pessimistic thoughts. On the astonished world the little five-word formula fell like a bombshell. The first four words he brought from the East, and the last word he brought from the West. All these are oft-repeated expressions, copy-book phrases both in the East and the West. And yet never in the annals of human thought was the juxtaposition accomplished before Vivekananda did it in this dynamic manner and obtained instantaneous recognition as a world's champion.

Vivekananda's gospel here is that of energism, of mastery over the world, of élan vital subduing conditions that surround life, of creative intelligence and will, of courage trampling down cowardice, of world-conquest. And those who are acquainted with the trends of world-thought since the middle of the nineteenth century are aware that it was just along these lines that the West was groping in the dark to find a solution. A most formidable exponent of these wants and shortcomings was the German man of letters and critic, Nietzsche (on whom the influence of Manu was powerful), whose works had awakened mankind to the need of a more positive, humane and joyous life's philosophy than that of the New Testament. This joy of life for which the religious, philosophical and social thought was anxiously waiting came suddenly from an unexpected quarter, from this unknown young man of India. And Vivekananda was acclaimed as a tremendous creative power, as the pioneer of a revolution—the positive and constructive counterpart to the destructive criticism of Nietzsche.

The key to Vivekananda's entire life is to be found in this Bhakti Yoga, energism, the vigour and strength of freedom. All his thoughts and activities are expressions of his energism. Like our Pauranik Vishwamitra or the Aeschylean Prometheus he wanted to create new worlds and distribute the fire of freedom, happiness, divinity and immortality among men and women.

~

His [Vivekananda] politics and economics are all to be found in his social philosophy. And in this domain we encounter Vivekananda as the messenger of modern materialism. It is possible to establish here an equation between Vivekananda and Immanuel Kant. What Kant did for Euro-America towards the end of the eighteenth century was accomplished for India towards the end of the nineteenth century by Vivekananda. Kant is the father of modern materialism for the West. Vivekananda is the father of modern materialism for India. It is to them that the world is indebted for the charters of dignity for Nature, matter, material science and material welfare. India like Europe was in need of a man who could say with all honesty he could command that Prakriti was no less sacred than Purusha and that the pursuit of material sciences and material prosperity was as godly as that of the sciences and activities bearing on the soul.

~

The combined intelligence of the entire world assembled at Chicago listened to this uninvited and perhaps unwelcome intruder [Swami Vivekananda] from the banks of the Southern Ganges and was convinced that a new power had arisen in the international sphere and that this new power was Young India. Vivekananda was acclaimed as the world-conqueror for Young India.

From 1757 down to 1893 for more than a hundred years —for nearly 140 years, the world had known almost nothing about Indian India, nothing of the creative Hindus and Mussulmans, nothing of Indian culture, nothing of India's constructive energism. In 1893 Vivekananda threw the first bombshell that announced to mankind in the two hemispheres, to the men and the women of America, of England, France, Germany, Russia, Italy, nay, to the yellows of Japan and China that India was once more to be a power among the powers of the world. Mankind came to realise 1893 as the year No.1 of a vast empire and to recognise the founder of that empire as Vivekananda.

Sarvepalli Radhakrishnan

When I was a student in the early years of this century, a student in high school and college classes, we used to read Swami Vivekananda's speeches and letters which were then passing from hand to hand in manuscript form, and they used to stir us a great deal and make us feel proud of our ancient culture. Though our externals were broken down, the spirit of our country is there and is everlastingly real—that was the message which we gathered from his speeches and writings when I was a young student.

There is nothing higher than humanity. But so far as we are concerned, a human individual is a lamp of Spirit on earth, the most concrete living embodiment of Spirit. By standing up for the great ideals of Hindu religion, the great ideals that alone can save humanity, by standing up for them, Swami Vivekananda tried to lead humanity to a nobler and better path than that which it found itself in. If you really believe in the divine spark in man, do not for a moment hesitate to accept the great tradition which has come to us, of which Swami Vivekananda was the greatest exponent.

~

We are today at a critical period not merely in the history of our country but in the history of the world. There are many people who think we are on the edge of an abyss. There is distortion of values, there is lowering of standards, there is widespread escapism, a good deal of mass hysteria, and people think of it and collapse in despair, frustration, hopelessness. These are the only things which are open to us. Such a kind of lack of faith in the spirit of Man is a treason to the dignity of man. It is an insult to human nature. It is human nature that has brought about all the great changes that have taken place in this world. And if there is any call which Vivekananda made to us, it is to rely on our own spiritual resources. Man has inexhaustible spiritual resources. His spirit is supreme, Man is unique. There is nothing inevitable in this world, and we can ward off the worst dangers and worst disabilities by which we are faced. Only we should not lose hope. He gave us fortitude in suffering, he gave us hope in distress, he gave us courage in despair. He told us: 'Do not be led away by the appearances. Deep down there is a providential will, there is a purpose in this universe. You must try to co-operate with that purpose and try to achieve it.

Jawaharlal Nehru

Rooted in the past and full of pride in India's prestige, Vivekananda was yet modern in his approach to life's problems and was a kind of bridge between the past of India and her present. He was a fine figure of a man, imposing, full of poise and dignity, sure of himself and his mission, and at the same time full of a dynamic and fiery energy and a passion to push India forward. He came as a tonic to the depressed and demoralised Hindu mind and gave it self-reliance and some roots in the past.

I do not know how many of the younger generation read the speeches and the writings of Swami Vivekananda. But I can tell you that many of my generation were very powerfully influenced by him and I think that it would do a great deal of good to the present generation if they also went through

Swami Vivekananda's writings and speeches, and they would learn much from them. That would, perhaps, as some of us did, enable us to catch a glimpse of that fire that raged in Swami Vivekananda's mind and heart and which ultimately consumed him at an early age. Because there was fire in his heart—the fire of a great personality coming out in eloquent and ennobling language—it was no empty talk that he was indulging in. He was putting his heart and soul into the words he uttered. Therefore, he became a great orator, not with the orators' flashes and flourishes but with a deep conviction and earnestness of spirit. And so he influenced powerfully the minds of many in India and two or three generations of young men and women have no doubt been influenced by him.

Much has happened which perhaps makes some forget those who came before and who prepared India and shaped India in those early and difficult days. If you read Swami Vivekananda's writings and speeches, the curious thing you will find is that they are not old. It was told 56* years ago, and they are fresh today because, what he wrote or spoke about dealt with certain fundamental matters and aspects of our problems or the world's problems. Therefore, they do not become old. They are fresh even though you read them now.

He gave us something which brings us, if I may use the word, a certain pride in our inheritance. He did not spare us. He talked of our weaknesses and our failings too. He did not wish to hide anything. Indeed he should not. Because we have to correct those failings, he deals with those failings also. Sometimes he strikes hard at us, but sometimes points out the great things for which India stood and which even in the days of India's downfall made her, in some measure, continue to be great.

So what Swamiji has written and said is of interest and must interest us and is likely to influence us for a long time

---

* Jawaharlal Nehru delivered this speech in 1949.

to come. He was no politician in the ordinary sense of the word and yet he was, I think, one of the great founders—if you like, you may use any other word—of the national modern movement of India, and a great number of people who took more or less an active part in that movement in a later date drew their inspiration from Swami Vivekananda. Directly or indirectly he has powerfully influenced the India of today. And I think that our younger generation will take advantage of this fountain of wisdom, of spirit and fire, that flows through Swami Vivekananda.

Men like Sri Ramakrishṇa Paramahansa, men like Swami Vivekananda and men like Mahatma Gandhi are great unifying forces, great constructive geniuses of the world not only in regard to the particular teachings that they taught, but their approach to the world and their conscious and unconscious influence on it is of the most vital importance to us.

Subhash Chandra Bose

Swamiji harmonised the East and the West, religion and science, past and present. And that is why he is great. Our countrymen have gained unprecedented self-respect, self-reliance and self-assertion from his teachings.

Jayaprakash Narayan

Swami Vivekananda belongs to the class of great seers of Truth. His intellect was great, but greater still was his heart. He once told his disciples at the Belur Math that if a conflict were to arise between the intellect and the heart, they should reject the intellect and follow the heart. Many a Mahatma has appeared in this land, and some of them understood that to meditate on the soul in the caves of the Himalayas was the correct path to follow. Swami Vivekananda's mind also was influenced by this tradition and there arose a conflict in him early in his career; his intellect advocating the traditional absorption in self-realisation and his heart bleeding for the miseries of the people around him. In the end he came to the conclusion that leaving the solitude he would enter into the soul of every being and worship his God by serving them.

What attracts the poor and lowly to him is this compassionate heart which ever bled for them and exhausted itself in their incessant service in thirty-nine brief years. It was this measureless feeling for the spiritual and material poverty and misery of his fellow men, particularly of his fellow countrymen, that drove him round the world like a tornado of moral energy and gave him no rest till the end. His life's campaigns in the East and West, including the founding of the Ramakrishna Math and Mission, were in response to this feeling.

His life was all purity and love; his coming to and going from this world was [were] quick, sudden. But in the short period of thirty-nine years he accomplished so much by way of stirring up and infusing new life and new hope into the people that in the history of our great country we do not find a second to stand equal to him in this, except, perhaps the great Shankaracharya.

Lal Bahadur Shastri

I remember that in my student days I have read the speeches of the Swami and was deeply attracted to it. Its impact on my mind was so great that my perceptions were all changed, and I started to have a different idea about life.

When the nation was in a deep slumber, he created the stir. He talked on the Vedanta; nevertheless, this sage-philosopher aroused the people. India was like an open picture before him. He wanted that the people of our country should embark on work and be active. His Advaitism was not a passivity, and he never directed to await luck or fate. He knew that if the people of the country were not ready for toil and sacrifice, India would hardly achieve wealth and prosperity. Subjugation of the country deeply troubled him. He called everyone to sacrifice for the attainment of a noble goal. Aspirants of wealth and power were deeply despised by him. In a country where millions of people were living in deprivation, individual enjoyments were considered unjust by him. His message was to awake, arise and stop not till the goal is reached. He was a seer and a God-commanded entity.

Indira Gandhi

I had had the good fortune to know about the life and teachings of Swami Vivekananda as well as about the activities of the Ramakrishna Mission. My parents and specially my mother were very close with the Ramakrishna Mission. And I must say that the teachings of Vivekananda had inspired all the members of the Nehru family both in their political activities and day-to-day lives. Swamiji's teachings, writings and speeches which appear on every page of his works, are indeed stimulant. Swamiji provides us courage, strength, and faith and teaches us how to be self-sufficient. These are the basic tenets of life which India needed most and which would be relevant for all time to come.

Swamiji has taught us that we are the inheritors of a glorious and sublime culture. He has at the same time shown us and analysed the root causes of our national malady. It was Swami Vivekananda who has given us the ways and means how to reconstruct a new India. Swamiji preached the message of universal brotherhood. And a single word which echoed and reached in all his speeches, was abhih *i.e.* fearlessness.

First Meeting With John D. Rockefeller

As told by Madame Emma Calve to Madame Drinette Verdier[*]

Mr. X, in whose home Swamiji was staying in Chicago, was a partner or an associate in some business with John D. Rockefeller. Many times John D. heard his friends talking about this extraordinary and wonderful

Hindu monk who was staying with them, and many times he had been invited to meet Swamiji but, for one reason or another, always refused. At that time Rockefeller was not yet at the peak of his fortune, but was already powerful and strong-willed, very difficult to handle and a hard man to advise.

But one day, although he did not want to meet Swamiji, he was pushed to it by an impulse and went directly to the house of his friends, brushing aside the butler who opened the door and saying that he wanted to see the Hindu monk.

The butler ushered him into the living room, and, not waiting to be announced, Rockefeller entered into Swamiji's adjoining study and was much surprised, I presume, to see Swamiji behind his writing table not even lifting his eyes to see who had entered.

---

* Excerpt from Madame Verdier's journal quoted in *New Discoveries*, Vol. 1, pp. 487–88.

After a while, as with Calve, Swamiji told Rockefeller much of his past that was not known to any but himself, and made him understand that the money he had already accumulated was not his, that he was only a channel and that his duty was to do good to the world—that God had given him all his wealth in order that he might have an opportunity to help and do good to people.

Rockefeller was annoyed that anyone dared to talk to him that way and tell him what to do. He left the room in irritation, not even saying goodbye. But about a week after, again without being announced, he entered Swamiji's study and, finding him the same as before, threw on his desk a paper which told of his plans to donate an enormous sum of money toward the financing of a public institution.

"Well, there you are", he said. "You must be satisfied now, and you can thank me for it."

Swamiji didn't even lift his eyes, did not move. Then taking the paper, he quietly read it, saying: "It is for you to thank me." That was all. This was Rockefeller's first large donation to the public welfare.

First Meeting With Madame Emma Calve

The story of Swami Vivekananda's first meeting with Madame Emma Calve, as told in her autobiography, My Life*

Swami Vivekananda was lecturing in Chicago one year when I was there; and as I was at that time greatly depressed in mind and body, I decided to go to him.

* *New Discoveries,* Vol. 1, pp. 484–86.

Before going I had been told not to speak until he addressed me. When I entered the room, I stood before him in silence for a moment. He was seated in a noble attitude of meditation, his robe of saffron yellow falling in straight lines to the floor, his head swathed in a turban bent forward, his eyes on the ground. After a pause he spoke without looking up.

"My child", he said, "what a troubled atmosphere you have about you. Be calm. It is essential."

Then in a quiet voice, untroubled and aloof, this man who did not even know my name talked to me of my secret problems and anxieties. He spoke of things that I thought were unknown even to my nearest friends. It seemed miraculous, supernatural.

"How do you know all this?" I asked at last. "Who has talked of me to you?"

He looked at me with his quiet smile as though I were a child who had asked a foolish question.

"No one has talked to me", he answered gently. "Do you think that it is necessary? I read in you as in an open book."

Finally it was time for me to leave.

"You must forget", he said as I rose. "Become gay and happy again. Build up your health. Do not dwell in silence upon your sorrows. Transmute your emotions into some form of external expression. Your spiritual health requires it. Your art demands it."

I left him deeply impressed by his words and his personality. He seemed to have emptied my brain of all its feverish complexities and placed there instead his clear and calming thoughts. I became once again vivacious and cheerful, thanks to the effect of his powerful will. He did not use any of the hypnotic or mesmeric influences. It was the strength of his character, the purity and intensity of his purpose that carried conviction. It seemed to me, when I came to know him better, that he lulled one's chaotic thoughts into a state of peaceful acquiescence, so that one could give complete and undivided attention to his words.

Jagadish Chandra Bose

What a void this makes! What great things were accomplished in these few years! How one man could have done it all! And how all is stilled now. And yet, when one is tired Great Thinkers on Vivekananda and weary, it is best that he should rest. I seem to see him just as I saw him in Paris two years ago—the strong man with the large hope, everything large about him.

[...I cannot tell you what a great sadness has come. I wish we could see beyond it. Our thoughts are in India with those who are suffering July 9th 1902. It seems to me that nothing is lost and all the great thoughts and work and service and hope remain embodied in and about the place which gave them birth. All our life is but an echo of a few great moments, an echo which reverberates through all time. That great soul is released; his heroic deeds on this earth are over. Can we realise what that work has been—how one man did all this? When one is tired it is best that he should sleep, but his deeds and teachings will walk the earth and waken and strengthen.

Munshi Premchand

Among the great souls who welcomed the Indian renaissance with sounds of conch shells, Vivekananda deserves the first place. His divine message has a clear pronouncement for spiritual progress—directed not for India alone but the world at large. The Swami is no more with us today, but the glow of spirituality he lighted will always illumine the World.

II

Lectures And Discourses

The Great Teachers Of The World

Delivered at the Shakespeare Club, Pasadena, California, 3 February 1900

The universe, according to the theory of the Hindus, is moving in cycles of wave forms. It rises, reaches its zenith, then falls and remains in the hollow, as it were, for some time, once more to rise, and so on, in wave after wave and fall after fall. What is true of the universe is true of every part of it. The march of human affairs is like that. The history of nations is like that: they rise and they fall; after the rise comes a fall, again out of the fall comes a rise, with greater power. This motion is always going on. In the religious world the same movement exists. In every nation's spiritual life, there is a fall as well as a rise. The nation goes down, and everything seems to go to pieces. Then, again, it gains strength, rises; a huge wave comes, sometimes a tidal wave—and always on the topmost crest of the wave is a shining soul, the Messenger. Creator and created by turns, he is the impetus that makes the wave rise, the nation rise: at the same time, he is created by the same forces which make the wave, acting and interacting by turns. He puts forth his tremendous power upon society; and society makes him what he is. These are the great world-thinkers. These are the Prophets of the world, the Messengers of life, the Incarnations of God.

Man has an idea that there can be only one religion, that there can be only one Prophet, and that there can be only one Incarnation; but that idea is not true. By studying the lives of all these great Messengers, we find that each, as it were, was destined to play a part, and a part only; that the harmony consists in the sum total, and not in one note. As in the life of races—no race is born to alone enjoy the world. None dare say no. Each race has a part to play in this divine harmony of nations. Each race has its mission to perform, its duty to fulfil. The sum total is the great harmony.

So, not any one of these Prophets is born to rule the world forever. None has yet succeeded and none is going to be the ruler forever. Each only contributes a part; and, as to that part, it is true that in the long run every Prophet will govern the world and its destinies.

Most of us are born believers in a personal religion. We talk of principles, we think of theories, and that is all right; but every thought and every movement, every one of our actions, shows that we can only understand the principle when it comes to us through a person. We can grasp an idea only when it comes to us through a materialised ideal person. We can understand the precept only through the example. Would to God that all of us were so developed that we would not require any example, would not require any person. But that we are not; and, naturally, the vast majority of mankind have put their souls at the feet of these extraordinary personalities, the Prophets, the Incarnations of God—Incarnations worshipped by the Christians, by the Buddhists, and by the Hindus. The Mohammedans from the beginning stood against any such worship. They would have nothing to do with worshipping the Prophets or the Messengers, or paying any homage to them; but, practically, instead of one Prophet, thousands upon thousands of saints are being worshipped. We cannot go against facts! We are bound to worship personalities, and it is good. Remember that word from your great Prophet to the query: "Lord, show us the Father", "He that hath seen me hath seen the Father." Which of us can imagine anything except that He is a man? We can only see Him in and through humanity. The vibration of light is everywhere in this room: why cannot we see it everywhere? You have to see it only in that lamp. God is an Omnipresent Principle—everywhere: but we are so constituted at present that we can see Him, feel Him, only in and through a human God. And when these great Lights come, then Man realises God. And they come in a different way from what we come. We come as beggars; they come as Emperors. We come here like orphans, as people who have lost their way and do not know it. What are we to do? We do not know what is the meaning of our lives. We cannot realise it. Today we are doing one thing, tomorrow another. We are like little bits of straw rocking to and fro in water, like feathers blown about in a hurricane.

But, in the history of mankind, you will find that there come these Messengers, and that from their very birth their mission is found and formed. The whole plan is there, laid down; and you see them swerving not one inch from that. Because they come with a mission, they come with a message, they do not want to reason. Did you ever hear or read of these great Teachers, or Prophets, reasoning out what they taught? No, not one of them did so. They speak direct. Why should they reason? They see the Truth. And not only do they see it but they show it! If you ask me, "Is there any God?" and I say "Yes", you immediately ask my grounds for saying so, and poor me has to exercise all his powers to provide you with some reason. If you had come to Christ and said, "Is there any God?" he would have said, "Yes"; and if you had asked, "Is there any proof?" he would have replied, "Behold the Lord!" And thus, you see, it is a direct perception, and not at all the ratiocination of reason. There is no groping in the dark, but there is the strength of direct vision. I see this table; no amount of reason can take that faith from me. It is a direct perception. Such is their faith—faith in their ideals, faith in their mission, faith in themselves, above all else. The great shining Ones believe in themselves as nobody else ever does. The people say, "Do you believe in God? Do you believe in a future life? Do you believe in this doctrine or that dogma?" But here the base is wanting: this belief in oneself. Ay, the man who cannot believe in himself, how can they expect him to believe in anything else? I am not sure of my own existence. One moment I think that I am existing and nothing can destroy me; the next moment I am quaking in fear of death. One minute I think I am immortal; the next minute, a spook appears, and then I don't know what I am, nor where I am. I don't know whether I am living or dead. One moment I think that I am spiritual, that I am moral; and the next moment, a blow comes, and I am thrown flat on my back. And why?—I have lost faith in myself, my moral backbone is broken.

But in these great Teachers you will always find this sign: that they have intense faith in themselves. Such intense faith"is unique,, and we cannot understand it. That is why we try to explain away in various ways what these Teachers speak of themselves; and people invent twenty thousand theories to explain what they say about their realisation. We do not think of ourselves in the same way, and, naturally, we cannot understand them.

Then again, when they speak, the world is bound to listen. When they speak, each word is direct; it bursts like a bomb-shell. What is in the word, unless it has the Power behind? What matters it what language you speak, and how you arrange your language? What matters it whether you speak correct grammar or with fine rhetoric? What matters it whether your language is ornamental or not? The question is whether or not you have anything to give. It is a question of giving and taking, and not listening. Have you anything to give?—that is the first question. If you have, then give.

Words but convey the gift: it is but one of the many modes. Sometimes we do not speak at all. There is an old Sanskrit verse which says, "I saw the Teacher sitting under a tree. He was a young man of sixteen, and the disciple was an old man of eighty. The preaching of the Teacher was silence, and the doubts of the disciple departed."

Sometimes they do not speak at all, but yet they convey the Truth from mind to mind. They come to give. They command, they are the Messengers; you have to receive the Command. Do you not remember in your own scriptures the authority with which Jesus speaks? "Go ye, therefore, and teach all nations teaching them to observe all things whatsoever I have commanded you." It runs through all his utterances, that tremendous faith in his own message. That you find in the life of all these great giants whom the world worships as its Prophets.

These great Teachers are the living Gods on this earth. Whom else should we worship? I try to get an idea of God in my mind, and I find what a false little thing I conceive; it would be a sin to worship that God. I open my eyes and look at the actual life of these great ones of the earth. They are higher than any conception of God that I could ever form. For, what conception of mercy could a man like me form who would go after a man if he steals anything from me and send him to jail? And what can be my highest idea of forgiveness? Nothing beyond myself. Which of you can jump out of your own bodies? Which of you can jump out of your own minds? Not one of you. What idea of divine love can you form except what you actually live? What we have never experienced we can form no idea of. So, all my best attempts at forming an idea of God would fail in every case. And here are plain facts, and not idealism—actual facts of love, of mercy, of purity, of which I can have no conception even. What wonder that I should fall at the feet of these men and worship them as God? And what else can anyone do? I should like to see the man who can do anything else, however much he may talk. Talking is not actuality. Talking about God and the Impersonal, and this and that, is all very good; but these man-Gods are the real Gods of all nations and all races. These divine men have been worshipped and will be worshipped so long as Man is Man. Therein is our faith, therein is our hope, of a reality. Of what avail is a mere mystical principle!

The purpose and intent of what I have to say to you is this, that I have found it possible in my life to worship all of them, and to be ready for all that are yet to come. A mother recognises her son in any dress in which he may appear before her; and if one does not do so, I am sure she is not the mother of that man. Now, as regards those of you that think that you understand Truth and Divinity, and God in only one Prophet in the world, and not in any other, naturally, the conclusion which I draw is that you do not understand Divinity in anybody; you have simply swallowed words and identified yourself with one sect, just as you would in party politics, as a matter of opinion; but that is no religion at all. There are some fools in this world who use brackish water although there is excellent sweet water near by, because, they say, the brackish-water well was dug by their father. Now, in my little experience I have collected this knowledge—that for all the devilry that religion is blamed with, religion is not at all in fault: no religion ever persecuted men, no religion ever burnt witches, no religion ever did any of these things. What then incited people to do these things? Politics, but never religion; and if such politics takes the name of religion whose fault is that?

So, when each man stands and says "My Prophet is the only true Prophet," he is not correct—he knows not the alpha of religion. Religion is neither talk, nor theory, nor intellectual consent. It is realisation in the heart of our hearts; it is touching God; it is feeling, realising that I am a spirit in relation with the Universal Spirit and all Its great manifestations. If you have really entered the house of the Father, how can you have seen His children and not known them? And if you do not recognise them, you have not entered the house of the Father. The mother recognises her child in any dress and knows him however disguised. Recognise all the great, spiritual men and women in every age and country, and see that they are not really at variance with one another. Wherever there has been actual religion—this touch of the Divine, the soul coming in direct sense-contact with the Divine—there has always been a broadening of the mind which enables it to see the light everywhere. Now, some Mohammedans are the crudest in this respect, and the most sectarian. Their watchword is: "There is one God, and Mohammed is His Prophet." Everything beyond that not only is bad, but must be destroyed forthwith; at a moment's notice, every man or woman who does not exactly believe in that must be killed; everything that does not belong to this worship must be immediately broken; every book that teaches anything else must be burnt. From the Pacific to the Atlantic, for five hundred years blood ran all over the world. That is Mohammedanism! Nevertheless, among these Mohammedans, wherever there was a philosophic man, he was sure to protest against these cruelties. In that he showed the touch of the Divine and realised a fragment of the truth; he was not playing with his religion; for it was not his father's religion he was talking, but spoke the truth direct like a man.

Side by side with the modern theory of evolution there is another thing: atavism. There is a tendency in us to revert to old ideas in religion. Let us think something new, even if it be wrong. It is better to do that. Why should you not try to hit the mark? We become wiser through failures. Time is infinite. Look at the wall. Did the wall ever tell a lie? It is always the wall. Man tells a lie—and becomes a god too. It is better, to do something; never mind even if it proves to be wrong; it is better than doing nothing. The cow never tells a lie, but she remains a cow, all the time. Do something! Think some thought; it doesn't matter whether you are right or wrong. But think something! Because my forefathers did not think this way, shall I sit down quietly and gradually lose my sense of feeling and my own thinking faculties? I may as well be dead! And what, is life worth if we have no living ideas, no convictions of our own about religion? There is some hope for the atheists, because though they differ from others, they think for themselves. The people who never think anything for themselves are not yet born into the world of religion; they have a mere jelly-fish existence. They will not think; they do not care for religion. But the disbeliever, the atheist, cares, and he is struggling. So think something! Struggle God-ward! Never mind if you fail, never mind if you get hold of a queer theory. If you are afraid to be called queer, keep it in your own mind—you need not go and preach it to others. But do something! Struggle God-ward! Light must come. If a man feeds me every day of my life, in the long run I shall lose the use of my hands. Spiritual death is the result of following each other like a flock of sheep. Death is the result of inaction. Be active; and wherever there is activity, there must be difference. Difference is the sauce of life; it is the beauty, it is the art of everything. Difference makes all beautiful here. It is variety that is the source of life, the sign of life. Why should we be afraid of it?

Now, we are coming into a position to understand about the Prophets. Now, we see that the historical evidence is—apart from the jelly-fish existence in religion—that where there has been any real thinking, any real love for God, the soul has grown God-ward and has got, as it were, a glimpse now and then, has come into direct perception, even for a second, even once in its life. Immediately, "All doubts vanish forever, and all the crookedness of the heart is made straight, and all bondages vanish, and the results of action and Karma fly when He is seen who is the nearest of the near and the farthest of the far." That is religion, that is all of religion; the rest is mere theory, dogma, so many ways of going to that state of direct perception. Now we are fighting over the basket and the fruits have' fallen into the ditch.

If two men quarrel about religion, just ask them the question: "Have you seen God? Have you seen these things?" One man says that Christ is the only Prophet: well, has he seen Christ? "Has your father seen Him?" "No, Sir." "Has your grandfather seen Him?" "No, Sir." "Have you seen Him?" "No, Sir." "Then what are you quarrelling for? The fruits have fallen into the ditch, and you are quarrelling over the basket!" Sensible men and woman should be ashamed to go on quarrelling in that way!

These great Messengers and Prophets are great and true. Why? Because, each one has come to preach a great idea. Take the Prophets of India, for instance. They are the oldest of the founders of religion. We take, first, Krishna. You who have read the *Gita* see all through the book that the one idea is non-attachment. Remain unattached. The heart's love is due to only One. To whom? To Him who never changeth. Who is that One? It is God. Do not make the mistake of giving the heart to anything that is changing, because that is misery. You may give it to a man; but if he dies, misery is the result. You may give it to a friend, but he may tomorrow become your enemy. If you give it to your husband, he may one day quarrel with you. You may give it to your wife, and she may die the day after tomorrow. Now, this is the way the world is going on. So says Krishna in the *Gita*: The Lord is the only One who never changes. His love never fails. Wherever we are and whatever we do, He is ever and ever the same merciful, the same loving heart. He never changes, He is never angry, whatever we do. How can God be angry with us? Your babe does many mischievous things: are you angry with that babe? Does not God know what we are going to be? He knows we are all going to be perfect, sooner or later. He has patience, infinite patience. We must love Him, and everyone that lives—only in and through Him. This is the keynote. You must love the wife, but not for the wife's sake. "Never, O Beloved, is the husband loved on account of the husband, but because the Lord is in the husband." The Vedanta philosophy says that even in the love of the husband and wife, although the wife is thinking that she is loving the husband, the real attraction is the Lord, who is present there. He is the only attraction, there is no other; but the wife in most cases does not know that it is so, but ignorantly she is doing the right thing, which is, loving the Lord. Only, when one does it ignorantly, it may bring pain. If one does it knowingly, that is salvation. This is what our scriptures say. Wherever there is love, wherever there is a spark of joy, know that to be a spark of His presence because He is joy, blessedness, and love itself. Without that there cannot be any love.

This is the trend of Krishna's instruction all the time. He has implanted that upon his race, so that when a Hindu does anything, even if he drinks water, he says, "If there is virtue in it, let it go to the Lord." The Buddhist says, if he, does any good deed, "Let the merit of the good deed belong to the world; if there is any virtue in what I do, let it go to the world, and let the evils of the world come to me." The Hindu says he is a great believer in; the Hindu says that God is omnipotent and that He is the Soul of every soul everywhere; the Hindu says, "If I give all my virtues unto Him, that is the greatest sacrifice, and they will go to the whole universe."

Now, this is one phase; and what is the other message of Krishna? "Whosoever lives in the midst of the world, and works, and gives up all the fruit of his action unto the Lord, he is never touched with the evils of the world. Just as the lotus, born under the water, rises up and blossoms above the water, even so is the man who is engaged in the activities of the world, giving up all the fruit of his activities unto the Lord."

Krishna strikes another note as a teacher of intense activity. Work, work, work day and night, says the *Gita*. You may ask, "Then, where is peace? If all through life I am to work like a cart-horse and die in harness, what am I here for?" Krishna says, "Yes, you will find peace. Flying from work is never the way to find peace." Throw off your duties if you can, and go to the top of a mountain; even there the mind is going—whirling, whirling, whirling. Someone asked a Sannyasin, "Sir, have you found a nice place? How many years have you been travelling in the Himalayas?" "For forty years," replied the Sannyasin. "There are many beautiful spots to select from, and to settle down in: why did you not do so?" "Because for these forty years my mind would not allow me to do so." We all say, "Let us find peace"; but the mind will not allow us to do so.

You know the story of the man who caught a Tartar. A soldier was outside the town, and he cried out when he came near the barracks, "I have caught a Tartar." A voice called out, "Bring him in." "He won't come in, Sir." "Then you come in." "He won't let me come in, Sir." So, in this mind of ours, we have "caught a Tartar": neither can we tone it down, nor will it let us be toned down. We have all "caught Tartars". We all say, be quiet, and peaceful, and so forth. But every baby can say that and thinks he can do it. However, that is very difficult. I have tried. I threw overboard all my duties and fled to the tops of mountains; I lived in caves and deep forests—but all the same, I "caught a Tartar", because I had my world with me all the time. The "Tartar" is what I have in my own mind, so we must not blame poor people outside. "These circumstances are good, and these are bad," so we say, while the "Tartar" is here, within; if we can quiet him down, we shall be all right.

Therefore, Krishna teaches us not to shirk our duties, but to take them up manfully, and not think of the result. The servant has no right to question. The soldier has no right to reason. Go forward, and do not pay too much attention to the nature of the work you have to do. Ask your mind if you are unselfish. If you are, never mind anything, nothing can resist you! Plunge in! Do the duty at hand. And when you have done this, by degrees you will realise the Truth: "Whosoever in the midst of intense activity finds intense peace, whosoever in the midst of the greatest peace finds the greatest activity, he is a Yogi, he is a great soul, he has arrived at perfection."

Now, you see that the result of this teaching is that all the duties of the world are sanctified. There is no duty in this world which we have any right to call menial: and each man's work is quite as good as that of the emperor on his throne.

Listen to Buddha's message—a tremendous message. It has a place in our heart. Says Buddha, "Root out selfishness, and everything that makes you selfish. Have neither wife, child, nor family. Be not of the world; become perfectly unselfish." A worldly man thinks he will be unselfish, but when he looks at the face of his wife it makes him selfish. The mother thinks she will be perfectly unselfish, but she looks at her baby, and immediately selfishness comes. So with everything in this world. As soon as selfish desires arise, as soon as some selfish pursuit is followed, immediately the whole man, the real man, is gone: he is like a brute, he is a slave, he forgets his fellow men. No more does he say, "You first and I afterwards," but it is "I first and let everyone else look out for himself."

We find that Krishna's message has also a place for us. Without that message, we cannot move at all. We cannot conscientiously and with peace, joy, and happiness, take up any duty of our lives without listening to the message of Krishna: "Be not afraid even if there is evil in your work, for there is no work which has no evil." "Leave it unto the Lord, and do not look for the results."

On the other hand, there is a corner in the heart for the other message: Time flies, this world is finite and all misery. With your good food, nice clothes, and your comfortable home, O sleeping man and woman, do you ever think of the millions that are starving and dying? Think of the great fact that it is all misery, misery, misery! Note the first utterance of the child: when it enters into the world, it weeps. That is the fact—the child weeps. This is a place for weeping! If we listen to the Messenger, we should not be selfish.

Behold another Messenger, He of Nazareth. He teaches, "Be ready, for the Kingdom of Heaven is at hand." I have pondered over the message of Krishna, and am trying to work without attachment, but sometimes I forget. Then, suddenly comes to me the message of Buddha: "Take care, for everything in the world is evanescent, and there is always misery in this life." I listen to that, and I am uncertain which to accept. Then again comes, like a thunderbolt, the message: "Be ready, for the Kingdom of Heaven is at hand." Do not delay a moment. Leave nothing for tomorrow. Get ready for the final event, which may overtake you immediately, even now. That message, also, has a place, and we acknowledge it. We salute the Messenger, we salute the Lord.

And then comes Mohammed, the Messenger of equality You ask, "What good can there be in his religion?" If there were no good, how could it live? The good alone lives, that alone survives; because the good alone is strong, therefore, it survives. How long is the life of an impure man, even in this life? Is not the life of the pure Man much longer? Without doubt, for purity is strength, goodness is strength. How could Mohammedanism have lived, had there been nothing good in its teaching? There is much good. Mohammed was the Prophet of equality, of the brotherhood of man, the brotherhood of all Mussulmans.

So we see that each Prophet, each Messenger, has a particular message. When you first listen to that message, and then look at his life, you see his whole life stands explained, radiant.

Now, ignorant fools start twenty thousand theories, and put forward, according to their own mental development, explanations to suit their own ideas, and ascribe them to these great Teachers. They take their teachings and put their misconstruction upon them. With every great Prophet his life is the only commentary. Look at his life: what he did will bear out the texts. Read the *Gita,* and you will find that is exactly borne out by the life of the Teacher.

Mohammed by his life showed that amongst Mohammedans there should be perfect equality and brotherhood. There was no question of race, caste, creed, colour, or sex. The Sultan of Turkey may buy a Negro from the mart of Africa, and bring him in chains to Turkey; but should he become a Mohammedan and have sufficient merit and abilities, he might even marry the daughter of the Sultan. Compare this with the way in which the Negroes and the American Indians are treated in this country! And what do Hindus do? If one of your missionaries chance to touch the food of an orthodox person, he would throw it away. Notwithstanding our grand philosophy, you note our weakness in practice; but there you see the greatness of the Mohammedan beyond other races, showing itself in equality, perfect equality regardless of race or colour.

Will other and greater Prophets come? Certainly they will come in this world. But do not look forward to that. I should better like that each one of you became a Prophet of this real New Testament, which is made up of all the Old Testaments. Take all the old messages, supplement them with your own realisations, and become a Prophet unto others. Each one of these Teachers has been great; each has left something for us; they have been our Gods. We salute them, we are their servants; and, all the same, we salute ourselves; for if they have been Prophets and children of God, we also are the same. They reached their perfection, and we are going to attain ours now. Remember the words of Jesus: "The Kingdom of Heaven is at hand!" This very moment let every one of us make a staunch resolution: "I will become a Prophet, I will become a messenger of Light, I will become a child of God, nay, I will become a God!"

The Sages Of India

In speaking of the sages of India, my mind goes back to those periods of which history has no record, and tradition tries in vain to bring the secrets out of the gloom of the past. The sages of India have been almost innumerable, for what has the Hindu nation been doing for thousands of years except producing sages? I will take, therefore, the lives of a few of the most brilliant ones, the epoch-makers, and present them before you, that is to say, my study of them.

In the first place, we have to understand a little about our scriptures. Two ideals of truth are in our scriptures; the one is, what we call the eternal, and the other is not so authoritative, yet binding under particular circumstances, times, and places. The eternal relations which deal with the nature of the soul, and of God, and the relations between souls and God are embodied in what we call the Shrutis, the Vedas. The next set of truths is what we call the Smritis, as embodied in the words of Manu. Yajnavalkya, and other writers and also in the Puranas, down to the Tantras. The second class of books and teachings is subordinate to the Shrutis, inasmuch as whenever any one of these contradicts anything in the Shrutis, the Shrutis must prevail. This is the law. The idea is that the framework of the destiny and goal of Man has been all delineated in the Vedas, the details have been left to be worked out in the Smritis and Puranas. As for general directions, the Shrutis are enough; for spiritual life, nothing more can be said, nothing more can be known. All that is necessary has been known, all the advice that is necessary to lead the soul to perfection has been completed in the Shrutis; the details alone were left out, and these the Smritis have supplied from time to time.

Another peculiarity is that these Shrutis have many sages as the recorders of the truths in them, mostly men, even some women. Very little is known of their personalities, the dates of their birth, and so forth, but their best thoughts, their best discoveries, I should say, are preserved there, embodied in the sacred literature of our country, the Vedas. In the Smritis, on the other hand, personalities are more in evidence. Startling, gigantic, impressive, world-moving persons stand before us, as it were, for the first time, sometimes of more magnitude even than their teachings.

This is a peculiarity which we have to understand—that our religion preaches an Impersonal Personal God. It preaches any amount of impersonal laws plus any amount of personality, but the very fountain-head of our religion is in the Shrutis, the Vedas, which are perfectly impersonal; the persons all come in the Smritis and Puranas—the great Avataras, the Incarnations of God, Prophets, and so forth. And this ought also to be observed that except our religion, every other religion in the world depends upon the life or lives of some personal founder or founders. Christianity is built upon the life of Jesus Christ, Mohammedanism upon Mohammed, Buddhism upon Buddha, Jainism upon the Jinas, and so on. It naturally follows that there must be in all these religions a good deal of fight about what they call the historical evidences of these great personalities. If at any time the historical evidences about the existence of these personages in ancient times become weak, the whole building of the religion tumbles down and is broken to pieces.

We escaped this fate because our religion is not based upon persons but on principles. That you obey your religion is not because it came through the authority of a sage, no, not even of an Incarnation. Krishna is not the authority of the Vedas, but the Vedas are the authority of Krishna himself. His glory is that he is the greatest preacher of the Vedas that ever existed. So with the other Incarnations; so with all our sages. Our first principle is that all that is necessary for the perfection of Man and for attaining unto freedom is there in the Vedas. You cannot find anything new. You cannot go beyond a perfect unity, which is the goal of all knowledge; this has been already reached there, and it is impossible to go beyond the unity. Religious knowledge became complete when Tat Twam Asi (Thou art That) was discovered, and that was in the Vedas. What remained was the guidance of people from time to time according to different times and places, according to different circumstances and environments; people had to be guided along the old, old path, and for this these great teachers came, these great sages. Nothing can bear out more clearly this position than the celebrated saying of Shri Krishna in the *Gita*: "Whenever virtue subsides and irreligion prevails, I create Myself for the protection of the good; for the destruction of all immorality I am coming from time to time." This is the idea in India.

What follows? That on the one hand, there are these eternal principles which stand upon their own foundations without depending on any reasoning even, much less on the authority of sages however great, of Incarnations however brilliant they may have been. We may remark that as this is the unique position in India, our claim is that the Vedanta only can be the universal religion, that it is already the existing universal religion in the world, because it teaches principles and not persons. No religion built upon a person can be taken up as a type by all the races of mankind. In our own country we find that there have been so many grand characters; in even a small city many persons are taken up as types by the different minds in that one city. How is it possible that one person as Mohammed or Buddha or Christ, can be taken up as the one type for the whole world, nay, that the whole of morality, ethics, spirituality, and religion can be true only from the sanction of that one person, and one person alone? Now, the Vedantic religion does not require any such personal authority. Its sanction is the eternal nature of man, its ethics are based upon the eternal spiritual solidarity of man, already existing, already attained and not to be attained. On the other hand, from the very earliest times, our sages have been feeling conscious of this fact that the vast majority of mankind require a personality. They must have a Personal God in some form or other. The very Buddha who declared against the existence of a Personal God had not died fifty years before his disciples manufactured a Personal God out of him. The Personal God is necessary, and at the same time we know that instead of and better than vain imaginations of a Personal God, which in ninety-nine cases out of a hundred are unworthy of human worship, we have in this world, living and walking in our midst, living Gods, now and then. These are more worthy of worship than any imaginary God, any creation of our imagination, that is to say, any idea of God which we can form. Shri Krishna is much greater than idea of God you or I can have. Buddha is a much higher idea, a more living and idolised idea, than the ideal you or I can conceive of in our minds; and, therefore, it is that they always command the worship of mankind even to the exclusion of all imaginary deities.

This our sages knew, and, therefore, left it open to all Indian people to worship such great personages, such Incarnations. Nay, the greatest of these Incarnations goes further: "Wherever an extraordinary spiritual power is manifested by external man, know that I am there; it is from Me that that manifestation comes." That leaves the door open for the Hindu to worship the Incarnations of all the countries in the world. The Hindu can worship any sage and any saint from any country whatsoever, and as a fact we know that we go and worship many times in the churches of the Christians, and many, many times in the Mohammedan mosques, and that is good. Why not? Ours, as I have said, is the universal religion. It is inclusive enough, it is broad enough to include all the ideals. All the ideals of religion that already exist in the world can be immediately included, and we can patiently wait for all the ideals that are to come in the future to be taken in the same fashion, embraced in the infinite arms of the religion of the Vedanta.

This, more or less, is our position with regard to the great sages, the Incarnations of God. There are also secondary characters. We find the word Rishi again and again mentioned in the Vedas, and it has become a common word at the present time. The Rishi is the great authority. We have to understand that idea. The definition is that the Rishi is the Mantra Drashta, the seer of thought. What is the proof of religion?—this was asked in very ancient times. There is no proof in the senses was the declaration, यतो वाचो निवर्तन्ते अप्राप्य मनसा सह —"From whence words reflect back with thought without reaching the goal." न तत्र चक्षुर्गच्छति न वाग्गच्छति नो मन: ।—"There the eyes cannot reach, neither can speech, nor the mind"—that has been the declaration for ages and ages. Nature outside cannot give us any answer as to the existence of the soul, the existence of God, the eternal life, the goal of man, and all that. This mind is continually changing, always in a state of flux; it is finite, it is broken into pieces. How can nature tell of the Infinite, the Unchangeable, the Unbroken, the Indivisible, the Eternal? It never can. And whenever mankind has striven to get an answer from dull dead matter, history shows how disastrous the results have been. How comes, then, the knowledge which the Vedas declare? It comes through being a Rishi. This knowledge is not in the senses; but are the senses the be-all and the end-all of the human being? Who dare say that the senses are the all-in-all of man?

Even in our lives, in the life of every one of us here, there come moments of calmness, perhaps, when we see before us the death of one we loved, when some shock comes to us, or when extreme blessedness comes to us. Many other occasions there are when the mind, as it were, becomes calm, feels for the moment its real nature; and a glimpse of the Infinite beyond, where words cannot reach nor the mind go, is revealed to us. This happens in ordinary life, but it has to be heightened, practised, perfected. Men found out ages ago that the soul is not bound or limited by the senses, no, not even by consciousness. We have to understand that this consciousness is only the, name of one link in the infinite chain. Being is not identical with consciousness, but consciousness is only one part of Being. Beyond consciousness is where the bold search lies. Consciousness is bound by the senses. Beyond that, beyond the senses, men must go in order to arrive at truths of the spiritual world, and there are even now persons who succeed in going beyond the bounds of the senses. These are called Rishis, because they come face to face with spiritual truths.

The proof, therefore, of the Vedas is just the same as the proof of this table before me, Pratyaksha, direct perception. This I see with the senses, and the truths of spirituality we also see in a superconscious state of the human soul. This Rishi-state is not limited by time or place, by sex or race. Vatsyayana boldly declares that this Rishihood is the common property of the descendants of the sage, of the Aryan, of the non-Aryan, of even the Mlechchha. This is the sage-ship of the Vedas, and constantly we ought to remember this ideal of religion in India, which I wish other nations of the world would also remember and learn, so that there may be less fight and less quarrel. Religion is not in books, nor in theories, nor in dogmas, nor in talking, not even in reasoning.

It is being and becoming. Ay, my friends, until each one of you has become a Rishi and come face to face with spiritual facts, religious life has not begun for you.

Until the superconscious opens for you, religion is mere talk, it is nothing but preparation. You are talking second-hand, third-hand, and here applies that beautiful saying of Buddha when he had a discussion with some Brahmins. They came discussing about the nature of Brahman, and the great sage asked, "Have you seen Brahman?" "No", said the Brahmin; "Or your father?" "No, neither has he"; "Or your grandfather?" "I don't think even he saw Him." "My friend, how can you discuss about a person whom your father and grandfather never saw, and try to put each other down?" That is what the whole world is doing. Let us say in the language of the Vedanta, "This Atman is not to be reached by too much talk, no, not even by the highest intellect, no, not even by the study of the Vedas themselves."

Let us speak to all the nations of the world in the language of the Vedas: Vain are your fights and your quarrels; have you seen God whom you want to preach? If you have not seen, vain is your preaching; you do not know what you say; and if you have seen God, you will not quarrel, your very face will shine. An ancient sage of the Upanishads sent his son out to learn about Brahman, and the child came back, and the father asked, "What have you learnt?" The child replied he had learnt so many sciences. But the father said, "That is nothing, go back." And the son went back, and when he returned again the father asked the same question, and the same answer came from the child. Once more he had to go back. And the next time he came, his whole face was shining; and his father stood up and declared, "Ay, today, my child, your face shines like a knower of Brahman." When you have known God, your very face will be changed, your voice will be changed, your whole appearance will be changed. You will be a blessing to mankind; none will be able to resist the Rishi.

This is the Rishihood, the ideal in our religion. The rest, all these talks and reasonings and philosophies and dualisms and monisms, and even the Vedas themselves are but preparations, secondary things. The other is primary. The Vedas, grammar, astronomy, etc., all these are secondary; that is supreme knowledge which makes us realise the Unchangeable One. Those who realised are the sages whom we find in the Vedas; and we understand how this Rishi is the name of a type, of a class, which every one of us, as true Hindus, is expected to become at some period of our life, and becoming which, to the Hindu, means salvation. Not belief in doctrines, not going to thousands of temples, nor bathing in all the rivers in the world, but becoming the Rishi, the Mantra Drashta—that is freedom, that is salvation.

Coming down to later times, there have been great world-moving sages, great Incarnations of whom there have been many; and according to the *Bhagavad,* they also are infinite in number, and those that are worshipped most in India are Rama and Krishna. Rama, the ancient idol of the heroic ages, the embodiment of truth, of morality, the ideal son, the ideal husband, the ideal father, and above all, the ideal king, this Rama has been presented before us by the great sage Valmiki. No language can be purer, none chaster, none more beautiful and at the same time simpler than the language in which the great poet has depicted the life of Rama. And what to speak of Sita? You may exhaust the literature of the world that is past, and I may assure you that you will have to exhaust the literature of the world of the future, before finding another Sita. Sita is unique; that character was depicted once and for all. There may have been several Ramas, perhaps, but never more than one Sita! She is the very type of the true Indian woman, for all the Indian ideals of a perfected woman have grown out of that one life of Sita; and here she stands these thousands of years, commanding the worship of every man, woman, and child throughout the length and breadth of the land of Aryavarta. There she will always be, this glorious Sita, purer than purity itself, all patience, and all suffering. She who suffered that life of suffering without a murmur, she the ever-chaste and ever-pure wife, she the ideal of the people, the ideal of the gods, the great Sita, our national God she must always remain. And every one of us knows her too well to require much delineation. All our mythology may vanish, even our Vedas may depart, and our Sanskrit language may vanish forever, but so long as there will be five Hindus living here, even if only speaking the most vulgar patois, there will be the story of Sita present. Mark my words: Sita has gone into the very vitals of our race. She is there in the blood of every Hindu man and woman; we are all children of Sita. Any attempt to modernise our women, if it tries to take our women away from that ideal of Sita, is immediately a failure, as we see every day. The women of India must grow and develop in the footprints of Sita, and that is the only way.

The next is He who is worshipped in various forms, the favourite ideal of men as well as of women, the ideal of children, as well as of grown-up men. I mean He whom the writer of the *Bhagavad* was not content to call an Incarnation but says, "The other Incarnations were but parts of the Lord. He, Krishna, was the Lord Himself. And it is not strange that such adjectives are applied to him when we marvel at the many-sidedness of his character. He was the most wonderful Sannyasin, and the most wonderful householder in one; he had the most wonderful amount of Rajas, power, and was at the same time living in the midst of the most wonderful renunciation. Krishna can never be understood until you have studied the *Gita*, for he was the embodiment of his own teaching. Every one of these Incarnations came as a living illustration of what they came to preach. Krishna, the preacher of the *Gita*, was all his life the embodiment of that Song Celestial; he was the great illustration of non-attachment. He gives up his throne and never cares for it. He, the leader of India, at whose word kings come down from their thrones, never wants to be a king. Lie is the simple Krishna, ever the same Krishna who played with the Gopis. Ah, that most marvellous passage of his life, the most difficult to understand, and which none ought to attempt to understand until he has become perfectly chaste and pure, that most marvellous expansion of love, allegorised and expressed in that beautiful play at Vrindaban, which none can understand but he who has become mad with love, drunk deep of the cup of love! Who can understand the throes of the love of the Gopis—the very ideal of love, love that wants nothing, love that even does not care for heaven, love that does not care for anything in this world or the world to come? And here, my friends, through this love of the Gopis has been found the only solution of the conflict between the Personal and the Impersonal God. We know how the Personal God is the highest point of human life; we know that it is philosophical to believe in an Impersonal God immanent in the universe, of whom everything is but a manifestation. At the same time our souls hanker after something concrete, something which we want to grasp, at whose feet we can pour out our soul, and so on. The Personal God is, therefore, the highest conception of human nature. Yet reason stands aghast at such an idea. It is the same old, old question which you find discussed in the *Brahma Sutras,* which you find Draupadi discussing with Yudhishthira in the forest: If there is a Personal God, all-merciful, all-powerful, why is the hell of an earth here, why did He create this?—He must be a partial God. There was no solution, and the only solution that can be found is what you read about the love of the Gopis. They hated every adjective that was applied to Krishna; they did not care to know that he was the Lord of creation, they did not care to know that he was almighty, they did not care to know that he was omnipotent, and so forth. The only thing they understood was that he was infinite Love, that was all. The

Gopis understood Krishna only as the Krishna of Vrindaban. He, the leader of the hosts, the King of kings, to them was the shepherd, and the shepherd forever. "I do not want wealth, nor many people, nor do I want learning; no, not even do I want to go to heaven. Let me be born again and again, but Lord, grant me this, that I may have love for Thee, and that for love's sake." A great landmark in the history of religion is here, the ideal of love for love's sake, work for work's sake, duty for duty's sake, and it for the first time fell from the lips of the greatest of Incarnations, Krishna, and for the first time in the history of humanity, upon the soil of India. The religions of fear and of temptations were gone forever, and in spite of the fear of hell and temptation of enjoyment in heaven, came the grandest of ideals, love for love's sake, duty for duty's sake, work for work's sake.

And what a love! I have told you just now that it is very difficult to understand the love of the Gopis. There are not wanting fools, even in the midst of us, who cannot understand the marvellous significance of that most marvellous of all episodes. There are, let me repeat, impure fools, even born of our blood, who try to shrink from that as if from something impure. To them I have only to say, first make yourselves pure; and you must remember that he who tells the history of the love of the Gopis is none else but Shuka Deva. The historian who records this marvellous love of the Gopis is one who was born pure, the eternally pure Shuka, the son of Vyasa. So long as there is selfishness in the heart, so long is love of God impossible; it is nothing but shopkeeping: "I give you something; O Lord, you give me something in return"; and says the Lord, "If you do not do this, I will take good care of you when you die. I will roast you all the rest of your lives, perhaps", and so on. So long as such ideas are in the brain, how can one understand the mad throes of the Gopis' love? "O for one, one kiss of those lips! One who has been kissed by Thee, his thirst for Thee increases forever, all sorrows vanish, and he forgets love for everything else but for Thee and Thee alone." Ay, forget first the love for gold, and name and fame, and for this little trumpery world of ours. Then, only then, you will understand the love of the Gopis, too holy to be attempted without giving up everything, too sacred to be understood until the soul has become perfectly pure. People with ideas of sex, and of money, and of fame, bubbling up every minute in the heart, daring to criticise and understand the love of the Gopis! That is the very essence of the Krishna Incarnation. Even the *Gita*, the great philosophy itself, does not compare with that madness, for in the *Gita* the disciple is taught slowly how to walk towards the goal, but here is the madness of enjoyment, the drunkenness of love, where disciples and teachers and teachings and books and all these things have become one; even the ideas of fear, and God, and heaven—everything has been thrown away. What remains is the madness of love. It is forgetfulness of everything, and the lover sees nothing in the world except that Krishna and Krishna alone, when the face of every being becomes a Krishna, when his own face looks like Krishna, when his own soul has become tinged with the Krishna colour. That was the great Krishna!

Do not waste your time upon little details. Take up the framework, the essence of the life. There may be many historical discrepancies, there may be interpolations in the life of Krishna. All these things may be true; but, at the same time, there must have been a basis, a foundation for this new and tremendous departure. Taking the life of any other sage or prophet, we find that that prophet is only the evolution of what had gone before him, we find that that prophet is only preaching the ideas that had been scattered about his own country even in his own times. Great doubts may exist even as to whether that prophet existed or not. But here, I challenge any one to show whether these things, these ideals—work for work's sake, love for love's sake, duty for duty's sake, were not original ideas with Krishna, and as such, there must have been someone with whom these ideas originated. They could not have been borrowed from anybody else. They were not floating about in the atmosphere when Krishna was born. But the Lord Krishna was the first preacher of this; his disciple Vyasa took it up and preached it unto mankind. This is the highest idea to picture. The highest thing we can get out of him is Gopijanavallabha, the Beloved of the Gopis of Vrindaban. When that madness comes in your brain, when you understand the blessed Gopis, then you will understand what love is. When the whole world will vanish, when all other considerations will have died out, when you will become pure-hearted with no other aim, not even the search after truth, then and then alone will come to you the madness of that love, the strength and the power of that infinite love which the Gopis had, that love for love's sake. That is the goal. When you have got that, you have got everything.

To come down to the lower stratum—Krishna, the preacher of the *Gita*. Ay, there is an attempt in India now which is like putting the cart before the horse. Many of our people think that Krishna as the lover of the Gopis is something rather uncanny, and the Europeans do not like it much. Dr. So-and-so does not like it. Certainly then, the Gopis have to go! Without the sanction of the Europeans how can Krishna live? He cannot! In the Mahabharata there is no mention of the Gopis except in one or two places, and those not very remarkable places. In the prayer of Draupadi, there is mention of a Vrindaban life, and in the speech of Shishupala there is again mention of this Vrindaban. All these are interpolations! What the Europeans do not want must be thrown off. They are interpolations, the mention of the Gopis and of Krishna too! Well, with these men, steeped in commercialism, where even the ideal of religion has become commercial, they are all trying to go to heaven by doing something here; the bania wants compound interest; wants to lay by something here and enjoy it there. Certainly the Gopis have no place in such a system of thought. From that ideal lover we come down to the lower stratum of Krishna, the preacher of the *Gita*. Than the *Gita* no better commentary on the Vedas has been written or can be written. The essence of the Shrutis, or of the Upanishads, is hard to be understood, seeing that there are so many commentators, each one trying to interpret in his own way. Then the Lord Himself comes, He who is the inspirer of the Shrutis, to show us the meaning of them, as the preacher of the *Gita*, and today India wants nothing better, the world wants nothing better than that method of interpretation. It is a wonder that subsequent interpreters of the scriptures, even commenting upon the *Gita*, many times could not catch the meaning, many times could not catch the drift. For what do you find in the *Gita*, and what in modern commentators? One non-dualistic commentator takes up an Upanishad; there are so many dualistic passages, and he twists and tortures them into some meaning, and wants to bring them all into a meaning of his own. If a dualistic commentator comes, there are so many non-dualistic texts which he begins to torture, to bring them all round to dualistic meaning. But you find in the *Gita* there is no attempt at torturing any one of them. They are all right, says the Lord; for slowly and gradually the human soul rises up and up, step after step, from the gross to the fine, from the fine to the finer, until it reaches the Absolute, the goal. That is what is in the *Gita*. Even the Karma Kanda is taken up, and it is shown that although it cannot give salvation direct, but only indirectly, yet that is also valid; images are valid indirectly; ceremonies, forms, everything is valid only with one condition, purity of the heart. For worship is valid and leads to the goal if the heart is pure and the heart is sincere; and all these various modes of worship are necessary, else why should they be there? Religions and sects are not the work of hypocrites and wicked people who invented all these to get a little money, as some of our modern men want to think. However reasonable that explanation may seem, it is not true, and they were not invented that way at all. They are the outcome of the necessity of the human soul. They are all here to satisfy the hankering and thirst of different classes of human minds, and you need not preach against them. The day when that necessity will cease, they will vanish along with the cessation of that necessity; and so long as that necessity remains, they must be there in spite of your preaching, in spite of your criticism. You may bring the sword or the gun into play, you may deluge the world with human blood, but so long as there is a necessity for idols, they must remain. These forms, and all the various steps in religion will remain, and we understand from the Lord Shri Krishna why they should.

A rather sadder chapter of India's history comes now. In the *Gita* we already hear the distant sound of the conflicts of sects, and the Lord comes in the middle to harmonise them all; He, the great preacher of harmony, the greatest teacher of harmony, Lord Shri Krishna. He says, "In Me they are all strung like pearls upon a thread." We already hear the distant sounds, the murmurs of the conflict, and possibly there was a period of harmony and calmness when it broke out anew, not only on religious grounds, but most possibly on caste grounds—the fight between the two powerful factors in our community, the kings and the priests. And from the topmost crest of the wave that deluged India for nearly a thousand years, we see another glorious figure, and that was our Gautama Shakyamuni. You all know about his teachings and preachings. We worship him as God incarnate, the greatest, the boldest preacher of morality that the world ever saw, the greatest Karma-Yogi; as disciple of himself, as it were, the same Krishna came to show how to make his theories practical. There came once again the same voice that in the *Gita* preached, "Even the least bit done of this religion saves from great fear." "Women, or Vaishyas, or even

Shudras, all reach the highest goal." Breaking the bondages of all, the chains of all, declaring liberty to all to reach the highest goal, come the words of the Git, foils like thunder the mighty voice of Krishna: "Even in this life they have conquered relativity, whose minds are firmly him. I have told you a few points about the state of things that existed in India. All these horrors that you are trying to reform are the outcome of that-reign of degradation, The Tartars and the Baluchis and all the hideous races of mankind came to India and became Buddhists, and assimilated with us, and brought their national customs, and the whole of our national life became a huge page of the most horrible and the most bestial customs. That was the inheritance which that boy got from the Buddhists, and from that time to this, the whole work in India is a reconquest of this Buddhistic degradation by the Vedanta. It is still going on, it is not yet finished. Shankara came, a great philosopher, and showed that the real essence of Buddhism and that of the Vedanta are not very different, but that the disciples did not understand the Master and have degraded themselves, denied the existence of the soul and of God, and have become atheists. That was what Shankara showed, and all the Buddhists began to come back to the old religion. But then they had become accustomed to all these forms; what could be done?

Then came the brilliant Ramanuja. Shankara, with his great intellect, I am afraid, had not as great a heart. Ramanuja's heart was greater. He felt for the downtrodden, he sympathised with them. He took up the ceremonies, the accretions that had gathered, made them pure so far as they could be, and instituted new ceremonies, new methods of worship, for the people who absolutely required them. At the same time he opened the door to the highest spiritual worship from the Brahmin to the Pariah. That was Ramanuja's work. That work rolled on, invaded the North, was taken up by some great leaders there; but that was much later, during the Mohammedan rule; and the brightest of these prophets of comparatively modern times in the North was Chaitanya.

You may mark one characteristic since the time of Ramanuja—the opening of the door of spirituality to every one. That has been the watchword of all prophets succeeding Ramanuja, as it had been the watchword of all the prophets before Shankara. I do not know why Shankara should be represented as rather exclusive; I do not find anything in his writings which is exclusive. As in the case of the declarations of the Lord Buddha, this exclusiveness that has been attributed to Shankara's teachings is most possibly not due to his teachings, but to the incapacity of his disciples. This one great Northern sage, Chaitanya, represented the mad love of the Gopis. Himself a Brahmin, born of one of the most rationalistic families of the day, himself a professor of logic fighting and gaining a word-victory—for, this he had learnt from his childhood as the highest ideal of life and yet through the mercy of some sage the whole life of that man became changed; he gave up his fight, his quarrels, his professorship of logic and became one of the greatest teachers of Bhakti the world has ever known—mad Chaitanya. His Bhakti rolled over the whole land of Bengal, bringing solace to every one. His love knew no bounds. The saint or the sinner, the Hindu or the Mohammedan, the pure or the impure, the prostitute, the streetwalker—all had a share in his love, all had a share in his mercy; and even to the present day, although greatly degenerated, as everything does become in time, his sect is the refuge of the poor, of the downtrodden, of the outcast, of the weak, of those who have been rejected by all society. But at the same time I must remark for truth's sake that we find this: In the philosophic sects we find wonderful liberalism. There is not a man who follows Shankara who will say that all the different sects of India are really different. At the same time he was a tremendous upholder of exclusiveness as regards caste. But with every Vaishnavite preacher we find a wonderful liberalism as to the teaching of caste questions, but exclusiveness as regards religious questions.

The one had a great head, the other a large heart, and the time was ripe for one to be born, the embodiment of both this head and heart; the time was ripe for one to be born who in one body would have the brilliant intellect of Shankara and the wonderfully expansive, infinite heart of Chaitanya; one who would see in every sect the same spirit working, the same God; one who would see God in every being, one whose heart would weep for the poor, for the weak, for the outcast, for the downtrodden, for every one in this world, inside India or outside India; and at the same time whose grand brilliant intellect would conceive of such noble thoughts as would harmonise all conflicting sects, not only in India but outside of India, and bring a marvellous harmony, the universal religion of head and heart into existence. Such a man was born, and I had the good fortune to sit at his feet for years. The time was ripe, it was necessary that such a man should be born, and he came; and the most wonderful part of it was that his life's work was just near a city which was full of Western thought, a city which had run mad after these occidental ideas, a city which had become more Europeanised than any other city in India. There he lived, without any book-learning whatsoever; this great intellect never learnt even to write his own name, but the most brilliant graduates of our university found in him an intellectual giant. He was a strange man, this Sri Ramakrishna Paramahamsa. It is a long, long story, and I have no time to tell anything about him tonight. Let me now only mention the great Sri Ramakrishna, the fulfilment of the Indian sages, the sage for the time, one whose teaching is just now, in the present time, most beneficial. And mark the divine power working behind the man. The son of a poor priest, born in an out-of-the-way village, unknown and unthought of, today is worshipped literally by thousands in Europe and America, and tomorrow will be worshipped by thousands more. Who knows the plans of the Lord!

Now, my brothers, if you do not see the hand, the finger of Providence, it is because you are blind, born blind indeed. If time comes, and another opportunity, I will speak to you more fully about him. Only let me say now that if I have told you one word of truth, it was his and his alone, and if I have told you many things which were not true, which were not correct, which were not beneficial to the human race, they were all mine, and on me is the responsibility.

The Ramayana

Delivered at the Shakespeare Club, Pasadena, California, 31 January 1900

There are two great epics in the Sanskrit language, which are very ancient. Of course, there are hundreds of other epic poems. The Sanskrit language and literature have been continued down to the present day, although, for more than two thousand years, it has ceased to be a spoken language. I am now going to speak to you of the two most ancient epics, called the Ramayana and the Mahabharata. They embody the manners and customs, the state of society, civilisation, etc., of the ancient Indians. The oldest of these epics is called Ramayana, "The Life of Rama." There was some poetical literature before this —most of the Vedas, the sacred books of the Hindus, are written, in a sort of metre—but this book is held by common consent in India as the very beginning of poetry.

The name of the poet or sage was Valmiki. Later on, a great many poetical stories were fastened moon that ancient poet: and subsequently, it became a very general practice to attribute to his authorship very many verses that were, not his. Notwithstanding all these interpolations, it comes down to us as a very beautiful arrangement, without equal in the literatures of the world.

There was a young man that could not in anyway support his family. He was strong and vigorous and, finally, became a highway robber; he attacked persons in the street and robbed them, and with that money he supported his father, mother, wife, and children. This went on continually, until one day a great saint called Narada was passing by, and the robber attacked him. The sage asked the robber, "Why are you going to rob me? It is a great sin to rob human beings and kill them. What do you incur all this sin for?" The robber said, "Why, I want to support my family with this money." "Now", said the sage, "do you think that they take a share of your sin also?" "Certainly they do," replied the robber. "Very good," said the sage, "make me safe by tying me up here, while you go home and ask your people whether they will share your sin in the same way as they share the money you make." The man accordingly went to his father, and asked, "Father, do you know how I support you?" He answered, "No, I do not." "I am a robber, and I kill persons and rob them." "What? You do that, my son? Get away! You outcast!" He then went to his mother and asked her, "Mother, do you know how I support you?" "No," she replied. "Through robbery and murder." "How horrible it is!" cried the mother. "But, do you partake in my sin?" said the son. "Why should I? I never committed a robbery," answered the mother. Then, he went to his wife and questioned her, "Do you know how I maintain you all?" "No," she responded. "Why, I am a highwayman," he rejoined, "and for years have been robbing people; that is how I support and maintain you all. And what I now want to know is, whether you are ready to share in my sin." "By no means. You are my husband, and it is your duty to support me."

The eyes of the robber were opened. "That is the way of the world—even my nearest relatives, for whom I have been robbing, will not share in my destiny." He came back to the place where he had bound the sage, unfastened his bonds, fell at his feet, recounted everything and said, "Save me! What can I do?" The sage said, "Give up your present course of life. You see that none of your family really loves you, so give up all these delusions. They will share your prosperity; but the moment you have nothing, they will desert you. There is none who will share in your evil, but they will all share in your good. Therefore, worship Him who alone stands by us whether we are doing good or evil. He never leaves us, for love never drags down, knows no barter, no selfishness."

Then the sage taught him how to worship. And this man left everything and went into a forest. There he went on praying and meditating until he forgot himself so entirely that the ants came and built ant-hills around him, and he was quite unconscious of it. After many years had passed, a voice came saying, "Arise, O sage!" Thus aroused he exclaimed, "Sage? I am a robber!" "No more 'robber'," answered the voice, "a purified sage art thou. Thine old name is gone. But now, since thy meditation was so deep and great that thou didst not remark even the anthills which surrounded thee, henceforth, thy name shall be Valmiki—he that was born in the anthill." So, he became a sage.

And this is how he became a poet. One day as this sage, Valmiki, was going to bathe in the holy river Ganga, he saw a pair of doves wheeling round and round, and kissing each other. The sage looked up and was pleased at the sight, but in a second an arrow whisked past him and killed the male dove. As the dove fell down on the ground, the female dove went on whirling round and round the dead body of its companion in grief. In a moment the poet became miserable, and looking round, he saw the hunter. "Thou art a wretch," he cried, "without the smallest mercy! Thy slaying hand would not even stop for love!" "What is this? What am I saying?" the poet thought to himself, "I have never spoken in this sort of way before." And then a voice came: "Be not afraid. This is poetry that is coming out of your mouth. Write the life of Rama in poetic language for-the benefit of the world' And that is how the poem first began. The first verse sprang out of pity from the mouth of Valmiki, the first poet. And it was after that, that he wrote the beautiful Ramayana, "The Life of Rama."

There was an ancient Indian town called Ayodhya—and it exists even in modern times. The province in which it is still located is called Oudh, and most of you may have noticed it in the map of India. That was the ancient Ayodhya. There, in ancient times, reigned a king called Dasharatha. He had three queens, but the king had not any children by them. And like good Hindus, the king and the queens, all went on pilgrimages fasting and praying, that they might have children and, in good time, four sons were born. The eldest of them was Rama.

Now, as it should be, these four brothers were thoroughly educated in all branches of learning. To avoid future quarrels there was in ancient India a custom for the king in his own lifetime to nominate his eldest son as his successor, the Yuvaraja, young king, as he is called.

Now, there was another king, called Janaka, and this king had a beautiful daughter named Sita. Sita was found in a field; she was a daughter of the Earth, and was born without parents. The word "Sita" in ancient Sanskrit means the furrow made by a plough. In the ancient mythology of India you will find persons born of one parent only, or persons born without parents, born of sacrificial fire, born in the field, and so on—dropped from the clouds as it were. All those sorts of miraculous birth were common in the mythological lore of India.

Sita, being the daughter of the Earth, was pure and immaculate. She was brought up by King Janaka. When she was of a marriageable age, the king wanted to find a suitable husband for her.

There was an ancient Indian custom called Svayamvara, by which the princesses used to choose husbands. A number of princes from different parts of the country were invited, and the princess in splendid array, with a garland in her hand, and accompanied by a crier who enumerated the distinctive claims of each of the royal suitors, would pass in the midst of those assembled before her, and select the prince she liked for her husband by throwing the garland of flowers round his neck. They would then be married with much pomp and grandeur.

There were numbers of princes who aspired for the hand of Sita; the test demanded on this occasion was the breaking of a huge bow, called Haradhanu. All the princes put forth all their strength to accomplish this feat, but failed. Finally, Rama took the mighty bow in his hands and with easy grace broke it in twain. Thus Sita selected Rama, the son of King Dasharatha for her husband, and they were wedded with great rejoicings. Then, Rama took his bride to his home, and his old father thought that the time was now come for him to retire and appoint Rama as Yuvaraja. Everything was accordingly made ready for the ceremony, and the whole country was jubilant over the affair, when the younger queen Kaikeyi was reminded by one of her maidservants of two promises made to her by the king long ago. At one time she had pleased the king very much, and he offered to grant her two boons: "Ask any two things in my power and I will grant them to you," said he, but she made no request then. She had forgotten all about it; but the evil-minded maidservant in her employ began to work upon her jealousy with regard to Rama being installed on the throne, and insinuated to her how nice it would be for her if her own son had succeeded the king, until the queen was almost mad with jealousy. Then the servant suggested to her to ask from the king the two promised boons: one would be that her own son Bharata should be placed on the throne, and the other, that Rama should be sent to the forest and be exiled for fourteen years.

Now, Rama was the life and the soul of the old king and when this wicked request was made to him, he as a king felt he could not go back on his word. So he did not know what to do. But Rama came to the rescue and willingly offered to give up the throne and go into exile, so that his father might not be guilty of falsehood. So Rama went into exile for fourteen years, accompanied by his loving wife Sita and his devoted brother Lakshmana, who would on no account be parted from him.

The Aryans did not know who were the inhabitants of these wild forests. In those days the forest tribes they called "monkeys", and some of the so-called "monkeys", if unusually strong and powerful, were called "demons".

So, into the forest, inhabited by demons and monkeys, Rama, Lakshmana, and Sita went. When Sita had offered to accompany Rama, he exclaimed, "How can you, a princess, face hardships and accompany me into a forest full of unknown dangers!" But Sita replied, "Wherever Rama goes, there goes Sita. How can you talk of 'princess' and 'royal birth' to me? I go before you!" So, Sita went. And the younger brother, he also went with them. They penetrated far into the forest, until they reached the river Godavari. On the banks of the river they built little cottages, and Rama and Lakshmana used to hunt deer and collect fruits. After they had lived thus for some time, one day there came a demon giantess. She was the sister of the giant king of Lanka (Ceylon). Roaming through the forest at will, she came across Rama, and seeing that he was a very handsome man, she fell in love with him at once. But Rama was the purest of men, and also he was a married man; so of course he could not return her love. In revenge, she went to her brother, the giant king, and told him all about the beautiful Sita, the wife of Rama.

Rama was the most powerful of mortals; there were no giants or demons or anybody else strong enough to conquer him. So, the giant king had to resort to subterfuge. He got hold of another giant who was a magician and changed him into a beautiful golden deer; and the deer went prancing round about the place where Rama lived, until Sita was fascinated by its beauty and asked Rama to go and capture the deer for her. Rama went into the forest to catch the deer, leaving his brother in charge of Sita. Then Lakshmana laid a circle of fire round the cottage, and he said to Sita, "Today I see something may befall you; and, therefore, I tell you not to go outside of this magic circle. Some danger may befall you if you do." In the meanwhile, Rama had pierced the magic deer with his arrow, and immediately the deer, changed into the form of a man, and died.

Immediately, at the cottage was heard the voice of Rama, crying, "Oh, Lakshmana, come to my help!" and Sita said, "Lakshmana, go at once into the forest to help Rama!" "That is not Rama's voice," protested Lakshmana. But at the entreaties of Sita, Lakshmana had to go in search of Rama. As soon as he went away, the giant king, who had taken the form of a mendicant monk, stood at the gate and asked for alms. "Wait awhile," said Sita, "until my husband comes back and I will give you plentiful alms." "I cannot wait, good lady," said he, "I am very hungry, give me anything you have." At this, Sita, who had a few fruits in the cottage, brought them out. But the mendicant monk after many persuasions prevailed upon her to bring the alms to him, assuring her that she need have no fear as he was a holy person. So Sita came out of the magic circle, and immediately the seeming monk assumed his giant body, and grasping Sita in his arms he called his magic chariot, and putting her therein, he fled with the weeping Sita. Poor Sita! She was utterly helpless, nobody was there to come to her aid. As the giant was carrying her away, she took off a few of the ornaments from her arms and at intervals dropped them to the ground.

She was taken by Ravana to his kingdom, Lanka, the island of Ceylon. He made proposals to her to become his queen, and tempted her in many ways to accede to his request. But Sita was chastity itself, would not even speak to the giant; and he to punish her, made her live under a tree, day and night, until she should consent to be his wife.

When Rama and Lakshmana returned to the cottage and found that Sita was not there, their grief knew no bounds. They could not imagine what had become of her. The two brothers went on, seeking, seeking everywhere for Sita, but could find no trace of her. After long searching, they came across a group of "monkeys", and in the midst of them was Hanuman, the "Divine Monkey". Hanuman, the best of the monkeys, became the most faithful servant of Rama and helped him in rescuing Sita, as we shall see later on. His devotion to Rama was so great that he is still worshipped by the Hindus as the ideal of a true servant of the Lord. You see, by the "monkeys" and "demons" are meant the aborigines of South India.

So, Rama, at last, fell in with these monkeys. They told him that they had seen flying through the sky a chariot, in which was seated a demon who was carrying away a most beautiful lady, and that she was weeping bitterly, and as the chariot passed over their heads she dropped one of her ornaments to attract their attention. Then they showed Rama the ornament. Lakshmana took up the ornament, and said, "I do not know whose ornament this is." Rama took it from him and recognised it at once, saying "Yes, it is Sita's." Lakshmana could not recognise the ornament, because in India the wife of the elder brother was held in so much reverence that he had never looked upon the arms and the neck of Sita. So you see, as it was a necklace, he did not know whose it was. There is in this episode a touch of the old Indian custom. Then, the monkeys told Rama who this demon king was and where he lived, and then they all went to seek for him.

Now, the monkey-king Vali and his younger brother Sugriva were then fighting amongst themselves for the kingdom. The younger brother was helped by Rama, and he regained the kingdom from Vali, who had driven him away; and he, in return, promised to help Rama. They searched the country all round, but could not find Sita.

At last Hanuman leaped by one bound from the coast of India to the island of Ceylon, and there went looking all over Lanka for Sita, but nowhere could he find her.

You see, this giant king had conquered the gods, the men, in fact the whole world; and he had collected all the beautiful women and made them his concubines. So, Hanuman thought to himself, "Sita cannot be with them in the palace. She would rather die than be in such a place." So Hanuman went to seek for her elsewhere. At last, he found Sita under a tree, pale and thin, like the new moon that lies low in the horizon. Now Hanuman took the form of a little monkey and settled on the tree, and there he witnessed how giantesses sent by Ravana came and tried to frighten Sita into submission, but she would not even listen to the name of the giant king.

Then, Hanuman came nearer to Sita and told her how he became the messenger of Rama, who had sent him to find out where Sita was; and Hanuman showed to Sita the signet ring which Rama had given as a token for establishing his identity. He also informed her that as soon as Rama would know her whereabouts, he would come with an army and conquer the giant and recover her. However, he suggested to Sita that if she wished it, he would take her on his shoulders and could with one leap clear the ocean and get back to Rama. But Sita could not bear the idea, as she was chastity itself, and could not touch the body of any man except her husband. So, Sita remained where she was. But she gave him a jewel from her hair to carry to Rama; and with that Hanuman returned.

Learning everything about Sita from Hanuman, Rama collected an army, and with it marched towards the southernmost point of India. There Rama's monkeys built a huge bridge, called Setu Bandha, connecting India with

Ceylon. In very low water even now it is possible to cross from India to Ceylon over the sandbanks there.

Now Rama was God incarnate, otherwise, how could he have done all these things? He was an Incarnation of God, according to the Hindus. They in India believe him to be the seventh Incarnation of God.

The monkeys removed whole hills, placed them in the sea and covered them with stones and trees, thus making a huge embankment. A little squirrel, so it is said, was there rolling himself in the sand and running backwards and forwards on to the bridge and shaking himself. Thus in his small way he was working for the bridge of Rama by putting in sand. The monkeys laughed, for they were bringing whole mountains, whole forests, huge loads of sand for the bridge—so they laughed at the little squirrel rolling in the sand and then shaking himself. But Rama saw it and remarked: "Blessed be the little squirrel; he is doing his work to the best of his ability, and he is, therefore, quite as great as the greatest of you." Then he gently stroked the squirrel on the back, and the marks of Rama's fingers, running lengthways, are seen on the squirrel's back to this day.

Now, when the bridge was finished, the whole army of monkeys, led by Rama and his brother entered Ceylon. For several months afterwards tremendous war and bloodshed followed. At last, this demon king, Ravana, was conquered and killed; and his capital, with all the palaces and everything, which were entirely of solid gold, was taken. In faraway villages in the interior of India, when I tell them that I have been in Ceylon, the simple folk say, "There, as our books tell, the houses are built of gold." So, all these golden cities fell into the hands of Rama, who gave them over to Vibhishana, the younger brother of Ravana, and seated him on the throne in the place of his brother, as a return for the valuable services rendered by him to Rama during the war.

Then Rama with Sita and his followers left Lanka. But there ran a murmur among his followers. "The test! The test!" they cried, "Sita has not given the test that she was perfectly pure in Ravana's household." "Pure! She is chastity itself!" exclaimed Rama. "Never mind! We want the test," persisted the people. Subsequently, a huge sacrificial fire was made ready, into which Sita had to plunge herself. Rama was in agony, thinking that Sita was lost; but in a moment, the God of fire himself appeared with a throne upon his head, and upon the throne was Sita. Then, there was universal rejoicing, and everybody was satisfied.

Early during the period of exile, Bharata, the younger brother had come and informed Rama, of the death of the old king and vehemently insisted on his occupying the throne. During Rama's exile Bharata would on no account ascend the throne and out of respect placed a pair of Rama's wooden shoes on it as a substitute for his brother. Then Rama returned to his capital, and by the common consent of his people, he became the king of Ayodhya.

After Rama regained his kingdom, he took the necessary vows which in olden times the king had to take for the benefit of his people. The king was the slave of his people, he had to bow to public opinion, as we shall see later on. Rama passed a few years in happiness with Sita, when the people again began to murmur that Sita had been stolen by a demon and carried across the ocean. They were not satisfied with the former test and clamoured for another test, otherwise she must be banished.

In order to satisfy the demands of the people, Sita was banished, and left to live in the forest, where was the hermitage of the sage and poet Valmiki. The sage found poor Sita weeping and forlorn, and hearing her sad story, sheltered her in his Ashrama. Sita was expecting soon to become a mother, and she gave birth to twin boys. The poet never told the children who they were. He brought them up together in the Brahmacharin life. He then composed the poem known as Ramayana, set it to music, and dramatised it.

The drama, in India, was a very holy thing. Drama and music are themselves held to be religion. Any song—whether it be a love-song or otherwise—if one's whole soul is in that song, one attains salvation, one has nothing else to do. They say it leads to the same goal as meditation.

So, Valmiki dramatised "The Life of Rama", and taught Rama's two children how to recite and sing it.

There came a time when Rama was going to perform a huge sacrifice, or Yajna, such as the old kings used to celebrate. But no ceremony in India can be performed by a married man without his wife: he must have the wife with him, the Sahadharmini, the "co-religionist"—that is the expression for the wife. The Hindu householder has to perform hundreds of ceremonies, but not one can be duly performed according to the Shastras, if he has not a wife to complement it with her part in it.

Now Rama's wife was not with him then, as she had been banished. So, the people asked him to marry again. But at this request Rama for the first time in his life stood against the people. He said, "This cannot be. My life is Sita's." So, as a substitute, a golden statue of Sita was made, in order that the ceremony could be accomplished. They arranged even a dramatic entertainment, to enhance the religious feeling in this great festival. Valmiki, the great sage-poet, came with his pupils, Lava and Kusha, the unknown sons of Rama. A stage had been erected and everything was ready for the performance. Rama and his brothers attended with all his nobles and his people—a vast audience. Under the direction of Valmiki, the life of Rama was sung by Lava and Kusha, who fascinated the whole assembly by their charming voice and appearance. Poor Rama was nearly maddened, and when in the drama, the scene of Sita's exile came about, he did not know what to do. Then the sage said to him, "Do not be grieved, for

I will show you Sita." Then Sita was brought upon the stage and Rama delighted to see his wife. All of a sudden, the old murmur arose: "The test! The test!" Poor Sita was so terribly overcome by the repeated cruel slight on her reputation that it was more than she could bear. She appealed to the gods to testify to her innocence, when the Earth opened and Sita exclaimed, "Here is the test", and vanished into the bosom of the Earth. The people were taken aback at this tragic end. And Rama was overwhelmed with grief.

A few days after Sita's disappearance, a messenger came to Rama from the gods, who intimated to him that his mission on earth was finished and he was to return to heaven. These tidings brought to him the recognition of his own real Self. He plunged into the waters of Sarayu, the mighty river that laved his capital, and joined Sita in the other world.

This is the great, ancient epic of India. Rama and Sita are the ideals of the Indian nation. All children, especially girls, worship Sita. The height of a woman's ambition is to be like Sita, the pure, the devoted, the all-suffering! When you study these characters, you can at once find out how different is the ideal in India from that of the West. For the race, Sita stands as the ideal of suffering. The West says, 'Do! Show your power by doing." India says, "Show your power by suffering." The West has solved the problem of how much a man can have: India has solved the problem of how little a man can have. The two extremes, you see. Sita is typical of India—the idealised India. The question is not whether she ever lived, whether the story is history or not, we know that the ideal is there. There is no other Pauranika story that has so permeated the whole nation, so entered into its very life, and has so tingled in every drop of blood of the race, as this ideal of Sita. Sita is the name in India for everything that is good, pure and holy—everything that in woman we call womanly. If a priest has to bless a woman he says, "Be Sita!" If he blesses a child, he says "Be Sita!" They are all children of Sita, and are struggling to be Sita, the patient, the all-suffering, the ever-faithful, the ever-pure wife. Through all this suffering she experiences, there is not one harsh word against Rama. She takes it as her own duty, and performs her own part in it. Think of the terrible injustice of her being exiled to the forest! But Sita knows no bitterness. That is, again, the Indian ideal. Says the ancient Buddha, "When a man hurts you, and you turn back to hurt him, that would not cure the first injury; it would only create in the world one more wickedness." Sita was a true Indian by nature; she never returned injury.

Who knows which is the truer ideal? The apparent power and strength, as held in the West, or the fortitude in suffering, of the East?

The West says, "We minimise evil by conquering it." India says, "We destroy evil by suffering, until evil is nothing to us, it becomes positive enjoyment." Well, both are great ideals. Who knows which will survive in the long run? Who knows which attitude will really most benefit humanity? Who knows which will disarm and conquer animality? Will it be suffering, or doing?

In the meantime, let us not try to destroy each other's ideals. We are both intent upon the same work, which is the annihilation of evil. You take up your method; let us take up our method. Let us not destroy the ideal. I do not say to the West, "Take up our method." Certainly not. The goal is the same, but the methods can never be the same. And so, after hearing about the ideals of India, I hope that you will say in the same breath to India, "We know, the goal, the ideal, is all right for us both. You follow your own ideal. You follow your method in your own way, and Godspeed to you!" My message in life is to ask the East and West not to quarrel over different ideals, but to show them that the goal is the same in both cases, however opposite it may appear. As we wend our way through this mazy vale of life, let us bid each other Godspeed.

The Mahabharata

Delivered at the Shakespeare Club, Pasadena, California, 1 February 1900

The other epic about which I am going to speak to you this evening, is called the Mahabharata. It contains the story of a race descended from King Bharata, who was the son of Dushyanta and Shakuntala. Maha means great, and Bharata means the descendants of Bharata, from whom India has derived its name, Bharata. Mahabharata means Great India, or the story of the great descendants of Bharata. The scene of this epic is the ancient kingdom of the Kurus, and the story is based on the great war which took place between the Kurus and the Panchalas. So the region of the quarrel is not very big. This epic is the most popular one in India; and it exercises the same authority in India as Homer's poems did over the Greeks. As ages went on, more and more matter was added to it, until it has become a huge book of about a hundred thousand couplets. All sorts of tales, legends and myths, philosophical treatises, scraps of history, and various discussions have been added to it from time to time, until it is a vast, gigantic mass of literature; and through it all runs the old, original story. The central story of the Mahabharata is of a war between two families of cousins, one family, called the Kauravas, the other the Pandavas—for the empire of India.

The Aryans came into India in small companies. Gradually, these tribes began to extend, until, at last, they became the undisputed rulers Of India, and then arose this fight to gain the mastery, between two branches of the same family. Those of you who have studied the *Gita* know how the book opens with a description of the battlefield, with two armies arrayed one against the other. That is the war of the Mahabharata.

There were two brothers, sons of the emperor. The elder one was called Dhritarashtra, and the other was called Pandu. Dhritarashtra, the elder one, was born blind. According to Indian law, no blind, halt, maimed, consumptive, or any other constitutionally diseased person, can inherit. He can only get a maintenance. So, Dhritarashtra could not ascend the throne, though he was the elder son, and Pandu became the emperor.

Dhritarashtra had a hundred sons, and Pandu had only five. After the death of Pandu at an early age, Dhritarashtra became king of the Kurus and brought up the sons of Pandu along with his own children. When they grew up, they were placed under the tutorship of the great priest-warrior, Drona, and were well trained in the various material arts and sciences befitting princes. The education of the princes being finished, Dhritarashtra put Yudhishthira, the eldest of the sons of Pandu, on the throne of his father. The sterling virtues of Yudhishthira and the valour and devotion of his other brothers aroused jealousies in the hearts of the sons of the blind king, and at the instigation of Duryodhana, the eldest of them, the five Pandava brothers were prevailed upon to visit Varanavata, on the plea of a religious festival that was being held there. There they were accommodated in a palace made under Duryodhana's instructions, of hemp, resin, and lac, and other, inflammable materials, which were subsequently set fire to secretly. But the good Vidura, the step-brother of Dhritarashtra, having become cognisant of the evil intentions of Duryodhana and his party, had warned the Pandavas of the plot, and they managed to escape without anyone's knowledge. When the Kurus saw the house was reduced to ashes, they heaved a sigh of relief and thought all obstacles were now removed out of their path. Then the children of Dhritarashtra got hold of the kingdom. The five Pandava brothers had fled to the forest with their mother, Kunti. They lived there by begging, and went about in disguise giving themselves but as Brahmana students. Many were the hardships and adventures they encountered in the wild forests, but their fortitude of mind, and strength, and valour made them conquer all dangers. So things went on until they came to hear of the approaching marriage of the princess of a neighbouring country.

I told you last night of the peculiar form of the ancient Indian marriage. It was called Svayamvara, that is, the choosing of the husband by the princess. A great gathering of princes and nobles assembled, amongst whom the princess would choose her husband. Preceded by her trumpeters and heralds she would approach, carrying a garland of flowers in her hand. At the throne of each candidate for her hand, the praises of that prince and all his great deeds in battle would be declared by the heralds. And when the princess decided which prince she desired to have for a husband, she would signify the fact by throwing the marriage-garland round his neck. Then the ceremony would turn into a wedding. King Drupada was a great king, king of the Panchalas and his daughter, Draupadi, famed far and wide for her beauty and accomplishments, was going to choose a hero.

At a Svayamvara there was always a great feat of arms or something of the kind. On this occasion, a mark in the form of a fish was set up high in the sky; under that fish was a wheel with a hole in the centre, continually turning round, and beneath was a tub of water. A man looking at the reflection of the fish in the tub of water was asked to send an arrow and hit the eye of the fish through the Chakra or wheel, and he who succeeded would be married to the princess. Now, there came kings and princes from different parts of India, all anxious to win the hand of the princess, and one after another they tried their skill, and every one of them failed to hit the mark.

You know, there are four castes in India: the highest caste is that of the hereditary priest, the Brahmana; next is the caste of the Kshatriya, composed of kings and fighters; next, the Vaishyas, the traders or businessmen, and then Shudras, the servants. Now, this princess was, of course, a Kshatriya, one of the second caste.

When all those princes failed in hitting the mark, then the son of King Drupada rose up in the midst of the court and said: "The Kshatriya, the king caste has failed; now the contest is open to the other castes. Let a Brahmana, even a Shudra, take part in it; whosoever hits the mark, marries Draupadi."

Among the Brahmanas were seated the five Pandava brothers. Arjuna, the third brother, was the hero of the bow. He arose and stepped forward. Now, Brahmanas as a caste are very quiet and rather timid people. According to the law, they must not touch a warlike weapon, they must not wield a sword, they must not go into any enterprise that is dangerous. Their life is one of contemplation, study, and control of the inner nature. Judge, therefore, how quiet and peaceable a people they are. When the Brahmanas saw this man get up, they thought this man was going to bring the wrath of the Kshatriyas upon them, and that they would all be killed. So they tried to dissuade him, but Arjuna did not listen to them, because he was a soldier. He lifted the bow in his hand, strung it without any effort, and drawing it, sent the arrow right through the wheel and hit the eye of the fish.

Then there was great jubilation. Draupadi, the princess, approached Arjuna and threw the beautiful garland of flowers over his head. But there arose a great cry among the princes, who could not bear the idea that this beautiful princess who was a Kshatriya should be won by a poor Brahmana, from among this huge assembly of kings and princes. So, they wanted to fight Arjuna and snatch her from him by force. The brothers had a tremendous fight with the warriors, but held their own, and carried off the bride in triumph.

The five brothers now returned home to Kunti with the princess. Brahmanas have to live by begging. So they, who lived as Brahmanas, used to go out, and what they got by begging they brought home and the mother divided it among them. Thus the five brothers, with the princess, came to the cottage where the mother lived. They shouted out to her jocosely, "Mother, we have brought home a most wonderful alms today." The mother replied, "Enjoy it in common, all of you, my children." Then the mother seeing the princess, exclaimed, "Oh! What have I said! It is a girl!" But what could be done! The mother's word was spoken once for all. It must not be disregarded. The mother's words must be fulfilled. She could not be made to utter an untruth, as she never had done so. So Draupadi became the common wife of all the five brothers.

Now, you know, in every society there are stages of development. Behind this epic there is a wonderful glimpse of the ancient historic times. The author of the poem mentions the fact of the five brothers marrying the same woman, but he tries to gloss it over, to find an excuse and a cause for such an act: it was the mother's command, the mother sanctioned this strange betrothal, and so on. You know, in every nation there has been a certain stage in society that allowed polyandry—all the brothers of a family would marry one wife in common. Now, this was evidently a glimpse of the past polyandrous stage.

In the meantime, the brother of the princess was perplexed in his mind and thought: "Who are these people? Who is this man whom my sister is going to marry? They have not any chariots, horses, or anything. Why, they go on foot!" So he had followed them at a distance, and at night overheard their conversation and became fully convinced that they were really Kshatriyas. Then King Drupada came to know who they were and was greatly delighted.

Though at first much objection was raised, it was declared by Vyasa that such a marriage was allowable for these princes, and it was permitted. So the king Drupada had to yield to this polyandrous marriage, and the princess was married to the five sons of Pandu.

Then the Pandavas lived in peace and prosperity and became more powerful every day. Though Duryodhana and his party conceived of fresh plots to destroy them, King Dhritarashtra was prevailed upon by the wise counsels of the elders to make peace with the Pandavas; and so he invited them home amidst the rejoicings of the people and gave them half of the kingdom. Then, the five brothers built for themselves a beautiful city, called Indraprastha, and extended their dominions, laying all the people under tribute to them. Then the eldest, Yudhishthira, in order to declare himself emperor over all the kings of ancient India, decided to perform a Rajasuya Yajna, or Imperial Sacrifice, in which the conquered kings would have to come with tribute and swear allegiance, and help the performance of the sacrifice by personal services. Shri Krishna, who had become their friend and a relative, came to them and approved of the idea. But there was one obstacle to its performance. A king, Jarasandha by name, who intended to offer a sacrifice of a hundred kings, had eighty-six of them kept as captives with him. Shri Krishna counselled an attack on Jarasandha. So he, Bhima, and Arjuna challenged the king, who accepted the challenge and was finally conquered by Bhima after fourteen days' continuous wrestling. The captive kings were then set free.

Then the four younger brothers went out with armies on a conquering expedition, each in a different direction, and brought all the kings under subjection to Yudhishthira.

Returning, they laid all the vast wealth they secured at the feet of the eldest brother to meet the expenses of the great sacrifice.

So, to this Rajasuya sacrifice all the liberated kings came, along with those conquered by the brothers, and rendered homage to Yudhishthira. King Dhritarashtra and his sons were also invited to come and take a share in the performance of the sacrifice. At the conclusion of the sacrifice, Yudhishthira was crowned emperor, and declared as lord paramount. This was the sowing of the future feud. Duryodhana came back from the sacrifice filled with jealousy against Yudhishthira, as their sovereignty and vast splendour and wealth were more than he could bear; and so he devised plans to effect their fall by guile, as he knew that to overcome them by force was beyond his power. This king, Yudhishthira, had the love of gambling, and he was challenged at an evil hour to play dice with Shakuni, the crafty gambler and the evil genius of Duryodhana. In ancient India, if a man of the military caste was challenged to fight, he must at any price accept the challenge to uphold his honour. And if he was challenged to play dice, it was a point of honour to play, and dishonourable to decline the challenge. King Yudhishthira, says the Epic, was the incarnation of all virtues. Even he, the great sage-king, had to accept the challenge. Shakuni and his party had made false dice. So Yudhishthira lost game after game, and stung with his losses, he went on with the fatal game, staking everything he had, and losing all, until all his possessions, his kingdom and everything, were lost. The last stage came when, under further challenge, he had no other resources left but to stake his brothers, and then himself, and last of all, the fair Draupadi, and lost all. Now they were completely at the mercy of the Kauravas, who cast all sorts of insults upon them, and subjected Draupadi to most inhuman treatment. At last through the intervention of the blind king, they got their liberty, and were asked to return home and rule their kingdom. But Duryodhana saw the danger and forced his father to allow one more throw of the dice in which the party which would lose, should retire to the forests for twelve years, and then live unrecognised in a city for one year; but if they were found out, the same term of exile should have to be undergone once again and then only the kingdom was to be restored to the exiled. This last game also Yudhishthira lost, and the five Pandava brothers retired to the forests with Draupadi, as homeless exiles. They lived in the forests and mountains for twelve years. There they performed many deeds of virtue and valour, and would go out now and then on a long round of pilgrimages, visiting many holy places. That part of the poem is very interesting and instructive, and various are the incidents, tales, and legends with which this part of the book is replete. There are in it beautiful and sublime stories of ancient India, religious and philosophical. Great sages came to see the brothers in their exile and narrated to them many telling stories of ancient India, so as to make them bear lightly the burden of their exile. One only I will relate to you here.

There was a king called Ashvapati. The king had a daughter, who was so good and beautiful that she was called Savitri, which is the name of a sacred prayer of the Hindus. When Savitri grew old enough, her father asked her to choose a husband, for herself. These ancient Indian princesses were very independent, you see, and chose their own princely suitors.

Savitri consented and travelled in distant regions, mounted in a golden chariot, with her guards and aged courtiers to whom her father entrusted her, stopping at different courts, and seeing different princes, but not one of them could win the heart of Savitri. They came at last to a holy hermitage in one of those forests that in ancient India were reserved for animals, and where no animals were allowed to be killed. The animals lost the fear of man—even the fish in the lakes came and took food out of the hand. For thousands of years no one had killed anything therein. The sages and the aged went there to live among the deer and the birds. Even criminals were safe there. When a man got tired of life, he would go to the forest; and in the company of sages, talking of religion and meditating thereon, he passed the remainder of his life.

Now it happened that there was a king, Dyumatsena, who was defeated by his enemies and was deprived of his kingdom when he was struck with age and had lost his sight. This poor, old, blind king, with his queen and his son, took refuge in the forest and passed his life in rigid penance. His boy's name was Satyavan.

It came to pass that after having visited all the different royal courts, Savitri at last came to this hermitage, or holy place. Not even the greatest king could pass by the hermitages, or ashramas as they were called, without going to pay homage to the sages, for such honour and respect was felt for these holy men. The greatest emperor of India would be only too glad to trace his descent to some sage who lived in a forest, subsisting on roots and fruits, and clad in rags. We are all children of sages. That is the respect that is paid to religion. So, even kings, when they pass by the hermitages, feel honoured to go in and pay their respects to the sages. If they approach on horseback, they descend and walk as they advance towards them. If they arrive in a chariot, chariot and armour must be left outside when they enter. No fighting man can enter unless he comes in the manner of a religious man, quiet and gentle.

So Savitri came to this hermitage and saw there Satyavan, the hermit's son, and her heart was conquered. She had escaped all the princes of the palaces and the courts, but here in the forest-refuge of the King Dyumatsena, his son, Satyavan, stole her heart.

When Savitri returned to her father's house, he asked her, "Savitri, dear daughter, speak. Did you see anybody whom you would like to marry?" Then softly with blushes, said Savitri, "Yes, father." "What is the name of the prince?" "He is no prince, but the son of King Dyumatsena who has lost his kingdom—a prince without a patrimony, who lives a monastic life, the life of a Sannyasin in a forest, collecting roots and herbs, helping and feeding his old father and mother, who live in a cottage."

On hearing this the father consulted the Sage Narada, who happened to be then present there, and he declared it was the most ill-omened choice that was ever made. The king then asked him to explain why it was so. And Narada said, "Within twelve months from this time the young man will die." Then the king started with terror, and spoke, "Savitri, this young man is going to die in twelve months, and you will become a widow: think of that! Desist from your choice, my child, you shall never be married to a short-lived and fated bridegroom." "Never mind, father; do not ask me to marry another person and sacrifice the chastity of mind, for I love and have accepted in my mind that good and brave Satyavan only as my husband. A maiden chooses only once, and she never departs from her troth." When the king found that Savitri was resolute in mind and heart, he complied. Then Savitri married prince Satyavan, and she quietly went from the palace of her father into the forest, to live with her chosen husband and help her husband's parents. Now, though Savitri knew the exact date when Satyavan was to die, she kept it hidden from him. Daily he went into the depths of the forest, collected fruits and flowers, gathered faggots, and then came back to the cottage, and she cooked the meals and helped the old people. Thus their lives went on until the fatal day came near, and three short days remained only.

She took a severe vow of three nights' penance and holy fasts, and kept her hard vigils. Savitri spent sorrowful and sleepless nights with fervent prayers and unseen tears, till the dreaded morning dawned. That day Savitri could not I bear him out of her sight, even for a moment. She begged permission from his parents to accompany her husband, when he went to gather the usual herbs and fuel, and gaining their consent she went. Suddenly, in faltering accents, he complained to his wife of feeling faint, "My head is dizzy, and my senses reel, dear Savitri, I feel sleep stealing over me; let me rest beside thee for a while." In fear and trembling she replied, "Come, lay your head upon my lap, my dearest lord." And he laid his burning head in the lap of his wife, and ere long sighed and expired. Clasping him to her, her eyes flowing with tears, there she sat in the lonesome forest, until the emissaries of Death approached to take away the soul of Satyavan. But they could not come near to the place where Savitri sat with the dead body of her husband, his head resting in her lap. There was a zone of fire surrounding her, and not one of the emissaries of Death could come within it. They all fled back from it, returned to King Yama, the God of Death, and told him why they could not obtain the soul of this man.

Then came Yama, the God of Death, the Judge of the dead. He was the first man that died—the first man that died on earth—and he had become the presiding deity over all those that die. He judges whether, after a man has died, he is to be punished or rewarded. So he came himself. Of course, he could go inside that charmed circle, as he was a god. When he came to Savitri, he said, "Daughter, give up this dead body, for know, death is the fate of mortals, and I am the first of mortals who died. Since then, everyone has had to die. Death is the fate of man." Thus told, Savitri walked off, and Yama drew the soul out. Yama having possessed himself of the soul of the young man proceeded on his way. Before he had gone far, he heard footfalls upon the dry leaves. He turned back. "Savitri, daughter, why are you following me? This is the fate of all mortals." "I am not following thee, Father," replied Savitri, "but this is, also, the fate of woman, she follows where her love takes her, and the Eternal Law separates not loving man and faithful wife." Then said the

God of Death, "Ask for any boon, except the life of your husband." "If thou art pleased to grant a boon, Lord of Death, I ask that my father-in-law may be cured of his blindness and made happy." "Let thy pious wish be granted, duteous daughter." And then the King of Death travelled on with the soul of Satyavan. Again the same footfall was heard from behind. He looked round. "Savitri, my daughter, you are still following me?" "Yes, my Father; cannot help doing so; I am trying all the time to go back, but the mind goes after my husband and the body follows. The soul has already gone, for in that soul is also mine; and when you take the soul, the body follows, does it not?" "Pleased am I with your words, fair Savitri. Ask yet another boon of me, but it must not be the life of your husband." "Let my father-in-law regain his lost wealth and kingdom, Father, if thou art pleased to grant another supplication." "Loving daughter," Yama answered, "this boon I now bestow; but return home, for living mortal cannot go with King Yama." And then Yama pursued his way. But Savitri, meek and faithful, still followed her departed husband. Yama again turned back. "Noble Savitri, follow not in hopeless woe." "I cannot choose but follow where thou takest my beloved one." "Then suppose, Savitri, that your husband was a sinner and has to go to hell. In that case goes Savitri with the one she loves?" "Glad am I to follow where he goes, be it life or death, heaven or hell," said the loving wife. "Blessed are your words, my child, pleased am I with you, ask yet another boon, but the dead come not to life again." "Since you so permit me, then, let the imperial line of my father-in-law be not destroyed; let his kingdom descend to Satyavan's sons." And then the God of Death smiled. "My daughter, thou shalt have thy desire now: here is the soul of thy husband, he shall live again. He shall live to be a father and thy children also shall reign in due course. Return home. Love has conquered Death! Woman never loved like thee, and thou art the proof that even I, the God of Death, am powerless against the power of the true love that abideth!"

This is the story of Savitri, and every girl in India must aspire to be like Savitri, whose love could not be conquered by death, and who through this tremendous love snatched back from even Yama, the soul of her husband.

The book is full of hundreds of beautiful episodes like this. I began by telling you that the Mahabharata is one of the greatest books in the world and consists of about a hundred thousand verses in eighteen Parvas, or volumes.

To return to our main story. We left the Pandava brothers in exile. Even there they were not allowed to remain unmolested from the evil plots of Duryodhana; but all of them were futile.

A story of their forest life, I shall tell you here. One day the brothers became thirsty in the forest. Yudhishthira bade his brother, Nakula to go and fetch water. He quickly proceeded towards the place where there was water and soon came to a crystal lake, and was about to drink of it, when he heard a voice utter these words: "Stop, O child. First answer my questions and then drink of this water." But Nakula, who was exceedingly thirsty, disregarded these words, drank of the water, and having drunk of it, dropped down dead. As Nakula did not return, King Yudhishthira told Sahadeva to seek his brother and bring back water with him. So Sahadeva proceeded to the lake and beheld his brother lying dead. Afflicted at the death of his brother and suffering severely from thirst, he went towards the water, when the same words were heard by him: "O child, first answer my questions and then drink of the water." He also disregarded these words, and having satisfied his thirst, dropped down dead. Subsequently Arjuna and Bhima were sent, one after the other, on a similar quest; but neither returned, having drunk of the lake and dropped down dead. Then Yudhishthira rose up to go in search of his brothers. At length, he came to the beautiful lake and saw his brothers lying dead. His heart was full of grief at the sight, and he began to lament. Suddenly he heard the same voice saying, "Do not, O child, act rashly. I am a Yaksha living as a crane on tiny fish. It is by me that thy younger brothers have been brought under the sway of the Lord of departed spirits. If thou, O Prince, answer not the questions put by me, even thou shalt number the fifth corpse. Having answered my questions first, do thou, O Kunti's son, drink and carry away as much as thou requirest." Yudhishthira replied, "I shall answer thy questions according to my intelligence. Do thou ask me!" The Yaksha then asked him several questions, all of which Yudhishthira answered satisfactorily. One of the questions asked was: "What is the most wonderful fact in this world?" "We see our fellow-beings every moment falling off around us; but those that are left behind think that they will never die. This is the most curious fact: in face of death, none believes that he will die!" Another question was: "What is the path of knowing the secret of religion?" And Yudhishthira answered, "By argument nothing can be settled; doctrines there are many; various are the scriptures, one part contradicting the other. There are not two sages who do not differ in their opinions. The secret of religion is buried deep, as it were, in dark caves. So the path to be followed is that which the great ones have trodden." Then the Yaksha said, "I am pleased. I am Dharma, the God of Justice in the form of a crane. I came to test you. Now, your brothers, see, not one of them is dead. It is all my magic. Since abstention from injury is regarded by thee as higher than both profit and pleasure, therefore, let all thy brothers live, O Bull of the Bharata race." And at these words of the Yaksha, the Pandavas rose up.

Here is a glimpse of the nature of King Yudhishthira. We find by his answers that he was more of a philosopher, more of a Yogi, than a king.

Now, as the thirteenth year of the exile was drawing nigh, the Yaksha bade them go to Virata's kingdom and live there in such disguises as they would think best.

So, after the term of the twelve years' exile had expired, they went to the kingdom of Virata in different disguises to spend the remaining one year in concealment, and entered into menial service in the king's household. Thus Yudhishthira became a Brahmana courtier of the king, as one skilled in dice; Bhima was appointed a cook; Arjuna, dressed as a eunuch, was made a teacher of dancing and music to Uttara, the princess, and remained in the inner apartments of the king; Nakula became the keeper of the king's horses; and Sahadeva got the charge of the cows; and Draupadi, disguised as a waiting-woman was also admitted into the queen's household. Thus concealing their identity the Pandava brothers safely spent a year, and the search of Duryodhana to find them out was of no avail. They were only discovered just when the year was out.

Then Yudhishthira sent an ambassador to Dhritarashtra and demanded that half of the kingdom should, as their share, be restored to them. But Duryodhana hated his cousins and would not consent to their legitimate demands. They were even willing to accept a single province, nay, even five villages. But the headstrong Duryodhana declared that he would not yield without fight even as much land as a needle's point would hold. Dhritarashtra pleaded again and again for peace, but all in vain. Krishna also went and tried to avert the impending war and death of kinsmen, so did the wise elders of the royal court; but all negotiations for a peaceful partition of the kingdom were futile. So, at last, preparations were made on both sides for war, and all the warlike nations took part in it.

The old Indian customs of the Kshatriyas were observed in it. Duryodhana took one side, Yudhishthira, the other. From Yudhishthira messengers were at once sent to all the surrounding kings, entreating their alliance, since honourable men would grant the request that first reached them. So, warriors from all parts assembled to espouse the cause of either the Pandavas or the Kurus according to the precedence of their requests; and thus one brother joined this side, and the other that side, the father on one side, and the son on the other. The most curious thing was the code of war of those days; as soon as the battle for the day ceased and evening came, the opposing parties were good friends, even going to each other's tents; however, when the morning came, again they proceeded to fight each other. That was the strange trait that the Hindus carried down to the time of the Mohammedan invasion. Then again, a man on horseback must not strike one on foot; must not poison the weapon; must not vanquish the enemy in any unequal fight, or by dishonesty; and must never take undue advantage of the another, and so on. If any deviated from these rules he would be covered with dishonour and shunned. The Kshatriyas were trained in that way. And when the foreign invasion came from Central Asia, the Hindus treated the invaders in the selfsame way. They defeated them several times, and on as many occasions sent them back to their homes with presents, etc. The code laid down was that they must not usurp anybody's country; and when a man was beaten he must be sent back to his country with due regard to his position. The Mohammedan conquerors treated the Hindu kings differently, and when they got them once, they destroyed them without remorse.

Mind you, in those days—in the times of our story, the poem says—the science of arms was not the mere use of bows and arrows at all; it was magic archery in which the use of Mantras, concentration, etc., played a prominent part. One man could fight millions of men and burn them at will. He could send one arrow, and it would rain thousands of arrows and thunder; he could make anything burn, and so on—it was all divine magic. One fact is most curious in both these poems—the Ramayana and the Mahabharata—along with these magic arrows and all these things going on, you see the cannon already in use.

The cannon is an old, old thing, used by the Chinese and the Hindus. Upon the walls of the cities were hundreds of curious weapons made of hollow iron tubes, which filled with powder and ball would kill hundreds of men. The people believed that the Chinese, by magic, put the devil inside a hollow iron tube, and when they applied a little fire to a hole, the devil came out with a terrific noise and killed many people.

So in those old days, they used to fight with magic arrows. One man would be able to fight millions of others. They had their military arrangements and tactics: there were the foot soldiers, termed the Pada; then the cavalry, Turaga; and two other divisions which the moderns have lost and given up—there was the elephant corps—hundreds and hundreds of elephants, with men on their backs, formed into regiments and protected with huge sheets of iron mail; and these elephants would bear down upon a mass of the enemy—then, there were the chariots, of course (you have all seen pictures of those old chariots, they were used in every country). These were the four divisions of the army in those old days.

Now, both parties alike wished to secure the alliance of Krishna. But he declined to take an active part and fight in the war, but offered himself as charioteer to Arjuna, and as the friend and counsellor of the Pandavas, while to Duryodhana he gave his army of mighty soldiers.

Then was fought on the vast plain of Kurukshetra the great battle in which Bhishma, Drona, Karna, and the brothers of Duryodhana with the kinsmen on both sides and thousands of other heroes fell. The war lasted eighteen days. Indeed, out of the eighteen Akshauhinis of soldiers very few men were left. The death of Duryodhana ended the war in favour of the Pandavas. It was followed b the lament of Gandhari, the queen, and the widowed women, and the funerals of the deceased warriors.

The greatest incident of the war was the marvellous and immortal poem of the *Gita*, the Song Celestial. It is the popular scripture of India and the loftiest of all teachings. It consists of a dialogue held by Arjuna with Krishna, just before the commencement of the fight on the battle-field of Kurukshetra. I would advise those of you who have not read that book to read it. If you only knew how much it has influenced your own country even! If you want to know the source of Emerson's inspiration, it is this book, the *Gita*. He went to see Carlyle, and Carlyle made him a present of the *Gita*; and that little book is responsible for the Concord Movement. All the broad movements in America, in one way or other, are indebted to the Concord party.

The central figure of the *Gita* is Krishna. As you worship Jesus of Nazareth as God come down as man, so the Hindus worship many Incarnations of God. They believe in not one or two only, but in many, who have come down from time to time, according to the needs of the world, for the preservation of Dharma and destruction of wickedness. Each sect has one, and Krishna is one of them. Krishna, perhaps, has a larger number of followers in India than any other Incarnation of God. His followers hold that he was the most perfect of those Incarnations. Why? "Because," they say, "look at Buddha and other Incarnations; they were only monks, and they had no sympathy for married people. How could they have? But look at Krishna: he was great as a son, as a king, as a father, and all through his life he practised the marvellous teachings which he preached." "He who in the midst of the greatest activity finds the sweetest peace, and in the midst of the greatest calmness is most active, he has known the secret of life." Krishna shows the way how to do this—by being non-attached: do everything but do not get identified with anything. You are the soul, the pure, the free, all the time; you are the Witness. Our misery comes, not from work, but by our getting attached to something.

Take for instance, money: money is a great thing to have, earn it, says Krishna; struggle hard to get money, but don't get attached to it. So with children, with wife, husband, relatives, fame, everything; you have no need to shun them, only don't get attached. There is only one attachment and that belongs to the Lord, and to none other. Work for them, love them, do good to them, sacrifice a hundred lives, if need be, for them, but never be attached. His own life was the exact exemplification of that.

Remember that the book which delineates the life of Krishna is several thousand years old, and some parts of his life are very similar to those of Jesus of Nazareth. Krishna was of royal birth; there was a tyrant king, called Kamsa, and there was a prophecy that one would be born of such and such a family, who would be king. So Kamsa ordered all the male children to be massacred. The father and mother of Krishna were cast by King Kamsa into prison, where the child was born. A light suddenly shone in the prison and the child spoke saying, "I am the Light of the world, born for the good of the world." You find Krishna again symbolically represented with cows—"The Great Cowherd" as he is called. Sages affirmed that God Himself was born, and they went to pay him homage. In other parts of the story, the similarity between the two does not continue.

Shri Krishna conquered this tyrant Kamsa, but he never thought of accepting or occupying the throne himself. He had nothing to do with that. He had done his duty and there it ended.

After the conclusion of the Kurukshetra War, the great warrior and venerable grandsire, Bhishma, who fought ten days out of the eighteen days' battle, still lay on his deathbed and gave instructions to Yudhishthira on various subjects, such as the duties of the king, the duties of the four castes, the four stages of life, the laws of marriage, the bestowing of gifts, etc., basing them on the teachings of the ancient sages. He explained Sankhya philosophy and Yoga philosophy and narrated numerous tales and traditions about saints and gods and kings. These teachings occupy nearly one-fourth of the entire work and form an invaluable storehouse of Hindu laws and moral codes. Yudhishthira had in the meantime been crowned king. But the awful bloodshed and extinction of superiors and relatives weighed heavily on his mind; and then, under the advice of Vyasa, he performed the Ashvamedha sacrifice.

After the war, for fifteen years Dhritarashtra dwelt in peace and honour, obeyed by Yudhishthira and his brothers. Then the aged monarch leaving Yudhishthira on the throne, retired to the forest with his devoted wife and Kunti, the mother of the Pandava brothers, to pass his last days in asceticism.

Thirty-six years had now passed since Yudhishthira regained his empire. Then came to him the news that Krishna had left his mortal body. Krishna, the sage, his friend, his prophet, his counsellor, had departed. Arjuna hastened to Dwaraka and came back only to confirm the sad news that Krishna and the Yadavas were all dead. Then the king and the other brothers, overcome with sorrow, declared that the time for them to go, too, had arrived. So they cast off the burden of royalty, placed Parikshit, the grandson of Arjuna, on the throne, and retired to the Himalayas, on the Great Journey, the Mahaprasthana. This was a peculiar form of Sannyasa. It was a custom for old kings to become Sannyasins. In ancient India, when men became very old, they would give up everything. So did the kings. When a man did not want to live any more, then he went towards the Himalayas, without eating or drinking and walked on and on till the body failed. All the time thinking of God, he just marched on till the body gave way.

Then came the gods, the sages, and they told King Yudhishthira that he should go and reach heaven. To go to heaven one has to cross the highest peaks of the Himalayas. Beyond the Himalayas is Mount Meru. On the top of Mount Meru is heaven. None ever went there in this body. There the gods reside. And Yudhishthira was called upon by the gods to go there.

So the five brothers and their wife clad themselves in robes of bark, and set out on their journey. On the way, they were followed by a dog. On and on they went, and they turned their weary feet northward to where the Himalayas lifts his lofty peaks, and they saw the mighty Mount Meru in front of them. Silently they walked on in the snow, until suddenly the queen fell, to rise no more. To Yudhishthira who was leading the way, Bhima, one of the brothers said, "Behold, O King, the queen has fallen." The king shed tears, but he did not look back. "We are going to meet Krishna," he said. "No time to look back. March on." After a while, again Bhima said, "Behold, our brother, Sahadeva has fallen." The king shed tears; but paused not. "March on," he cried.

One after the other, in the cold and snow, all the four brothers dropped down, but unshaken, though alone, the king advanced onward. Looking behind, he saw the faithful dog was still following him. And so the king and the dog went on, through snow and ice, over hill and dale, climbing higher and higher, till they reached Mount Meru; and there they began to hear the chimes of heaven, and celestial flowers were showered upon the virtuous king by the gods. Then descended the chariot of the gods, and Indra prayed him, "Ascend in this chariot, greatest of mortals: thou that alone art given to enter heaven without changing the mortal body." But no, that Yudhishthira would not do without his devoted brothers and his queen; then Indra explained to him that the brothers had already gone thither before him.

And Yudhishthira looked around and said to his dog, "Get into the chariot, child." The god stood aghast. "What? The dog?" he cried. "Do thou cast off this dog! The dog goeth not to heaven! Great King, what dost thou mean? Art thou mad? Thou, the most virtuous of the human race, thou only canst go to heaven in thy body." "But he has been my devoted companion through the snow and ice. When all my brothers were dead, my queen dead, he alone never left me. How can I leave him now?" "There is no place in heaven for men with dogs. He has to be left behind. There is nothing unrighteous in this." "I do not go to heaven," replied the king, "without the dog. I shall never give up such a one who has taken refuge with me, until my own life is at an end. I shall never swerve from righteousness, nay, not even for the joys of heaven or the urging of a god." "Then," said Indra, "on one condition the dog goes to heaven. You have been the most virtuous of mortals and he has been a dog, killing and eating animals; he is sinful, hunting, and taking other lives. You can exchange heaven with him." "Agreed," says the king. "Let the dog go to heaven."

At once, the scene changed. Hearing these noble words of Yudhishthira, the dog revealed himself as Dharma; the dog was no other than Yama, the Lord of Death and Justice. And Dharma exclaimed, "Behold, O King, no man was ever so unselfish as thou, willing to exchange heaven with a little dog, and for his sake disclaiming all his virtues and ready to go to hell even for him. Thou art well born, O King of kings. Thou hast compassion for all creatures, O Bharata, of which this is a bright example. Hence, regions of undying felicity are thine! Thou has won them, O King, and thine is a celestial and high goal."

Then Yudhishthira, with Indra, Dharma, and other gods, proceeds to heaven in a celestial car. He undergoes some trials, bathes in the celestial Ganga, and assumes a celestial body. He meets his brothers who are now immortals, and all at last is bliss.

Thus ends the story of the Mahabharata, setting forth in a sublime poem the triumph of virtue and the defeat of vice.

In speaking of the Mahabharata to you, it is simply impossible for me to present the unending array of the grand and majestic characters of the mighty heroes depicted by the genius and mastermind of Vyasa. The internal conflicts between righteousness and filial affection in the mind of the god-fearing, yet feeble, old, blind King Dhritarashtra; the majestic character of the grandsire Bhishma; the noble and virtuous nature of the royal Yudhishthira, and of the other four brothers, as mighty in valour as in devotion and loyalty; the peerless character of Krishna, unsurpassed in human wisdom; and not less brilliant, the characters of the women—the stately queen Gandhari, the loving mother Kunti, the ever-devoted and all-suffering Draupadi—these and hundreds of other characters of this Epic and those of the Ramayana have been the cherished heritage of the whole Hindu world for the last several thousands of years and form the basis of their thoughts and of their moral and ethical ideas. In fact, the Ramayana and the Mahabharata are the two encyclopaedias of the ancient Aryan life and wisdom, portraying an ideal civilisation which humanity has yet to aspire after.

The *Gita* I

Delivered in San Francisco, on 26 May 1900

To understand the *Gita* requires its historical background. It is a commentary on the Upanishads. The Upanishads are the Bible of India. They occupy the same place as the New Testament does. There are more than a hundred books comprising the Upanishads, some very small and some big, each a separate treatise. The Upanishads do not reveal the life of any teacher, but simply teach principles. They are as it were shorthand notes taken down of discussion in learned assemblies, generally in the courts of kings. The word "Upanishad" may mean "sittings" or "sitting near a teacher". Those of you who may have studied some of the Upanishads can understand how they are condensed shorthand sketches. After long discussions had been held, they were taken down, possibly from memory. The difficulty is that you get very little of the background. Only the luminous points are mentioned there. The origin of ancient Sanskrit is 5000 BC; the Upanishads are at least two thousand years before that. Nobody knows exactly how old they are. The *Gita* takes the ideas of the Upanishads and in some cases the very words. They are strung together with the idea of bringing out, in a compact, condensed, and systematic form, the whole subject the Upanishads deal with.

The original scriptures of the Hindus are called the Vedas. They were so vast—the mass of writings—that if the texts alone were brought here, this room would not contain them. Many of them are lost. They were divided into branches, each branch put into the head of certain priests and kept alive by memory. Such men still exist. They will repeat book after book of the Vedas without missing a single intonation. The larger portion of the Vedas has disappeared. The small portion left makes a whole library by itself. The oldest of these contains the hymns of the Rig Veda. It is the aim of the modern scholar to restore the sequence of the Vedic compositions. The old, orthodox idea is quite different, as your orthodox idea of the Bible is quite different from the modern scholar's. The Vedas are divided into two portions: one the Upanishads, the philosophical portion, the other the work portion.

We will try to give a little idea of the work portion. It consists of rituals and hymns, various hymns addressed to various gods. The ritual portion is composed of ceremonies, some of them very elaborate. A great many priests are required. The priestly function became a science by itself, owing to the elaboration of the ceremonials. Gradually the popular idea of veneration grew round these hymns and rituals. The gods disappeared and in their place were left the rituals. That was the curious development in India. The orthodox Hindu the Mimamsaka does not believe in gods, the unorthodox believe in them. If you ask the orthodox Hindu what the meaning is of these gods in the Vedas, he will not be able to give any satisfactory answer. The priests sing these hymns and pour libations and offering into the fire. When you ask the orthodox Hindu the meaning of this, he says that words have the power to produce certain effects. That is all. There is all the natural and supernatural power that ever existed. The Vedas are simply words that have the mystical power to produce effects if the sound intonation is right. If one sound is wrong it will not do. Each one must be perfect. Thus what in other religions is called prayer disappeared and the Vedas became the gods. So you see the tremendous importance that was attached to the words of the Vedas. These are the eternal words out of which the whole universe has been produced. There cannot be any thought without the word. Thus whatever there is in this world is the manifestation of thought, and thought can only manifest itself through words. This mass of words by which the unmanifested thought becomes manifest, that is what is meant by the Vedas. It follows that the external existence of everything depends on the Vedas, for thought does not exist without the word. If the word "horse" did not exist, none could think of a horse. So there must be an intimate relation between thought, word, and the external object. What are these words in reality? The Vedas. They do not call it Sanskrit language at all. It is Vedic language, a divine language. Sanskrit is a degenerate form. So are all other languages. There is no language older than the Vedic. You may ask, "Who wrote the Vedas?" They were not written. The words are the Vedas. A word is Veda, if I can pronounce it rightly. Then it will immediately produce the desired effect.

This mass of Vedas eternally exists and all the world is the manifestation of this mass of words. Then when the cycle ends, all this manifestation of energy becomes finer and finer, becomes only words, then thought. In the next cycle, first the thought changes into words and then out of those words the whole universe is produced. If there is something here that is not in the Vedas, that is your delusion. It does not exist.

Numerous books upon that subject alone defend the Vedas. If you tell their authors that the Vedas must have been pronounced by men first, they will simply laugh. You never heard of any man uttering them for the first time. Take Buddha's words. There is a tradition that he lived and spoke these words many times before. If the Christian stands up and says, "My religion is a historical religion and, therefore, yours is wrong and ours is true," the Mimamsaka replies,

"Yours being historical, you confess that a man invented it nineteen hundred years ago. That which is true must be infinite and eternal. That is the one test of truth. It never decays, it is always the same. You confess your religion was created by such-and-such a man. The Vedas were not. By no prophets or anything. Only infinite words, infinite by their very nature, from which the whole universe comes and goes." In the abstract it is perfectly correct. The sound must be the beginning of creation. There must be germ sounds like germ plasm. There cannot be any ideas without the words. Wherever there are sensations, ideas, emotion, there must be words. The difficulty is when they say that these four books are the Vedas and nothing else. Then the Buddhist will stand up and say, "Ours are Vedas. They were revealed to us later on." That cannot be. Nature does not go on in that way. Nature does not manifest her laws bit by bit, an inch of gravitation today and another inch tomorrow. No, every law is complete. There is no evolution in law at all. It is given once and forever. It is all nonsense, this "new religion and better inspiration," and all that. It means nothing. There may be a hundred thousand laws and Man may know only a few today. We discover them—that is all. Those old priests with their tremendous claims about eternal words, having dethroned the gods, took the place of the gods. They said, "You do not understand the power of words. We know how to use them. We are the living gods of the world. Pay us; we will manipulate the words, and you will get what you want. Can you pronounce the words yourself? You cannot, for, mind you, one mistake will produce the opposite effect. You want to be rich, handsome, have a long life, a fine husband?" Only pay the priest and keep quiet!

Yet there is another side. The ideal of the first part of the Vedas is entirely different from the ideal of the other part, the Upanishads. The ideal of the first part coincides with that of all other religions of the world except the Vedanta.

The ideal is enjoyment here and hereafter—man and wife, husband and children. Pay your dollar, and the priest will give you a certificate, and you will have a happy time afterwards in heaven. You will find all your people there and have this merry-go-round without end. No tears, no weeping—only laughing. No stomach ache, but yet eating. No headache, but yet parties. That, considered the priests, was the highest goal of man.

There is another idea in this philosophy which is according to your modern ideas. Man is a slave of nature, and slave eternally he has got to remain. We call it Karma. Karma means law, and it applies everywhere. Everything is bound by Karma. "Is there no way out?" "No! Remain slaves all through the years—fine slaves. We will manipulate the words so that you will only have the good and not the bad side of all—if you will pay us enough." That was the ideal of the Mimamsakas. These are the ideals which are popular throughout the ages. The vast mass of mankind are never thinkers. Even if they try to think, the effect of the vast mass of superstitions on them is terrible. The moment they weaken, one blow comes, and the backbone breaks into twenty pieces. They can only be moved by lures and threats. They can never move of their own accord. They must be frightened, horrified, or terrorised, and they are your slaves forever. They have nothing else to do but to pay and obey. Everything else is done by the priest. How much easier religion becomes! You see, you have nothing to do. Go home and sit quietly. Somebody is doing the whole thing for you. Poor, poor animals!

Side by side, there was the other system. The Upanishads are diametrically opposite in all their conclusions. First of all, the Upanishads believe in God, the creator of the universe, its ruler. You find later on the idea of a benign Providence. It is an entirely opposite conception. Now, although we hear the priest, the ideal is much more subtle. Instead of many gods they made one God.

The second idea, that you are all bound by the law of Karma, the Upanishads admit, but they declare the way out. The goal of Man is to go beyond law. And enjoyment can never be the goal, because enjoyment can only be in nature.

In the third place, the Upanishads condemn all the sacrifices and say that is mummery. That may give you all you want, but it is not desirable, for the more you get, the more you want, and you run round and round in a circle eternally, never getting to the end—enjoying and weeping. Such a thing as eternal happiness is impossible anywhere. It is only a child's dream. The same energy becomes joy and sorrow.

I have changed my psychology a bit today. I have found the most curious fact. You have a certain idea and you do not want to have it, and you think of something else, and the idea you want to suppress is entirely suppressed. What is that idea? I saw it come out in fifteen minutes. It came out and staggered me. It was strong, and it came in such a violent and terrible fashion that I thought here was a madman. And when it was over, all that had happened was a suppression of the previous emotion. What came out? It was my own bad impression which had to be worked out. "Nature will have her way. What can suppression do?" That is a terrible statement in the *Gita*. It seems it may be a vain struggle after all. You may have a hundred thousand urges competing at the same time. You may repress them, but the moment the spring rebounds, the whole thing is there again.

But there is hope. If you are powerful enough, you can divide your consciousness into twenty parts all at the same time. I am changing my psychology. Mind grows. That is what the Yogis say. There is one passion and it rouses another, and the first one dies. If you are angry, and then happy, the next moment the anger passes away. Out of that anger you manufactured the next state. These states are always interchangeable. Eternal happiness and misery are a child's dream. The Upanishads point out that the goal of Man is neither misery nor happiness, but we have to be master of that out of which these are manufactured. We must be masters of the situation at its very root, as it were.

The other point of divergence is: the Upanishads condemn all rituals, especially those that involve the killing of animals. They declare those all nonsense. One school of old philosophers says that you must kill such an animal at a certain time if the effect is to be produced. You may reply, "But there is also the sin of taking the life of the animal; you will have to suffer for that." They say that is all nonsense. How do you know what is right and what is wrong? Your mind says so? Who cares what your mind says? What nonsense are you talking? You are setting your mind against the scriptures. If your mind says something and the Vedas say something else, stop your mind and believe in the Vedas. If they say, killing a man is right, that is right. If you say, "No, my conscience says otherwise," it won't do. The moment you believe in any book as the eternal word, as sacred, no more can you question. I do not see how you people here believe in the Bible whenever you say about it, "How wonderful those words are, how right and how good!" Because, if you believe in the Bible as the word of God, you have no right to judge at all. The moment you judge, you think you are higher than the Bible. Then what is the use of the Bible to you? The priests say, "We refuse to make the comparison with your Bible or anybody's. It is no use comparing, because—what is the authority? There it ends. If you think something is not right, go and get it right according to the Vedas."

The Upanishads believe in that, but they have a higher standard too. On the one hand, they do not want to overthrow the Vedas, and on the other they see these animal sacrifices and the priests stealing everybody's money. But in the psychology they are all alike. All the differences have been in the philosophy, regarding the nature of the soul. Has it a body and a mind? And is the mind only a bundle of nerves, the motor nerves and the sensory nerves? Psychology, they all take for granted, is a perfect science. There cannot be any difference there. All the fight has been regarding philosophy—the nature of the soul, and God, and all that.

Then another great difference between the priests and the Upanishads. The Upanishads say, renounce. That is the test of everything. Renounce everything. It is the creative faculty that brings us into all this entanglement. The mind is in its own nature when it is calm. The moment you can calm it, that very moment you will know the truth. What is it that is whirling the mind? Imagination, creative activity. Stop creation and you know the truth. All power of creation must stop, and then you know the truth at once.

On the other hand, the priests are all for creation. Imagine a species of life in which there is no creative activity. It is unthinkable. The people had to have a plan of evolving a stable society. A system of rigid selection was adopted. For instance, no people who are blind and halt can be married. As a result you will find so much less deformity in India than in any other country in the world. Epileptics and insane people are very rare there. That is owing to direct selection. The priests say, "Let them become Sannyasins." On the other hand, the Upanishads say, "Oh no, the earth's best and finest and freshest flowers should be laid upon the altar. The strong, the young, with sound intellect and sound body—they must struggle for the truth."

So with all these divergences of opinion, I have told you that the priests already differentiated themselves into a separate caste. The second is the caste of the kings. All the Upanishadic philosophy is from the brains of kings, not priests. There runs an economic struggle through every religious struggle. This animal called Man has some religious influence, but he is guided by economy. Individuals are guided by something else, but the mass of mankind never made a move unless economy was involved. You may preach a religion that may not be perfect in every detail, but if there is an economic background to it, and you have the most ardent champions to preach it, you can convince a whole country.

Whenever any religion succeeds, it must have economic value. Thousands of similar sects will be struggling for power, but only those who meet the real economic problem will have it. Man is guided by the stomach. He walks and the stomach goes first and the head afterwards. Have you not seen that? It will take ages for the head to go first. By the time a man is sixty years of age, he is called out of the world. The whole of life is one delusion, and just when you begin to see things the way they are, you are snatched off. So long as the stomach went first you were all right. When children's dreams begin to vanish and you begin to look at things the way they are, the head goes. Just when the head goes first, you go out.

For the religion of the Upanishads to be popularised was a hard task. Very little economy is there, but tremendous altruism.

The Upanishads had very little kingdom, although they were discovered by kings that held all the royal power in their hands. So the struggle began to be fiercer. Its culminating point came two thousand years after, in Buddhism. The seed of Buddhism is here, in the ordinary struggle between the king and the priest; and in the struggle all religion declined. One wanted to sacrifice religion, the other wanted to cling to the sacrifices, to Vedic gods, etc. Buddhism broke the chains of the masses. All castes and creeds alike became equal in a minute. So the great religious ideas in India exist, but have yet to be preached: otherwise they do no good.

In every country it is the priest who is conservative, for two reasons—because it is his bread and because he can only move with the people. All priests are not strong. If the people say, "Preach two thousand gods," the priests will do it. They are the servants of the congregation who pay them. God does not pay them. So blame yourselves before blaming the priests. You can only get the government and the religion and the priesthood you deserve, and no better.

So the great struggle began in India and it comes to one of its culminating points in the *Gita*. When it was causing fear that all India was going to be broken up between the two groups, there rose this man Krishna, and in the *Gita* he tries to reconcile the ceremony and the philosophy of the priests and the people. Krishna is loved and worshipped in the same way as you do Christ. The difference is only in the age. The Hindus keep the birthday of Krishna as you do Christ's. Krishna lived five thousand years ago and his life is full of miracles, some of them very similar to those in the life of Christ. The child was born in prison. The father took him away and put him with the shepherds. All children born in that year were ordered to be killed. He was killed; that was his fate.

Krishna was a married man. There are thousands of books about him. They do not interest me much. The Hindus are great in telling stories, you see. If the Christian missionaries tell one story from their Bible, the Hindus will produce twenty stories. You say the whale swallowed Jonah; the Hindus say someone swallowed an elephant. Since I was a child I have heard about Krishna's life. I take it for granted there must have been a man called Krishna, and his *Gita* shows he has left a wonderful book. I told you, you can understand the character of a man by analysing the fables about him. The fables have the nature of decorations. You must find they are all polished and manipulated to fit into the character. For instance, take Buddha. The central idea is sacrifice. There are thousands of folklore, but in every case the sacrifice must have been kept up. There are thousands of stories about Lincoln, about some characteristic of that great man. You take all the fables and find the general idea and know that that was the central character of the man. You find in Krishna that non-attachment is the central idea. He does not need anything. He does not want anything. He works for work's sake. "Work for work's sake. Worship for worship's sake. Do good because it is good to do good. Ask no more." That must have been the character of the man. Otherwise these fables could not be brought down to the one idea of non-attachment. The *Gita* is not his only sermon.

He is the most rounded man I know of, wonderfully developed equally in brain and heart and hand. Every moment of his is alive with activity, either as a gentleman, warrior, minister, or something else. Great as a gentleman, as a scholar, as a poet. This all-rounded and wonderful activity and combination of brain and heart you see in the *Gita* and other books. Most wonderful heart, exquisite language, and nothing can approach it anywhere. This tremendous activity of the man—the impression is still there. Five thousand years have passed and he has influenced millions and millions. Just think what an influence this man has over the whole world, whether you know it or not. My regard for him is for his perfect sanity. No cobwebs in that brain, no superstition. He knows the use of everything, and when it is necessary to assign a place to each, he is there. Those that talk, go everywhere, question about the mystery of the Vedas, etc., they do not know the truth. They are no better than frauds. There is a place in the Vedas even for superstition, for ignorance. The whole secret is to find out the proper place for everything.

Then that heart! He is the first man, way before Buddha, to open the door of religion to every caste. That wonderful mind! That tremendously active life! Buddha's activity was on one plane, the plane of teaching. He could not keep his wife and child and become a teacher at the same time. Krishna preached in the midst of the battlefield. "He who in the midst of intense activity finds himself in the greatest calmness, and in the greatest peace finds intense activity that is the greatest Yogi as well as the wisest man." It means nothing to this man—the flying of missiles about him. Calm and sedate he goes on discussing the problems of life and death. Each one of the prophets is the best commentary on his own teaching. If you want to know what is meant by the doctrine of the New Testament, you go to Mr. So-and-so. But read again and again the four Gospels and try to understand their import in the light of the wonderful life of the Master as depicted there. The great men think, and you and I also think. But there is a difference. We think and our bodies do not follow. Our actions do not harmonise with our thoughts. Our words have not the power of the words that become Vedas. Whatever they think must be accomplished. If they say, "I do this," the body does it. Perfect obedience. This is the end. You can think yourself God in one minute, but you cannot be God. That is the difficulty. They become what they think. We will become only by degrees.

You see, that was about Krishna and his time. In the next lecture we will know more of his book.

The *Gita* II

Delivered in San Francisco, on 28 May 1900

The *Gita* requires a little preliminary introduction. The scene is laid on the battlefield of Kurukshetra. There were two branches of the same race fighting for the empire of India about five thousand years ago. The Pandavas had the right, but the Kauravas had the might. The Pandavas were five brothers, and they were living in a forest. Krishna was the friend of the Pandavas. The Kauravas would not grant them as much land as would cover the point of a needle.

The opening scene is the battlefield, and both sides see their relatives and friends—one brother on one side and another on the other side; a grandfather on one side, grandson on the other side. When Arjuna sees his own friends and relatives on the other side and knows that he may have to kill them, his heart gives way and he says that he will not fight. Thus begins the *Gita*.

For all of us in this world life is a continuous fight. Many a time comes when we want to interpret our weakness and cowardice as forgiveness and renunciation. There is no merit in the renunciation of a beggar. If a person who can give a blow forbears, there is merit in that. If a person who has, gives up, there is merit in that. We know how often in our lives through laziness and cowardice we give up the battle and try to hypnotise our minds into the belief that we are brave.

The *Gita* opens with this very significant verse: "Arise, O Prince! Give up this faint-heartedness, this weakness! Stand up and fight!" Then Arjuna, trying to argue the matter with Krishna, brings higher moral ideas, how non-resistance is better than resistance, and so on. He is trying to justify himself, but he cannot fool Krishna. Krishna is the higher Self, or God. He sees through the argument at once. In this case the motive is weakness. Arjuna sees his own relatives and he cannot strike them.

There is a conflict in Arjuna's heart between his emotionalism and his duty. The nearer we are to beasts and birds, the more we are in the hells of emotion. We call it love. It is self-hypnotisation. We are under the control of our emotions like animals. A cow can sacrifice its life for its young. Every animal can. What of that? It is not the blind, birdlike emotion that leads to perfection. To reach the eternal consciousness, that is the goal of man! There emotion has no place, nor sentimentalism, nor anything that belongs to the senses—only the light of pure reason. There Man stands as spirit.

Now, Arjuna is under the control of this emotionalism. He is not what he should be—a great self-controlled, enlightened sage working through the eternal light of reason. He has become like an animal, like a baby, just letting his heart carry away his brain, making a fool of himself and trying to cover his weakness with the flowery names of "love" and so on. Krishna sees through that. Arjuna talks like a man of little learning and brings out many reasons, but at the same time he talks the language of a fool.

"The sage is not sorry for those that are living nor for those that die." Krishna says: "You cannot die nor can I. There was never a time when we did not exist. There will never be a time when we shall not exist. As in this life a man begins with childhood, and passes through youth and old age, so at death he merely passes into another kind of body. Why should a wise man be sorry?" And where is the beginning of this emotionalism that has got hold of you? It is in the senses. "It is the touch of the senses that brings all this quality of existence: heat and cold, pleasure and pain. They come and go." Man is miserable this moment, happy the next. As such he cannot experience the nature of the soul.

"Existence can never be non-existence, neither can non-existence ever become existence. Know, therefore, that that which pervades all this universe is without beginning or end. It is unchangeable. There is nothing in the universe that can change the Changeless. Though this body has its beginning and end, the dweller in the body is infinite and without end."

Knowing this, stand up and fight! Not one step back, that is the idea Fight it out, whatever comes. Let the stars move from the sphere! Let the whole world stand against us! Death means only a change of garment. What of it? Thus fight! You gain nothing by becoming cowards. Taking a step backward, you do not avoid any misfortune. You have cried to all the gods in the world. Has misery ceased? The masses in India cry to sixty million gods, and still die like dogs. Where are these gods? The gods come to help you when you have succeeded. So what is the use? Die game. This bending the knee to superstitions, this selling yourself to your own mind does not befit you, my soul. You are infinite, deathless, birthless. Because you are infinite spirit, it does not befit you to be a slave. Arise! Awake! Stand up and fight! Die if you must. There is none to help you. You are all the world. Who can help you?

"Beings are unknown to our human senses before birth and after death. It is only in the interim that they are manifest. What is there to grieve about?

"Some look at It the Self with wonder. Some talk of It as wonderful. Others hear of It as wonderful. Others, hearing of It, do not understand."

But if you say that killing all these people is sinful, then consider this from the standpoint of your own caste-duty: "Making pleasure and misery the same, making success and defeat the same, do thou stand up and fight."

This is the beginning of another peculiar doctrine of the *Gita*—the doctrine of non-attachment. That is to say, we have to bear the result of our own actions because we attach ourselves to them. "Only what is done as duty for duty's sake can scatter the bondage of Karma." There is no danger that you can overdo it. "If you do even a little of it, this Yoga will save you from the terrible round of birth and death.

"Know, Arjuna, the mind that succeeds is the mind that is concentrated. The minds that are taken up with two thousand subjects have their energies dispersed. Some can talk flowery language and think there is nothing beyond the Vedas. They want to go to heaven. They want good things through the power of the Vedas, and so they make sacrifices."Such will never attain any success in spiritual life unless they give up all these materialistic ideas.

That is another great lesson. Spirituality can never be attained unless all material ideas are given up. What is in the senses? The senses are all delusion. People wish to retain them in heaven even after they are dead—a pair of eyes, a nose. Some imagine they will have more organs than they have now. They want to see God sitting on a throne through all eternity—the material body of God. Such men's desires are for the body, for food and drink and enjoyment. It is the materialistic life prolonged. Man cannot think of anything beyond this life. This life is all for the body. "Such a man never comes to that concentration which leads to freedom."

"The Vedas only teach things belonging to the three Gunas, to Sattva, Rajas, and Tamas." The Vedas only teach about things in nature. People cannot think anything they do not see on earth. If they talk about heaven, they think of a king sitting on a throne, of people burning incense. It is all nature, nothing beyond nature. The Vedas, therefore, teach nothing but nature. "Go beyond nature, beyond the dualities of existence, beyond your own consciousness, caring for nothing, neither for good nor for evil."

We have identified ourselves with our bodies. We are only body, or rather, possessed of a body. If I am pinched, I cry. All this is nonsense, since I am the soul. All this chain of misery, imagination, animals, gods, and demons, everything, the whole world—all this comes from the identification of ourselves with the body. I am spirit. Why do I jump if you pinch me? Look at the slavery of it. Are you not ashamed? We are religious! We are philosophers! We are sages! Lord bless us! What are we? Living hells, that is what we are. Lunatics, that is what we are!

We cannot give up the idea of body. We are earth-bound. Our ideas are burial grounds. When we leave the body we are bound by thousands of elements to those ideas.

Who can work without any attachment? That is the real question. Such a man is the same whether his work succeeds or fails. His heart does not give one false beat even if his whole life-work is burnt to ashes in a moment. "This is the sage who always works for work's sake without caring for the results. Thus he goes beyond the pain of birth and death. Thus he becomes free." Then he sees that this attachment is all delusion. The Self can never be attached. Then he goes beyond all the scriptures and philosophies. If the mind is deluded and pulled into a whirlpool by books and scriptures, what is the good of all these scriptures? One says this, another says that. What book shall you take? Stand alone! See the glory of your own soul, and see that you will have to work. Then you will become a man of firm will.

Arjuna asks: "Who is a person of established will?"

Krishna answers: "The man who has given up all desires, who desires nothing, not even this life, nor freedom, nor gods, nor work, nor anything. When he has become perfectly satisfied, he has no more cravings." He has seen the glory of the Self and has found that the world, and the gods, and heaven are within his own Self. Then the gods become no gods; death becomes no death; life becomes no life. Everything has changed. "A man is said to be illumined if his will has become firm, if his mind is not disturbed by misery, if he does not desire any happiness, if he is free of all attachment, of all fear, of all anger.

"As the tortoise can draw in his legs, and if you strike him, not one foot comes out, even so the sage can draw all his sense-organs inside," and nothing can force them out. Nothing can shake him, no temptation or anything. Let the universe tumble about him, it does not make one single ripple in his mind.

Then comes a very important question. Sometimes people fast for days. When the worst man has fasted for twenty days, he becomes quite gentle. Fasting and torturing themselves have been practised by people all over the world. Krishna's idea is that this is all nonsense. He says that the senses will for the moment recede from the man who tortures himself, but will emerge again with twenty times more power, What should you do? The idea is to be natural—no asceticism. Go on, work, only mind that you are not attached. The will can never be fixed strongly in the man who has not learnt and practised the secret of non-attachment.

I go out and open my eyes. If something is there, I must see it. I cannot help it. The mind runs after the senses. Now the senses must give up any reaction to nature.

"Where it is dark night for the sense-bound world, the self controlled Man is awake. It is daylight for him. And where the world is awake, the sage sleeps." Where is the world awake? In the senses. People want to eat and drink and have children, and then they die a dog's death. They are always awake for the senses. Even their religion is just for that. They invent a God to help them, to give them more women, more money, more children—never a God to help them become more godlike! "Where the whole world is awake, the sage sleeps. But where the ignorant are asleep, there the sage keeps awake"—in the world-of light where Man looks upon himself not as a bird, not as an animal, not as a body, but as infinite spirit, deathless, immortal. There, where the ignorant are asleep, and do not have time, nor intellect, nor power to understand, there the sage is awake. That is daylight for him.

"As all the rivers of the world constantly pour their waters into the ocean, but the ocean's grand, majestic nature remains undisturbed and unchanged, so even though all the senses bring in sensations from nature, the ocean-like heart of the sage knows no disturbance, knows no fear." Let miseries come in millions of rivers and happiness in hundreds! I am no slave to misery! I am no slave to happiness!

The *Gita* III

Delivered in San Francisco, on 29 May 1900

Arjuna asks: "You just advised action, and yet you uphold knowledge of Brahman as the highest form of life. Krishna, if you think that knowledge is better than action, why do you tell me to act?"

Shri Krishna: "From ancient times these two systems have come down to us. The Sankhya philosophers advance the theory of knowledge. The Yogis advance the theory of work. But none can attain to peace by renouncing actions. None in this life can stop activity even for a moment. Nature's qualities Gunas will make him act. He who stops his activities and at the same time is still thinking about them attains to nothing; he only becomes a hypocrite. But he who by the power of his mind gradually brings his sense-organs under control, employing them in work, that man is better. Therefore, do thou work."

"Even if you have known the secret that you have no duty, that you are free, still you have to work for the good of others. Because whatever a great man does, ordinary people will do also. If a great man who has attained peace of mind and freedom ceases to work, then all the rest without that knowledge and peace will try to imitate him, and thus confusion would arise."

"Behold, Arjuna, there is nothing that I do not possess and nothing that I want to acquire. And yet I continue to work. If I stopped work for a moment, the whole universe would be destroyed. That which the ignorant do with desire for results and gain, let the wise do without any attachment and without any desire for results and gain."

Even if you have knowledge, do not disturb the childlike faith of the ignorant. On the other hand, go down to their level and gradually bring them up. That is a very powerful idea, and it has become the ideal in India. That is why you can see a great philosopher going into a temple and worshipping images. It is not hypocrisy.

Later on we read what Krishna says, "Even those who worship other deities are really worshipping me." It is God incarnate whom Man is worshipping. Would God be angry if you called Him by the wrong name? He would be no God at all! Can't you understand that whatever a man has in his own heart is God—even if he worships a stone? What of that!

We will understand more clearly if we once get rid of the idea that religion consists in doctrines. One idea of religion has been that the whole world was born because Adam ate the apple, and there is no way of escape. Believe in Jesus Christ—in a certain man's death! But in India there is quite a different idea. There religion means realisation, nothing else. It does not matter whether one approaches the destination in a carriage with four horses, in an electric car, or rolling on the ground. The goal is the same. For the Christians the problem is how to escape the wrath of the terrible God. For the Indians it is how to become what they really are, to regain their lost Selfhood.

Have you realised that you are spirit? When you say, "I do," what is meant by that—this lump of flesh called the body or the spirit, the infinite, ever blessed, effulgent, immortal? You may be the greatest philosopher, but as long as you have the idea that you are the body, you are no better than the little worm crawling under your foot! No excuse for you! So much the worse for you that you know all the philosophies and at the same time think you are the body! Body-gods, that is what you are! Is that religion?

Religion is the realisation of spirit as spirit. What are we doing now? Just the opposite, realising spirit as matter, Out of the immortal God we manufacture death and matter, and out of dead dull matter we manufacture spirit.

If you can realise Brahman by standing on your head, or on one foot, or by worshipping five thousand gods with three heads each—welcome to it! Do it any way you can! Nobody has any right to say anything. Therefore, Krishna says, if your method is better and higher, you have no business to say that another man's method is bad, however wicked you may think it.

Again, we must consider, religion is a matter of growth, not a mass of foolish words. Two thousand years ago a man saw God. Moses saw God in a burning bush. Does what Moses did when he saw God save you? No man's seeing God can help you the least bit except that it may excite you and urge you to do the same thing. That is the whole value of the ancients' examples. Nothing more. Just signposts on the way. No man's eating can satisfy another man. No man's seeing God can save another man. You have to see God yourself. All these people fighting about what God's nature is—whether He has three heads in one body or five heads in six bodies. Have you seen God? No. And they do not believe they can ever see Him. What fools we mortals be! Sure, lunatics!

In India it has come down as a tradition that if there is a God, He must be your God and my God. To whom does the sun belong! You say Uncle Sam is everybody's uncle. If there is a God, you ought to be able to see Him. If not, let Him go.

Each one thinks his method is best. Very good! But remember, it may be good for you. One food which is very indigestible to one is very digestible to another. Because it is good for you, do not jump to the conclusion that your method is everybody's method, that Jack's coat fits John and Mary. All the uneducated, uncultured, unthinking men and women have been put into that sort of strait jacket! Think for yourselves. Become atheists! Become materialists! That would be better. Exercise the mind! What right have you to say that this man's method is wrong? It may be wrong for you. That is to say, if you undertake the method, you will be degraded; but that does not mean that he will be degraded. Therefore, says Krishna, if you have knowledge and see a man weak, do not condemn him. Go to his level and help him if you can. He must grow. I can put five bucketfuls of knowledge into his head in five hours. But what good will it do? He will be a little worse than before.

Whence comes all this bondage of action? Because we chain the soul with action. According to our Indian system, there are two existences: nature on the one side and the Self, the Atman, on the other. By the word nature is meant not only all this external world, but also our bodies, the mind, the will, even down to what says "I". Beyond all that is the infinite life and light of the soul—the Self, the Atman. According to this philosophy the Self is entirely separate from nature, always was and always will be. There never was a time when the spirit could be identified even with the mind.

It is self-evident that the food you eat is manufacturing the mind all the time. It is matter. The Self is above any connection with food. Whether you eat or not does not matter. Whether you think or not does not matter. It is infinite light. Its light is the same always. If you put a blue or a green glass before a light, what has that to do with the light? Its colour is unchangeable. It is the mind which changes and gives the different colours. The moment the spirit leaves the body, the whole thing goes to pieces.

The reality in nature is spirit. Reality itself—the light of the spirit—moves and speaks and does everything through our bodies, minds, etc. It is the energy and soul and life of the spirit that is being worked upon in different ways by matter. The spirit is the cause of all our thoughts and body-action and everything, but it is untouched by good or evil, pleasure or pain, heat or cold, and all the dualism of nature, although it lends its light to everything.

"Therefore, Arjuna, all these actions are in nature. Nature is working out her own laws in our bodies and minds. We identify ourselves with nature and say, 'I am doing this.' This way delusion seizes us."

We always act under some compulsion. When hunger compels me, I eat. And suffering is still worse—slavery. That real "I" is eternally free. What can compel it to do anything? The sufferer is in nature. It is only when we identify ourselves with the body that we say, "I am suffering; I am Mr. So-and-so"—all such nonsense. But he who has known the truth, holds himself aloof. Whatever his body does, whatever his mind does, he does not care. But mind you, the vast majority of mankind are under this delusion; and whenever they do any good, they feel that they are the doers. They are not yet able to understand higher philosophy. Do not disturb their faith! They are shunning evil and doing good. Great idea! Let them have it! They are workers for good. By degrees they will think that there is greater glory than that of doing good. They will only witness, and things are done. Gradually they will understand. When they have shunned all evil and done all good, then they will begin to realise that they are beyond all nature. They are not the doers. They stand apart. They are the witness. They simply stand and look. Nature is begetting all the universe. They turn their backs. "In the beginning, O beloved, there only existed that Existence. Nothing else existed. And That brooding, everything else was created."*

* *Chhandogya Upanishad,* VI.2.2-3

"Even those who know the path act impelled by their own nature. Everyone acts according to his nature. He cannot transcend it." The atom cannot disobey the law. Whether it is the mental or the physical atom, it must obey the law. "What is the use of external restraint?"

What makes the value of anything in life? Not enjoyment, not possessions. Analyse everything. You will find there is no value except in experience, to teach us something. And in many cases it is our hardships that give us better experience than enjoyment. Many times blows give us better experience than the caresses of nature. Even famine has its place and value.

According to Krishna, we are not new beings just come into existence. Our minds are not new minds. In modern times we all know that every child brings with him all the past, not only of humanity, but of the plant life. There are all the past chapters, and this present chapter, and there are a whole lot of future chapters before him. Everyone has his path mapped and sketched and planned out for him. And in spite of all this darkness, there cannot be anything uncaused—no event, no circumstance. It is simply our ignorance. The whole infinite chain of causation is bound one link to another back to nature. The whole universe is bound by that sort of chain. It is the universal chain of cause and effect, you receiving one link, one part, I another And that part is our own nature.

Now Shri Krishna says: "Better die in your own path than attempt the path of another." This is my path, and I am down here. And you are way up there, and I am always tempted to give up my path thinking I will go there and be with you. And if I go up, I am neither there nor here. We must not lose sight of this doctrine. It is all a matter of growth. Wait and grow, and you attain everything; otherwise there will be great spiritual danger. Here is I the fundamental secret of teaching religion.

What do you mean by "saving people" and all believing in the same doctrine? It cannot be. There are the general ideas that can be taught to mankind. The true teacher will be able to find out for you what your own nature is. Maybe you do not know it. It is possible that I what you think is your own nature is all wrong. It has not developed to consciousness. The teacher is the person; who ought to know. He ought to know by a glance at your face and put you on your path. We grope about and struggle here and there and do all sorts of things and make no progress until the time comes when we fall into that life-current and are carried on. The sign is that the moment we are in that stream we will float. Then there is no more struggle. This is to be found out. Then die in that path rather than giving it up and taking hold of another.

Instead, we start a religion and make a set of dogmas and betray the goal of mankind and treat everyone as having the same nature. No two persons have the same mind or the same body. No two persons have the same religion.

If you want to be religious, enter not the gate of any organised religions. They do a hundred times more evil than good, because they stop the growth of each one's individual development. Study everything, but keep your own seat firm. If you take my advice, do not put your neck into the trap. The moment they try to put their noose on you, get your neck out and go somewhere else. As the bee culling honey from many flowers remains free, not bound by any flower, be not bound. Enter not the door of any organised religion. Religion is only between you and your God, and no third person must come between you. Think what these organised religions have done! What Napoleon was more terrible than these religious persecutions? If you and I organise, we begin to hate every person. It is better not to love, if loving only means hating others. That is no love. That is hell! If loving your own people means hating everybody else, it is the quintessence of selfishness and brutality, and the effect is that it will make you brutes. Therefore, better die working out your own natural religion than following another's natural religion, however great it may appear to you.

"Beware, Arjuna, lust and anger are the great I enemies. These are to be controlled. These cover the knowledge even of those who are wise. This fire of lust is unquenchable. Its location is in the sense-organs and in the mind. The Self desires nothing.

"This Yoga I taught in ancient times to Vivaswan; Vivaswan taught it to Manu. Thus it was that the knowledge descended from one thing to another. But in time this great Yoga was destroyed. That is why I am telling it to you again today."

Then Arjuna asks, "Why do you speak thus? You are a man born only the other day, and Vivaswan was born long before you. What do you mean that you taught him?"

Then Krishna says, "O Arjuna, you and I have run the cycle of births and deaths many times, but you are not conscious of them all. I am without beginning, birthless, the absolute Lord of all creation. I through my own nature take form. Whenever virtue subsides and wickedness prevails, I come to help mankind. For the salvation of the good, for the destruction of wickedness, for the establishment of spirituality I come from time to time. Whosoever wants to reach me through whatsoever ways, I reach him through that. But know, Arjuna, none can ever swerve from my path." None ever did. How can we? None swerves from His path.

All societies are based upon bad generalisation. The law can only be formed upon perfect generalisation. What is the old saying: Every law has its exception? If it is a law, it cannot be broken. None can break it. Does the apple break the law of gravitation? The moment a law is broken no more universe exists. There will come a time when you will break the law, and that moment your consciousness mind, and body will melt away.

There is a man stealing there. Why does he steal? You punish him. Why can you not make room for him and put his energy to work? You say, "You are a sinner," and many will say he has broken the law. All this herd of mankind is forced into uniformity and hence ail trouble, sin, and weakness. The world is not as bad as you think. It is we fools who have made it evil. We manufacture our own ghosts and demons, and then we cannot get rid of them. We put our hands before our eyes and cry: "Somebody give us light." Fools! Take your hands from your eyes! That is all there is to it. We call upon the gods to save us and nobody blames himself. That is the pity of it. Why is there so much evil in society? What is it they say? Flesh and the devil and the woman. Why make these things up? Nobody asks you to make them up. "None, O Arjuna, can swerve from my path." We are fools, and our paths are foolish. We have to go through all this Maya. God made the heaven, and Man made the hell for himself.

"No action can touch me. I have no desire for the results of action. Whosoever knows me thus knows the secret and is not bound by action. The ancient sages, knowing this secret could safely engage in action. Do thou work in the same fashion."

"He who sees in the midst of intense activity, intense calm, and in the midst of intensest peace is intensely active is wise indeed. This is the question: With every sense and every organ active, have you that tremendous peace so that nothing can disturb you? Standing on Market street, waiting for the car with all the rush going on around you, are you in meditation—calm and peaceful? In the cave, are you intensely active there with all quiet about you? If you are, you are a Yogi, otherwise not.

" The seers call him wise whose every attempt is free, I without any desire for gain, without any selfishness." Truth can never come to us as long as we are selfish. We colour everything with our own selves. Things come to us as they are. Not that they are hidden, not at all! We hide them. We have the brush. A thing comes, and we do not like it, and we brush a little and then look at it. We do not want to know. We paint everything with ourselves. In all action the motive power is selfishness. Everything is hidden by ourselves. We are like the caterpillar which takes the thread out of his own body and of that makes the cocoon, and behold, he is caught. By his own work he imprisons himself. That is what we are doing. The moment I say "me" the thread makes a turn. "I and mine," another turn. So it goes.

We cannot remain without action for a moment. Act! But just as when your neighbour asks you, "Come and help me!" have you exactly the same idea when you are helping yourself. No more. Your body is of no more value than that of John. Don't do anything more for your body than you do for John. That is religion.

"He whose efforts are bereft of all desire and selfishness has burnt all this bondage of action with the fire of knowledge. He is wise." Reading books cannot do that. The ass can be burdened with the whole library; that does not make him learned at all. What is the use of reading many books? "Giving up all attachment to work, always satisfied, not hoping for gain, the wise man acts and is beyond action."

Naked I came out of my mother's womb and naked I return. Helpless I came and helpless I go. Helpless I am now. And we do not know the goal. It is terrible for us to think about it. We get such odd ideas! We go to a medium and see if the ghost can help us. Think of the weakness! Ghosts, devils, gods, anybody—come on! And all the priests, all the charlatans! That is just the time they get hold of us, the moment we are weak. Then they bring in all the gods.

I see in my country a man becomes strong, educated, becomes a philosopher, and says, "All this praying and I bathing is nonsense." The man's father dies, and his mother dies. That is the most terrible shock a Hindu can have. You will find him bathing in every dirty pool, going into the temple, licking the dust. Help anyone! But we are helpless. There is no help from anyone. That is the truth. There have been more gods than human beings; and yet no help. We die like dogs—no help. Everywhere beastliness, famine, disease, misery, evil! And all are crying for help. But no help. And yet, hoping against hope, we are still screaming for help. Oh, the miserable condition! Oh, the terror of it! Look into your own heart! One half of the trouble is not our fault, but the fault of our parents. Born with this weakness, more and more of it was put into our heads. Step by step we go beyond it.

It is a tremendous error to feel helpless. Do not seek help from anyone. We are our own help. If we cannot help ourselves, there is none to help us. "Thou thyself art thy only friend, thou thyself thy only enemy. There is no other enemy but this self of mine, no other friend by myself." This is the last and greatest lesson, and Oh, what a time it takes to learn it! We seem to get hold of it, and the next moment the old wave comes. The backbone breaks. We weaken and again grasp for that superstition and help. Just think of that huge mass of misery, and all caused by this false idea of going to seek for help!

Possibly the priest says his routine words and expects something. Sixty thousand people look to the skies and pray and pay the priest. Month after month they still look, still pay and pray. Think of that! Is it not lunacy? What else is it? Who is responsible? You may preach religion, but to excite the minds of undeveloped children! You will have to suffer for that. In your heart of hearts, what are you? For every weakening thought you have put into anybody's head you will have to pay with compound interest. The law of Karma must have its pound of flesh.

There is only one sin. That is weakness. When I was a boy I read Milton's *Paradise Lost*. The only good man I had any respect for was Satan. The only saint is that soul that never weakens, faces everything, and determines to die game.

Stand up and die game! Do not add one lunacy to another. Do not add your weakness to the evil that is going to come. That is all I have to say to the world. Be strong! You talk of ghosts and devils. We are the living devils. The sign of life is strength and growth. The sign of death is weakness. Whatever is weak, avoid! It is death. If it is strength, go down into hell and get hold of it! There is salvation, only for the brave. "None but the brave deserves the fair." None but the bravest deserves salvation. Whose hell? Whose torture? Whose sin? Whose weakness? Whose death? Whose disease?

You believe in God. If you do, believe in the real God. "Thou art the man, thou the woman, thou the young man walking in the strength of youth, thou the old man tottering with his stick."* Thou art weakness. Thou art fear. Thou art heaven, and Thou art hell. Thou art the serpent that would sting. Come thou as fear! Come thou as death! Come thou as misery!

All weakness, all bondage is imagination. Speak one word to it, it must vanish. Do not weaken! There is no other way out. Stand up and be strong! No fear. No superstition. Face the truth as it is! If death comes—that is the worst of our miseries—let it come! We are determined to die game. That is all the religion I know. I have not attained to it, but I am struggling to do it. I may not, but you may. Go on!

Where one sees another, one hears another, so long as there are two, there must be fear, and fear is the mother of all misery. Where none sees another, where it is all One, there is none to be miserable, none to be unhappy.** There is only the One without a second. Therefore, be not afraid. Awake, arise, and stop not till the goal is reached!

---

* *Shvetashvatara Upanishad*, IV. 3.
** *Chhandogya Upanishad*, VII. 23-24.

Christ, The Messenger

Delivered at Los Angeles, California, 1900

The wave rises on the ocean, and there is a hollow. Again another wave rises, perhaps bigger than the former, to fall down again, similarly, again to rise, driving onward. In the march of events, we notice the rise and fall, and we generally look towards the rise, forgetting the fall. But both are necessary, and both are great. This is the nature of the universe. Whether in the world of our thoughts, the world of our relations in society, or in our spiritual affairs, the same movement of succession, of rises and falls, is going on. Hence great predominances in the march of events, the liberal ideals, are marshalled ahead, to sink down, to digest, as it were, to ruminate over the past—to adjust, to conserve, to gather strength once more for a rise and a bigger rise.

The history of nations also has ever been like that. The great soul, the Messenger we are to study this afternoon, came at a period of the history of his race which we may well designate as a great fall. We catch only little glimpses here and there of the stray records that have been kept of his sayings and doings; for verily it has been well said, that the doings and sayings of that great soul would fill the world if they had all been written down. And the three years of his ministry were like one compressed, concentrated age, which it has taken nineteen hundred years to unfold, and who knows how much longer it will yet take! Little men like you and me are simply the recipients of just a little energy. A few minutes, a few hours, a few years at best, are enough to spend it all, to stretch it out, as it were, to its fullest strength, and then we are gone forever. But mark this giant that came; centuries and ages pass, yet the energy that he left upon the world is not yet stretched, nor yet expended to its full. It goes on adding new vigour as the ages roll on.

Now what you see in the life of Christ is the life of all the past. The life of every man is, in a manner, the life of the past. It comes to him through heredity, through surroundings, through education, through his own reincarnation—the past of the race. In a manner, the past of the earth, the past of the whole world is there, upon every soul. What are we, in the present, but a result, an effect, in the hands of that infinite past? What are we but floating wavelets in the eternal current of events, irresistibly moved forward and onward and incapable of rest? But you and I are only little things, bubbles. There are always some giant waves in the ocean of affairs, and in you and me the life of the past race has been embodied only a little; but there are giants who embody, as it were, almost the whole of the past and who stretch out their hands for the future. These are the sign-posts here and there which point to the march of humanity; these are verily gigantic, their shadows covering the earth—they stand undying, eternal! As it has been said by the same Messenger, "No man hath seen God at any time, but through the Son." And that is true. And where shall we see God but in the Son? It is true that you and I, and the poorest of us, the meanest even, embody that God, even reflect that God. The vibration of light is everywhere, omnipresent; but we have to strike the light of the lamp before we can see the light. The Omnipresent God of the universe cannot be seen until He is reflected by these giant lamps of the earth—the Prophets, the man-Gods, the Incarnations, the embodiments of God.

We all know that God exists, and yet we do not see Him, we do not understand Him. Take one of these great Messengers of light, compare his character with the highest ideal of God that you ever formed, and you will find that your God falls short of the ideal, and that the character of the Prophet exceeds your conceptions. You cannot even form a higher ideal of God than what the actually embodied have practically realised and set before us as an example. Is it wrong, therefore, to worship these as God? Is it a sin to fall at the feet of these man-Gods and worship them as the only divine beings in the world? If they are really, actually, higher than all our conceptions of God, what harm is there in worshipping them? Not only is there no harm, but it is the only possible and positive way of worship. However much you may try to struggle, by abstraction, by whatsoever method you like, still so long as you are a man in the world of men, your world is human, your religion is human, and your God is human. And that must be so. Who is not practical enough to take up an actually existing thing and give up an idea which is only an abstraction which he cannot grasp, and is difficult of approach except through a concrete medium? Therefore, these Incarnations of God have been worshipped in all ages and in all countries.

We are now going to study a little of the life of Christ, the Incarnation of the Jews. When Christ was born, the Jews were in that state which I call a state of fall between two waves; a state of conservatism; a state where the human mind is, as it were, tired for the time being of moving forward and is taking care only of what it has already; a state when the attention is more bent upon particulars, upon details, than upon the great, general, and bigger problems of life; a state of stagnation, rather than a towing ahead; a state of suffering more than of doing. Mark you, I do not blame this state of things. We have no right to criticise it—because had it not been for this fall, the next rise, which was embodied in Jesus of Nazareth would have been impossible. The Pharisees and Sadducees might have been insincere, they might have been doing things which they ought not to have done; they might have been even hypocrites; but whatever they were, these factors were the very cause, of which the Messenger was the effect. The Pharisees and Sadducees at one end were the very impetus which came out at the other end as the gigantic brain of Jesus of Nazareth.

The attention to forms, to formulas, to the everyday details of religion, and to rituals, may sometimes be laughed at; but nevertheless, within them is strength. Many times in the rushing forward we lose much strength. As a fact, the fanatic is stronger than the liberal man. Even the fanatic, therefore, has one great virtue, he conserves energy, a tremendous amount of it. As with the individual so with the race, energy is gathered to be conserved. Hemmed in all around by external enemies, driven to focus in a centre by the Romans, by the Hellenic tendencies in the world of intellect, by waves from Persia, India, and Alexandria—hemmed in physically, mentally, and morally—there stood the race with an inherent, conservative, tremendous strength, which their descendants have not lost even today. And the race was forced to concentrate and focus all its energies upon Jerusalem and Judaism. But all power when once gathered cannot remain collected; it must expend and expand itself. There is no power on earth which can be kept long confined within a narrow limit. It cannot be kept compressed too long to allow of expansion at a subsequent period.

This concentrated energy amongst the Jewish race found its expression at the next period in the rise of Christianity. The gathered streams collected into a body. Gradually, all the little streams joined together, and became a surging wave on the top of which we find standing out the character of Jesus of Nazareth. Thus, every Prophet is a creation of his own times, the creation of the past of his race; he himself is the creator of the future. The cause of today is the effect of the past and the cause for the future.

In this position stands the Messenger. In him is embodied all that is the best and greatest in his own race, the meaning, the life, for which that race has struggled for ages; and he himself is the impetus for the future, not only to his own race but to unnumbered other races of the world.

We must bear another fact in mind: that my view of the great Prophet of Nazareth would be from the standpoint of the Orient. Many times you forget, also, that the Nazarene himself was an Oriental of Orientals. With all your attempts to paint him with blue eyes and yellow hair, the Nazarene was still an Oriental. All the similes, the imageries, in which the Bible is written—the scenes, the locations, the attitudes, the groups, the poetry, and symbol—speak to you of the Orient: of the bright sky, of the heat, of the sun, of the desert, of the thirsty men and animals; of men and women coming with pitchers on their heads to fill them at the wells; of the flocks, of the ploughmen, of the cultivation that is going on around; of the water-mill and wheel, of the mill-pond, of the millstones. All these are to be seen today in Asia.

The voice of Asia has been the voice of religion. The voice of Europe is the voice of politics. Each is great in its own sphere. The voice of Europe is the voice of ancient Greece. To the Greek mind, his immediate society was all in all: beyond that, it is Barbarian. None but the Greek has the right to live. Whatever the Greeks do is right and correct; whatever else there exists in the world is neither right nor correct, nor should be allowed to live. It is intensely human in its sympathies, intensely natural, intensely artistic, therefore. The Greek lives entirely in this world. He does not care to dream. Even his poetry is practical. His gods and goddesses are not only human beings, but intensely human, with all human passions and feelings almost the same as with any of us. He loves what is beautiful, but, mind you, it is always external nature; the beauty of the hills, of the snows, of the flowers, the beauty of forms and of figures, the beauty in the human face, and, more often, in the human form —that is what the Greeks liked. And the Greeks being the teachers of all subsequent Europeanism, the voice of Europe is Greek.

There is another type in Asia. Think of that vast, huge continent, whose mountain-tops go beyond the clouds, almost touching the canopy of heaven's blue; a rolling desert of miles upon miles where a drop of water cannot be found, neither will a blade of grass grow; interminable forests and gigantic rivers rushing down to the sea. In the midst of all these surroundings, the oriental love of the beautiful and of the sublime developed itself in another direction. It looked inside, and not outside. There is also the thirst for nature, and there is also the same thirst for power; there is also the same thirst for excellence, the same idea of the Greek and Barbarian, but it has extended over a larger circle. In Asia, even today, birth or colour or language never makes a race. That which makes a race is its religion. We are all Christians; we are all Mohammedans; we are all Hindus, or all Buddhists. No matter if a Buddhist is a Chinaman, or is a man from Persia, they think that they are brothers, because of their professing the same religion. Religion is the tie, unity of humanity. And then again, the Oriental, for the same reason, is a visionary, is a born dreamer. The ripples of the waterfalls, the songs of the birds, the beauties of the sun and moon and the stars and the whole earth are pleasant enough; but they are not sufficient for the oriental mind. He wants to dream a dream beyond. He wants to go beyond the present. The present, as it were, is nothing to him. The Orient has been the cradle of the human race for ages, and all the vicissitudes of fortune are there—kingdoms succeeding kingdoms, empires succeeding empires, human power, glory, and wealth, all rolling down there; a Golgotha of power and learning. That is the Orient: a Golgotha of power, of kingdoms, of learning. No wonder, the oriental mind looks with contempt upon the things of this world and naturally wants to see something that changeth not, something which dieth not, something which in the midst of this world of misery and death is eternal, blissful, undying. An oriental Prophet never tires of insisting upon these ideals; and, as for Prophets, you may also remember that without one exception, all the Messengers were Orientals.

We see, therefore, in the life of this great Messenger of life, the first watchword: "Not this life, but something higher"; and, like the true son of the Orient, he is practical in that. You people of the West are practical in your own department, in military affairs, and in managing political circles and other things. Perhaps the Oriental is not practical in those ways, but he is practical in his own field; he is practical in religion. If one preaches a philosophy, tomorrow there are hundreds who will struggle their best to make it practical in their lives. If a man preaches that standing on one foot would lead one to salvation, he will immediately get five hundred to stand on one foot. You may call it ludicrous; but, mark you, beneath that is their philosophy—that intense practicality. In the West, plans of salvation mean intellectual gymnastics—plans which are never worked out, never brought into practical life. In the West, the preacher who talks the best is the greatest preacher.

So, we find Jesus of Nazareth, in the first place, the true son of the Orient, intensely practical. He has no faith in this evanescent world and all its belongings. No need of text-torturing, as is the fashion in the West in modern times, no need of stretching out texts until they will not stretch any more. Texts are not Indian rubber, and even that has its limits. Now, no making of religion to pander to the sense vanity of the present day! Mark you, let us all be honest. If we cannot follow the ideal, let us confess our weakness, but not degrade it; let not any try to pull it down. One gets sick at heart at the different accounts of the life of the Christ that Western people give. I do not know what he was or what he was not! One would make him a great politician: another, perhaps, would make of him a great military general; another, a great patriotic Jew; and so on. Is there any warrant in the books for all such assumptions? The best commentary on the life of a great teacher is his own life. "The foxes have holes, the birds of the air have nests, but the Son of Man hath not where to lay his head." That is what Christ says as the only way to salvation; he lays down no other way. Let us confess in sackcloth and ashes that we cannot do that. We still have, fondness for "me and mine". We want property, money, wealth. Woe unto us! Let us confess and not put to shame that great Teacher of Humanity! He had no family ties. But do you think that, that Man had any physical ideas in him? Do you think that, this mass of light, this God and not-man, came down to earth, to be the brother of animals? And yet, people make him preach all sorts of things. He had no sex ideas! He was a soul! Nothing but a soul—just working a body for the good of humanity; and that was all his relation to the body. In the soul there is no sex. The disembodied soul has no relationship to the animal, no relationship to the body. The ideal may be far away beyond us. But never mind, keep to the ideal. Let us confess that it is our ideal, but we cannot approach it yet.

He had no other occupation in life, no other thought except that one, that he was a spirit. He was a disembodied, unfettered, unbound spirit. And not only so, but he, with his marvellous vision, had found that every man and woman, whether Jew or Gentile, whether rich or poor, whether saint or sinner, was the embodiment of the same undying spirit as himself. Therefore, the one work his whole life showed was to call upon them to realise their own spiritual nature. Give up, he says, these superstitious dreams that you are low and that you are poor. Think not that you are trampled upon and tyrannised over as if you were slaves, for within you is something that can never be tyrannised over, never be trampled upon, never be troubled, never be killed. You are all Sons of God, immortal spirit. "Know", he declared, "the Kingdom of Heaven is within you." "I and my Father are one." Dare you stand up and say, not only that "I am the Son of God", but I shall also find in my heart of hearts that "I and my Father are one"? That was what Jesus of Nazareth said. He never talks of this world and of this life. He has nothing to do with it, except that he wants to get hold of the world as it is, give it a push and drive it forward and onward until the whole world has reached to the effulgent Light of God, until everyone has realised his spiritual nature, until death is vanished and misery banished.

We have read different stories that have been written about him; we know the scholars and their writings, and the higher criticism; and we know all that has been done by study. We are not here to discuss how much of the New Testament is true, we are not here to discuss how much of that life is historical. It does not matter at all whether the New Testament was written within five hundred years of his birth, nor does it matter even, how much of that life is true. But there is something behind it, something we want to imitate. To tell a lie, you have to imitate a truth, and that truth is a fact. You cannot imitate that which never existed. You cannot imitate that which you never perceived. But there must have been a nucleus, a tremendous power that came down, a marvellous manifestation of spiritual power—and of that we "are speaking. It stands there. Therefore, we are not afraid of all the criticisms of the scholars. If I, as an Oriental, have to worship Jesus of Nazareth, there is only one way left to me, that 's, to worship him as God and nothing else. Have we no right to worship him in that way, do you mean to say? If we bring him down to our own level and simply pay him a little respect as a great man, why should we worship at all? Our scriptures say, "These great children of Light, who manifest the Light' themselves, who are Light themselves, they, being worshipped, become, as it were, one with us and we become one with them."

For, you see, in three ways Man perceives God. At first the undeveloped intellect of the uneducated man sees God as far away, up in the heavens somewhere, sitting on a throne as a great Judge. He looks upon Him as a fire, as a terror. Now, that is good, for there is nothing bad in it. You must remember that humanity travels not from error to truth, but from truth to truth; it may be, if you like it better, from lower truth to higher truth, but never from error to truth. Suppose you start from here and travel towards the sun in a straight line. From here the sun looks only small in size. Suppose you go forward a million miles, the sun will be much bigger. At every stage the sun will become bigger and bigger. Suppose twenty thousand photographs had been taken of the same sun, from different standpoints; these twenty thousand photographs will all certainly differ from one another. But can you deny that each is a photograph of the same sun? So all forms of religion, high or low, are just different stages toward that eternal state of Light, which is God Himself. Some embody a lower view, some a higher, and that is all the difference. Therefore, the religions of the unthinking masses all over the world must be; and have always been, of a God who is outside of the universe, who lives in heaven, who governs from that place, who is a punisher of the bad and a rewarder of the good, and so on. As Man advanced spiritually, he began to feel that God was omnipresent, that He must be in him, that He must be everywhere, that He was not a distant God, but clearly the Soul of all souls. As my soul moves my body, even so is God the mover of my soul. Soul within soul. And a few individuals who had developed enough and were pure enough, went still further, and at last found God. As the New Testament says, "Blessed are the pure in heart for they shall see God." And they found at last that they and the Father were one.

You find that all these three stages are taught by the Great Teacher in the New Testament. Note the Common Prayer he taught: "Our Father which art in Heaven, hallowed be Thy name," and so on—a simple prayer, a child's prayer. Mark you, it is the "Common Prayer" because it is intended for the uneducated masses. To a higher circle, to those who had advanced a little more, he gave a more elevated teaching: "I am in my Father, and ye in me, and I in you." Do you remember that? And then, when the Jews asked him who he was, he declared that he and his Father were one, and the Jews thought that that was blasphemy. What did he mean by that? This has been also told by your old Prophets, "Ye are gods and all of you are children of the Most High." Mark the same three stages. You will find that it is easier for you to begin with the first and end with the last.

The Messenger came to show the path: that the spirit is not in forms, that it is not through all sorts of vexations and knotty problems of philosophy that you know the spirit. Better that you had no learning, better that you never read a book in your life. These are not at all necessary for salvation—neither wealth, nor position nor power, not even learning; but what is necessary is that one thing, purity. "Blessed are the pure in heart," for the spirit in its own nature is pure. How can it be otherwise? It is of God, it has come from God. In the language of the Bible, "It is the breath of God." In the language of the Koran, "It is the soul of God." Do you mean to say that the Spirit of God can ever be impure? But, alas, it has been, as it were, covered over with the dust and dirt of ages, through our own actions, good and evil. Various works which were not correct, which were not true, have covered the same spirit with the dust and dirt of the ignorance of ages. It is only necessary to clear away the dust and dirt, and then the spirit shines immediately. "Blessed are the pure in heart, for they shall see God." "The Kingdom of Heaven is within you." Where goest thou to seek for the Kingdom of God, asks Jesus of Nazareth, when it is there, within you? Cleanse the spirit, and it is there. It is already yours. How can you get what is not yours? It is yours by right. You are the heirs of immortality, sons of the Eternal Father.

This is the great lesson of the Messenger, and another which is the basis of all religions, is renunciation. How can you make the spirit pure? By renunciation. A rich young man asked Jesus, "Good Master, what shall I do that I may inherit eternal life?" And Jesus said unto him, "One thing thou lackest; go thy way, sell whatsoever thou hast, and give to the poor, and thou shalt have treasures in heaven: and come, take up thy cross, and follow Me." And he was sad at that saying and went away grieved; for he had great possessions. We are all more or less like that. The voice is ringing in our ears day and night. In the midst of our pleasures and joys, in the midst of worldly things, we think that we have forgotten everything else. Then comes a moment's pause and the voice rings in our ears: "Give up all that thou hast and follow Me." "Whosoever will save his life shall lose it; and whosoever shall lose his life for My sake shall find it." For whoever gives up this life for His sake, finds the life immortal. In the midst of all our weakness there is a moment of pause and the voice rings: "Give up all that thou hast; give it to the poor and follow me." This is the one ideal he preaches, and this has been the ideal preached by all the great Prophets of the world: renunciation. What is meant by renunciation? That there is only one ideal in morality: unselfishness. Be selfless. The ideal is perfect unselfishness. When a man is struck on the right cheek, he turns the left also. When a man's coat is carried off, he gives away his cloak also.

We should work in the best way we can, without dragging the ideal down. Here is the ideal. When a man has no more self in him, no possession, nothing to call "me" or "mine", has given himself up entirely, destroyed himself as it were—in that man is God Himself; for in him self-will is gone, crushed out, annihilated. That is the ideal man. We cannot reach that state yet; yet, let us worship the ideal, and slowly struggle to reach the ideal, though, maybe, with faltering steps. It may be tomorrow, or it may be a thousand years hence; but that ideal has to be reached. For it is not only the end, but also the means. To be unselfish, perfectly selfless, is salvation itself; for the man within dies, and God alone remains.

One more point. All the teachers of humanity are unselfish. Suppose Jesus of Nazareth was teaching, and a man came and told him, "What you teach is beautiful. I believe that it is the way to perfection, and I am ready to follow it; but I do not care to worship you as the only begotten Son of God." What would be the answer of Jesus of Nazareth? "Very well, brother, follow the ideal and advance in your own way. I do not care whether you give me the credit for the teaching or not. I am not a shopkeeper. I do not trade in religion. I only teach truth, and truth is nobody's property. Nobody can patent truth. Truth is God Himself. Go forward." But what the disciples say nowadays is: "No matter whether you practise the teachings or not, do you give credit to the Man? If you credit the Master, you will be saved; if not, there is no salvation for you." And thus the whole teaching of the Master is degenerated, and all the struggle and fight is for the personality of the Man. They do not know that in imposing that difference, they are, in a manner, bringing shame to the very Man they want to honour—the very Man that would have shrunk with shame from such an idea. What did he care if there was one man in the world that remembered him or not? He had to deliver his message, and he gave it. And if he had twenty thousand lives, he would give them all up for the poorest man in the world. If he had to be tortured millions of times for a million despised Samaritans, and if for each one of them the sacrifice of his own life would be the only condition of salvation, he would have given his life. And all this without wishing to have his name known even to a single person. Quiet, unknown, silent, would he work, just as the Lord works. Now, what would the disciple say? He will tell you that you may be a perfect man, perfectly unselfish; but unless you give the credit to our teacher, to our saint, it is of no avail. Why? What is the origin of this superstition, this ignorance? The disciple thinks that the Lord can manifest Himself only once. There lies the whole mistake. God manifests Himself to you in man. But throughout nature, what happens once must have happened before, and must happen in future. There is nothing in nature which is not bound by law; and that means that whatever happens once must go on and must have been going on.

In India they have the same idea of the Incarnations of God. One of their great Incarnations, Krishna, whose grand sermon, the *Bhagavad Gita*, some of you might have read, says, "Though I am unborn, of changeless nature, and Lord of beings, yet subjugating My Prakriti, I come into being by My own Maya. Whenever virtue subsides and immorality prevails, then I body Myself forth. For the protection of the good, for the destruction of the wicked, and for the establishment of Dharma, I come into being, in every age." Whenever the world goes down, the Lord comes to help it forward; and so He does from time to time and place to place. In another passage He speaks to this effect: Wherever thou findest a great soul of immense power and purity struggling to raise humanity, know that he is born of My splendour, that I am there working through him.

Let us, therefore, find God not only in Jesus of Nazareth, but in all the great Ones that have preceded him, in all that came after him, and all that are yet to come. Our worship is unbounded and free. They are all manifestations of the same Infinite God. They are all pure and unselfish; they struggled and gave up their lives for us, poor human beings. They each and all suffer vicarious atonement for every one of us, and also for all that are to come hereafter.

In a sense you are all Prophets; every one of you is a Prophet, bearing the burden of the world on your own shoulders. Have you ever seen a man, have you ever seen a woman, who is not quietly, patiently, bearing his or her little burden of life? The great Prophets were giants—they bore a gigantic world on their shoulders. Compared with them we are pygmies, no doubt, yet we are doing the same task; in our little circles, in our little homes, we are bearing our little crosses. There is no one so evil, no one so worthless, but he has to bear his own cross. But with all our mistakes, with all our evil thoughts and evil deeds, there is a bright spot somewhere, there is still somewhere the golden thread through which we are always in touch with the divine. For, know for certain, that the moment the touch of the divine is lost there would be annihilation. And because none can be annihilated, there is always somewhere in our heart of hearts, however low and degraded we may be, a little circle of light which is in constant touch with the divine.

Our salutations go to all the past Prophets whose teachings and lives we have inherited, whatever might have been their race, clime, or creed! Our salutations go to all those Godlike men and women who are working to help humanity, whatever be their birth, colour, or race! Our salutations to those who are coming in the future—living Gods—to work unselfishly for our descendants.

Mohammed's Message To The World

Excerpts of Ida Ansell's first transcript of Swami Vivekananda's San Francisco lecture delivered Sunday, 25 March 1900

Each great messenger not only creates a new order of things, but is himself the creation of a certain order of things. There is no such thing as an independent, active cause. All causes are cause and effect in turn. Father is father and son in turn. Mother is mother and daughter in turn. It is necessary to understand the surroundings and circumstances into which they, the great messengers, come.

This is the peculiarity of civilisation. One wave of a race will go from its birthplace to a distant land and make a wonderful civilisation. The rest will be left in barbarism. The Hindus came into India and the tribes of Central Asia were left in barbarism. Others came to Asia Minor and Europe. Then, you remember the coming out of Egypt of the Israelites. Their home was the Arabian desert. Out of that springs a new work. All civilisations grow that way. A certain race becomes civilised. Then comes a nomad race. Nomads are always ready to fight. They come and conquer a race. They bring better blood, stronger physiques. They take up the mind of the conquered race and add that to their body and push civilisation still further. One race becomes cultured and civilised until the body is worn out. Then like a whirlwind comes a race strong in the physical, and they take up the arts and the sciences and the mind, and push civilisation further. This must be. Otherwise the world would not be.

~

The moment a great man rises, they build a beautiful mythology around him. Science and truth is all the religion that exists. Truth is more beautiful than any mythology in the world.

The old Greeks had disappeared already, the whole nation lay under the feet of the Romans who were learning their science and art. The Roman was a barbarian, a conquering man. He had no eye for poetry or art. He knew how to rule and how to get everything centralised into that system of Rome and to enjoy that. That was sweet. And that Roman Empire is gone, destroyed by all sorts of difficulties, luxury, a new foreign religion, and all that. Christianity had been already six hundred years in the Roman Empire.

Whenever a new religion tries to force itself upon another race, it succeeds if the race is uncultured. If the race is cultured, it will destroy the religion. The Roman Empire was a case in point, and the Persian people saw that. Christianity was another thing with the barbarians in the north. But the Christianity of the Roman Empire was a mixture of everything, something from Persia, from the Jews, from India, from Greece, everything.

~

The race is always killed by war. War takes away the best men, gets them killed, and the cowards are left at home. Thus comes the degeneration of the race. Men became small. Why? All the great men became warriors. That is how war kills races, takes their best into the battlefields.

Then the monasteries. They all went to the desert, to the caves for meditation. The monasteries gradually became the centres of wealth and luxury.

The Anglo-Saxon race would not be Anglo-Saxon but for these monasteries. Every weak man was worse than a slave. In that state of chaos these monasteries were centres of light and protection.

Where cultures differ very much they do not quarrel. All these warring, jarring elements were originally all one.

In the midst of all this chaos was born the Prophet.

On Lord Buddha

Delivered in Detroit

In every religion we find one type of self-devotion particularly developed. The type of working without a motive is most highly developed in Buddhism. Do not mistake Buddhism and Brahminism. In this country you are very apt to do so. Buddhism is one of our sects. It was founded by a great man called Gautama, who became disgusted at the eternal metaphysical discussions of his day, and the cumbrous rituals, and more especially with the caste system. Some people say that we are born to a certain state, and, therefore, we are superior to others who are not thus born. He was also against the tremendous priestcraft. He preached a religion in which there was no motive power, and was perfectly agnostic about metaphysics or theories about God. He was often asked if there was a God, and he answered, he did not know. When asked about right conduct, he would reply, "Do good and be good." There came five Brahmins, who asked him to settle their discussion. One said, "Sir, my book says that God is such and such, and that this is the way to come to God." Another said, "That is wrong, for my book says such and such, and this is the way to come to God"; and so the others. He listened calmly to all of them, and then asked them one by one, "Does any one of your books say that God becomes angry, that He ever injures anyone, that He is impure?" "No, Sir, they all teach that God is pure and good." "Then, my friends, why do you not become pure and good first, that you may know what God is?"

Of course I do not endorse all his philosophy. I want a good deal of metaphysics, for myself. I entirely differ in many respects, but, because I differ, is that any reason why I should not see the beauty of the man? He was the only man who was bereft of all motive power. There were other great men who all said they were the Incarnations of God Himself, and that those who would believe in them would go to heaven. But what did Buddha say with his dying breath? "None can help you; help yourself; work out your own salvation." He said about himself, "Buddha is the name of infinite knowledge, infinite as the sky; I, Gautama, have reached that state; you will all reach that too if you struggle for it." Bereft of all motive power, he did not want to go to heaven, did not want money; he gave up his throne and everything else and went about begging his bread through the streets of India, preaching for the good of men and animals with a heart as wide as the ocean.

He was the only man who was ever ready to give up his life for animals to stop a sacrifice. He once said to a king, "If the sacrifice of a lamb helps you to go to heaven, sacrificing a man will help you better; so sacrifice me." The king was astonished. And yet this man was without any motive power. He stands as the perfection of the active type, and the very height to which he attained shows that through the power of work we can also attain to the highest spirituality.

To many the path becomes easier it they believe in God. But the life of Buddha shows that even a man who does not believe in God, has no metaphysics, belongs to no sect, and does not go to any church, or temple, and is a confessed materialist, even he can attain to the highest. We have no right to judge him. I wish I had one infinitesimal part of Buddha's heart. Buddha may or may not have believed in God; that does not matter to me. He reached the same state of perfection to which others come by Bhakti—love of God—Yoga, or Jnana. Perfection does not come from belief or faith. Talk does not count for anything. Parrots can do that. Perfection comes through the disinterested performance of action.

Religion Is Self-Abnegation

One cannot divide the rights of the universe. To talk of "right" implies limitation. It is not "right" but "responsibility". Each is responsible for the evil anywhere in the world. No one can separate himself from his brother. All that unites with the universal is virtue; all that separates is sin. You are a part of the Infinite. This is your nature. Hence you are your brother's keeper.

The first end of life is knowledge; the second end of life is happiness. Knowledge and happiness lead to freedom. But not one can attain liberty until every being, ant or dog, has liberty. Not one can be happy until all are happy. When you hurt anyone you hurt yourself, for you and your brother are one. He is indeed a Yogi who sees himself in the whole universe and the whole universe in himself. Self-sacrifice, not self-assertion, is the law of the highest universe. The world is so evil because Jesus' teaching, "Resist not evil", has never been tried. Selflessness alone will solve the problem. Religion comes with intense self-sacrifice. Desire nothing for yourself. Do all for others. This is to live and move and have your being in God.

Religion Is Realisation

The greatest name man ever gave to God is Truth. Truth is the fruit of realisation; therefore, seek it within the soul. Get away from all books and forms and let your soul see its Self. "We are deluded and maddened by books," Shri Krishna declares. Be beyond the dualities of nature. The moment you think creed and form and ceremony the "be-all" and "end-all", then you are in bondage. Take part in them to help others, but take care they do not become a bondage. Religion is one, but its application must be various. Let each one, therefore, give his message; but find not the defects in other religions. You must come out from all form if you would see the Light. Drink deep of the nectar of the knowledge of God. The man who realises, "I am He," though clad in rags, is happy. Go forth into the Eternal and come back with eternal energy. The slave goes out to search for truth; he comes back free.

Response To Welcome At The World's Parliament Of Religions

Delivered in Chicago, 11 September 1893

Sisters and Brothers of America,

It fills my heart with joy unspeakable to rise in response to the warm and cordial welcome which you have given us. I thank you in the name of the most ancient order of monks in the world; I thank you in the name of the mother of religions; and I thank you in the name of millions and millions of Hindu people of all classes and sects.

My thanks, also, to some of the speakers on this platform who, referring to the delegates from the Orient, have told you that these men from far-off nations may well claim the honour of bearing to different lands the idea of toleration. I am proud to belong to a religion which has taught the world both tolerance and universal acceptance. We believe not only in universal toleration, but we accept all religions as true. I am proud to belong to a nation which has sheltered the persecuted and the refugees of all religions and all nations of the earth. I am proud to tell you that we have gathered in our bosom the purest remnant of the Israelites, who came to Southern India and took refuge with us in the very year in which their holy temple was shattered to pieces by Roman tyranny. I am proud to belong to the religion which has sheltered and is still fostering the remnant of the grand Zoroastrian nation. I will quote to you, brethren, a few lines from a hymn which I remember to have repeated from my earliest boyhood, which is every day repeated by millions of human beings: "As the different streams having their sources in different places all mingle their water in the sea, so, O Lord, the different paths which men take through different tendencies, various though they appear, crooked or straight, all lead to Thee."

The present convention, which is one of the most august assemblies ever held, is in itself a vindication, a declaration to the world of the wonderful doctrine preached in the *Gita*: "Whosoever comes to Me, through whatsoever form, I reach him; all men are struggling through paths which in the end lead to me." Sectarianism, bigotry, and its horrible descendant, fanaticism, have long possessed this beautiful earth. They have filled the earth with violence, drenched it often and often with human blood, destroyed civilisation and sent whole nations to despair. Had it not been for these horrible demons, human society would be far more advanced than it is now. But their time is come; and I fervently hope that the bell that tolled this morning in honour of this convention may be the death-knell of all fanaticism, of all persecutions with the sword or with the pen, and of all uncharitable feelings between persons wending their way to the same goal.

Why We Disagree

15 September 1893

I will tell you a little story. You have heard the eloquent speaker who has just finished say, "Let us cease from abusing each other," and he was very sorry that there should be always so much variance.

But I think I should tell you a story which would illustrate the cause of this variance. A frog lived in a well. It had lived there for a long time. It was born there and brought up there, and yet was a little, small frog. Of course the evolutionists were not there then to tell us whether the frog lost its eyes or not, but, for our story's sake, we must take it for granted that it had its eyes, and that it every day cleansed the water of all the worms and bacilli that lived in it with an energy that would do credit to our modern bacteriologists. In this way it went on and became a little sleek and fat. Well, one day another frog that lived in the sea came and fell into the well.

"Where are you from?"

"I am from the sea."

"The sea! How big is that? Is it as big as my well?" and he took a leap from one side of the well to the other.

"My friend," said the frog of the sea, "how do you compare the sea with your little well?"

Then the frog took another leap and asked, "Is your sea so big?"

"What nonsense you speak, to compare the sea with your well!"

"Well, then," said the frog of the well, "nothing can be bigger than my well; there can be nothing bigger than this. This fellow is a liar, so turn him out."

That has been the difficulty all the while.

I am a Hindu. I am sitting in my own little well and thinking that the whole world is my little well. The Christian sits in his little well and thinks the whole world is his well. The Mohammedan sits in his little well and thinks that is the whole world. I have to thank you of America for the great attempt you are making to break down the barriers of this little world of ours, and hope that, in the future, the Lord will help you to accomplish your purpose.

My Life And Mission

Delivered at the Shakespeare Club of Pasadena, California, on 27 January 1900

Now, ladies and gentlemen, the subject for this morning was to have been the Vedanta Philosophy. That subject itself is interesting, but rather dry and very vast.

Meanwhile, I have been asked by your president and some of the ladies and gentlemen here to tell them something about my work and what I have been doing. It may be interesting to some here, but not so much so to me. In fact, I do not quite know how to tell it to you, for this will have been the first time in my life that I have spoken on that subject.

Now, to understand what I have been trying to do, in my small way, I will take you, in imagination, to India. We have not time to go into all the details and all the ramifications of the subject; nor is it possible for you to understand all the complexities in a foreign race in this short time. Suffice it to say, I will at least try to give you a little picture of what India is like.

It is like a gigantic building all tumbled down in ruins. At first sight, then, there is little hope. It is a nation gone and ruined. But you wait and study, then you see something beyond that. The truth is that so long as the principle, the ideal, of which the outer man is the expression, is not hurt or destroyed, the man lives, and there is hope for that man. If your coat is stolen twenty times, that is no reason why you should be destroyed. You can get a new coat. The coat is unessential. The fact that a rich man is robbed does not hurt the vitality of the man, does not mean death. The man will survive.

Standing on this principle, we look in and we see—what? India is no longer a political power; it is an enslaved race. Indians have no say, no voice in their own government; they are three hundred millions of slaves—nothing more! The average income of a man in India is two shillings a month. The common state of the vast mass of the people is starvation, so that, with the least decrease in income, millions die. A little famine means death. So there, too, when I look on that side of India, I see ruin—hopeless ruin.

But we find that the Indian race never stood for wealth. Although they acquired immense wealth, perhaps more than any other nation ever acquired, yet the nation did not stand for wealth. It was a powerful race for ages, yet we find that that nation never stood for power, never went out of the country to conquer. Quite content within their own boundaries, they never fought anybody. The Indian nation never stood for imperial glory. Wealth and power, then, were not the ideals of the race.

What then? Whether they were wrong or right—that is not the question we discuss—that nation, among all the children of men, has believed, and believed intensely, that this life is not real. The real is God; and they must cling unto that God through thick and thin. In the midst of their degradation, religion came first. The Hindu man drinks religiously, sleeps religiously, walks religiously, marries religiously, robs religiously.

Did you ever see such a country? If you want to get up a gang of robbers, the leader will have to preach some sort of religion, then formulate some bogus metaphysics, and say that this method is the clearest and quickest way to get to God. Then he finds a following, otherwise not. That shows that the vitality of the race, the mission of the race is religion; and because that has not been touched, therefore, that race lives.

See Rome. Rome's mission was imperial power, expansion. And so soon as that was touched, Rome fell to pieces, passed out. The mission of Greece was intellect, as soon as that was touched, why, Greece passed out. So in modern times, Spain and all these modern countries. Each nation has a mission for the world. So long as that mission is not hurt, that nation lives, despite every difficulty. But as soon as its mission is destroyed, the nation collapses.

Now, that vitality of India has not been touched yet. They have not given up that, and it is still strong—in spite of all their superstitions. Hideous superstitions are there, most revolting some of them. Never mind. The national life—current is still there—the mission of the race.

The Indian nation never will be a powerful conquering people—never. They will never be a great political power; that is not their business, that is not the note India has to play in the great harmony of nations. But what has she to play? God, and God alone. She clings unto that like grim death. Still there is hope there.

So, then, after your analysis, you come to the conclusion that all these things, all this poverty and misery, are of no consequence—the man is living still, and, therefore, there is hope.

Well! You see religious activities going on all through the country. I do not recall a year that has not given birth to several new sects in India. The stronger the current, the more the whirlpools and eddies. Sects are not signs of decay; they are a sign of life. Let sects multiply, till the time comes when every one of us is a sect, each individual. We need not quarrel about that.

Now, take your country. I do not mean any criticism. Here the social laws, the political formation—everything is made to facilitate man's journey in this life. He may live very happily so long as he is on this earth. Look at your streets—how clean! Your beautiful cities! And in how many ways a man can make money! How many channels to get enjoyment in this life! But, if a man here should say, "Now look here, I shall sit down under this tree and meditate; I do not want to work," why, he would have to go to jail. See! There would be no chance for him at all. None. A man can live in this society only if he falls in line. He has to join in this rush for the enjoyment of good in this life, or he dies.

Now let us go back to India. There, if a man says, "I shall go and sit on the top of that mountain and look at the tip of my nose all the rest of my days," everybody says, "Go, and Godspeed to you!" He need not speak a word. Somebody brings him a little cloth, and he is all right. But if a man says, "Behold, I am going to enjoy a little of this life," every door is closed to him.

I say that the ideas of both countries are unjust. I see no reason why a man here should not sit down and look at the tip of his nose if he likes. Why should everybody here do just what the majority does? I see no reason.

Nor why, in India, a man should not have the goods of this life and make money. But you see how those vast millions are forced to accept the opposite point of view by tyranny. This is the tyranny of the sages. This is the tyranny of the great, tyranny of the spiritual, tyranny of the intellectual, tyranny of the wise. And the tyranny of the wise, mind you, is much more powerful than the tyranny of the ignorant. The wise, the intellectual, when they take to forcing their opinions upon others, know a hundred thousand ways to make bonds and barriers which it is not in the power of the ignorant to break.

Now, I say that this thing has got to stop. There is no use in sacrificing millions and millions of people to produce one spiritual giant. If it is possible to make a society where the spiritual giant will be produced and all the rest of the people will be happy as well, that is good; but if the millions have to be ground down, that is unjust. Better that the one great man should suffer for the salvation of the world.

In every nation you will have to work through their methods. To every man you will have to speak in his own language. Now, in England or in America, if you want to preach religion to them, you will have to work through political methods—make organisations, societies, with voting, balloting, a president, and so on, because that is the language, the method of the Western race. On the other hand, if you want to speak of politics in India, you must speak through the language of religion. You will have to tell them something like this: "The man who cleans his house every morning will acquire such and such an amount of merit, he will go to heaven, or he comes to God." Unless you put it that way, they will not listen to you. It is a question of language. The thing done is the same. But with every race, you will have to speak their language in order to reach their hearts. And that is quite just. We need not fret about that.

In the Order to which I belong we are called Sannyasins. The word means "a man who has renounced". This is a very, very, very ancient Order. Even Buddha, who was 560 years before Christ, belonged to that Order. He was one of the reformers of his Order. That was all. So ancient! You find it mentioned way back in the Vedas, the oldest book in the world. In old India there was the regulation that every man and woman, towards the end of their lives, must get out of social life altogether and think of nothing except God and their own salvation. This was to get ready for the great event—death. So old people used to become Sannyasins in those early days. Later on, young people began to give up the world. And young people are active. They could not sit down under a tree and think all the time of their own death, so they went about preaching and starting sects, and so on. Thus, Buddha, being young, started that great reform. Had he been an old man, he would have looked at the tip of his nose and died quietly.

The Order is not a church, and the people who join the Order are not priests. There is an absolute difference between the priests and the Sannyasins. In India, priesthood, like every other business in a social life, is a hereditary profession. A priest's son will become a priest, just as a carpenter's son will be a carpenter, or a blacksmith's son a blacksmith. The priest must always be married. The Hindu does not think a man is complete unless he has a wife. An unmarried man has no right to perform religious ceremonies.

The Sannyasins do not possess property, and they do not marry. Beyond that there is no organisation. The only bond that is there is the bond between the teacher and the taught—and that is peculiar to India. The teacher is not a man who comes just to teach me, and I pay him so much, and there it ends. In India it is really like an adoption. The teacher is more than my own father, and I am truly his child, his son in every respect. I owe him obedience and reverence first, before my own father even; because, they say, the father gave me this body, but the teacher showed me the way to salvation, he is greater than father. And we carry this love, this respect for our teacher all our lives. And that is the only organisation that exists. I adopt my disciples. Sometimes the teacher will be a young man and the disciple a very old man. But never mind, he is the son, and he calls me "Father", and I have to address him as my son, my daughter, and so on.

Now, I happened to get an old man to teach me, and he was very peculiar. He did not go much for intellectual scholarship, scarcely studied books; but when he was a boy he was seized with the tremendous idea of getting to truth direct. First he tried by studying his own religion. Then he got the idea that he must get the truth of other religions; and with that idea he joined all the sects, one after another. For the time being he did exactly what they told him to do—lived with the devotees of these different sects in turn, until inter-penetrated with the particular ideal of that sect. After a few years he would go to another sect. When he had gone through with all that, he came to the conclusion that they were all good. He had no criticism to offer to any one; they are all so many paths leading to the same goal. And then he said, "That is a glorious thing, that there should be so many paths, because if there were only one path, perhaps it would suit only an individual man. The more the number of paths, the more the chance for every one of us to know the truth. If I cannot be taught in one language, I will try another, and so on." Thus his benediction was for every religion.

Now, all the ideas that I preach are only an attempt to echo his ideas. Nothing is mine originally except the wicked ones, everything I say which is false and wicked. But every word that I have ever uttered which is true and good is simply an attempt to echo his voice. Read his life by Prof. Max Muller. (*Ramakrishna: His Life and Sayings.*)

Well, there at his feet I conceived these ideas—there with some other young men. I was just a boy. I went there when I was about sixteen. Some of the other boys were still younger, some a little older—about a dozen or more. And together we conceived that this ideal had to be spread. And not only spread, but made practical. That is to say, we must show the spirituality of the Hindus, the mercifulness of the Buddhists, the activity of the Christians, the brotherhood of the Mohammedans, by our practical lives. "We shall start a universal religion now and here," we said, "we will not wait."

Our teacher was an old man who would never touch a coin with his hands. He took just the little food offered, just so many yards of cotton cloth, no more. He could never be induced to take any other gift. With all these marvellous ideas, he was strict, because that made him free. The monk in India is the friend of the prince today, dines with him; and tomorrow he is with the beggar, sleeps under a tree. He must come into contact with everyone, must always move about. As the saying is, "The rolling stone gathers no moss." The last fourteen years of my life, I have never been for three months at a time in any one place—continually rolling. So do we all.

Now, this handful of boys got hold of these ideas, and all the practical results that sprang out of these ideas. Universal religion, great sympathy for the poor, and all that are very good in theory, but one must practise.

Then came the sad day when our old teacher died. We nursed him the best we could. We had no friends. Who would listen to a few boys, with their crank notions? Nobody. At least, in India, boys are nobodies. Just think of it—a dozen boys, telling people vast, big ideas, saying they are determined to work these ideas out in life. Why, everybody laughed. From laughter it became serious; it became persecution. Why, the parents of the boys came to feel like spanking every one of us. And the more we were derided, the more determined we became.

Then came a terrible time—for me personally and for all the other boys as well. But to me came such misfortune! On the one side was my mother, my brothers. My father died at that time, and we were left poor. Oh, very poor, almost starving all the time! I was the only hope of the family, the only one who could do anything to help them. I had to stand between my two worlds. On the one hand, I would have to see my mother and brothers starve unto death; on the other, I had believed that this man's ideas were for the good of India and the world, and had to be preached and worked out. And so the fight went on in my mind for days and months. Sometimes I would pray for five or six days and nights together without stopping. Oh, the agony of those days! I was living in hell! The natural affections of my boy's heart drawing me to my family—I could not bear to see those who were the nearest and dearest to me suffering. On the other hand, nobody to sympathise with me. Who would sympathise with the imaginations of a boy—imaginations that caused so much suffering to others? Who would sympathise with me? None—except one.

That one's sympathy brought blessing and hope. She was a woman. Our teacher, this great monk, was married when he was a boy and she a mere child. When he became a young man, and all this religious zeal was upon him, she came to see him. Although they had been married for long, they had not seen very much of each other until they were grown up. Then he said to his wife, "Behold, I am your husband; you have a right to this body. But I cannot live the sex life, although I have married you. I leave it to your judgment." And she wept and said, "God speed you! The Lord bless you! Am I the woman to degrade you? If I can, I will help you. Go on in your work."

That was the woman. The husband went on and became a monk in his own way; and from a distance the wife went on helping as much as she could. And later, when the man had become a great spiritual giant, she came—really, she was the first disciple—and she spent the rest of her life taking care of the body of this man. He never knew whether he was living or dying, or anything. Sometimes, when talking, he would get so excited that if he sat on live charcoals, he did not know it. Live charcoals! Forgetting all about his body, all the time.

Well, that lady, his wife, was the only one who sympathised with the idea of those boys. But she was powerless. She was poorer than we were. Never mind! We plunged into the breach. I believed, as I was living, that these ideas were going to rationalise India and bring better days to many lands and foreign races. With that belief, came the realisation that it is better that a few persons suffer than that such ideas should die out of the world. What if a mother or two brothers die? It is a sacrifice. Let it be done. No great thing can be done without sacrifice. The heart must be plucked out and the bleeding heart placed upon the altar. Then great things are done. Is there any other way? None have found it. I appeal to each one of you, to those who have accomplished any great thing. Oh, how much it has cost! What agony! What torture! What terrible suffering is behind every deed of success in every life! You know that, all of you.

And thus we went on, that band of boys. The only thing we got from those around us was a kick and a curse—that was all. Of course, we had to beg from door to door for our food: got hips and haws—the refuse of everything—a piece of bread here and there. We got hold of a broken-down old house, with hissing cobras living underneath; and because that was the cheapest, we went into that house and lived there.

Thus we went on for some years, in the meanwhile making excursions all over India, trying to bring about the idea gradually. Ten years were spent without a ray of light! Ten more years! A thousand times despondency came; but there was one thing always to keep us hopeful—the tremendous faithfulness to each other, the tremendous love between us. I have got a hundred men and women around me; if I become the devil himself tomorrow, they will say, "Here we are still! We will never give you up!" That is a great blessing. In happiness, in misery, in famine, in pain, in the grave, in heaven, or in hell who never gives me up is my friend. Is such friendship a joke? A man may have salvation through such friendship. That brings salvation if we can love like that. If we have that faithfulness, why, there is the essence of all concentration. You need not worship any gods in the world if you have that faith, that strength, that love. And that was there with us all throughout that hard time. That was there. That made us go from the Himalayas to Cape Comorin, from the Indus to the Brahmaputra.

This band of boys began to travel about. Gradually we began to draw attention: ninety per cent was antagonism, very little of it was helpful. For we had one fault: we were boys—in poverty and with all the roughness of boys. He who has to make his own way in life is a bit rough, he has not much time to be smooth and suave and polite—"my lady and my gentleman", and all that. You have seen that in life, always. He is a rough diamond, he has not much polish, he is a jewel in an indifferent casket.

And there we were. "No compromise!" was the watchword. "This is the ideal, and this has got to be carried out. If we meet the king, though we die, we must give him a bit of our minds; if the peasant, the same." Naturally, we met with antagonism.

But, mind you, this is life's experience; if you really want the good of others, the whole universe may stand against you and cannot hurt you. It must crumble before your power of the Lord Himself in you if you are sincere and really unselfish. And those boys were that. They came as children, pure and fresh from the hands of nature. Said our Master: I want to offer at the altar of the Lord only those flowers that have not even been smelled, fruits that have not been touched with the fingers. The words of the great man sustained us all. For he saw through the future life of those boys that he collected from the streets of Calcutta, so to say. People used to laugh at him when he said, "You will see—this boy, that boy, what he becomes." His faith was unalterable: "Mother showed it to me. I may be weak, but when She says this is so—She can never make mistakes—it must be so."

So things went on and on for ten years without any light, but with my health breaking all the time. It tells on the body in the long run: sometimes one meal at nine in the evening, another time a meal at eight in the morning, another after two days, another after three days—and always the poorest and roughest thing. Who is going to give to the beggar the good things he has? And then, they have not much in India. And most of the time walking, climbing snow peaks, sometimes ten miles of hard mountain climbing, just to get a meal. They eat unleavened bread in India, and sometimes they have it stored away for twenty or thirty days, until it is harder than bricks; and then they will give a square of that. I would have to go from house to house to collect sufficient for one meal. And then the bread was so hard, it made my mouth bleed to eat it. Literally, you can break your teeth on that bread. Then I would put it in a pot and pour over it water from the river. For months and months I existed that way—of course it was telling on the health.

Then I thought, I have tried India: it is time for me to try another country. At that time your Parliament of Religions was to be held, and someone was to be sent from India. I was just a vagabond, but I said, "If you send me, I am going. I have not much to lose, and I do not care if I lose that." It was very difficult to find the money, but after a long struggle they got together just enough to pay for my passage—and I came. Came one or two months earlier, so that I found myself drifting about in the streets here, without knowing anybody.

But finally the Parliament of Religions opened, and I met kind friends, who helped me right along. I worked a little, collected funds, started two papers, and so on. After that I went over to England and worked there. At the same time I carried on the work for India in America too.

My plan for India, as it has been developed and centralised, is this: I have told you of our lives as monks there, how we go from door to door, so that religion is brought to everybody without charge, except, perhaps, a broken piece of bread. That is why you see the lowest of the low in India holding the most exalted religious ideas. It is all through the work of these monks. But ask a man, "Who are the English?"—he does not know. He says perhaps, "They are the children of those giants they speak of in those books, are they not?" "Who governs you?" "We do not know." "What is the government?" They do not know. But they know philosophy. It is a practical want of intellectual education about life on this earth they suffer from. These millions and millions of people are ready for life beyond this world—is not that enough for them? Certainly not. They must have a better piece of bread and a better piece of rag on their bodies. The great question is: How to get that better bread and better rag for these sunken millions.

First, I must tell you, there is great hope for them, because, you see, they are the gentlest people on earth. Not that they are timid. When they want to fight, they fight like demons. The best soldiers the English have are recruited from the peasantry of India. Death is a thing of no importance to them. Their attitude is: "Twenty times I have died before, and I shall die many times after this. What of that?" They never turn back. They are not given to much emotion, but they make very good fighters.

Their instinct, however, is to plough. If you rob them, murder them, tax them, do anything to them, they will be quiet and gentle, so long as you leave them free to practise their religion. They never interfere with the religion of others. "Leave us the liberty to worship our gods, and take everything else!" That is their attitude. When the English touch them there, trouble starts. That was the real cause of the 1857 Mutiny—they would not bear religious repression. The great Mohammedan governments were simply blown up because they touched the Indians' religion.

But aside from that, they are very peaceful, very quiet, very gentle, and, above all, not given to vice. The absence of any strong drink, oh, it makes them infinitely superior to the mobs of any other country. You cannot compare the decency of life among the poor in India with life in the slums here. A slum means poverty, but poverty does not mean sin, indecency, and vice in India. In other countries, the opportunities are such that only the indecent and the lazy need be poor. There is no reason for poverty unless one is a fool or a blackguard—the sort who want city life and all its luxuries. They will not go into the country. They say, "We are here with all the fun, and you must give us bread." But that is not the case in India, where the poor fellows work hard from morning to sunset, and somebody else takes the bread out of their hands, and their children go hungry. Notwithstanding the millions of tons of wheat raised in India, scarcely a grain passes the mouth of a peasant. He lives upon the poorest corn, which you would not feed to your canary-birds.

Now there is no reason why they should suffer such distress—these people; oh, so pure and good! We hear so much talk about the sunken millions and the degraded women of India—but none come to our help. What do they say? They say, "You can only be helped, you can only be good by ceasing to be what you are. It is useless to help Hindus." These people do not know the history of races. There will be no more India if they change their religion and their institutions, because that is the vitality of that race. It will disappear; so, really, you will have nobody to help.

Then there is the other great point to learn: that you can never help really. What can we do for each other? You are growing in your own life, I am growing in my own. It is possible that I can give you a push in your life, knowing that, in the long run, all roads lead to Rome. It is a steady growth. No national civilisation is perfect yet. Give that civilisation a push, and it will arrive at its own goal: do not strive to change it. Take away a nation's institutions, customs, and manners, and what will be left? They hold the nation together.

But here comes the very learned foreign man, and he says, "Look here; you give up all those institutions and customs of thousands of years, and take my tomfool tinpot and be happy." This is all nonsense.

We will have to help each other, but we have to go one step farther: the first thing is to become unselfish in help. "If you do just what I tell you to do, I will help you; otherwise not." Is that help?

And so, if the Hindus want to help you spiritually, there will be no question of limitations: perfect unselfishness.

I give, and there it ends. It is gone from me. My mind, my powers, my everything that I have to give, is given: given with the idea to give, and no more. I have seen many times people who have robbed half the world, and they gave $20,000 "to convert the heathen". What for? For the benefit of the heathen, or for their own souls? Just think of that.

And the Nemesis of crime is working. We men try to hoodwink our own eyes. But inside the heart, He has remained, the real Self. He never forgets. We can never delude Him. His eyes will never be hoodwinked. Whenever there is any impulse of real charity, it tells, though it be at the end of a thousand years. Obstructed, it yet wakens once more to burst like a thunderbolt. And every impulse where the motive is selfish, self-seeking—though it may be launched forth with all the newspapers blazoning, all the mobs standing and cheering—it fails to reach the mark.

I am not taking pride in this. But, mark you, I have told the story of that group of boys. Today there is not a village, not a man, not a woman in India that does not know their work and bless them. There is not a famine in the land where these boys do not plunge in and try to work and rescue as many as they can. And that strikes to the heart. The people come to know it. So help whenever you can, but mind what your motive is. If it is selfish, it will neither benefit those you help, nor yourself. If it is unselfish, it will bring blessings upon them to whom it is given, and infinite blessings upon you, sure as you are living. The Lord can never be hoodwinked. The law of Karma can never be hoodwinked.

Well then, my plans are, therefore, to reach these masses of India. Suppose you start schools all over India for the poor, still you cannot educate them. How can you? The boy of four years would better go to the plough or to work, than to your school. He cannot go to your school. It is impossible. Self-preservation is the first instinct. But if the mountain does not go to Mohammed, then Mohammed can come to the mountain. Why should not education go from door to door, say I. If a ploughman's boy cannot come to education, why not meet him at the plough, at the factory, just wherever he is? Go along with him, like his shadow. But there are these hundreds and thousands of monks, educating the people on the spiritual plane; why not let these men do the same work on the intellectual plane? Why should they not talk to the masses a little about history—about many things? The ears are the best educators. The best principles in our lives were those which we heard from our mothers through our ears. Books came much later. Book-learning is nothing. Through the ears we get the best formative principles. Then, as they get more and more interested, they may come to your books too. First, let it roll on and on—that is my idea.

Well, I must tell you that I am not a very great believer in monastic systems. They have great merits, and also great defects. There should be a perfect balance between the monastics and the householders. But monasticism has absorbed all the power in India. We represent the greatest power. The monk is greater than the prince. There is no reigning sovereign in India who dares to sit down when the "yellow cloth" is there. He gives up his seat and stands. Now, that is bad, so much power, even in the hands of good men—although these monastics have been the bulwark of the people. They stand between the priestcraft and knowledge. They are the centres of knowledge and reform. They are just what the prophets were among the Jews. The prophets were always preaching against the priests, trying to throw out superstitions. So are they in India. But all the same so much power is not good there; better methods should be worked out. But you can only work in the line of least resistance. The whole national soul there is upon monasticism. You go to India and preach any religion as a householder: the Hindu people will turn back and go out. If you have given up the world, however, they say, "He is good, he has given up the world. He is a sincere man, he wants to do what he preaches." What I mean to say is this, that it represents a tremendous power. What we can do is just to transform it, give it another form. This tremendous power in the hands of the roving Sannyasins of India has got to be transformed, and it will raise the masses up.

Now, you see, we have brought the plan down nicely on paper; but I have taken it, at the same time, from the regions of idealism. So far the plan was loose and idealistic. As years went on, it became more and more condensed and accurate; I began to see by actual working its defects, and all that.

What did I discover in its working on the material plane? First, there must be centres to educate these monks in the method of education. For instance, I send one of my men, and he goes about with a camera: he has to be taught in those things himself. In India, you will find every man is quite illiterate, and that teaching requires tremendous centres. And what does all that mean? Money. From the idealistic plane you come to everyday work. Well, I have worked hard, four years in your country, and two in England. And I am very thankful that some friends came to the rescue. One who is here today with you is amongst them. There are American friends and English friends who went over with me to India, and there has been a very rude beginning. Some English people came and joined the orders. One poor man worked hard and died in India. There are an Englishman and an Englishwoman who have retired; they have some means of their own, and they have started a centre in the Himalayas, educating the children. I have given them one of the papers I have started—a copy you will find there on the table—The Awakened India. And there they are instructing and working among the people. I have another centre in Calcutta. Of course, all great movements must proceed from the capital. For what is a capital? It is the heart of a nation. All the blood comes into the heart and thence it is distributed; so all the wealth, all the ideas, all the education, all spirituality will converge towards the capital and spread from it.

I am glad to tell you I have made a rude beginning. But the same work I want to do, on parallel lines, for women. And my principle is: each one helps himself. My help is from a distance. There are Indian women, English women, and I hope American women will come to take up the task. As soon as they have begun, I wash my hands of it. No man shall dictate to a woman; nor a woman to a man. Each one is independent. What bondage there may be is only that of love. Women will work out their own destinies—much better, too, than men can ever do for them. All the mischief to women has come because men undertook to shape the destiny of women. And I do not want to start with any initial mistake. One little mistake made then will go on multiplying; and if you succeed, in the long run that mistake will have assumed gigantic proportions and become hard to correct. So, if I made this mistake of employing men to work out this women's part of the work, why, women will never get rid of that—it will have become a custom. But I have got an opportunity. I told you of the lady who was my Master's wife. We have all great respect for her. She never dictates to us. So it is quite safe.

That part has to be accomplished.

III

Vedanta, Bhakti And Culture

Practical Vedanta

Delivered in London, 10 November 1896

I have been asked to say something about the practical position of the Vedanta philosophy. As I have told you, theory is very good indeed, but how are we to carry it into practice? If it be absolutely impracticable, no theory is of any value whatever, except as intellectual gymnastics. The Vedanta, therefore, as a religion must be intensely practical. We must be able to carry it out in every part of our lives. And not only this, the fictitious differentiation between religion and the life of the world must vanish, for the Vedanta teaches oneness—one life throughout. The ideals of religion must cover the whole field of life, they must enter into all our thoughts, and more and more into practice. I will enter gradually on the practical side as we proceed. But this series of lectures is intended to be a basis, and so we must first apply ourselves to theories and understand how they are worked out, proceeding from forest caves to busy streets and cities; and one peculiar feature we find is that many of these thoughts have been the outcome, not of retirement into forests, but have emanated from persons whom we expect to lead the busiest lives—from ruling monarchs.

Shvetaketu was the son of Aruni, a sage, most probably a recluse. He was brought up in the forest, but he went to the city of the Panchalas and appeared at the court of the king,

Pravahana Jaivali. The king asked him, "Do you know how beings depart hence at death?" "No, Sir." "Do you know how they return hither?" "No, Sir." "Do you know the way of the fathers and the way of the gods?" "No, Sir." Then the king asked other questions. Shvetaketu could not answer them. So the king told him that he knew nothing. The boy went back to his father, and the father admitted that he himself could not answer these questions. It was not that he was unwilling to answer these questions. It was not that he was unwilling to teach the boy, but he did not know these things. So he went to the king and asked to be taught these secrets. The king said that these things had been hitherto known only among kings; the priests never knew them. He, however, proceeded to teach him what he desired to know. In various Upanishads we find that this Vedanta philosophy is not the outcome of meditation in the forests only, but that the very best parts of it were thought out and expressed by brains which were busiest in the everyday affairs of life. We cannot conceive any man busier than an absolute monarch, a man who is ruling over millions of people, and yet, some of these rulers were deep thinkers.

Everything goes to show that this philosophy must be very practical; and later on, when we come to the *Bhagavad Gita*—most of you, perhaps, have read it, it is the best commentary we have on the Vedanta philosophy—curiously enough the scene is laid on the battlefield, where Krishna teaches this philosophy to Arjuna; and the doctrine which stands out luminously in every page of the *Gita* is intense activity, but in the midst of it, eternal calmness. This is the secret of work, to attain which is the goal of the Vedanta. Inactivity, as we understand it in the sense of passivity, certainly cannot be the goal. Were it so, then the walls around us would be the most intelligent; they are inactive. Clods of earth, stumps of trees, would be the greatest sages in the world; they are inactive. Nor does inactivity become activity when it is combined with passion. Real activity, which is the goal of Vedanta, is combined with eternal calmness, the calmness which cannot be ruffled, the balance of mind which is never disturbed, whatever happens. And we all know from our experience in life that that is the best attitude for work.

I have been asked many times how we can work if we do not have the passion which we generally feel for work. I also thought in that way years ago, but as I am growing older, getting more experience, I find it is not true. The less passion there is, the better we work. The calmer we are, the better for us, and the more the amount of work we can do. When we let loose our feelings, we waste so much energy, shatter our nerves, disturb our minds, and accomplish very little work. The energy which ought to have gone out as work is spent as mere feeling, which counts for nothing. It is only when the mind is very calm and collected that the whole of its energy is spent in doing good work. And if you read the lives of the great workers which the world has produced, you will find that they were wonderfully calm men. Nothing, as it were, could throw them off their balance. That is why the man who becomes angry never does a great amount of work, and the man whom nothing can make angry accomplishes so much. The man who gives way to anger, or hatred, or any other passion, cannot work; he only breaks himself to pieces, and does nothing practical. It is the calm, forgiving, equable, well-balanced mind that does the greatest amount of work.

The Vedanta preaches the ideal; and the ideal, as we know, is always far ahead of the real, of the practical, as we may call it. There are two tendencies in human nature: one to harmonise the ideal with the life, and the other to elevate the life to the ideal. It is a great thing to understand this, for the former tendency is the temptation of our lives. I think that I can only do a certain class of work. Most of it, perhaps, is bad; most of it, perhaps, has a motive power of passion behind it, anger, or greed, or selfishness. Now if any man comes to preach to me a certain ideal, the first step towards which is to give up selfishness, to give up self-enjoyment, I think that is impractical. But when a man brings an ideal which can be reconciled with my selfishness, I am glad at once and jump at i t. That is the ideal for me. As the word "orthodox" has been manipulated into various forms, so has been the word "practical". "My doxy is orthodoxy; your doxy is heterodoxy." So with practicality. What I think is practical, is to me the only practicality in the world. If I am a shopkeeper, I think shopkeeping the only practical pursuit in the world. If I am a thief, I think stealing is the best means of being practical; others are not practical. You see how we all use this word practical for things *we* like and can do. Therefore, I will ask you to understand that Vedanta, though it is intensely practical, is always so in the sense of the ideal. It does not preach an impossible ideal, however high it be, and it is high enough for an ideal. In one word, this ideal is that you are divine, "Thou art That." This is the essence of Vedanta; after all its ramifications and intellectual gymnastics, you know the human soul to be pure and omniscient, you see that such superstitions as birth and death would be entire nonsense when spoken of in connection with the soul. The soul was never born and will never die, and all these ideas that we are going to die and are afraid to die are mere superstitions. And all such ideas as that we can do this or cannot do that are superstitions. We can do everything. The Vedanta teaches men to have faith in themselves first. As certain religions of the world say that a man who does not believe in a Personal God outside of himself is an atheist, so the Vedanta says, a man who does not believe in himself is an atheist. Not believing in the glory of our own soul is what the Vedanta calls atheism. To many this is, no doubt, a terrible idea; and most of us think that this ideal can never be reached; but the Vedanta insists that it can be realised by every one. There is neither man nor woman or child, nor difference of race or sex, nor anything that stands as a bar to the realisation of the ideal, because Vedanta shows that it is realised already, it is already there.

All the powers in the universe are already ours. It is we who have put our hands before our eyes and cry that it is dark. Know that there is no darkness around us. Take the hands away and there is the light which was from the beginning. Darkness never existed, weakness never existed. We who are fools cry that we are weak; we who are fools cry that we are impure. Thus Vedanta not only insists that the ideal is practical, but that it has been so all the time; and this Ideal, this Reality, is our own nature. Everything else that you see is false, untrue. As soon as you say, "I am a little mortal being," you are saying something which is not true, you are giving the lie to yourselves, you are hypnotising yourselves into something vile and weak and wretched.

The Vedanta recognises no sin, it only recognises error. And the greatest error, says the Vedanta, is to say that you are weak, that you are a sinner, a miserable creature, and that you have no power and you cannot do this and that. Every time you think in that way, you, as it were, rivet one more link in the chain that binds you down, you add one more layer of hypnotism on to your own soul. Therefore, whosoever thinks he is weak is wrong, whosoever thinks he is impure is wrong, and is throwing a bad thought into the world. This we must always bear in mind that in the Vedanta there is no attempt at reconciling the present life—the hypnotised life, this false life which we have assumed—with the ideal; but this false life must go, and the real life which is always existing must manifest itself, must shine out. No man becomes purer and purer, it is a matter of greater manifestation. The veil drops away and the native purity of the soul begins to manifest itself. Everything is ours already—infinite purity, freedom, love, and power.

The Vedanta also says that not only can this be realised in the depths of forests or caves, but by men in all possible conditions of life. We have seen that the people who discovered these truths were neither living in caves nor forests, nor following the ordinary vocations of life, but men who, we have every reason to believe, led the busiest of lives, men who had to command armies, to sit on thrones, and look to the welfare of millions—and all these, in the days of absolute monarchy, and not as in these days when a king is to a great extent a mere figurehead. Yet they could find time to think out all these thoughts, to realise them, and to teach them to humanity. How much more then should it be practical for us whose lives, compared with theirs, are lives of leisure? That we cannot realise them is a shame to us, seeing that we are comparatively free all the time, having very little to do. My requirements are as nothing compared with those of an ancient absolute monarch. My wants are as nothing compared with the demands of Arjuna on the battlefield of Kurukshetra, commanding a huge army; and yet he could find time in the midst of the din and turmoil of battle to talk the highest philosophy and to carry it into his life also. Surely we ought to be able to do as much in this life of ours—comparatively free, easy, and comfortable. Most of us here have more time than we think we have, if we really want to use it for good. With the amount of freedom we have we can attain to two hundred ideals in this life, if we will, but we must not degrade the ideal to the actual. One of the most insinuating things comes to us in the shape of persons who apologise for our mistakes and teach us how to make special excuses for all our foolish wants and foolish desires; and we think that their ideal is the only ideal we need have. But it is not so. The Vedanta teaches no such thing. The actual should be reconciled to the ideal, the present life should be made to coincide with life eternal.

For you must always remember that the one central ideal of Vedanta is this oneness. There are no two in anything, no two lives, nor even two different kinds of life for the two worlds. You will find the Vedas speaking of heavens and things like that at first; but later on, when they come to the highest ideals of their philosophy, they brush away all these things. There is but one life, one world, one existence. Everything is that One, the difference is in degree and not in kind. The difference between our lives is not in kind. The Vedanta entirely denies such ideas as that animals are separate from men, and that they were made and created by God to be used for our food.

Some people have been kind enough to start an anti-vivisection society. I asked a member, "Why do you think, my friend, that it is quite lawful to kill animals for food, and not to kill one or two for scientific experiments?" He replied, "Vivisection is most horrible, but animals have been given to us for food." Oneness includes all animals. If man's life is immortal, so also is the animal's. The difference is only in degree and not in kind. The amoeba and I are the same, the difference is only in degree; and from the standpoint of the highest life, all these differences vanish. A man may see a great deal of difference between grass and a little tree, but if you mount very high, the grass and the biggest tree will appear much the same. So, from the standpoint of the highest ideal, the lowest animal and the highest man are the same. If you believe there is a God, the animals and the highest creatures must be the same. A God who is partial to his children called men, and cruel to his children called brute beasts, is worse than a demon. I would rather die a hundred times than worship such a God. My whole life would be a fight with such a God. But there is no difference, and those who say there is, are irresponsible, heartless people who do not know. Here is a case of the word "practical" used in a wrong sense. I myself may not be a very strict vegetarian, but I understand the ideal. When I eat meat I know it is wrong. Even if I am bound to eat it under certain circumstances, I know it is cruel. I must not drag my ideal down to the actual and apologise for my weak conduct in this way. The ideal is not to eat flesh, not to injure any being, for all animals are my brothers. If you can think of them as your brothers, you have made a little headway towards the brotherhood of all souls, not to speak of the brotherhood of man! That is child's play. You generally find that this is not very acceptable to many, because it teaches them to give up the actual, and go higher up to the ideal. But if you bring out a theory which is reconciled with their present conduct, they regard it as entirely practical.

There is this strongly conservative tendency in human nature: we do not like to move one step forward. I think of mankind just as I read of persons who become frozen in snow; all such, they say, want to go to sleep, and if you try to drag them up, they say, "Let me sleep; it is so beautiful to sleep in the snow", and they die there in that sleep. So is our nature. That is what we are doing all our life, getting frozen from the feet upwards, and yet wanting to sleep. Therefore, you must struggle towards the ideal, and if a man comes who wants to bring that ideal down to your level, and teach a religion that does not carry that highest ideal, do not listen to him. To me that is an impracticable religion. But if a man teaches a religion which presents the highest ideal, I am ready for him. Beware when anyone is trying to apologise for sense vanities and sense weaknesses. If anyone wants to preach that way to us, poor, sense-bound clods of earth as we have made ourselves by following that teaching, we shall never progress. I have seen many of these things, I have had some experience of the world, and my country is the land where religious sects grow like mushrooms. Every year new sects arise. But one thing I have marked, that it is only those that never want to reconcile the man of flesh with the man of truth that make progress. Wherever there is this false idea of reconciling fleshly vanities with the highest ideals, of dragging down God to the level of man, there comes decay.

Man should not be degraded to worldly slavery, but should be raised up to God.

At the same time, there is another side to the question. We must not look down with contempt on others. All of us are going towards the same goal. The difference between weakness and strength is one of degree; the difference between virtue and vice is one of degree; the difference between heaven and hell is one of degree; the difference between life and death is one of degree; all differences in this world are of degree, and not of kind, because oneness is the secret of everything. All is One, which manifests Itself, either as thought, or life, or soul, or body, and the difference is only in degree. As such, we have no right to look down with contempt upon those who are not developed exactly in the same degree as we are. Condemn none; if you can stretch out a helping hand, do so. If you cannot, fold your hands, bless your brothers, and let them go their own way. Dragging down and condemning is not the way to work. Never is work accomplished in that way. We spend our energies in condemning others. Criticism and condemnation is a vain way of spending our energies, for in the long run we come to learn that all are seeing the same thing, are more or less approaching the same ideal, and that most of our differences are merely differences of expression.

Take the idea of sin. I was telling you just now the Vedantic idea of it, and the other idea is that Man is a sinner. They are practically the same, only the one takes the positive and the other the negative side. One shows to Man his strength and the other his weakness. There may be weakness, says the Vedanta, but never mind, we want to grow. Disease was found out as soon as Man was born. Everyone knows his disease; it requires no one to tell us what our diseases are. But thinking all the time that we are diseased will not cure us—medicine is necessary. We may forget anything outside, we may try to become hypocrites to the external world, but in our heart of hearts we all know our weaknesses. But, says the Vedanta, being reminded of weakness does not help much; give strength, and strength does not come by thinking of weakness all the time. The remedy for weakness is not brooding over weakness, but thinking of strength. Teach men of the strength that is already within them. Instead of telling them they are sinners, the Vedanta takes the opposite position, and says, "You are pure and perfect, and what you call sin does not belong to you." Sins are very low degrees of Self-manifestation; manifest your Self in a high degree. That is the one thing to remember; all of us can do that. Never say, "No", never say, "I cannot", for you are infinite. Even time and space are as nothing compared with your nature. You can do anything and everything, you are almighty.

These are the principles of ethics, but we shall now come down lower and work out the details. We shall see how this Vedanta can be carried into our everyday life, the city life, the country life, the national life, and the home life of every nation. For, if a religion cannot help Man wherever he may be, wherever he stands, it is not of much use; it will remain only a theory for the chosen few. Religion, to help mankind, must be ready and able to help him in whatever condition he is, in servitude or in freedom, in the depths of degradation or on the heights of purity; everywhere, equally, it should be able to come to his aid. The principles of Vedanta, or the ideal of religion, or whatever you may call it, will be fulfilled by its capacity for performing this great function.

The ideal of faith in ourselves is of the greatest help to us. If faith in ourselves had been more extensively taught and practised, I am sure a very large portion of the evils and miseries that we have would have vanished. Throughout the history of mankind, if any motive power has been more potent than another in the lives of all great men and women, it is that of faith in themselves. Born with the consciousness that they were to be great, they became great. Let a man go down as low as possible; there must come a time when out of sheer desperation he will take an upward curve and will learn to have faith in himself. But it is better for us that we should know it from the very first. Why should we have all these bitter experiences in order to gain faith in ourselves? We can see that all the difference between Man and Man is owing to the existence of non-existence of faith in himself. Faith in ourselves will do everything. I have experienced it in my own life, and am still doing so; and as I grow older that faith is becoming stronger and stronger. He is an atheist who does not believe in himself. The old religions said that he was an atheist who did not believe in God. The new religion says that he is the atheist who does not believe in himself. But it is not selfish faith, because the Vedanta, again, is the doctrine of oneness. It means faith in all, because you are all. Love for yourselves means love for all, love for animals, love for everything, for you are all one. It is the great faith which will make the world better. I am sure of that. He is the highest man who can say with truth, "I know all about myself." Do you know how much energy, how many powers, how many forces are still lurking behind that frame of yours? What scientist has known all that is in man? Millions of years have passed since Man first came here, and yet but one infinitesimal part of his powers has been manifested. Therefore, you must not say that you are weak. How do you know what possibilities lie behind that degradation on the surface? You know but little of that which is within you. For behind you is the ocean of infinite power and blessedness.

"This Atman is first to be heard of." Hear day and night that you are that Soul. Repeat it to yourselves day and night till it enters into your very veins, till it tingles in every drop of blood, till it is in your flesh and bone. Let the whole body be full of that one ideal, "I am the birthless, the deathless, the blissful, the omniscient, the omnipotent, ever-glorious Soul." Think on it day and night; think on it till it becomes part and parcel of your life. Meditate upon it, and out of that will come work. "Out of the fullness of the heart the mouth speaketh," and out of the fullness of the heart the hand worketh also. Action will come. Fill yourselves with the idea; whatever you do, think well on it. All your actions will be magnified, transformed, deified, by the very power of the thought. If matter is powerful, thought is omnipotent. Bring this thought to bear upon your life, fill yourselves with the thought of your almightiness, your majesty, and your glory. Would to God no superstitions had been put into your head! Would to God we had not been surrounded from our birth by all these superstitious influences and paralysing ideas of our weakness and vileness! Would to God that mankind had had an easier path through which to attain to the noblest and highest truths! But Man had to pass through all this; do not make the path more difficult for those who are coming after you.

These are sometimes terrible doctrines to teach. I know people who get frightened at these ideas, but for those who want to be practical, this is the first thing to learn. Never tell yourselves or others that you are weak. Do good if you can, but do not injure the world. You know in your inmost heart that many of your limited ideas, this humbling of yourself and praying and weeping to imaginary beings are superstitions. Tell me one case where these prayers have been answered. All the answers that came were from your own hearts. You know there are no ghosts, but no sooner are you in the dark than you feel a little creepy sensation. That is so because in our childhood we have had all these fearful ideas put into our heads. But do not teach these things to others through fear of society and public opinion, through fear of incurring the hatred of friends, or for fear of losing cherished superstitions. Be masters of all these. What is there to be taught more in religion than the oneness of the universe and faith in one's self? All the works of mankind for thousands of years past have been towards this one goal, and mankind is yet working it out. It is your turn now and you already know the truth.

For it has been taught on all sides. Not only philosophy and psychology, but materialistic sciences have declared it. Where is the scientific man today who fears to acknowledge the truth of this oneness of the universe? Who is there who dares talk of many worlds? All these are superstitions. There is only one life and one world, and this one life and one world is appearing to us as manifold. This manifoldness is like a dream. When you dream, one dream passes away and another comes. You do not live in your dreams. The dreams come one after another, scene after scene unfolds before you. So it is in this world of ninety per cent misery and ten per cent happiness. Perhaps after a while it will appear as ninety per cent happiness, and we shall call it heaven, but a time comes to the sage when the whole thing vanishes, and this world appears as God Himself, and his own soul as God. It is not, therefore, that there are many worlds, it is not that there are many lives. All this manifoldness is the manifestation of that One. That One is manifesting Himself as many, as matter, spirit, mind, thought, and everything else. It is that One, manifesting Himself as many. Therefore, the first step for us to take is to teach the truth to ourselves and to others.

Let the world resound with this ideal, and let superstitions vanish. Tell it to men who are weak and persist in telling it. You are the Pure One; awake and arise, O mighty one, this sleep does not become you. Awake and arise, it does not befit you. Think not that you are weak and miserable. Almighty, arise and awake, and manifest your own nature. It is not fitting that you think yourself a sinner. It is not fitting that you think yourself weak. Say that to the world, say it to yourselves, and see what a practical result comes, see how with an electric flash everything is manifested, how everything is changed. Tell that to mankind, and show them their power. Then we shall learn how to apply it in our daily lives.

To be able to use what we call viveka, to learn how in every moment of our lives, in every one of our actions, to discriminate between what is right and wrong, true and false, we shall have to know the test of truth, which is purity, oneness. Everything that makes for oneness is truth. Love is truth, and hatred is false, because hatred makes for multiplicity. It is hatred that separates Man from Man; therefore, it is wrong and false. It is a disintegrating power; it separates and destroys.

Love binds, love makes for that oneness. You become one, the mother with the child, families with the city, the whole world becomes one with the animals. For love is Existence, God Himself; and all this is the manifestation of that One Love, more or less expressed. The difference is only in degree, but it is the manifestation of that One Love throughout. Therefore, in all our actions we have to judge whether it is making for diversity or for oneness. If for diversity we have to give it up, but if it makes for oneness we are sure it is good. So with our thoughts; we have to decide whether they make for disintegration, multiplicity, or for oneness, binding soul to soul and bringing one influence to bear. If they do this, we will take them up, and if not, we will throw them off as criminal.

The whole idea of ethics is that it does not depend on anything unknowable, it does not teach anything unknown, but in the words of St. Paul (The Acts, 17:23): "The God whom you worship as an unknown God, the same I preach unto thee." It is through the Self that you know anything. I see the chair; but to see the chair, I have first to perceive myself and then the chair. It is in and through the Self that the chair is perceived. It is in and through the Self that you are known to me, that the whole world is known to me; and, therefore, to say this Self is unknown is sheer nonsense. Take off the Self and the whole universe vanishes. In and through the Self all knowledge comes. Therefore, it is the best known of all. It is yourself, that which you call I. You may wonder how this I of me can be the I of you. You may wonder how this limited I can be the unlimited Infinite, but it is so. The limited is a mere fiction. The Infinite has been covered up, as it were, and a little of It is manifesting as the I. Limitation can never come upon the unlimited; it is a fiction. The Self is known, therefore, to every one of us—man, woman, or child—and even to animals. Without knowing Him we can neither live nor move, nor have our being; without knowing this Lord of all, we cannot breathe or live a second. The God of the Vedanta is the most known of all and is not the outcome of imagination.

If this is not preaching a practical God, how else could you teach a practical God? Where is there a more practical God than He whom I see before me—a God omnipresent, in every being, more real than our senses? For you are He, the Omnipresent God Almighty, the Soul of your souls, and if I say you are not, I tell an untruth. I know it, whether at all times I realise it or not. He is the Oneness, the Unity of all, the Reality of all life and all existence.

These ideas of the ethics of Vedanta have to be worked out in detail, and, therefore, you must have patience. As I have told you, we want to take the subject in detail and work it up thoroughly, to see how the ideas grow from very low ideals, and how the one great Ideal of oneness has developed and become shaped into the universal love; and we ought to study these in order to avoid dangers. The world cannot find time to work it up from the lowest steps. But what is the use of our standing on higher steps if we cannot give the truth to others coming afterwards? Therefore, it is better to study it in all its workings; and first, it is absolutely necessary to clear the intellectual portion, although we know that intellectuality is almost nothing; for it is the heart that is of most importance. It is through the heart that the Lord is seen, and not through the intellect. The intellect is only the street-cleaner, cleansing the path for us, a secondary worker, the policeman; but the policeman is not a positive necessity for the workings of society. He is only to stop disturbances, to check wrong-doing, and that is all the work required of the intellect. When you read intellectual books, you think when you have mastered them, "Bless the Lord that I am out of them", because the intellect is blind and cannot move of itself, it has neither hands nor feet. It is feeling that works, that moves with speed infinitely superior to that of electricity or anything else.

Do you feel?—that is the question. If you do, you will see the Lord: It is the feeling that you have today that will be intensified, deified, raised to the highest platform, until it feels everything, the oneness in everything, till it feels God in itself and in others. The intellect can never ' do that. "Different methods of speaking words, different methods of explaining the texts of books, these are for the enjoyment of the learned, not for the salvation of the soul." (*Vivekachudamani*, 58).

Those of you who have read Thomas à Kempis know how in every page he insists on this, and almost every holy man in the world has insisted on it. Intellect is necessary, for without it we fall into crude errors and make all sorts of mistakes. Intellect checks these; but beyond that, do not try to build anything upon it. It is an inactive, secondary help; the real help is feeling, love. Do you feel for others? If you do, you are growing in oneness. If you do not feel for others, you may be the most intellectual giant ever born, but you will be nothing; you are but dry intellect, and you will remain so. And if you feel, even if you cannot read any book and do not know any language, you are in the right way. The Lord is yours.

Do you not know from the history of the world where the power of the prophets lay? Where was it? In the intellect? Did any of them write a fine book on philosophy, on the most intricate ratiocinations of logic? Not one of them. They only spoke a few words. Feel like Christ and you will be a Christ; feel like Buddha and you will be a Buddha. It is feeling that is the life, the strength, the vitality, without which no amount of intellectual activity can reach God. Intellect is like limbs without the power of locomotion. It is only when feeling enters and gives them motion that they move and work on others. That is so all over the world, and it is a thing which you must always remember. It is one of the most practical things in Vedantic morality, for it is the teaching of the Vedanta that you are all prophets, and all must be prophets. The book is not the proof of your conduct, but you are the proof of the book. How do you know that a book teaches truth? Because you are truth and feel it. That is what the Vedanta says. What is the proof of the Christs and Buddhas of the world? That you and I feel like them. That is how you and I understand chat they were true. Our prophet-soul is the proof of their prophet-soul. Your godhead is the proof of God Himself. If you are not a prophet, there never has been anything true of God. If you are not God, there never was any God, and never will be. This, says the Vedanta, is the ideal to follow. Every one of us will have to become a prophet, and you are that already. Only *know* it. Never think there is anything impossible for the soul. It is the greatest heresy to think so. If there is sin, this is the only sin—to say that you are weak, or others are weak.

The Vedanta In All Its Phases

Delivered in Calcutta

Away back, where no recorded history, nay, not even the dim light of tradition, can penetrate, has been steadily shining the light, sometimes dimmed by external circumstances, at others effulgent, but undying and steady, shedding its lustre not only over India, but permeating the whole thought-world with its power, silent, unperceived, gentle, yet omnipotent, like the dew that falls in the morning, unseen and unnoticed, yet bringing into bloom the fairest of roses: this has been the thought of the Upanishads, the philosophy of the Vedanta. Nobody knows when it first came to flourish on the soil of India. Guesswork has been vain. The guesses, especially of Western writers, have been so conflicting that no certain date can be ascribed to them. But we Hindus, from the spiritual standpoint, do not admit that they had any origin. This Vedanta, the philosophy of the Upanishads, I would make bold to state, has been the first as well as the final thought on the spiritual plane that has ever been vouchsafed to man.

From this ocean of the Vedanta, waves of light from time to time have been going Westward and Eastward. In the days of yore it travelled Westward and gave its impetus to the mind of the Greeks, either in Athens, or in Alexandria, or in Antioch. The Sankhya system must clearly have made its mark on the minds of the ancient Greeks; and the Sankhya and all other systems in India had that one authority the Upanishads, the Vedanta. In India, too, in spite of all these jarring sects that we see today and all those that have been in the past, the one authority, the basis of all these systems, has yet been the Upanishads, the Vedanta. Whether you are a dualist, or a qualified monist, an Advaitist, or a Vishishtadvaitist, a Shuddhadvaitist, or any other Advaitist, or Dvaitist, or whatever you may call yourself, there stand behind you as authority, your Shastras, your scriptures, the Upanishads. Whatever system in India does not obey the Upanishads cannot be called orthodox, and even the systems of the Jains and the Buddhists have been rejected from the soil of India only because they did not bear allegiance to the Upanishads. Thus the Vedanta, whether we know it or not, has penetrated all the sects of India, and what we call Hinduism, this mighty banyan with its immense, almost infinite ramifications, has been throughout inter-penetrated by the influence of the Vedanta. Whether we are conscious of it or not, we think the Vedanta, we live in the Vedanta, we breathe the Vedanta, and we die in the Vedanta, and every Hindu does that. To preach Vedanta in the land of India, and before an Indian audience, seems, therefore, to be an anomaly. But it is the one thing that has to be preached, and it is the necessity of the age that it must be preached. For, as I have just told you, all the Indian sects must bear allegiance to the Upanishads; but among these sects there are many apparent contradictions. Many times the great sages of yore themselves could not understand the underlying harmony of the Upanishads. Many times, even sages quarrelled, so much so that it became a proverb that there are no sages who do not differ. But the time requires that a better interpretation should be given to this underlying harmony of the Upanishadic texts, whether they are dualistic, or non-dualistic, quasi-dualistic, or so forth. That has to be shown before the world at large, and this work is required as much in India as outside of India; and I, through the grace of God, had the great good fortune to sit at the feet of one whose whole life was such an interpretation, whose life, a thousandfold more than whose teaching, was a living commentary on the texts of the Upanishads, was in fact the spirit of the Upanishads living in a human form. Perhaps I have got a little of that harmony; I do not know whether I shall be able to express it or not. But this is my attempt, my mission in life, to show that the Vedantic schools are not contradictory, that they all necessitate each other, all fulfil each other, and one, as it were, is the stepping-stone to the other, until the goal, the Advaita, the Tat Tvam Asi, is reached. There was a time in India when the Karma Kanda had its sway. There are many grand ideals, no doubt, in that portion of the Vedas. Some of our present daily worship is still according to the precepts of the Karma Kanda. But with all that, the Karma Kanda of the Vedas has almost disappeared from India. Very little of our life today is bound and regulated by the orders of the Karma Kanda of the Vedas. In our ordinary lives we are mostly Pauranikas or Tantrikas, and, even where some Vedic texts are used by the Brahmins of India, the adjustment of the texts is mostly not according to the Vedas, but according to the Tantras or the Puranas. As such, to call ourselves Vaidikas in the sense of following the Karma Kanda of the Vedas, I do not think, would be proper. But the other fact stands that we are all of us Vedantists. The people who call themselves Hindus had better be called Vedantists, and, as I have shown you, under that one name Vaidantika come in all our various sects, whether dualists or non-dualists.

The sects that are at the present time in India come to be divided in general into the two great classes of dualists and monists. The little differences which some of these sects insist upon, and upon the authority of which want to take new names as pure Advaitists, or qualified Advaitists, and so forth, do not matter much. As a classification, either they are dualists or monists, and of the sects existing at the present time, some of them are very new, and others seem to be reproductions of very ancient sects. The one class I would present by the life and philosophy of Ramanuja, and the other by Shankaracharya.

Ramanuja is the leading dualistic philosopher of later India, whom all the other dualistic sects have followed, directly or indirectly, both in the substance of their teaching and in the organisation of their sects even down to some of the most minute points of their organisation. You will be astonished if you compare Ramanuja and his work with the other dualistic Vaishnava sects in India, to see how much they resemble each other in organisation, teaching, and method. There is the great Southern preacher Madhva Muni, and following him, our great Chaitanya of Bengal who took up the philosophy of the Madhvas and preached it in Bengal. There are some other sects also in Southern India, as the qualified dualistic Shaivas. The Shaivas in most parts of India are Advaitists, except in some portions of Southern India and in Ceylon. But they also only substitute Shiva for Vishnu and are Ramanujists in every sense of the term except in the doctrine of the soul. The followers of Ramanuja hold that the soul is Anu, like a particle, very small, and the followers of Shankaracharya hold that it is Vibhu, omnipresent. There have been several non-dualistic sects. It seems that there have been sects in ancient times which Shankara's movement has entirely swallowed up and assimilated. You find sometimes a fling at Shankara himself in some of the commentaries, especially in that of Vijnana Bhikshu who, although an Advaitist, attempts to upset the Mayavada of Shankara. It seems there were schools who did not believe in this Mayavada, and they went so far as to call Shankara a crypto-Buddhist, Prachchhanna Bauddha, and they thought this Mayavada was taken from the Buddhists and brought within the Vedantic fold. However that may be, in modern times the Advaitists have all ranged themselves under Shankaracharya; and Shankaracharya and his disciples have been the great preachers of Advaita both in Southern and in Northern India. The influence of Shankaracharya did not penetrate much into our country of Bengal and in Kashmir and the Punjab, but in Southern India the Smartas are all followers of Shankaracharya, and with Varanasi as the centre, his influence is simply immense even in many parts of Northern India.

Now both Shankara and Ramanuja laid aside all claim to originality. Ramanuja expressly tells us he is only following the great commentary of Bodhayana. भगवद्बोधायनकृतां विस्तीर्णां ब्रह्मसूत्रवृत्तिं पूर्वाचार्याः संचिक्षिपुः तन्मतानुसारेण सूत्रक्षराणि व्याख्यास्यन्ते। "Ancient teachers abridged that extensive commentary on the *Brahma Sutras* which was composed by the Bhagvan Bodhayana; in accordance with their opinion, the words of the Sutra are explained." That is what Ramanuja says at the beginning of his commentary, the *Shri Bhasya.* He takes it up and makes of it a Samkshepa, and that is what we have today. I myself never had an opportunity of seeing this commentary of Bodhayana. The late Swami Dayananda Saraswati wanted to reject every other commentary of the *Vyasa Sutras* except that of Bodhayana; and although he never lost an opportunity of having a fling at Ramanuja, he himself could never produce the Bodhayana. I have sought for it all over India, and never yet have been able to see it. But Ramanuja is very plain on the point, and he tells us that he is taking the ideas, and sometimes the very passages out of Bodhayana, and condensing them into the present Ramanuja Bhashya. It seems that Shankaracharya was also doing the same. There are a few places in his *Bhasya* which mention older commentaries, and when we know that his Guru and his Guru's Guru had been Vedantists of the same school as he, sometimes even more thoroughgoing, bolder even than Shankara himself on certain points, it seems pretty plain that he also was not preaching anything very original, and that even in his *Bhasya* he himself had been doing the same work that Ramanuja did with Bodhayana, but from what *Bhasya*, it cannot be discovered at the present time.

All these Darshanas that you have ever seen or heard of are based upon Upanishadic authority. Whenever they want to quote a Shruti, they mean the Upanishads. They are always quoting the Upanishads. Following the Upanishads there come other philosophies of India, but every one of them failed in getting that hold on India which the philosophy of Vyasa got, although the philosophy of Vyasa is a development out of an older one, the Sankhya, and every philosophy and every system in India—I meant throughout the world—owes much to Kapila, perhaps the greatest name in the history of India in psychological and philosophical lines. The influence of Kapila is everywhere seen throughout the world. Wherever there is a recognised system of thought, there you can trace his influence; even if it be thousands of years back, yet he stands there, the shining, glorious, wonderful Kapila. His psychology and a good deal of his philosophy have been accepted by all the sects of India with but very little differences. In our own country, our Naiyayika philosophers could not make much impression on the philosophical world of India. They were too busy with little things like species and genus, and so forth, and that most cumbersome terminology, which it is a life's work to study. As such, they were very busy with logic and left philosophy to the Vedantists, but every one of the Indian philosophic sects in modern times has adopted the logical terminology of the Naiyayikas of Bengal. Jagadisha, Gadadhara, and Shiromani are as well known at Nadia as in some of the cities in Malabar. But the philosophy of Vyasa, the *Vyasa Sutras,* is firm-seated and has attained the permanence of that which it intended to present to men, the Brahman of the Vedantic side of philosophy. Reason was entirely subordinated to the Shrutis, and as Shankaracharya declares, Vyasa did not care to reason at all. His idea in writing the Sutras was just to bring together, and with one thread to make a garland of the flowers of Vedantic texts. His Sutras are admitted so far as they are subordinate to the authority of the Upanishads, and no further.

And, as I have said, all the sects of India now hold these *Vyasa Sutras* to be the great authority, and every new sect in India starts with a fresh commentary on the *Vyasa Sutras* according to its light. The difference between some of these commentators is sometimes very great, sometimes the text-torturing is quite disgusting. The *Vyasa Sutras* have got the place of authority, and no one can expect to found a sect in India until he can write a fresh commentary on the *Vyasa-Sutras.*

Next in authority is the celebrated *Gita*. The great glory of Shankaracharya was his preaching of the *Gita*. It is one of the greatest works that this great man did among the many noble works of his noble life—the preaching of the *Gita* and writing the most beautiful commentary upon it. And he has been followed by all founders of the orthodox sects in India, each of whom has written a commentary on the *Gita*.

The Upanishads are many, and said to be one hundred and eight, but some declare them to be still larger in number. Some of them are evidently of a much later date, as for instance, the Allopanishad in which Allah is praised and Mohammed is called the Rajasulla. I have been told that this was written during the reign of Akbar to bring the Hindus and Mohammedans together, and sometimes they got hold of some word, as Allah, or Ila in the Samhitas, and made an Upanishad on it. So in this Allopanishad, Mohammed is the Rajasulla, whatever that may mean. There are other sectarian Upanishads of the same species, which you find to be entirely modern, and it has been so easy to write them, seeing that this language of the Samhita portion of the Vedas is so archaic that there is no grammar to it. Years ago I had an idea of studying the grammar of the Vedas and I began with all earnestness to study Panini and the *Mahabhashya,* but to my surprise I found that the best part of the Vedic grammar consists only of exceptions to rules. A rule is made, and after that comes a statement to the effect, "This rule will be an exception." So you see what an amount of liberty there is for anybody to write anything, the only safeguard being the dictionary of Yaska. Still, in this you will find, for the most part, but a large number of synonyms. Given all that, how easy it is to write any number of Upanishads you please. Just have a little knowledge of Sanskrit, enough to make words look like the old archaic words, and you have no fear of grammar. Then you bring in Rajasulla or any other Sulla you like. In that way many Upanishads have been manufactured, and I am told that that is being done even now. In some parts of India, I am perfectly certain, they are trying to manufacture such Upanishads among the different sects. But among the Upanishads are those, which, on the face of them, bear the evidence of genuineness, and these have been taken up by the great commentators and commented upon, especially by Shankar a, followed by Ramanuja and all the rest.

There are one or two more ideas with regard to the Upanishads which I want to bring to your notice, for these are an ocean of knowledge, and to talk about the Upanishads, even for an incompetent person like myself, takes years and not one lecture only. I want, therefore, to bring to your notice one or two points in the study of the Upanishads. In the first place, they are the most wonderful poems in the world. If you read the Samhita portion of the Vedas, you now and then find passages of most marvellous beauty. For instance, the famous Shloka which describes Chaos—तम आसीत्तमसा गूढमग्र etc.,—"When darkness was hidden in darkness", so on it goes. One reads and feels the wonderful sublimity of the poetry. Do you mark this that outside of India, and inside also, there have been attempts at painting the sublime. But outside, it has always been the infinite in the muscles, the external world, the infinite of matter, or of space. When Milton or Dante, or any other great European poet, either ancient or modern, wants to paint a picture of the infinite, he tries to soar outside, to make you feel the infinite through the muscles. That attempt has been made here also. You find it in the Samhitas, the infinite of extension most marvellously painted and placed before the readers, such as has been done nowhere else. Mark that one sentence तम आसीत् तमसा गूढम् and now mark the description of darkness by three poets. Take our own Kalidasa—"Darkness which can be penetrated with the point of a needle"; then Milton—"No light but rather darkness visible"; but come now to the Upanishad, "Darkness was covering darkness", "Darkness was hidden in darkness" We who live in the tropics can understand it, the sudden outburst of the monsoon, when in a moment, the horizon becomes darkened and clouds become covered with more rolling black clouds. So on, the poem goes; but yet, in the Samhita portion, all these attempts are external. As everywhere else, the attempts at finding the solution of the great problems of life have been through the external world. Just as the Greek mind or the modern European mind wants to find the solution of life and of all the sacred problems of Being by searching into the eternal world, so also did our forefathers, and just as the Europeans failed, they failed also. But the Western people never made a move more, they remained there, they failed in the search for the solution of the great problems of life and death in the external world, and there they remained, stranded; our forefathers also found it impossible, but were bolder in declaring the utter helplessness of the senses to find the solution. Nowhere else was the answer better put than in the Upanishad: यतो वाचो निवर्तन्ते अप्राप्य मनसा सह। —"From whence words come back reflected, together with the mind"; न तत्रचक्षुर्गच्छति न वाग्गच्छति। —"There the eye cannot go, nor can speech reach." There are various sentences which declare the utter helplessness of the senses, but they did not stop there; they fell back upon the internal nature of man, they went to get the answer from their own soul, they became introspective; they gave up external nature as a failure, as nothing could be done there, as no hope, no answer could be found; they discovered that dull, dead matter would not give them truth, and they fell back upon the shining soul of man, and there the answer was found.

तमेवैकं जानथ आत्मानम् अन्या वाचो विमुञ्चथ।—"Know this Atman alone," they declared, "give up all other vain words, and hear no other." In the Atman they found the solution—the greatest of all Atmans, the God, the Lord of this universe, His relation to the Atman of man, our duty to Him, and through that our relation to each other. And herein you find the most sublime poetry in the world. No more is the attempt made to paint this Atman in the language of matter. Nay, for it they have given up even all positive language. No more is there any attempt to come to the senses to give them the idea of the infinite, no more is there an external, dull, dead, material, spacious, sensuous infinite, but instead of that comes something which is as fine as even that mentioned in the saying—

न तत्र सूर्यो भाति न चन्द्रतारकं नेमा विद्युतो भान्ति कुतोऽयमग्निः।
तमेव भान्तमनुभाति सर्वं तस्य भासा सर्वमिदं विभाति।।

What poetry in the world can be more sublime than this! "There the sun cannot illumine, nor the moon, nor the stars, there this flash of lightning cannot illumine; what to speak of this mortal fire!" Such poetry you find nowhere else. Take that most marvellous Upanishad, the Katha. What a wonderful finish, what a most marvellous art displayed in that poem! How wonderfully it opens with that little boy to whom Shraddha came, who wanted to see Yama, and how that most marvellous of all teachers, Death himself, teaches him the great lessons of life and death!

And what was his quest? To know the secret of death. The second point that I want you to remember is the perfectly impersonal character of the Upanishads. Although we find many names, and many speakers, and many teachers in the Upanishads, not one of them stands as an authority of the Upanishads, not one verse is based upon the life of any one of them. These are simply figures like shadows moving in the background, unfelt, unseen, unrealised, but the real force is in the marvellous, the brilliant, the effulgent texts of the Upanishads, perfectly impersonal. If twenty Yajnavalkyas came and lived and died, it does not matter; the texts are there. And yet it is against no personality; it is broad and expansive enough to embrace all the personalities that the world has yet produced, and all that are yet to come. It has nothing to say against the worship of persons, or Avataras, or sages. On the other hand, it is always upholding it. At the same time, it is perfectly impersonal. It is a most marvellous idea, like the God it preaches, the impersonal idea of the Upanishads. For the sage, the thinker, the philosopher, for the rationalist, it is as much impersonal as any modern scientist can wish. And these are our scriptures. You must remember that what the Bible is to the Christians, what the Koran is to the Mohammedans, what the Tripitaka is to the Buddhist, what the Zend Avesta is to the Parsees, these Upanishads are to us. These and nothing but these are our scriptures. The Puranas, the Tantras, and all the other books, even the *Vyasa Sutras,* are of secondary, tertiary authority, but primary are the Vedas. Manu, and the Puranas, and all the other books are to be taken so far as they agree with the authority of the Upanishads, and when they disagree they are to be rejected without mercy. This we ought to remember always, but unfortunately for India, at the present time we have forgotten it. A petty village custom seems now the real authority and not the teaching of the Upanishads. A petty idea current in a wayside village in Bengal seems to have the authority of the Vedas, and even something better. And that word "orthodox", how wonderful its influence! To the villager, the following of every little bit of the Karma Kanda is the very height of "orthodoxy", and one who does not do it is told, "Go away, you are no more a Hindu." So there are, most unfortunately in my motherland, persons who will take up one of these Tantras and say, that the practice of this Tantra is to be obeyed; he who does not do so is no more orthodox in his views. Therefore, it is better for us to remember that in the Upanishads is the primary authority, even the Grihya and *Shrauta Sutras* are subordinate to the authority of the Vedas. They are the words of the Rishis, our forefathers, and you have to believe them if you want to become a Hindu. You may even believe the most peculiar ideas about the Godhead, but if you deny the authority of the Vedas, you are a Nastika. Therein lies the difference between the scriptures of the Christians or the Buddhists and ours; theirs are all Puranas, and not scriptures, because they describe the history of the deluge, and the history of kings and reigning families, and record the lives of great men, and so on. This is the work of the Puranas, and so far as they agree with the Vedas, they are good. So far as the Bible and the scriptures of other nations agree with the Vedas, they are perfectly good, but when they do not agree, they are no more to be accepted. So with the Koran. There are many moral teachings in these, and so far as they agree with the Vedas they have the authority of the Puranas, but no more. The idea is that the Vedas were never written; the idea is, they never came into existence. I was told once by a Christian missionary that their scriptures have a historical character, and, therefore, are true, to which I replied, "Mine have no historical character and, therefore, they are true; yours being historical, they were evidently made by some man the other day. Yours are man-made and mine are not; their non-historicity is in their favour." Such is the relation of the Vedas with all the other scriptures at the present day.

We now come to the teachings of the Upanishads.

Various texts are there. Some are perfectly dualistic, while others are monistic. But there are certain doctrines which are agreed to by all the different sects of India. First, there is the doctrine of Samsara or reincarnation of the soul. Secondly, they all agree in their psychology; first there is the body, behind that, what they call the Sukshma Sharira, the mind, and behind that even, is the Jiva. That is the great difference between Western and Indian psychology; in the Western psychology the mind is the soul, here it is not. The Antahkarana, the internal instrument, as the mind is called, is only an instrument in the hands of that Jiva, through which the Jiva works on the body or on the external world. Here they all agree, and they all also agree that this Jiva or Atman, Jivatman as it is called by various sects, is eternal, without beginning; and that it is going from birth to birth, until it gets a final release. They all agree in this, and they also all agree in one other most vital point, which alone marks characteristically, most prominently, most vitally, the difference between the Indian and the Western mind, and it is this, that everything is in the soul. There is no inspiration, but properly speaking, expiration. All powers and all purity and all greatness—everything is in the soul. The Yogi would tell you that the Siddhis—Anima, Laghima, and so on—that he wants to attain to are not to be attained, in the proper sense of the word, but are already there in the soul; the work is to make them manifest. Patanjali, for instance, would tell you that even in the lowest worm that crawls under your feet, all the eightfold Yogi's powers are already existing. The difference has been made by the body. As soon as it gets a better body, the powers will become manifest, but they are there. निमित्तमप्रयोजकं प्रकृतीनां वरणभेदस्तु ततः क्षेत्रिकवत्। "Good and bad deeds are not the direct causes in the transformations of nature, but they act as breakers of obstacles to the evolutions of nature: as a farmer breaks the obstacles to the course of water, which then runs down by its own nature." Here Patanjali gives the celebrated example of the cultivator bringing water into his field from a huge tank somewhere. The tank is already filled and the water would flood his land in a moment, only there is a mud wall between the tank and his field. As soon as the barrier is broken, in rushes the water out of its own power and force. This mass of power and purity and perfection is in the soul already. The only difference is the Avarana—this veil—that has been cast over it. Once the veil is removed, the soul attains to purity, and its powers become manifest. This, you ought to remember, is the great difference between Eastern and Western thought. Hence you find people teaching such awful doctrines as that we are all born sinners, and because we do not believe in such awful doctrines we are all born wicked. They never stop to think that if we are by our very nature wicked, we can never be good—for how can nature change? If it changes, it contradicts itself; it is not nature. We ought to remember this. Here the dualist, and the Advaitist, and all others in India agree.

The next point, which all the sects in India believe in, is God. Of course their ideas of God will be different. The dualists believe in a Personal God, and a personal only. I want you to understand this word personal a little more. This word personal does not mean that God has a body, sits on a throne somewhere, and rules this world, but means Saguna, with qualities. There are many descriptions of the Personal God. This Personal God as the Ruler, the Creator, the Preserver, and the Destroyer of this universe is believed in by all the sects. The Advaitists believe something more. They believe in a still higher phase of this Personal God, which is personal-impersonal. No adjective can illustrate where there is no qualification, and the Advaitist would not give Him any qualities except the three—Sat-Chid-Ananda, Existence, Knowledge, and Bliss Absolute. This is what Shankara did.

But in the Upanishads themselves you find they penetrate even further, and say, nothing can be predicated of it except Neti, Neti, "Not this, Not this."

Here all the different sects of India agree. But taking the dualistic side, as I have said, I will take Ramanuja as the typical dualist of India, the great modern representative of the dualistic system. It is a pity that our people in Bengal know so very little about the great religious leaders in India, who have been born in other parts of the country; and for the matter of that, during the whole of the Mohammedan period, with the exception of our Chaitanya, all the great religious leaders were born in Southern India, and it is the intellect of Southern India that is really governing India now; for even Chaitanya belonged to one of these sects, a sect of the Madhvas. According to Ramanuja, these three entities are eternal—God, and soul, and nature. The souls are eternal, and they will remain eternally existing, individualised through eternity, and will retain their individuality all through. Your soul will be different from my soul through all eternity, says Ramanuja, and so will this nature—which is an existing fact, as much a fact as the existence of soul or the existence of God—remain always different. And God is inter-penetrating, the essence of the soul, He is the Antaryamin. In this sense Ramanuja sometimes thinks that God is one with the soul, the essence of the soul, and these souls—at the time of Pralaya, when the whole of nature becomes what he calls Sankuchita, contracted—become contracted and minute and remain so for a time. And at the beginning of the next cycle they all come out, according to their past Karma, and undergo the effect of that Karma. Every action that makes the natural inborn purity and perfection of the soul get contracted is a bad action, and every action that makes it come out and expand itself is a good action, says Ramanuja. Whatever helps to make the Vikasha of the soul is good, and whatever makes it Sankuchita is bad. And thus the soul is going on, expanding or contracting in its actions, till through the grace of God comes salvation. And that grace comes to all souls, says Ramanuja, that are pure and struggle for that grace.

There is a celebrated verse in the Shrutis, आहारशुद्धौ सत्त्वशुद्धिः सत्त्वशुद्धौ ध्रुवास्मृतिः "When the food is pure, then the Sattva becomes pure; when the Sattva is pure, then the Smriti"—the memory of the Lord, or the memory of our own perfection—if you are an Advaitist—"becomes truer, steadier, and absolute". Here is a great discussion. First of all, what is this Sattva? We know that according to the Sankhya—and it has been admitted by all our sects of philosophy—the body is composed of three sorts,of materials—not qualities. It is the general idea that Sattva, Rajas, and Tamas are qualities. Not at all, not qualities but the materials of this universe, and with Ahara Shuddhi, when the food is pure, the Sattva material becomes pure. The one theme of the Vedanta is to get this Sattva. As I have told you, the soul is already pure and perfect, and it is, according to the Vedanta, covered up by Rajas and Tamas particles. The Sattva particles are the most luminous, and the effulgence of the soul penetrates through them as easily as light through glass. So if the Rajas and Tamas particles go, and leave the Sattva particles, in this state the power and purity of the soul will appear, and leave the soul more manifest.

Therefore, it is necessary to have this Sattva. And the text says, "When Ahara becomes pure." Ramanuja takes this word Ahara to mean food, and he has made it one of the turning points of his philosophy. Not only so, it has affected the whole of India, and all the different sects. Therefore, it is necessary for us to understand what it means, for that, according to Ramanuja, is one of the principal factors in our life, Ahara Shuddhi. What makes food impure? asks Ramanuja. Three sorts of defects make food impure—first, Jati Dosha, the defect in the very nature of the class to which the food belongs, as the smell in onions, garlic, and suchlike. The next is Ashraya Dosha, the defect in the person from whom the food comes; food coming from a wicked person will make you impure. I myself have seen many great sages in India following strictly that advice-all their lives. Of course they had the power to know who brought the food, and even who had touched the food, and I have seen it in my own life, not once, but hundreds of times. Then Nimitta Dosha, the defect of impure things or influences coming in contact with food is another. We had better attend to that a little more now. It has become too prevalent in India to take food with dirt and dust and bits of hair in it. If food is taken from which these three defects have been removed, that makes Sattva Shuddhi, purifies the Sattva. Religion seems to be a very easy task then. Then every one can have religion if it comes by eating pure food only. There is none so weak or incompetent in this world, that I know, who cannot save himself from these defects. Then comes Shankaracharya, who says this word Ahara means thought collected in the mind; when that becomes pure, the Sattva becomes pure, and not before that. You may eat what you like. If food alone would purify the Sattva, then feed the monkey with milk and rice all its life; would it become a great Yogi? Then the cows and the deer would be great Yogis. As has been said, "If it is by bathing much that heaven is reached, the fishes will get to heaven first. If by eating vegetables a man gets to heaven, the cows and the deer will get to heaven first."

But what is the solution? Both are necessary. Of course the idea that Shankaracharya gives us of Ahara is the primary idea. But pure food, no doubt, helps pure thought; it has an intimate connection; both ought to be there. But the defect is that in modern India we have forgotten the advice of Shankaracharya and taken only the "pure food" meaning. That is why people get mad with me when I say, religion has got into the kitchen; and if you had been in Madras with me, you would have agreed with me. The Bengalis are better than that. In Madras they throw away food if anybody looks at it. And with all this, I do not see that the people are any the better there. If only eating this and that sort of food and saving it from the looks of this person and that person would give them perfection, you would expect them all to be perfect men, which they are not.

Thus, although these are to be combined and linked together to make a perfect whole, do not put the cart before the horse. There is a cry nowadays about this and that food and about Varnashrama, and the Bengalis are the most vociferous in these cries. I would ask every one of you, what do you know about this Varnashrama? Where are the four castes today in this country? Answer me; I do not see the four castes. Just as our Bengali proverb has it, "A headache without a head", so you want to make this Varnashrama here. There are not four castes here. I see only the Brahmin and the Shudra. If there are the Kshatriyas and the Vaishyas, where are they and why do not you Brahmins order them to take the Yajnopavita and study the Vedas, as every Hindu ought to do? And if the Vaishyas and the Kshatriyas do not exist, but only the Brahmins and the Shudras, the Shastras say that the Brahmin must not live in a country where there are only Shudras; so depart bag and baggage! Do you know what the Shastras say about people who have been eating Mlechchha food and living under a government of the Mlechchhas, as you have for the past thousand years? Do you know the penance for that? The penance would be burning oneself with one's own hands. Do you want to pass as teachers and walk like hypocrites? If you believe in your Shastras, burn yourselves first like the one great Brahmin did who went with Alexander the Great and burnt himself because he thought he had eaten the food of a Mlechchha. Do like that, and you will see that the whole nation will be at your feet. You do not believe in your own Shastras and yet want to make others believe in them. If you think you are not able to do that in this age, admit your weakness and excuse the weakness of others, take the other castes up, give them a helping hand, let them study the Vedas and become just as good Aryans as any other Aryans in the world, and be you likewise Aryans, you Brahmins of Bengal.

Give up this filthy Vamachara that is killing your country. You have not seen the other parts of India. When I see how much the Vamachara has entered our society, I find it a most disgraceful place with all its boast of culture. These Vamachara sects are honeycombing our society in Bengal. Those who come out in the daytime and preach most loudly about Achara, it is they who carry on the horrible debauchery at night and are backed by the most dreadful books. They are ordered by the books do to these things. You who are of Bengal know it. The Bengali Shastras are the Vamachara Tantras. They are published by the cart-load, and you poison the minds of your children with them instead of teaching them your Shrutis. Fathers of Calcutta, do you not feel ashamed that such horrible stuff as these Vamachara Tantras, with translations too, should be put into the hands of your boys and girls, and their minds poisoned, and that they should be brought up with the idea that these are the Shastras of the Hindus? If you are ashamed, take them away from your children, and let them read the true Shastras, the Vedas, the *Gita*, the Upanishads.

According to the dualistic sects of India, the individual souls remain as individuals throughout, and God creates the universe out of pre-existing material only as the efficient cause. According to the Advaitists, on the other hand, God is both the material and the efficient cause of the universe. He is not only the Creator of the universe, but He creates it out of Himself. That is the Advaitist position. There are crude dualistic sects who believe that this world has been created by God out of Himself, and at the same time God is eternally separate from the universe, and everything is eternally subordinate to the Ruler of the universe. There are sects too who also believe that out of Himself God has evolved this universe, and individuals in the long run attain to Nirvana to give up the finite and become the Infinite. But these sects have disappeared. The one sect of Advaitists that you see in modern India is composed of the followers of Shankara. According to Shankara, God is both the material and the efficient cause through Maya, but not in reality. God has not become this universe; but the universe is not, and God is. This is one of the highest points to understand of Advaita Vedanta, this idea of Maya. I am afraid I have no time to discuss this one most difficult point in our philosophy. Those of you who are acquainted with Western philosophy will find something very similar in Kant. But I must warn you, those of you who have studied Professor Max Muller's writings on Kant, that there is one idea most misleading. It was Shankara who first found out the idea of the identity of time, space, and causation with Maya, and I had the good fortune to find one or two passages in Shankara's commentaries and send them to my friend the Professor. So even that idea was here in India. Now this is a peculiar theory—this Maya theory of the Advaita Vedantists. The Brahman is all that exists, but differentiation has been caused by this Maya. Unity, the one Brahman, is the ultimate, the goal, and herein is an eternal dissension again between Indian and Western thought. India has thrown this challenge to the world for thousands of years, and the challenge has been taken up by different nations, and the result is that they all succumbed and you live. This is the challenge that this world is a delusion, that it is all Maya, that whether you eat off the ground with your fingers or dine off golden plates, whether you live in palaces and are one of the mightiest monarchs or are the poorest of beggars, death is the one result; it is all the same, all Maya. That is the old Indian theme, and again and again nations are springing up trying to unsay it, to disprove it; becoming great, with enjoyment as their watchword, power in their hands, they use that power to the utmost, enjoy to the utmost, and the next moment they die. We stand forever because we see that everything is Maya. The children of Maya live forever, but the children of enjoyment die.

Here again is another great difference. Just as you find the attempts of Hegel and Schopenhauer in German philosophy, so you will find the very same ideas brought forward in ancient India. Fortunately for us, Hegelianism was nipped in the bud and not allowed to sprout and cast its baneful shoots over this motherland of ours. Hegel's one idea is that the one, the absolute, is only chaos, and that the individualised form is the greater. The world is greater than the non-world, Samsara is greater than salvation. That is the one idea, and the more you plunge into this Samsara the more your soul is covered with the workings of life, the better you are. They say, do you not see how we built houses, cleanse the streets, enjoy the senses? Ay, behind that they may hide rancour, misery, horror—behind every bit of that enjoyment.

On the other hand, our philosophers have from the very first declared that every manifestation, what you call evolution, is vain, a vain attempt of the unmanifested to manifest itself. Ay, you the mighty cause of this universe, trying to reflect yourself in little mud puddles! But after making the attempt for a time you find out it was all in vain and beat a retreat to the place from whence you came. This is Vairagya, or renunciation, and the very beginning of religion. How can religion or morality begin without renunciation itself? The Alpha and Omega is renunciation. "Give up," says the Veda, "give up". That is the one way, "Give up." न प्रजया धनेन त्यागेनैकेऽमृतत्वमानशुः—"Neither through wealth, nor through progeny, but by giving up alone that immortality is to be reached." That is the dictate of the Indian books. Of course, there have been great givers-up of the world, even sitting on thrones. But even (King) Janaka himself had to renounce; who was a greater renouncer than he? But in modern times we all want to be called Janakas! They are all Janakas (literally: fathers) of children—unclad, ill-fed, miserable children. The word "Janaka" can be applied to them in that sense only; they have none of the shining, Godlike thoughts as the old Janaka had. These are our modern Janakas! A little less of this Janakism now, and come straight to the mark! If you can give up, you will have religion. If you cannot, you may read all the books that are in the world, from East to West, swallow all the libraries, and become the greatest of Pandits, but if you have Karma Kanda only, you are nothing; there is no spirituality. Through renunciation alone this immortality is to be reached. It is the power, the great power, that cares not even for the universe; then it is that ब्रह्माण्डम् गोष्पदायते। "The whole universe becomes like a hollow made by a cow's foot."

Renunciation, that is the flag, the banner of India, floating over the world, the one undying thought which India sends again and again as a warning to dying races, as a warning to all tyranny, as a warning to wickedness in the world. Ay, Hindus, let not your hold of that banner go. Hold it aloft. Even if you are weak and cannot renounce, do not lower the ideal. Say, "I am weak and cannot renounce the world", but do not try to be hypocrites, torturing texts, and making specious arguments, and trying to throw dust in the eyes of people who are ignorant. Do not do that, but own you are weak. For the idea is great, that of renunciation. What matters it if millions fail in the attempt, if ten soldiers or even two return victorious! Blessed be the millions dead! Their blood has bought the victory. This renunciation is the one ideal throughout the different Vedic sects except one, and that is the Vallabhacharya sect in Bombay Presidency, and most of you are aware what comes where renunciation does not exist. We want orthodoxy—even the hideously orthodox, even those who smother themselves with ashes, even those who stand with their hands uplifted. Ay, we want them, unnatural though they be, for standing for that idea of giving up, and acting as a warning to the race against succumbing to the effeminate luxuries that are creeping into India, eating into our very vitals, and tending to make the whole race a race of hypocrites. We want to have a little of asceticism. Renunciation conquered India in days of yore, it has still to conquer India. Still it stands as the greatest and highest of Indian ideals—this renunciation. The land of Buddha, the land of Ramanuja, of Ramakrishna Paramahamsa, the land of renunciation, the land where, from the days of yore, Karma Kanda was preached against, and even today there are hundreds who have given up everything, and become Jivanmuktas—ay, will that land give up its ideals? Certainly not. There may be people whose brains have become turned by the Western luxurious ideals; there may be thousands and hundreds of thousands who have drunk deep of enjoyment, this curse of the West—the senses—the curse of the world; yet for all that, there will be other thousands in this motherland of mine to whom religion will ever be a reality, and who will be ever ready to give up without counting the cost, if need be.

Another ideal very common in all our sects, I want to place before you; it is also a vast subject. This unique idea that religion is to be realised is in India alone. नायमात्मा प्रवचनेन लभ्यो न मेधया न बहुना श्रुतेन—"This Atman is not to be reached by too much talking, nor is it to be reached by the power of the intellect, nor by much study of the scriptures." Nay, ours is the only scripture in the world that declares, not even by the study of the scriptures can the Atman be realised—not talks, not lecturing, none of that, but It is to be realised. It comes from the teacher to the disciple. When this insight comes to the disciple, everything is cleared up and realisation follows.

One more idea. There is a peculiar custom in Bengal, which they call Kula Guru, or hereditary Guruship. "My father was your Guru, now I shall be your Guru. My father was the Guru of your father, so shall I be yours." What is a Guru? Let us go back to the Shrutis—"He who knows the secret of the Vedas," not bookworms, not grammarians, not Pandits in general, but he who knows the meaning. यथा

खरश्चन्दनभारवाही भारस्य वेत्ता न तु चन्दनस्य a load of sandalwood knows only the weight of the wood, but not its precious qualities"; so are these Pandits. We do not want such. What can they teach if they have no realisation? When I was a boy here, in this city of Calcutta, I used to go from place to place in search of religion, and everywhere I asked the lecturer after hearing very big lectures, "Have you seen God?" The man was taken aback at the idea of seeing God; and the only man who told me, "I have", was Ramakrishna Paramahamsa, and not only so, but he said, "I will put you in the way of seeing Him too." The Guru is not a man who twists and tortures texts, वाग्वैखरी शब्दझरी शास्त्रव्ख्यानकौशलं वैदुष्यं विदुषां तद्वद्भुक्तये न तु मुक्तये। —"Different ways of throwing out words, different ways of explaining texts of the scriptures, these are for the enjoyment of the learned, not for freedom." Shrotriya, he who knows the secret of the Shrutis, Avrijina, the sinless, and Akamahata, unpierced by desire—he who does not want to make money by teaching you—he is the Shanta, the Sadhu, who comes as the spring which brings the leaves and blossoms to various plants but does not ask anything from the plant, for its very nature is to do good. It does good and there it is. Such is the Guru, तीर्णाः स्वयं भीमभवार्णवं जनानहेतुनान्यानपि तारयन्तः "Who has himself crossed this terrible ocean of life, and without any idea of gain to himself, helps others also to cross the ocean." This is the Guru, and mark that none else can be a Guru, for अविद्यायामन्तरे वर्तमानाः स्वयं धीराः पण्डितम्मन्यमानाः। दन्द्रम्यमाणाः परियन्ति मूढा अन्धेनैव नीयमाना यथान्धाः —"Themselves steeped in darkness, but in the pride of their hearts, thinking they know everything, the fools want to help others, and they go round and round in many crooked ways, staggering to and fro, and thus like the blind leading the blind, both fall into the ditch." Thus say the Vedas. Compare that and your present custom. You are Vedantists, you are very orthodox, are you not? You are great Hindus and very orthodox. Ay, what I want to do is to make you more orthodox. The more orthodox you are, the more sensible; and the more you think of modern orthodoxy, the more foolish you are. Go back to your old orthodoxy, for in those days every sound that came from these books, every pulsation, was out of a strong, steady, and sincere heart; every note was true. After that came degradation in art, in science, in religion, in everything, national degradation. We have no time to discuss the causes, but all the books written about that period breathe of the pestilence—the national decay; instead of vigour, only wails and cries. Go back, go back to the old days when there was strength and vitality. Be strong once more, drink deep of this fountain of yore, and that is the only condition of life in India.

According to the Advaitist, this individuality which we have today is a delusion. This has been a hard nut to crack all over the world. Forthwith you tell a man he is not an individual, he is so much afraid that his individuality, whatever that may be, will be lost! But the Advaitist says there never has been an individuality, you have been changing every moment of your life. You were a child and thought in one way, now you are a man and think another way, again you will be an old man and think differently. Everybody is changing. If so, where is your individuality? Certainly not in the body, or in the mind, or in thought. And beyond that is your Atman, and, says the Advaitist, this Atman is the Brahman Itself. There cannot be two infinites. There is only one individual and it is infinite. In plain words, we are rational beings, and we want to reason. And what is reason? More or less of classification, until you cannot go on any further. And the finite can only find its ultimate rest when it is classified into the infinite. Take up a finite thing and go on analysing it, but you will find rest nowhere until you reach the ultimate or infinite, and that infinite, says the Advaitist, is what alone exists. Everything else is Maya, nothing else has real existence; whatever is of existence in any material thing is this Brahman; we are this Brahman, and the shape and everything else is Maya. Take away the form and shape, and you and I are all one. But we have to guard against the word, "I". Generally people say, "If I am the Brahman, why cannot I do this and that?" But this is using the word in a different sense. As soon as you think you are bound, no more you are Brahman, the Self, who wants nothing, whose light is inside. All His pleasures and bliss are inside; perfectly satisfied with Himself, He wants nothing, expects nothing, perfectly fearless, perfectly free. That is Brahman. In That we are all one.

Now this seems, therefore, to be the great point of difference between the dualist and the Advaitist. You find even great commentators like Shankaracharya making meanings of texts, which, to my mind, sometimes do not seem to be justified. Sometimes you find Ramanuja dealing with texts in a way that is not very clear. The idea has been even among our Pandits that only one of these sects can be true and the rest must be false, although they have the idea in the Shrutis, the most wonderful idea that India has yet to give to the world: एकं सद्विप्रा बहुधा वदन्ति।—"That which exists is One; sages call It by various names." That has been the theme, and the working out of the whole of this life-problem of the nation is the working out of that theme—एकं सद्विप्रा बहुधा वदन्ति। Yea, except a very few learned men, I mean, barring a very few spiritual men, in India, we always forget this. We forget this great idea, and you will find that there are persons among Pandits—I should think ninety-eight per cent—who are of opinion that either the Advaitist will be true, or the Vishishtadvaitist will be true, or the Dvaitist will be true; and if you go to Varanasi, and sit for five minutes in one of the Ghats there, you will have demonstration of what I say. You will see a regular bullfight going on about these various sects and things.

Thus it remains. Then came one whose life was the explanation, whose life was the working out of the harmony that is the background of all the different sects of India, I mean

Ramakrishna Paramahamsa. It is his life that explains that both of these are necessary, that they are like the geocentric and the heliocentric theories in astronomy. When a child is taught astronomy, he is taught the geocentric first, and works out similar ideas of astronomy to the geocentric. But when he comes to finer points of astronomy, the heliocentric will be necessary, and he will understand it better. Dualism is the natural idea of the senses; as long as we are bound by the senses we are bound to see a God who is only Personal, and nothing but Personal, we are bound to see the world as it is. Says Ramanuja, "So long as you think you are a body, and you think you are a mind, and you think you are a Jiva, every act of perception will give you the three—Soul, and nature, and something as causing both." But yet, at the same time, even the idea of the body disappears where the mind itself becomes finer and finer, till it has almost disappeared, when all the different things that make us fear, make us weak, and bind us down to this body-life have disappeared. Then and then alone one finds out the truth of that grand old teaching. What is the teaching?

इहैव तैर्जितः सर्गो येषां साम्ये स्थितं मनः।
निर्दोषं हि समं ब्रह्म तस्माद्ब्रह्मणि ते स्थिताः।।

"Even in this life they have conquered the round of birth and death whose minds are firm-fixed on the sameness of everything, for God is pure and the same to all, and, therefore, such are said to be living in God."

समं पश्यन् हि सर्वत्र समवस्थितमीश्वरम्।
न हिनस्त्यात्मनात्मानं ततो याति परां गतिम्।।

"Thus seeing the Lord the same everywhere, he, the sage, does not hurt the Self by the self, and so goes to the highest goal."

The Forms Of Love Manifestation

Here are some of the forms in which love manifests itself. First there is reverence. Why do people show reverence to temples and holy places? Because He is worshipped there, and His presence is associated with all such places. Why do people in every country pay reverence to teachers of religion? It is natural for the human heart to do so, because all such teachers preach the Lord. At bottom, reverence is a growth out of love; we can none of us revere him whom we do not love. Then comes Priti—pleasure in God. What an immense pleasure men take in the objects of the senses. They go anywhere, run through any danger, to get the thing which they love, the thing which their senses like. What is wanted of the Bhakta is this very kind of intense love which has, however, to be directed to God. Then there is the sweetest of pains, Viraha, the intense misery due to the absence of the beloved. When a man feels intense misery because he has not attained to God, has not known that which is the only thing worthy to be known, and becomes in consequence very dissatisfied and almost mad—then there is Viraha; and this state of the mind makes him feel disturbed in the presence of anything other than the beloved (Ekarativichikitsa). In earthly love we see how often this Viraha comes. Again, when men are really and intensely in love with women or women with men, they feel a kind of natural annoyance in the presence of all those whom they do not love. Exactly the same state of impatience in regard to things that are not loved conies to the mind when Para Bhakti holds sway over it; even to talk about things other than God becomes distasteful then. "Think of Him, think of Him alone, and give up all other vain words"—अन्या वाचो विमुंचथ। Those who talk of Him alone, the Bhakta finds to be friendly to him; while those who talk of anything else appear to him to be unfriendly. A still higher stage of love is reached when life itself is maintained for the sake of the one Ideal of Love, when life itself is considered beautiful and worth living only on account of that Love (तदर्थप्राणसंस्थानं). Without it, such a life would not remain even for a moment. Life is sweet, because it thinks of the Beloved. Tadiyata (His-ness) comes when a man becomes perfect according to Bhakti—when he has become blessed, when he has attained God, when he has touched the feet of God, as it were. Then his whole nature is purified and completely changed. All his purpose in life then becomes fulfilled. Yet many such Bhaktas live on just to worship Him. That is the bliss, the only pleasure in life which they will not give up. "O king, such is the blessed quality of Hari that even those who have become satisfied with everything, all the knots of whose hearts have been cut asunder, even they love the Lord for love's sake"—the Lord "Whom all the gods worship—all the lovers of liberation, and all the knowers of the Brahman"—यं सर्वे देवा नमन्ति मुमुक्षवो ब्रह्मवादिनश्चेति *(Nri. Tap. Up.)*. Such is the power of love. When a man has forgotten, himself altogether, and does not feel that anything belongs to him, then he acquires the state of Tadiyata; everything is sacred to him, because it belongs to the Beloved. Even in regard to earthly love, the lover thinks that everything belonging to his beloved is sacred and so dear to him. He loves even a piece of cloth belonging to the darling of his heart. In the same way, when a person loves the Lord, the whole universe becomes dear to him, because it is all His.

The God Of Love Is His Own Proof

What is the ideal of the lover who has quite passed beyond the idea of selfishness, of bartering and bargaining, and who knows no fear? Even to the great God such a man will say, "I will give You my all, and I do not want anything from You; indeed there is nothing that I can call my own." When a man has acquired this conviction, his ideal becomes one of perfect love, one of perfect fearlessness of love. The highest ideal of such a person has no narrowness of particularity about it; it is love universal, love without limits and bonds, love itself, absolute love. This grand ideal of the religion of love is worshipped and loved absolutely as such without the aid of any symbols or suggestions. This is the highest form of Para Bhakti—the worship of such an all-comprehending ideal as the ideal; all the other forms of Bhakti are only stages on the way to reach it.

All our failures and all our successes in following the religion of love are on the road to the realisation of that one ideal. Object after object is taken up, and the inner ideal is successively projected on them all; and all such external objects are found inadequate as exponents of the ever-expanding inner ideal and are naturally rejected one after another. At last the aspirant begins to think that it is vain to try to realise the ideal in external objects, that all external objects are as nothing when compared with the ideal itself; and, in course of time, he acquires the power of realising the highest and the most generalised abstract ideal entirely as an abstraction that is to him quite alive and real. When the devotee has reached this point, he is no more impelled to ask whether God can be demonstrated or not, whether He is omnipotent and omniscient or not. To him He is only the God of Love; He is the highest ideal of love, and that is sufficient for all his purposes. He, as love, is self-evident. It requires no proofs to demonstrate the existence of the beloved to the lover. The, magistrate-Gods of other forms of religion may require a good deal of proof to prove Them, but the Bhakta does not and cannot think of such Gods at all. To him God exists entirely as love. "None, O beloved, loves the husband for the husband's sake, but it is for the sake of the Self who is in the husband that the husband is loved; none, O beloved, loves the wife for the wife's sake, but it is for the sake of the Self who is in the wife that the wife is loved."

It is said by some that selfishness is the only motive power in regard to all human activities. That also is love lowered by being particularised. When I think of myself as comprehending the Universal, there can surely be no selfishness in me; but when I, by mistake, think that I am a little something, my love becomes particularised and narrowed. The mistake consists in making the sphere of love narrow and contracted. All things in the universe are of divine origin and deserve to be loved; it has, however, to be borne in mind that the love of the whole includes the love of the parts. This whole is the God of the Bhaktas, and all the other Gods, Fathers in Heaven, or Rulers, or Creators, and all theories and doctrines and books have no purpose and no meaning for them, seeing that they have through their supreme love and devotion risen above those things altogether. When the heart is purified and cleansed and filled to the brim with the divine nectar of love, all other ideas of God become simply puerile and are rejected as being inadequate or unworthy. Such is indeed the power of Para Bhakti or Supreme Love; and the perfected Bhakta no more goes to see God in temples and churches; he knows no place where he will not find Him. He finds Him in the temple as well as out of the temple, he finds Him in the saint's saintliness as well as in the wicked man's wickedness, because he has Him already seated in glory in his own heart as the one Almighty inextinguishable Light of Love which is ever shining and eternally present.

Narada Bhakti Sutras

A translation dictated by Swami Vivekananda in America

CHAPTER I

1. Bhakti is intense love for God.

2. It is the nectar of love;

3. Getting which Man becomes perfect, immortal, and satisfied forever;

4. Getting which Man desires no more, does not become jealous of anything, does not take pleasure in vanities:

5. Knowing which Man becomes filled with spirituality, becomes calm, and finds pleasure only in God.

6. It cannot be used to fill any desire, itself being the check to all desires.

7. Sannyasa is giving up both the popular and the scriptural forms of worship.

8. The Bhakti Sannyasin is the one whose whole soul goes unto God, and whatever militates against love to God, he rejects.

9. Giving up all other refuge, he takes refuge in God.

10. Scriptures are to be followed as long as one's life has not become firm;

11. Or else there is danger of doing evil in the name of liberty.

12. When love becomes established, even social forms are given up, except those which are necessary for the preservation of life.

13. There have been many definitions of love, but Narada gives these as the signs of love: When all thoughts, all words, and all deeds are given up unto the Lord, and the least forgetfulness of God makes one intensely miserable, then *love has begun*.

14. As the Gopis had it—

15. Because, although worshipping God as their lover, they never forgot his God-nature;

16. Otherwise they would have committed the sin of unchastity.

17. This is the highest form of love, because there is no desire of reciprocity, which desire is in all human love.

CHAPTER II

1. Bhakti is greater than Karma, greater than Jnana, greater than Yoga (Raja Yoga), because Bhakti itself is its result, because Bhakti is both the means and the end (fruit).

2. As a man cannot satisfy his hunger by simple knowledge or sight of food, so a man cannot be satisfied by the knowledge or even the perception of God until love comes; therefore, love is the highest.

CHAPTER III

1. These, however, the Masters have said about Bhakti:

2. One who wants this Bhakti must give up sense-enjoyments and even the company of people.

3. Day and night he must think about Bhakti and nothing else.

4. (He must) go where they sing or talk of God.

5. The principle cause of Bhakti is the mercy of a great (or free) soul.

6. Meeting with a great soul is hard to obtain, and never fails to save the soul.

7. Through the mercy of God we get such Gurus.

8. There is no difference between Him and His (own) ones.

9. Seek, therefore, for this.

10. Evil company is always to be shunned;

11. Because it leads to lust and anger, illusion, forgetfulness of the goal, destruction of the will (lack of perseverance), and destruction of everything.

12. These disturbances may at first be like ripples, but evil company at last makes them like the sea.

13. He gets across Maya who gives up all attachment, serves the great ones, lives alone, cuts the bondages of this world, goes beyond the qualities of nature, and depends upon the Lord for even his living.

14. He who gives up the fruits of work, he who gives up all work and the dualism of joy and misery, who gives up even the scriptures, gets that unbroken love for God;

15. He crosses this river and helps others to cross it.

CHAPTER IV

1. The nature of love is inexpressible.

2. As the dumb man cannot express what he tastes, but his actions betray his feelings, so Man cannot express this love in words, but his actions betray it.

3. In some rare persons it is expressed.

4. Beyond all qualities, all desires, ever increasing, unbroken, the finest perception is love.

5. When a man gets this love, he sees love everywhere, he hears love everywhere, he talks love everywhere, he thinks love everywhere.

6. According to the qualities or conditions, this love manifests itself differently.

7. The qualities are: Tamas (dullness, heaviness), Rajas (restlessness, activity), Sattva (serenity, purity); and the

conditions are: Arta (afflicted), Artharthi (wanting something), Jijnasu (searching truth), Jnani (knower).

8. Of these the latter are higher than the preceding ones.

9. Bhakti is the easiest way of worship.

10. It is its own proof and does not require any other.

11. Its nature is peace and perfect bliss.

12. Bhakti never seeks to injure anyone or anything, not even the popular modes of worship.

13. Conversation about lust, or doubt of God or about one's enemies must not be listened to.

14. Egotism, pride, etc. must be given up.

15. If those passions cannot be controlled, place them upon God, and place all your actions on Him.

16. Merging the trinity of Love, Lover, and Beloved, worship God as His eternal servant, His eternal bride—thus love is to be made unto God.

CHAPTER V

1. That love is highest which is concentrated upon God.

2. When such speak of God, their voices stick in their throats, they cry and weep; and it is they who give holy places their holiness; they make good works, good books better, because they are permeated with God.

3. When a man loves God so much, his forefathers rejoice, the gods dance, and the earth gets a Master!

4. To such lovers there is no difference of caste, sex, knowledge, form, birth, or wealth;

5. Because they are all God's.

6. Arguments are to be avoided;

7. Because there is no end to them, and they lead to no satisfactory result.

8. Read books treating of this love, and do deeds which increase it.

9. Giving up all desires of pleasure and pain, gain and loss, worship God day and night. Not a moment is to be spent in vain.

10. Ahimsa (non-killing), truthfulness, purity, mercy, and godliness are always to be kept.

11. Giving up all other thoughts, the whole mind should day and night worship God. Thus being worshipped day and night, He reveals Himself and makes His worshippers feel Him.

12. In past, present, and future, *Love is greatest!*

Thus following the ancient sages, we have dared to preach the doctrine of *Love,* without fearing the jeers of the world.

On Art

In art, interest must be centred on the principal theme. Drama is the most difficult of all arts. In it two things are to be satisfied—first, the ears, and second, the eyes. To paint a scene, if one thing be painted, it is easy enough; but to paint different things and yet to keep up the central interest is very difficult. Another difficult thing is stage-management, that is, combining different things in such a manner as to keep the central interest intact.

On Music

There is science in Dhrupad, Kheyal, etc., but it is in Kirtana, *i.e.* in Mathura and Viraha and other like compositions that there is real music—for there is feeling. Feeling is the soul, the secret of everything. There is more music in common people's songs, and they should be collected together. The science of Dhrupad etc., applied to the music of Kirtana will produce the perfect music.

On Food

You preach to others to be men but cannot give them good food. I have been thinking over this problem for the last four years. I wish to make an experiment whether something of the nature of flattened rice can be made out of wheat. Then we can get a different food every day. About drinking water, I searched for a filter which would suit our country. I found one pan-like porcelain vessel through which water was made to pass, and all the bacilli remained in the porcelain pan. But gradually that filter would itself become the hotbed of all germs. This is the danger of all filters. After continued searching I found one method by which water was distilled and then oxygen was passed into it. After this the water became so pure, that great improvement of health was sure to result from its use.

IV

PHILOSOPHY

On Professor Max Muller

Written for the Brahmavadin, *1896*

Though the ideal of work of our *Brahmavadin* should always be "कर्मण्येवाधिकारस्ते मा फलेषु कदाचन—To work thou hast the right, but never to the fruits thereof", yet no sincere worker passes out of the field of activity without making himself known and catching at least a few rays of light.

The beginning of our work has been splendid, and the steady earnestness shown by our friends is beyond all praise. Sincerity of conviction and purity of motive will surely gain the day; and even a small minority, armed with these, is surely destined to prevail against all odds.

Keep away from all insincere claimants to supernatural illumination; not that such illumination is impossible, but, my friends, in this world of ours "lust, or gold, or fame" is the hidden motive behind ninety per cent of all such claims, and of the remaining ten per cent, nine per cent are cases which require the tender care of physicians more than the attention of metaphysicians.

The first great thing to accomplish is to establish a character, to obtain, as we say, the प्रतिष्ठिता प्रज्ञा (established in Wisdom). This applies equally to individuals and to organised bodies of individuals. Do not fret because the world looks with suspicion at every new attempt, even though it be in the path of spirituality. The poor world, how often has it been cheated! The more the संसार, that is, the worldly aspect of life, looks at any growing movement with eyes of suspicion, or, even better still, presents to it a semi-hostile front, so much the better is it for the movement. If there is any truth this movement has to disseminate, any need it is born to supply, soon will condemnation be changed into praise, and contempt converted into love. People in these days are apt to take up religion as a means to some social or political end. Beware of this. Religion is its own end. That religion which is only a means to worldly well-being is not religion, whatever else it may be; and it is sheer blasphemy against God and Man to hold that Man has no other end than the free and full enjoyment of all the pleasure of his senses.

Truth, purity, and unselfishness—wherever these are present, there is no power below or above the sun to crush the possessor thereof. Equipped with these, one individual is able to face the whole universe in opposition.

Above all, beware of compromises. I do not mean that you are to get into antagonism with anybody, but you have to hold on to your own principles in weal or woe and never adjust them to others' "fads" through the greed of getting supporters. Your Atman is the support of the universe—whose support do you stand in need of? Wait with patience and love and strength; if helpers are not ready now, they will come in time. Why should we be in a hurry? The real working force of all great work is in its almost unperceived beginnings.

Whoever could have thought that the life and teachings of a boy born of poor Brahmin parents in a wayside Bengal village would, in a few years, reach such distant lands as our ancestors never even dreamed of? I refer to Bhagvan Ramakrishna. Do you knew that Prof. Max Muller has already written an article on Sri Ramakrishna for the *Nineteenth Century,* and will be very glad to write a larger and fuller account of his life and teachings if sufficient materials are forthcoming? What an extraordinary man is Prof. Max Muller! I paid a visit to him a few days ago, I should say, that I went to pay my respects to him, for whosoever loves Sri Ramakrishna, whatever be his or her sect, or creed, or nationality, my visit to that person I hold as a pilgrimage. "मद्भक्तानां च ये भक्तास्ते मे भक्ततमा मताः—They who are devoted to those who love Me—they are My best devotees." Is that not true?

The Professor was first induced to inquire about the power behind, which led to sudden and momentous changes in the life of the late Keshab Chandra Sen, the great Brahmo leader; and since then, he has been an earnest student and admirer of the life and teachings of Sri Ramakrishna. "Ramakrishna is worshipped by thousands today, Professor", I said. "To whom else shall worship be accorded, if not to such", was the answer. The Professor was kindness itself, and asked Mr. Sturdy and myself to lunch with him. He showed us several colleges in Oxford and the Bodleian library. He also accompanied us to the railway station; and all this he did because, as he said, "It is not every day one meets a disciple of Ramakrishna Paramahamsa."

The visit was really a revelation to me. That nice little house in its setting of a beautiful garden, the silver-headed sage, with a face calm and benign, and forehead smooth as a child's in spite of seventy winters, and every line in that face speaking of a deep-seated mine of spirituality somewhere behind; that noble wife, the helpmate of his life through his long and arduous task of exciting interest, overriding opposition and contempt, and at last creating a respect for the thoughts of the sages of ancient India—the trees, the flowers, the calmness, and the clear sky—all these sent me back in imagination to the glorious days of Ancient India, the days of our Brahmarishis and Rajarishis, the days of the great Vanaprasthas, the days of Arundhatis and Vasishthas.

It was neither the philologist nor the scholar that I saw, but a soul that is every day realising its oneness with the Brahman, a heart that is every moment expanding to reach oneness with the Universal. Where others lose themselves in the desert of dry details, he has struck the well-spring of life. Indeed his heartbeats have caught the rhythm of the Upanishads "तमेवैकं जानथ आत्मानमन्यथा वाचो विमुञ्चथ—Know the Atman alone, and leave off all other talk."

Although a world-moving scholar and philosopher, his learning and philosophy have only led him higher and higher to the realisation of the Spirit, his अपरा विद्या (lower knowledge) has indeed helped him to reach the परा विद्या (higher knowledge). This is real learning. विद्या ददाति विनयम् —"Knowledge gives humility." Of what use is knowledge if it does not show us the way to the Highest?

And what love he bears towards India! I wish I had a hundredth part of that love for my own motherland! Endued with an extraordinary, and at the same time intensely active mind, he has lived and moved in the world of Indian thought for fifty years or more, and watched the sharp interchange of light and shade in the interminable forest of Sanskrit literature with deep interest and heartfelt love, till they have all sunk into his very soul and coloured his whole being.

Max Muller is the Vedantist of Vedantists. He has, indeed, caught the real soul of the melody of the Vedanta, in the midst of all its settings of harmonies and discords—the one light that lightens the sects and creeds of the world, the Vedanta, the one principle of which all religions are only applications. And what was Ramakrishna Paramahamsa? The practical demonstration of this ancient principle, the embodiment of India that is past, and a foreshadowing of the India that is to be, the bearer of spiritual light unto nations. The jeweller alone can understand the worth of jewels; this is an old proverb. Is it a wonder that this Western sage does study and appreciate every new star in the firmament of Indian thought, before even the Indians themselves realise its magnitude?

"When are you coming to India? Every heart there would welcome one who has done so much to place the thoughts of their ancestors in the true light", I said. The face of the aged sage brightened up—there was almost a tear in his eyes, a gentle nodding of the head, and slowly the words come out: "I would not return then; you would have to cremate me there." Further questions seemed an unwarrantable intrusion into realms wherein are stored the holy secrets of man's heart. Who knows but that it was what the poet has said—

तच्चेतसा स्मरति नूनमबोधपूर्वं।
भावस्थिराणि जननान्तरसौहृदानि।।

—"He remembers with his mind the friendships of former births, firmly rooted in his heart."

His life has been a blessing to the world; and may it be many, many years more, before he changes the present plane of his existence!

On Dr. Paul Deussen

Written for the Brahmavadin, *1896*

More than a decade has passed since a young German student, one of eight children of a not very well-to-do clergyman, heard on a certain day Professor Lassen lecturing on a language and literature new—very new even at that time—to European scholars, namely, Sanskrit. The lectures were of course free; for even now it is impossible for any one in any European University to make a living by teaching Sanskrit, unless indeed the University backs him.

Lassen was almost the last of that heroic band of German scholars, the pioneers of Sanskrit scholarship in Germany. Heroic certainly they were—what interest except their pure and unselfish love of knowledge could German scholars have had at that time in Indian literature? The veteran Professor was expounding a chapter of *Shakuntala;* and on that day there was no one present more eagerly and attentively listening to Lassen's exposition than our young student. The subject-matter of the exposition was of course interesting and wonderful, but more wonderful was the strange language, the strange sounds of which, although uttered with all those difficult peculiarities that Sanskrit consonants are subjected to in the mouths of unaccustomed Europeans, had strange fascination for him. He returned to his lodgings, but that night sleep could not make him oblivious of what he had heard. A glimpse of a hitherto unknown land had been given to him, a land far more gorgeous in its colours than any he had yet seen, and having a power of fascination never yet experienced by his young and ardent soul.

Naturally his friends were anxiously looking forward to the ripening of his brilliant parts, and expected that he would soon enter a learned profession which might bring him respect, fame, and, above all, a good salary and a high position. But then there was this Sanskrit! The vast majority of European scholars had not even heard of it then; as for making it pay—I have already said that such a thing is impossible even now. Yet his desire to learn it was strong.

It has unfortunately become hard for us modern Indians to understand how it could be like that; nevertheless, there are to be met with in Varanasi and Nadia and other places even now, some old as well as young persons among our Pandits, and mostly among the Sannyasins, who are mad with this kind of thirst for knowledge for its own sake. Students, not placed in the midst of the luxurious surroundings and materials of the modern Europeanised Hindu, and with a thousand times less facilities for study, poring over manuscripts in the flickering light of an oil lamp, night after night, which alone would have been enough to completely destroy the eye-sight of the students of any other nation; travelling on foot hundreds of miles, begging their way all along, in search of a rare manuscript or a noted teacher; and wonderfully concentrating all the energy of their body and mind upon their one object of study, year in and year out, till the hair turns grey and the infirmity of age overtakes them—such students have not, through God's mercy, as yet disappeared altogether from our country. Whatever India now holds as a proud possession, has been undeniably the result of such labour on the part of her worthy sons in days gone by; and the truth of this remark will become at once evident on comparing the depth and solidity as well as the unselfishness and the earnestness of purpose of India's ancient scholarship with the results attained by our modern Indian Universities. Unselfish and genuine zeal for real scholarship and honest earnest thought must again become dominant in the life of our countrymen if they are ever to rise to occupy among nations a rank worthy of their own historic past. It is this kind of desire for knowledge which has made Germany what she is now—one of the foremost, if not the foremost, among the nations of the world.

Yes, the desire to learn Sanskrit was strong in the heart of this German student. It was long, uphill work—this learning of Sanskrit; with him too it was the same world-old story of successful scholars and their hard work, their privations and their indomitable energy—and also the same glorious conclusion of a really heroic achievement. He thus achieved success; and now—not only Europe, but all India knows this man, Paul Deussen, who is the Professor of Philosophy in the University of Kiel. I have seen professors of Sanskrit in America and in Europe. Some of them are very sympathetic towards Vedantic thought. I admire their intellectual acumen and their lives of unselfish labour. But Paul Deussen—or as he prefers to be called in Sanskrit, Deva Sena—and the veteran Max Muller have impressed me as being the truest friends of India and Indian thought. It will always be among the most pleasing episodes in my life—my first visit to this ardent Vedantist at Kiel, his gentle wife who travelled with him in India, and his little daughter, the darling of his heart—and our travelling together through Germany and Holland, to London, and the pleasant meetings we had in and about London.

The earliest schools of Sanskritists in Europe entered into the study of Sanskrit with more imagination than critical ability. They knew a little, expected much from that little, and often tried to make too much of what little they knew. Then, in those days even, such vagaries as the estimation of *Shakuntala* as forming the high watermark of Indian philosophy were not altogether unknown! These were naturally followed by a reactionary band of superficial critics, more than real scholars of any kind, who knew little or nothing of Sanskrit, expected nothing from Sanskrit studies, and ridiculed everything from the East. While criticising the unsound imaginativeness of the early school to whom everything in Indian literature was rose and musk, these, in their turn, went into speculations which, to say the least, were equally highly unsound and indeed very venturesome. And their boldness was very naturally helped by the fact that these over-hasty and unsympathetic scholars and critics were addressing an audience whose entire qualification for pronouncing any judgment in the matter was their absolute ignorance of Sanskrit. What a medley of results from such critical scholarship! Suddenly, on one fine morning, the poor Hindu woke up to find that everything that was his was gone; one strange race had snatched away from him his arts, another his architecture, and a third, whatever there was of his ancient sciences; why, even his religion was not his own! Yes—that too had migrated into India in the wake of a Pehlevi cross of stone! After a feverish period of such treading-on-each-other's-toes of original research, a better state of things has dawned. It has now been found out that mere adventure without some amount of the capital of real and ripe scholarship produces nothing but ridiculous failure even in the business of Oriental research, and that the traditions in India are not to be rejected with supercilious contempt, as there is really more in them than most people ever dream of.

There is now happily coming into existence in Europe a new type of Sanskrit scholars, reverential, sympathetic, and learned—reverential because they are a better stamp of men, and sympathetic because they are learned. And the link which connects the new portion of the chain with the old one is, of course, our Max Muller. We Hindus certainly owe more to him than to any other Sanskrit scholar in the West, and I am simply astonished when I think of the gigantic task which he, in his enthusiasm, undertook as a young man and brought to a successful conclusion in his old age. Think of this man without any help, poring over old manuscripts, hardly legible to the Hindus themselves, and in a language to acquire which takes a lifetime even in India—without even the help of any needy Pandit whose "brains could be picked", as the Americans say, for ten shillings a month, and a mere mention of his name in the introduction to some book of "very new researches" —think of this man, spending days and sometimes months in elucidating the correct reading and meaning of a word or a sentence in the commentary of Sayana (as he has himself told me), and in the end succeeding in making an easy road through the forest of Vedic literature for all others to go along; think of him and his work, and then say what he really is to us! Of course we need not all agree with him in all that he says in his many writings; certainly such an agreement is impossible. But agreement or no agreement, the fact remains that this one man has done a thousand times more for the preservation, spreading, and appreciation of the literature of our forefathers than any of us can ever hope to do, and he has done it all with a heart which is full of the sweet balm of love and veneration.

If Max Muller is thus the old pioneer of the new movement, Deussen is certainly one of its younger advance-guard. Philological interest had hidden long from view the gems of thought and spirituality to be found in the mine of our ancient scriptures. Max Muller brought out a few of them and exhibited them to the public gaze, compelling attention to them by means of his authority as the foremost philologist. Deussen, unhampered by any philological leanings and possessing the training of a philosopher singularly well versed in the speculations of ancient Greece and modern Germany, took up the cue and plunged boldly into the metaphysical depths of the Upanishads, found them to be fully safe and satisfying, and then—equally boldly declared that fact before the whole world. Deussen is certainly the freest among scholars in the expression of his opinion about the Vedanta. He never stops to think about the "What they would say" of the vast majority of scholars. We indeed require bold men in this world to tell us bold words about truth; and nowhere is this more true now than in Europe where, through the fear of social opinion and such other causes, there has been enough in all conscience of the whitewashing and apologising attitude among scholars towards creeds and customs which, in all probability, not many among them really believe in. The greater is the glory, therefore, to Max Muller and to Deussen for their bold and open advocacy of truth! May they be as bold in showing to us our defects, the later corruptions in our thought-systems in India, especially in their application to our social needs! Just now we very much require the help of such genuine friends as these to check the growing virulence of the disease,'very prevalent in India, of running either to the one extreme of slavish panegyrists who cling to every village superstition as the innermost essence of the Shastras, or to the other extreme of demoniacal denouncers who see no good in us and in our history, and will, if they can, at once dynamite all the social and spiritual organisations of our ancient land of religion and philosophy.

Hinduism And Sri Ramakrishna

Translated from the Bengali

By the word "Shastras" the Vedas without beginning or end are meant. In matters of religious duty the Vedas are the only capable authority.

The Puranas and other religious scriptures are all denoted by the word "Smriti". And their authority goes so far as they follow the Vedas and do not contradict them.

Truth is of two kinds: (1) that which is cognisable by the five ordinary senses of man, and by reasonings based thereon; (2) that which is cognisable by the subtle, supersensuous power of Yoga.

Knowledge acquired by the first means is called science; and knowledge acquired by the second is called the Vedas.

The whole body of supersensuous truths, having no beginning or end, and called by the name of the Vedas, is ever-existent. The Creator Himself is creating, preserving, and destroying the universe with the help of these truths.

The person in whom this supersensuous power is manifested is called a Rishi, and the supersensuous truths which he realises by this power are called the Vedas.

This Rishihood, this power of supersensuous perception of the Vedas, is real religion. And so long as this does not develop in the life of an initiate, so long is religion a mere empty word to him, and it is to be understood that he has not taken yet the first step in religion.

The authority of the Vedas extends to all ages, climes and persons; that is to say, their application is not confined to any particular place, time, and persons.

The Vedas are the only exponent of the universal religion.

Although the supersensuous vision of truths is to be met with in some measure in our Puranas and Itihasas and in the religious scriptures of other races, still the fourfold scripture known among the Aryan race as the Vedas being the first, the most complete, and the most undistorted collection of spiritual truths, deserve to occupy the highest place among all scriptures, command the respect of all nations of the earth, and furnish the rationale of all their respective scriptures.

With regard to the whole Vedic collection of truths discovered by the Aryan race, this also has to be understood that those portions alone which do not refer to purely secular matters and which do not merely record tradition or history, or merely provide incentives to duty, form the Vedas in the real sense.

The Vedas are divided into two portions, the Jnana Kanda (knowledge-portion) and the Karma Kanda (ritual-portion). The ceremonies and the fruits of the Karma Kanda are confined within the limits of the world of Maya, and, therefore, they have been undergoing and will undergo transformation according to the law of change which operates through time, space, and personality.

Social laws and customs likewise, being based on this Karma Kanda, have been changing and will continue to change hereafter. Minor social usages also will be recognised and accepted when they are compatible with the spirit of the true scriptures and the conduct and example of holy sages. But blind allegiance only to usages such as are repugnant to the spirit of the Shastras and the conduct of holy sages has been one of the main causes of the downfall of the Aryan race.

It is the Jnana Kanda or the Vedanta only that has for all time commanded recognition for leading men across Maya and bestowing salvation on them through the practice of Yoga, Bhakti, Jnana, or selfless work; and as its validity and authority remain unaffected by any limitations of time, place or persons, it is the only exponent of the universal and eternal religion for all mankind.

The Samhitas of Manu and other sages, following the lines laid down, in the Karma Kanda, have mainly ordained rules of conduct conducive to social welfare, according to the exigencies of time, place, and persons. The Puranas etc., have taken up the truths embedded in the Vedanta and have explained them in detail in the course of describing the exalted life and deeds of Avataras and others. They have each emphasised, besides, some out of the infinite aspects of the Divine Lord to teach men about them.

But when by the process of time, fallen from the true ideals and rules of conduct and devoid of the spirit of renunciation, addicted only to blind usages, and degraded in intellect, the descendants of the Aryans failed to appreciate even the spirit of these Puranas etc., which taught men of ordinary intelligence the abstruse truths of the Vedanta in concrete form and diffuse language and appeared antagonistic to one another on the surface, because of each inculcating with special emphasis only particular aspects of the spiritual ideal—

And when, as a consequence, they reduced India, the fair land of religion, to a scene of almost infernal confusion by breaking up piecemeal the one Eternal Religion of the Vedas (Sanatana Dharma), the grand synthesis of all the aspects of the spiritual ideal, into conflicting sects and by seeking to sacrifice one another in the flames of sectarian hatred and intolerance—

Then it was that Sri Bhagvan Ramakrishna incarnated himself in India, to demonstrate what the true religion of the

Aryan race is; to show where amidst all its many divisions and offshoots, scattered over the land in the course of its immemorial history, lies the true unity of the Hindu religion, which by its overwhelming number of sects discordant to superficial view, quarrelling constantly with each other and abounding in customs divergent in every way, has constituted itself a misleading enigma for our countrymen and the butt of contempt for foreigners; and above all, to hold up before men, for their lasting welfare, as a living embodiment of the Sanatana Dharma, his own wonderful life into which he infused the universal spirit and character of this Dharma, so long cast into oblivion by the process of time.

In order to show how the Vedic truths—eternally existent as the instrument with the Creator in His work of creation, preservation, and dissolution—reveal themselves spontaneously in the minds of the Rishis purified from all impressions of worldly attachment, and because such verification and confirmation of the scriptural truths will help the revival, reinstatement, and spread of religion—the Lord, though the very embodiment of the Vedas, in this His new incarnation has thoroughly discarded all external forms of learning.

That the Lord incarnates again and again in human form for the protection of the Vedas or the true religion, and of Brahminhood or the ministry of that religion—is a doctrine well established in the Puranas etc.

The waters of a river falling in a cataract acquire greater velocity, the rising wave after a hollow swells higher; so after every spell of decline, the Aryan society recovering from all the evils by the merciful dispensation of Providence has risen the more glorious and powerful—such is the testimony of history.

After rising from every fall, our revived society is expressing more and more its innate eternal perfection, and so also the omnipresent Lord in each successive incarnation is manifesting Himself more and more. Again and again has our country fallen into a swoon, as it were, and again and again has India's Lord, by the manifestation of Himself, revivified her.

But greater than the present deep dismal night, now almost over, no pall of darkness had ever before enveloped this holy land of ours. And compared with the depth of this fall, all previous falls appear like little hoof-marks.

Therefore, before the effulgence of this new awakening, the glory of all past revivals in her history will pale like stars before the rising sun; and compared with this mighty manifestation of renewed strength, all the many past epochs of such restoration will be as child's play.

The various constituent ideals of the Religion Eternal, during its present state of decline, have been lying scattered here and there for want of competent men to realise them—some being preserved partially among small sects and some completely lost.

But strong in the strength of this new spiritual renaissance, men, after reorganising these scattered and disconnected spiritual ideals, will be able to comprehend and practise them in their own lives and also to recover from oblivion those that are lost. And as the sure pledge of this glorious future, the all-merciful Lord has manifested in the present age, as stated above, an incarnation which in point of completeness in revelation, its synthetic harmonising of all ideals, and its promoting of every sphere of spiritual culture, surpasses the manifestations of all past ages.

So at the very dawn of this momentous epoch, the reconciliation of all aspects and ideals of religious thought and worship is being proclaimed; this boundless, all-embracing idea had been lying inherent, but so long concealed, in the Religion Eternal and its scriptures, and now rediscovered, it is being declared to humanity in a trumpet voice.

This epochal new dispensation is the harbinger of great good to the whole world, specially to India; and the inspirer of this dispensation, Sri Bhagvan Ramakrishna, is the reformed and remodelled manifestation of all the past great epoch-makers in religion. O man, have faith in this, and lay it to heart.

The dead never return; the past night does not reappear; a spent-up tidal wave does not rise anew; neither does Man inhabit the same body over again. So from the worship of the dead past, O man, we invite you to the worship of the living present; from the regretful brooding over bygones, we invite you to the activities of the present; from the waste of energy in retracing lost and demolished pathways, we call you back to broad new-laid highways lying very near. He that is wise, let him understand.

Of that power, which at the very first impulse has roused distant echoes from all the four quarters of the globe, conceive in your mind the manifestation in its fullness; and discarding all idle misgivings, weaknesses, and the jealousies characteristic of enslaved peoples, come and help in the turning of this mighty wheel of new dispensation!

With the conviction firmly rooted in your heart that you are the servants of the Lord, His children, helpers in the fulfilment of His purpose, enter the arena of work.

Sri Ramakrishna: The Significance Of His Life And Teachings

In a narrow society there is depth and intensity of spirituality. The narrow stream is very rapid. In a catholic society, along with the breadth of vision we find a proportionate loss in depth and intensity. But the life of Sri Ramakrishna upsets all records of history. It is a remarkable phenomenon that in Sri Ramakrishna there has been an assemblage of ideas deeper than the sea and vaster than the skies.

We must interpret the Vedas in the light of the experience of Sri Ramakrishna. Shankaracharya and all other commentators made the tremendous mistake to think that the whole of the Vedas spoke the same truth. Therefore, they were guilty of torturing those of the apparently conflicting Vedic texts which go against their own doctrines, into the meaning of their particular schools. As, in the olden times, it was the Lord alone, the deliverer of the *Gita*, who partially harmonised these apparently conflicting statements, so with a view to completely settling this dispute, immensely magnified in the process of time, He Himself has come as Sri Ramakrishna. Therefore, no one can truly understand the Vedas and Vedanta, unless one studies them in the light of the utterances of Sri Ramakrishna who first exemplified in his life and taught that these scriptural statements which appear to the cursory view as contradictory, are meant for different grades of aspirants and are arranged in the order of evolution. The whole world will undoubtedly forget its fights and disputes and be united in a fraternal tie in religious and other matters as a consequence of these teachings.

If there is anything which Sri Ramakrishna has urged us to give up as carefully as lust and wealth, it is the limiting of the infinitude of God by circumscribing it within narrow bounds. Whoever, therefore, will try to limit the infinite ideals of Sri Ramakrishna in that way, will go against him and be his enemy.

One of his own utterances is that those who have seen the chameleon only once, know only one colour of the animal, but those who have lived under the tree, know all the colours that it puts on. For this reason, no saying of Sri Ramakrishna can be accepted as authentic, unless it is verified by those who constantly lived with him and whom he brought up to fulfil his life's mission.

Such a unique personality, such a synthesis of the utmost of Jnana, Yoga, Bhakti and Karma, has never before appeared among mankind. The life of Sri Ramakrishna proves that the greatest breadth, the highest catholicity and the utmost intensity can exist side by side in the same individual, and that society also can be constructed like that, for society is nothing but an aggregate of individuals.

He is the true disciple and follower of Sri Ramakrishna, whose character is perfect and all-sided like this. The formation of such a perfect character is the ideal of this age, and everyone should strive for that alone.

On Sri Ramakrishna And His Views

By force, think of one thing at least as Brahman. Of course it is easier to think of Ramakrishna as God, but the danger is that we cannot form Ishvara Buddhi (Vision of Divinity) in others. God is eternal, without any form, omnipresent. To think of Him as possessing any form is blasphemy. But the secret of image-worship is that you are trying to develop your vision of Divinity in one thing.

Sri Ramakrishna used to consider himself as an Incarnation in the ordinary sense of the term, though I could not understand it. I used to say that he was Brahman in the Vedantic sense; but just before his passing away, when he was suffering from the characteristic difficulty in breathing, he said to me as I was cogitating in my mind whether he could even in that pain say that he was an Incarnation, "He who was Rama and Krishna has now actually become Ramakrishna—but not in your Vedantic sense!" He used to love me intensely, which made many quite jealous of me. He knew one's character by sight, and never changed his opinion. He could perceive, as it were, supersensual things, while we try to know one's character by reason, with the result that our judgments are often fallacious. He called some persons his Antarangas or "belonging to the inner circle", and he used to teach them the secrets of his own nature and those of Yoga. To the outsiders or Bahirangas he taught those parables now known as "Sayings". He used to prepare those young men (the former class) for his work, and though many complained to him about them, he paid no heed. I may have perhaps a better opinion of a Bahiranga than an Antaranga through his actions, but I have a superstitious regard for the latter. "Love me, love my dog", as they say. I love that Brahmin priest intensely, and, therefore, love whatever he used to love, whatever he used to regard! He was afraid about me that I might create a sect, if left to myself.

He used to say to some, "You will not attain spirituality in this life." He sensed everything, and this will explain his apparent partiality to some. He, as a scientist, used to see that different people required different treatment. None except those of the "inner circle" were allowed to sleep in his room. It is not true that those who have not seen him will not attain salvation; neither is it true that a man who has seen him thrice will attain Mukti (liberation).

Devotion as taught by Narada, he used to preach to the masses, those who were incapable of any higher training.

He used generally to teach dualism. As a rule, he never taught Advaitism. But he taught it to me. I had been a dualist before.

Sri Ramakrishna: The Nation's Ideal

In order that a nation may rise, it must have a high ideal. Now, that ideal is, of course, the abstract Brahman. But as you all cannot be inspired by an abstract ideal, you must have a personal ideal. You have got that, in the person of Sri Ramakrishna. The reason why other personages cannot be our ideal now is, that their days are gone; and in order that Vedanta may come to everyone, there must be a person who is in sympathy with the present generation. This is fulfilled in Sri Ramakrishna. So now you should place him before everyone. Whether one accepts him as a Sadhu or an Avatara does not matter.

He said he would come once more with us. Then, I think, he will embrace Videha Mukti (absolute emancipation). If you wish to work, you must have such an Ishta Devata, or Guardian Angel, as the Christian nations call it. I sometimes imagine that different nations have different Ishta Devatas, and these are each trying for supremacy. Sometimes I fancy, such an Ishta Devata becomes powerless to do service to a nation.

Sri Ramakrishna's Disciple

*Mrs. Edith Allan described a teacher-student exchange in one of Swami Vivekananda's San Francisco classes**

Swami Vivekananda: I am the disciple of a man who could not write his own name, and I am not worthy to undo his shoes. How often have I wished I could take my intellect and throw it into the Ganges!

Student: But, Swami, that is the part of you I like best.

Swami Vivekananda: That is because you are a fool, Madam—like I am.

---

* *New Discoveries*, Vol. 6, p. 12.

The Soul And God

Delivered in San Francisco, 23 March 1900

Whether it was fear or mere inquisitiveness which first led man to think of powers superior to himself, we need not discuss. These raised in the mind peculiar worship tendencies, and so on. There never have been times in the history of mankind without some ideal of worship. Why? What makes us all struggle for something beyond what we see—whether it be a beautiful morning or a fear of dead spirits? We need not go back into prehistoric times, for it is a fact present today as it was two thousand years ago. We do not find satisfaction here. Whatever our station in life—even if we are powerful and wealthy—we cannot find satisfaction.

Desire is infinite. Its fulfilment is very limited. There is no end to our desires; but when we go to fulfil them, the difficulty comes. It has been so with the most primitive minds, when their desires were few. Even these could not be accomplished. Now, with our arts and sciences improved and multiplied, our desires cannot be fulfilled either. On the other hand, we are struggling to perfect means for the fulfilment of desires, and the desires are increasing.

The most primitive man naturally wanted help from outside for things which he could not accomplish. He desired something, and it could not be obtained. He wanted help from other powers. The most ignorant and primitive man and the most cultivated man today, each appealing to God and asking for the fulfilment of some desire, are exactly the same. What difference? Some people find a great deal of difference. We are always finding much difference in things when there is no difference at all. Both the primitive man and the cultivated man plead to the same power. You may call it God or Allah or Jehovah. Human beings want something and cannot get it by their own powers, and are after someone who will help them. This is primitive, and it is still present with us. We are all born savages and gradually civilise ourselves. All of us here, if we search, will find the same fact. Even now this fear does not leave us. We may talk big, become philosophers and all that; but when the blow comes, we find that we must beg for help. We believe in all the superstitions that ever existed. But there is no superstition in the world that does not have some basis of truth. If I cover my face and only the tip of my nose is showing, still it is a bit of my face. So with the superstitions—the little bits are true.

You see, the lowest sort of manifestation of religion came with the burial of the departed. First they wrapped them up and put them in mounds, and the spirits of the departed came and lived in the mounds, at night. Then they began to bury them. At the gate stands a terrible goddess with a thousand teeth. Then came the burning of the body and the flames bore the spirit up. The Egyptians brought food and water for the departed.

The next great idea was that of the tribal gods. This tribe had one god and that tribe another. The Jews had their God Jehovah, who was their own tribal god and fought against all the other gods and tribes. That god would do anything to please his own people. If he killed a whole tribe not protected by him, that was all right, quite good. A little love was given, but that love was confined to a small section.

Gradually, higher ideals came. The chief of the conquering tribe was the Chief of chiefs, God of gods.

So with the Persians when they conquered Egypt. The Persian emperor was the Lord of lords, and before the emperor nobody could stand. Death was the penalty for anyone who looked at the Persian emperor.

Then came the ideal of God Almighty and All-powerful, the omnipotent, omniscient Ruler of the universe: He lives in heaven, and Man pays special tribute to his Most Beloved, who creates everything for man. The whole world is for man. The sun and moon and stars are for him. All who have those ideas are primitive men, not civilised and not cultivated at all. All the superior religions had their growth between the Ganga and the Euphrates—outside of India we will find no further development of religion beyond this idea of God in heaven. That was the highest knowledge ever obtained outside of India. There is the local heaven where he is and where the faithful shall go when they die. As far as I have seen, we should call it a very primitive idea. Mumbo jumbo in Africa and God in heaven—the same. He moves the world, and of course his will is being done everywhere.

The old Hebrew people did not care for any heaven. That is one of the reasons they opposed Jesus of Nazareth—because he taught life after death. Paradise in Sanskrit means land beyond this life. So the paradise was to make up for all this evil. The primitive man does not care about evil. He never questions why there should be any.

The word "devil" is a Persian word. The Persians and Hindus share the Aryan ancestry upon religious grounds, and they spoke the same language, only the words one sect uses for good the other uses for bad. The word "Deva" is an old Sanskrit word for God, the same word in the Aryan languages. Here the word means the devil.

Later on, when Man developed his inner life, he began to question, and to say that God is good. The Persians said that there were two gods—one was bad and one was good. Their idea was that everything in this life was good: beautiful country, where there was spring almost the whole year round and nobody died; there was no disease, everything was fine. Then came this Wicked One, and he touched the land, and then came death and disease and mosquitoes and tigers and lions. Then the Aryans left their fatherland and migrated southward. The old Aryans must have lived way to the north. The Jews learnt it the idea of the devil from the Persians. The Persians also taught that there will come a day when this wicked god will be killed, and it is our duty to stay with the good god and add our force to him in this eternal struggle between him and the wicked one. The whole world will be burnt out and everyone will get a new body.

The Persian idea was that even the wicked will be purified and not be bad any more. The nature of the Aryan was love and poetry. They cannot think of their being burnt for eternity. They will all receive new bodies. Then no more death. So that is the best about religious ideas outside of India.

Along with that is the ethical strain. All that Man has to do is to take care of three things: good thought, good word, good deed. That is all. It is a practical, wise religion. Already there has come a little poetry in it. But there is higher poetry and higher thought.

In India we see this Satan in the most ancient part of the Vedas. He just appears and immediately disappears. In the Vedas the bad god got a blow and disappeared. He is gone, and the Persians took him. We are trying to make him leave the world altogether. Taking the Persian idea, we are going to make a decent gentleman of him; give him a new body. There was the end of the Satan idea in India.

But the idea of God went on; but mind you, here comes another fact. The idea of God grew side by side with the idea of materialism until you have traced it up to the emperor of Persia. But on the other hand comes in metaphysics, philosophy. There is another line of thought, the idea of the non-dual Atman, man's own soul. That also grows. So, outside of India ideas about God had to remain in that concrete form until India came to help them out a bit. The other nations stopped with that old concrete idea. In this country, America, there are millions who believe that God is [has?] a body. Whole sects say it. They believe that He rules the world, but there is a place where He has a body. He sits upon a throne. They light candles and sing songs just as they do in our temples.

But in India they are sensible enough never to make their God a physical being. You never see in India a temple of Brahma. Why? Because the idea of the soul always existed. The Hebrew race never questioned about the soul. There is no soul idea in the Old Testament at all. The first is in the New Testament. The Persians, they became so practical—wonderfully practical people—a fighting, conquering race. They were the English people of the old time, always fighting and destroying their neighbours—too much engaged in that sort of thing to think about the soul.

The oldest idea of the soul was that of a fine body inside this gross one. The gross one disappears and the fine one appears. In Egypt that fine one also dies, and as soon as the gross body disintegrates, the fine one also disintegrates. That is why they built those pyramids and embalmed the dead bodies of their ancestors, thus hoping to secure immortality for the departed.

The Indian people have no regard for the dead body at all. Their attitude is: "Let us take it and burn it." The son has to set fire to his father's body.

There are two sorts of races, the divine and the demonic. The divine think that they are soul and spirit. The demonic think that they are bodies. The old Indian philosophers tried to insist that the body is nothing. "As a man emits his old garment and takes a new one, even so the old body is shed and he takes a new one." In my case, all my surroundings and education were trying to make me the other way. I was always associated with Mohammedans and Christians, who take more care of the body.

It is only one step from the body to the spirit. In India they became insistent on this ideal of the soul. It became synonymous with the idea of God. If the idea of the soul begins to expand, Man must arrive at the conclusion that it is beyond name and form, The Indian idea is that the soul is formless. Whatever is form must break some time or other. There cannot be any form unless it is the result of force and matter; and all combinations must dissolve. If such is the case, if your soul is made of name and form, it disintegrates, and you die, and you are no more immortal. If it is double, it has form and it belongs to nature and it obeys nature's laws of birth and death. They find that this soul is not the mind neither a double.

Thoughts can be guided and controlled. The Yogis of India practised to see how far the thoughts can be guided and controlled. By dint of hard work, thoughts may be silenced altogether. If thoughts were the real man, as soon as thought ceases, he ought to die. Thought ceases in meditation; even the mind's elements are quite quiet. Blood circulation stops. His breath stops, but he is not dead. If thought were he, the whole thing ought to go, but they find it does not go. That is practical proof. They came to the conclusion that even mind and thought were not the real man. Then speculation showed that it could not be.

I come, I think and talk. In the midst of all this activity is this unity of the Self. My thought and action are varied, manifold but in and through them runs that one unchangeable One. It cannot be the body. That is changing every minute. It cannot be the mind; new and fresh thoughts come all the time. It is neither the body nor the mind. Both body and mind belong to nature and must obey nature's laws. A free mind never will.

Now, therefore, this real man does not belong to nature. It is the person whose mind and body belong to nature. So much of nature we are using. Just as you come to use the pen and ink and chair, so he uses so much of nature in fine and in gross form; gross form, the body, and fine form, the mind. If it is simple, it must be formless. In nature alone are forms. That which is not of nature cannot have any forms, fine or gross. It must be formless. It must be omnipresent. Understand this. Take this glass on the table. The glass is form and the table is form. So much of the glass-ness goes off, so much of table-ness when they break.

The soul is nameless because it is formless. It will neither go to heaven nor to hell any more than it will enter this glass. It takes the form of the vessel it fills. If it is not in space, either of two things is possible. Either the soul permeates space or space is in it. You are in space and must have a form. Space limits us, binds us, and makes a form of us. If you are not in space, space is in you. All the heavens and the world are in the person.

So it must be with God. God is omnipresent. "Without hands he grasps everything; without feet he can move."* He is the formless, the deathless, the eternal. The idea of God came. He is the Lord of souls, just as my soul is the lord of my body. If my soul left the body, the body would not be for a moment. If He left my soul, the soul would not exist. He is the creator of the universe; of everything that dies He is the destroyer. His shadow is death; His shadow is life.

The ancient Indian philosophers thought: This filthy world is not fit for man's attention. There is nothing in the universe that is permanent—neither good nor evil.

I told you Satan did not have much chance in India. Why? Because they were very bold in religion. They were not babies. Have you seen that characteristic of children? They

---

* *Shvetashvatara Upanishad*, 111.19.

are always trying to throw the blame on someone else. Baby minds are trying, when they make a mistake, to throw the blame upon someone else. On the one hand, we say, "Give me this; give me that." On the other hand, we say, "I did not do this; the devil tempted me. The devil did it." That is the history of mankind, weak mankind.

Why is evil? Why is the world the filthy, dirty hole? We have made it. Nobody is to blame. We put our hand in the fire. The Lord bless us, Man gets just what he deserves. Only He is merciful. If we pray to Him, He helps us. He gives Himself to us.

That is their idea. They are of a poetic nature. They go crazy over poetry. Their philosophy is poetry. This philosophy is a poem. All high thought in the Sanskrit is written in poetry. Metaphysics, astronomy—all in poetry.

We are responsible, and how do we come to mischief? You may say, "I was born poor and miserable. I remember the hard struggle all my life." Philosophers say that you are to blame. You do not mean to say that all this sprang up without any cause whatever? You are a rational being. Your life is not without cause, and you are the cause. You manufacture your own life all the time. You make and mould your own life. You are responsible for yourself. Do not lay the blame upon anybody, any Satan. You will only get punished a little more.

A man is brought up before God, and He says, "Thirty-one stripes for you," when comes another man. He says, "Thirty stripes: fifteen for that fellow, and fifteen for the teacher—that awful man who taught him." That is the awful thing in teaching. I do not know what I am going to get. I go all over the world. If I have to get fifteen for each one I have taught!

We have to come to this idea: "This My Maya is divine." It is My activity, My divinity. "My Maya is hard to cross, but those that take refuge in me go beyond Maya." But you find out that it is very difficult to cross this ocean of Maya by yourself. You cannot. It is the old question—hen and egg.

If you do any work, that work becomes the cause and produces the effect. That effect again becomes the cause and produces the effect. And so on. If you push this down, it never stops. Once you set a thing in motion, there is no more stopping. I do some work, good or bad, and it sets up a chain reaction, I cannot stop now.

It is impossible for us to get out from this bondage by ourselves. It is only possible if there is someone more powerful than this law of causation, and if he takes mercy on us and drags us out.

And we declare that there is such a one—God. There is such a being, all merciful. If there is a God, then it is possible for me to be saved. How can you be saved by your own will? Do you see the philosophy of the doctrine of salvation by grace? You Western people are wonderfully clever, but when you undertake to explain philosophy, you are so wonderfully complicated. How can you save yourself by work, if by salvation you mean that you will be taken out of all this nature? Salvation means just standing upon God, but if you understand what is meant by salvation, then you are the Self. You are not nature. You are the only thing outside of souls and gods and nature. These are the external existences, and God is inter-penetrating both nature and soul.

Therefore, just as my soul is to my body, we, as it were, are the bodies of God. God-souls-nature—it is one. The One, because, as I say, I mean the body, soul, and mind. But, we have seen, the law of causation pervades every bit of nature, and once you have got caught you cannot get out. When once you get into the meshes of law, a possible way of escape is not through work done by you. You can build hospitals for every fly and flea that ever lived. All this you may do, but it would never lead to salvation.

Hospitals go up and they come down again. Salvation is only possible if there is some being whom nature never caught, who is the Ruler of nature. He rules nature instead of being ruled by nature. He wills law instead of being downed by law. He exists and he is all merciful. The moment you seek Him He will save you.

Why has He not taken us out? You do not want Him. You want everything but Him. The moment you want Him, that moment you get Him. We never want Him. We say, "Lord, give me a fine house." We want the house, not Him. "Give me health! Save me from this difficulty!" When a man wants nothing but Him, he gets Him. "The same love which wealthy men have for gold and silver and possessions, Lord, may I have the same love for Thee. I want neither earth nor heaven, nor beauty nor learning. I do not want salvation. Let me go to hell again and again. But one thing I want: to love Thee, and for love's sake—not even for heaven."

Whatever Man desires, he gets. If you always dream of having a body, you will get another body. When this body goes away he wants another, and goes on begetting body after body. Love matter and you become matter. You first become animals. When I see a dog gnawing a bone, I say, "Lord help us!" Love body until you become dogs and cats! Still degenerate, until you become minerals—all body and nothing else.

There are other people, who would have no compromise. The road to salvation is through truth. That was another watchword.

Man began to progress spiritually when he kicked the devil out. He stood up and took the responsibility of the misery of the world upon his own shoulders. But whenever he looked at the past and future and at the law of causation, he knelt down and said, "Lord, save me, thou who art our creator, our father, and dearest friend." That is poetry, but not very good poetry, I think. Why not? It is the painting of the Infinite no doubt. You have it in every language how they paint the Infinite. But it is the infinite of the senses, of the muscles.

"Him the sun does not illumine, nor the moon, nor the stars, nor the flash of lightning."* That is another painting of the Infinite, by negative language. And the last Infinite is painted in the spirituality of the Upanishads. Not only is Vedanta the highest philosophy in the world, but it is the greatest poem.

Mark today, this is the difference between the first part of the Vedas and the second. In the first, it is all in the domain of sense. But all religions are only concerned with the infinite of the external world—nature and nature's God. Not so Vedanta. This is the first light that the human mind throws back of all that. No satisfaction comes of the infinite in space. "The Self-existent One has created the senses as turned to the outer world. Those, therefore, who seek outside will never find that which is within. There are the few who, wanting to know the truth, turn their eyes inward and in their own souls behold the glory of the Self."**

It is not the infinite of space, but the real Infinite, beyond space, beyond time. Such is the world missed by the Occident. Their minds have been turned to external nature and nature's God. Look within yourself and find the truth that you had forgotten. Is it possible for mind to come out of this dream without the help of the gods? Once you start the action, there is no help unless the merciful Father takes us out.

That would not be freedom, even at the hands of the merciful God. Slavery is slavery. The chain of gold is quite as bad as the chain of iron. Is there a way out?

You are not bound. No one was ever bound. The Self is beyond. It is the all. You are the One; there are no two. God was your own reflection cast upon the screen of Maya. The real God is the Self. He whom Man ignorantly worships is that reflection. They say that the Father in heaven is God.

---

* *Katha Upanishad,* II.ii.15.

** *Katha Upanishad,* II.i.1.

Why God? It is because He is your own reflection that He is God. Do you see how you are seeing God all the time? As you unfold yourself, the reflection grows clearer.

"Two beautiful birds are there sitting upon the same tree. The one is calm, silent, majestic; the one below the individual self, is eating the fruits, sweet and bitter, and becoming happy and sad. But when the individual self beholds the worshipful Lord as his own true Self, he grieves no more."*

Do not say "God". Do not say "Thou". Say "I". The Language of non-dualism says, "God, Thou, my Father." The language of non-dualism says, "Dearer unto me than I am myself. I would have no name for Thee. The nearest I can use is I.

"God is true. The universe is a dream. Blessed am I that I know this moment that I have been and] shall be free all eternity; that I know that I am worshipping only myself; that no nature, no delusion, had any hold on me. Vanish nature from me, vanish these gods; vanish worship; vanish superstitions, for I know myself. I am the Infinite. All these—Mrs. So-and-so, Mr. So-and-so, responsibility, happiness, misery—have vanished. I am the Infinite. How can there be death for me, or birth? Whom shall I fear? I am the One. Shall I be afraid of myself? Who is to be afraid of whom? I am the one Existence. Nothing else exists. I am everything."

It is only the question of memory, of your true nature, not salvation by work. Do you *get* salvation? You are already free.

Go on saying, "I am free." Never mind if the next moment delusion comes and says, "I am bound." De-hypnotise the whole thing.

This truth is first to be heard. Hear it first. Think on it day and night. Fill the mind with it day and night: "I am It. I am the Lord of the universe. Never was there any delusion." Meditate upon it with all the strength of the mind

---

* *Mundaka Upanishad,* III.i.1-2.

till you actually see these walls, houses, everything, melt away—until body, everything, vanishes. "I will stand alone. I am the One." Struggle on! "Who cares! We want to be free; [we] do not want any powers. Worlds we renounce; heavens we renounce; hells we renounce. What do I care about all these powers, and this and that! What do I care if the mind is controlled or uncontrolled! Let it run on. What of that! I am not the mind, Let it go on!"

The sun shines on the just and on the unjust. Is he touched by the defective character of anyone? "I am He. Whatever [my] mind does, I am not touched. The sun is not touched by shining on filthy places, I am Existence."

This is the religion of non-dual philosophy. It is difficult. Struggle on! Down with all superstitions! Neither teachers nor scriptures nor gods exist. Down with temples, with priests, with gods, with incarnations, with God himself? I am all the God that ever existed! There, stand up philosophers! No fear! Speak no more of God and the superstition of the world. Truth alone triumphs, and this is true. I am the Infinite.

All religious superstitions are vain imaginations. This society, that I see you before me, and that I am talking to you—this is all superstition; all must be given up. Just see what it takes to become a philosopher! This is the path of Jnana Yoga, the way through knowledge. The other paths are easy, slow, but this is pure strength of mind. No weakling can follow this path of knowledge. You must be able to say: "I am the Soul, the ever free; I never was bound. Time is in me, not I in time. God was born in my mind. God the Father, Father of the universe—he is created by me in my own mind."

Do you call yourselves philosophers? Show it! Think of this, talk of this, and help each other in this path, and give up all superstition!

Steps To Realisation

A class-lecture delivered in America

First among the qualifications required of the aspirant for Jnana, or wisdom, come Shama and Dama, which may be taken together. They mean the keeping of the organs in their own centres without allowing them to stray out. I shall explain to you first what the word "organ" means. Here are the eyes; the eyes are not the organs of vision but only the instruments. Unless the organs also are present, I cannot see, even if I have eyes. But, given both the organs and the instruments, unless the mind attaches itself to these two, no vision takes place. So, in each act of perception, three things are necessary—first, the external instruments, then, the internal organs, and lastly, the mind. If any one of them be absent, then there will be no perception. Thus the mind acts through two agencies—one external, and the other internal. When I see things, my mind goes out, becomes externalised; but suppose I close my eyes and begin to think, the mind does not go out, it is internally active. But, in either case, there is activity of the organs. When I look at you and speak to you, both the organs and the instruments are active. When I close my eyes and begin to think, the organs are active, but not the instruments. Without the activity of these organs, there will be no thought. You will find that none of you can think without some symbol. In the case of the blind man, he has also to think through some figure. The organs of sight and hearing are generally very active.

You must bear in mind that by the word "organ" is meant the nerve centre in the brain. The eyes and ears are only the instruments of seeing and hearing, and the organs are inside. If the organs are destroyed by any means, even if the eyes or the ears be there, we shall not see or hear. So in order to control the mind, we must first be able to control these organs. To restrain the mind from wandering outward or inward, and keep the organs in their respective centres, is what is meant by the words "Shama" and "Dama". Shama consists in not allowing the mind to externalise, and Dama, in checking the external instruments.

Now comes Uparati which consists in not thinking of things of the senses. Most of our time is spent in thinking about sense-objects, things which we have seen, or we have heard, which we shall see or shall hear, things which we have eaten, or are eating, or shall eat, places where we have lived, and so on. We think of them or talk of them most of our time. One who wishes to be a Vedantin must give up this habit.

Then comes the next preparation (it is a hard task to be a philosopher!), Titiksha, the most difficult of all. It is nothing less than the ideal forbearance—"Resist not evil." This requires a little explanation. We may not resist an evil, but at the same time we may feel very miserable. A man may say very harsh things to me, and I may not outwardly hate him for it, may not answer him back, and may restrain myself from apparently getting angry, but anger and hatred may be in my mind, and I may feel very badly towards that man. That is not non-resistance; I should be without any feeling of hatred or anger, without any thought of resistance; my mind must then be as calm as if nothing had happened. And only when I have got to that state, have I attained to non-resistance, and not before. Forbearance of all misery, without even a thought of resisting or driving it out, without even any painful feeling in the mind, or any remorse—this is Titiksha. Suppose I do not resist, and some great evil comes thereby; if I have Titiksha, I should not feel any remorse for not having resisted. When the mind has attained to that state, it has become established in Titiksha. People in India do extraordinary things in order to practise this Titiksha. They bear tremendous heat and cold without caring, they do not even care for snow, because they take no thought for the body; it is left to itself, as if it were a foreign thing.

The next qualification required is Shraddha, faith. One must have tremendous faith in religion and God. Until one has it, one cannot aspire to be a Jnani. A great sage once told me that not one in twenty millions in this world believed in God. I asked him why, and he told me, "Suppose there is a thief in this room, and he gets to know that there is a mass of gold in the next room, and only a very thin partition between the two rooms; what will be the condition of that thief?" I answered, "He will not be able to sleep at all; his brain will be actively thinking of some means of getting at the gold, and he will think of nothing else." Then he replied, "Do you believe that a man could believe in God and not go mad to get him? If a man sincerely believes that there is that immense, infinite mine of Bliss, and that It can be reached, would not that man go mad in his struggle to reach it?" Strong faith in God and the consequent eagerness to reach Him constitute Shraddha.

Then comes Samadhana, or constant practice, to hold the mind in God. Nothing is done in a day. Religion cannot be swallowed in the form of a pill. It requires hard and constant practice. The mind can be conquered only by slow and steady practice.

Next is Mumukshutva, the intense desire to be free. Those of you who have read Edwin Arnold's *Light of Asia* remember his translation of the first sermon of Buddha, where Buddha says,

Ye suffer from yourselves. None else compels.

None other holds you that ye live and die,
And whirl upon the wheel, and hug and kiss
Its spokes of agony,
Its tire of tears, its nave of nothingness.

All the misery we have is of our own choosing; such is our nature. The old Chinaman, who having been kept in prison for sixty years was released on the coronation of a new emperor, exclaimed, when he came out, that he could not live; he must go back to his horrible dungeon among the rats and mice; he could not bear the light. So he asked them to kill him or send him back to the prison, and he was sent back. Exactly similar is the condition of all men. We run headlong after all sorts of misery, and are unwilling to be freed from them. Every day we run after pleasure, and before we reach it, we find it is gone, it has slipped through our fingers. Still we do not cease from our mad pursuit, but on and on we go, blinded fools that we are.

In some oil mills in India, bullocks are used that go round and round to grind the oil-seed. There is a yoke on the bullock's neck. They have a piece of wood protruding from the yoke, and on that is fastened a wisp of straw. The bullock is blindfolded in such a way that it can only look forward, and so it stretches its neck to get at the straw; and in doing so, it pushes the piece of wood out a little further; and it makes another attempt with the same result, and yet another, and so on. It never catches the straw, but goes round and round in the hope of getting it, and in so doing, grinds out the oil. In the same way you and I who are born slaves to nature, money and wealth, wives and children, are always chasing a wisp of straw, a mere chimera, and are going through an innumerable round of lives without obtaining what we seek. The great dream is love; we are all going to love and be loved, we are all going to be happy and never meet with misery, but the more we go towards happiness, the more it goes away from us. Thus the world is going on, society goes on, and we, blinded slaves, have to pay for it without knowing. Study your own lives, and find how little of happiness there is in them, and how little in truth you have gained in the course of this wild-goose chase of the world.

Do you remember the story of Solon and Croesus? The king said to the great sage that Asia Minor was a very happy place. And the sage asked him, "Who is the happiest man? I have not seen anyone very happy." "Nonsense," said Croesus, "I am the happiest man in the world." "Wait, Sir, till the end of your life; don't be in a hurry," replied the sage and' went away. In course of time that king was conquered by the Persians, and they ordered him to be burnt alive. The funeral pyre was prepared and when poor Croesus saw it, he cried aloud "Solon! Solon!" On being asked to whom he referred, he told his story, and the Persian emperor was touched, and saved his life.

Such is the life-story of each one of us; such is the tremendous power of nature over us. It repeatedly kicks us away, but still we pursue it with feverish excitement. We are always hoping against hope; this hope, this chimera maddens us; we are always hoping for happiness.

There was a great king in ancient India who was once asked four questions, of which one was: "What is the most wonderful thing in the world?" "Hope," was the answer. This is the most wonderful thing. Day and night we see people dying around us, and yet we think we shall not die; we never think that we shall die, or that we shall suffer. Each man thinks that success will be his, hoping against hope, against all odds, against all mathematical reasoning. Nobody is ever really happy here. If a man be wealthy and have plenty to eat, his digestion is out of order, and he cannot eat. If a man's digestion be good, and he have the digestive power of a cormorant, he has nothing to put into his mouth. If he be rich, he has no children. If he be hungry and poor, he has a whole regiment of children, and does not know what to do with them. Why is it so? Because happiness and misery are the obverse and reverse of the same coin; he who takes happiness, must take misery also.

We all have this foolish idea that we can have happiness without misery, and it has taken such possession of us that we have no control over the senses.

When I was in Boston, a young man came up to me, and gave me a scrap of paper of which he had written a name and address, followed by these words: "All the wealth and all the happiness of the world are yours, if you only know how to get them. If you come to me, I will teach you how to get them. Charge $5." He gave me this and said, "What do you think of this?" I said, "Young man, why don't you get the money to print this? You have not even enough money to get this printed!" He did not understand this. He was infatuated with the idea that he could get immense wealth and happiness without any trouble. There are two extremes into which men are running; one is extreme optimism, when everything is rosy and nice and good; the other, extreme pessimism, when everything seems to be against them. The majority of men have more or less undeveloped brains. One in a million we see with a well-developed brain; the rest either have peculiar idiosyncrasies, or are monomaniacs.

Naturally we run into extremes. When we are healthy and young, we think that all the wealth of the world will be ours, and when later we get kicked about by society like footballs and get older, we sit in a comer and croak and throw cold water on the enthusiasm of others. Few men know that with pleasure there is pain, and with pain, pleasure; and as pain is disgusting, so is pleasure, as it is the twin brother of pain. It is derogatory to the glory of man that he should be going after pain, and equally derogatory, that he should be going after pleasure. Both should be turned aside by men whose reason is balanced. Why will not men seek freedom from being played upon? This moment we are whipped, and when we begin to weep, nature gives us a dollar; again we are whipped, and when we weep, nature gives us a piece of gingerbread, and we begin to laugh again.

The sage wants liberty; he finds that sense-objects are all vain and that there is no end to pleasures and pains. How many rich people in the world want to find fresh pleasures! All pleasures are old, and they want new ones. Do you not see how many foolish things they are inventing every day, just to titillate the nerves for a moment, and that done, how there comes a reaction? The majority of people are just like a flock of sheep. If the leading sheep falls into a ditch, all the rest follow and break their necks. In the same way, what one leading member of a society does, all the others do, without thinking what they are doing. When a man begins to see the vanity of worldly things, he will feel he ought not to be thus played upon or borne along by nature. That is slavery. If a man has a few kind words said to him, he begins to smile, and when he hears a few harsh words, he begins to weep. He is a slave to a bit of bread, to a breath of air; a slave to dress, a slave to patriotism, to country, to name, and to fame. He is thus in the midst of slavery and the real man has become buried within, through his bondage. What you call Man is a slave. When one realises all this slavery, then comes the desire to be free; an intense desire comes. If a piece of burning charcoal be placed on a man's head, see how he struggles to throw it off. Similar will be the struggles for freedom of a man who really understands that he is a slave of nature.

We have now seen what Mumukshutva, or the desire to be free, is. The next training is also a very difficult one. Nityanitya Viveka—discriminating between that which is true and that which is untrue, between the eternal and the transitory. God alone is eternal, everything else is transitory. Everything dies; the angels die, men die, animals die, earths die, sun, moon, and stars, all die; everything undergoes constant change. The mountains of today were the oceans of yesterday and will be oceans tomorrow. Everything is in a state of flux. The whole universe is a mass of change. But there is One who never changes, and that is God; and the nearer we get to Him, the less will be the change for us, the less will nature be able to work on us; and when we reach Him, and stand with Him, we shall conquer nature, we shall be masters of these phenomena of nature, and they will have no effect on us.

You see, if we really have undergone the above discipline, we really do not require anything else in this world. All knowledge is within us. All perfection is there already in the soul. But this perfection has been covered up by nature; layer after layer of nature is covering this purity of the soul. What have we to do? Really we do not develop our souls at all. What can develop the perfect? We simply take the evil off; and the soul manifests itself in its pristine purity, its natural, innate freedom.

Now begins the inquiry: Why is this discipline so necessary? Because religion is not attained through the ears, nor through the eyes, nor yet through the brain. No scriptures can make us religious. We may study all the books that are in the world, yet we may not understand a word of religion or of God. We may talk all our lives and yet may not be the better for it; we may be the most intellectual people the world ever saw, and yet we may not come to God at all. On the other hand, have you not seen what irreligious men have been produced from the most intellectual training? It is one of the evils of your Western civilisation that you are after intellectual education alone, and take no care of the heart. It only makes men ten times more selfish, and that will be your destruction. When there is conflict between the heart and the brain, let the heart be followed, because intellect has only one state, reason, and within that, intellect works, and cannot get beyond. It is the heart which takes one to the highest plane, which intellect can never reach; it goes beyond intellect, and reaches to what is called inspiration.

Intellect can never become inspired; only the heart when it is enlightened, becomes inspired. An intellectual, heartless man never becomes an inspired man. It is always the heart that speaks in the Man of love; it discovers a greater instrument than intellect can give you, the instrument of inspiration. Just as the intellect is the instrument of knowledge, so is the heart the instrument of inspiration. In a lower state it is a much weaker instrument than intellect. An ignorant man knows nothing, but he is a little emotional by nature. Compare him with a great professor—what wonderful power the latter possesses! But the professor is bound by his intellect, and he can be a devil and an intellectual man at the same time; but the man of heart can never be a devil; no man with emotion was ever a devil. Properly cultivated, the heart can be changed, and will go beyond intellect; it will be changed into inspiration. Man will have to go beyond intellect in the end. The knowledge of man, his powers of perception, of reasoning and intellect and heart, all are busy churning this milk of the world. Out of long churning comes butter, and this butter is God. Men of heart get the "butter", and the "buttermilk" is left for the intellectual.

These are all preparations for the heart, for that love, for that intense sympathy appertaining to the heart. It is not at all necessary to be educated or learned to get to God. A sage once told me, "To kill others one must be equipped with swords and shields, but to commit suicide a needle is sufficient; so to teach others, much intellect and learning are necessary, but not so for your own self-illumination." Are you pure? If you are pure, you will reach God. "Blessed are the pure in heart, for they shall see God." If you are not pure, and you know all the sciences in the world, that will not help you at all; you may be buried in all the books you read, but that will not be of much use. It is the heart that reaches the goal. Follow the heart. A pure heart sees beyond the intellect; it gets inspired; it knows things that reason can never know, and whenever there is conflict between the pure heart and the intellect, always side with the pure heart, even if you think what your heart is doing is unreasonable. When it is desirous of doing good to others, your brain may tell you that it is not politic to do so, but follow your heart, and you will find that you make less mistakes than by following your intellect. The pure heart is the best mirror for the reflection of truth, so all these disciplines are for the purification of the heart. And as soon as it is pure, all truths flash upon it in a minute; all truth in the universe will manifest in your heart, if you are sufficiently pure.

The great truths about atoms, and the finer elements, and the fine perceptions of men, were discovered ages ago by men who never saw a telescope, or a microscope, or a laboratory. How did they know all these things? It was through the heart; they purified the heart. It is open to us to do the same today; it is the culture of the heart, really, and not that of the intellect that will lessen the misery of the world.

Intellect has been cultured with the result that hundreds of sciences have been discovered, and their effect has been that the few have made slaves of the many—that is all the good that has been done. Artificial wants have been created; and every poor man, whether he has money or not, desires to have those wants satisfied, and when he cannot, he struggles, and dies in the struggle. This is the result. Through the intellect is not the way to solve the problem of misery, but through the heart. If all this vast amount of effort had been spent in making men purer, gentler, more forbearing, this world would have a thousand-fold more happiness than it has today. Always cultivate the heart; through the heart the Lord speaks, and through the intellect you yourself speak.

You remember in the Old Testament where Moses was told, "Take off thy shoes from off thy feet, for the place whereon thou standest is holy ground." We must always approach the study of religion with that reverent attitude. He who comes with a pure heart and a reverent attitude, his heart will be opened; the doors will open for him, and he will see the truth.

If you come with intellect only, you can have a little intellectual gymnastics, intellectual theories, but not truth. Truth has such a face that any one who sees that face becomes convinced. The sun does not require any torch to show it; the sun is self-effulgent. If truth requires evidence, what will evidence that evidence? If something is necessary as witness for truth, where is the witness for that witness? We must approach religion with reverence and with love, and our heart will stand up and say, this is truth, and this is untruth.

The field of religion is beyond our senses, beyond even our consciousness. We cannot *sense* God. Nobody has seen God with his eyes or ever will see; nobody has God in his consciousness. I am not conscious of God, nor you, nor anybody. Where is God? Where is the field of religion? It is beyond the senses, beyond consciousness. Consciousness is only one of the many planes in which we work; you will have to transcend the field of consciousness, to go beyond the senses, approach nearer and nearer to your own centre, and as you do that, you will approach nearer and nearer to God. What is the proof of God? Direct perception, Pratyaksha. The proof of this wall is that I perceive it. God has been perceived that way by thousands before, and will be perceived by all who want to perceive Him. But this perception is no sense-perception at all; it is supersensuous, superconscious, and all this training is needed to take us beyond the senses. By means of all sorts of past work and bondages we are being dragged downwards; these preparations will make us pure and light. Bondages will fall off by themselves, and we shall be buoyed up beyond this plane of sense-perception to which we are tied down, and then we shall see, and hear, and feel things which men in the three ordinary states (viz. waking, dream, and sleep) neither feel, nor see, nor hear. Then we shall speak a strange language, as it were, and the world will not understand us, because it does not know anything but the senses. True religion is entirely transcendental. Every being that is in the universe has the potentiality of transcending the senses; even the little worm will one day transcend the senses and reach God. No life will be a failure; there is no such thing as failure in the universe. A hundred times Man will hurt himself, a thousand times he will tumble, but in the end he will realise that he is God. We know there is no progress in a straight line. Every soul moves, as it were, in a circle, and will have to complete it, and no soul can go so low but there will come a time when it will have to go upwards. No one will be lost. We are all projected from one common centre, which is God. The highest as well as the lowest life God ever projected, will come back to the Father of all lives. "From whom all beings are projected, in whom all live, and unto whom they all return; that is God."

On Sannyasa And Family Life

Talking of the respective duties of a monk and a householder, Swamiji said:

A Sannyasin should avoid the food, bedding, etc., which have been touched or used by householders, in order to save himself—not from hatred towards them—so long as he has not risen to the highest grade, that is, become a Paramahamsa. A householder should salute him with "Namo Narayanaya", and a Sannyasin should bless the former.

मेरुसर्षपयोर्यद्‌यत् सूर्यखद्योतयोरिव।
सरित्सागरयोर्यद्‌यत् यथा भिक्षुगृहस्थयोः।।

—Like the difference between the biggest mountain and a mustard seed, between the sun and a glow-worm, between the ocean and a streamlet, is the wide gulf between a Sannyasin and a householder.

Swami Vivekananda made everyone utter this and, chanting some Vedanta stanzas, said, "You should always repeat to yourselves these Shlokas. 'Shravana' not only means hearing from the Guru, but also repetition to our own selves. आवृत्तिरसकृदुपदेशात्—Scriptural truth should be often repeated for such has been repeatedly enjoined'—In this Sutra of Vedanta, Vyasa lays stress on repetition."

On Mantra And Mantra Chaitanya

The Mantra Shastris (upholders of the Mantra theory) believe that some words have been handed down through a succession of teachers and disciples, and the mere utterance of them will lead to some form of realisation. There are different meanings of the words "Mantra Chaitanya". According to some, if you practise the repetition of a certain Mantra, you will see the Ishta Devata who is the object or deity of that Mantra. But according to others, the word means that if you practise the repetition of a certain Mantra received from a Guru not competent, you will have to perform certain ceremonials by which that Mantra will become Chetana or living, and then its repetition will be successful. Different Mantras, when they are thus "living", show different signs, but the general sign is that one will be able to repeat it for a long time without feeling any strain and that his mind will very soon be concentrated. This is about the Tantrika Mantras.

From the time of the Vedas, two different opinions have been held about Mantras. Yaska and others say that the Vedas have meanings, but the ancient Mantra Shastris say that they have no meaning, and that their use consists only in uttering them in connection with certain sacrifices, when they will surely produce effect in the form of various material enjoyments or spiritual knowledge. The latter arises from the utterance of the Upanishads.

Sadhanas Or Preparations For Higher Life

If atavism gains, you go down; if evolution gains, you go on. Therefore, we must not allow atavism to take place. Here, in my own body, is the first work of the study. We are too busy trying to mend the ways of our neighbours, that is the difficulty. We must begin with our own bodies. The heart, the liver, etc., are all atavistic; bring them back into consciousness, control them, so that they will obey your commands and act up to your wishes. There was a time when we had control of the liver; we could shake the whole skin, as can the cow. I have seen many people bring the control back by sheer hard practice. Once an impress is made, it is there. Bring back all the submerged activities—the vast ocean of action. This is the first part of the great study, and it is absolutely necessary for our social wellbeing. On the other hand, only the consciousness need not be studied all the time.

Then there is the other part of the study, not so necessary in our social life, which tends to liberation. Its direct action is to free the soul, to take the torch into the gloom, to clean out what is behind, to shake it up or even defy it, and to make us march onward piercing the gloom. That is the goal—the superconscious. Then when that state is reached, this very man becomes divine, becomes free. And to the mind thus trained to transcend all, gradually this universe will begin to give up its secrets; the book of nature will be read chapter after chapter, till the goal is attained, and we pass from this valley of life and death to that One, where death and life do not exist, and we know the Real and become the Real.

The first thing necessary is a quiet and peaceable life. If I have to go about the world the whole day to make a living, it is hard for me to attain to anything very high in this life. Perhaps in another life I shall be born under more propitious circumstances. But if I am earnest enough, these very circumstances will change even in this birth. Was there anything you did not get which you really wanted? It could not be. For it is the want that creates the body. It is the light that has bored the holes, as it were, in your head, called the eyes. If the light had not existed, you would have had no eyes. It is sound that had made the ears. The object of perception existed first, before you made the organ. In a few hundred thousand years or earlier, we may have other organs to perceive electricity and other things. There is no desire for a peaceful mind. Desire will not come unless there is something outside to fulfill it. The outside something just bores a hole in the body, as it were, and tries to get into the mind. So, when the desire will arise to have a peaceful, quiet life, that shall come where everything shall be propitious for the development of the mind—you may take that as my experience. It may come after thousands of lives, but it must come. Hold on to that, the desire. You cannot have the strong desire if its object was not outside for you already. Of course, you must understand, there is a difference between desire and desire. The master said, "My child, if you desire after God, God shall come to you." The disciple did not understand his master fully. One day both went to bathe in a river, and the master said, "Plunge in," and the boy did so. In a moment the master was upon him, holding him down. He would not let the boy come up. When the boy struggled and was exhausted, he let him go. "Yes, my child, how did you feel there?" "Oh, the desire for a breath of air!" "Do you have that kind of desire for God?" "No, Sir." "Have that kind of desire for God, and you shall have God."

That, without which we cannot live, must come to us. If it did not come to us, life could not go on.

If you want to be a Yogi, you must be free and place yourself in circumstances where you are alone and free from all anxiety. He who desires for a comfortable and nice life and at the same time wants to realise the Self is like the fool who, wanting to cross the river, caught hold of a crocodile mistaking it for a log of wood. "Seek ye first the Kingdom of God and His righteousness, and all these things shall be added unto you." Unto him comes everything who does not care for anything. Fortune is like a flirt; she cares not for him who wants her, but she is at the feet of him who does not care for her. Money comes and showers itself upon one who does not care for it; so does fame come in abundance until it is a trouble and a burden. They always come to the Master. The slave never gets anything. The Master is he who can live in spite of them, whose life does not depend upon the little, foolish things of the world. Live for an ideal, and that one ideal alone. Let it be so great, so strong, that there may be nothing else left in the mind; no place for anything else, no time for anything else.

How some people give all their energies, time, brain, body, and everything, to become rich! They have no time for breakfast! Early in the morning they are out and at work! They die in the attempt—ninety per cent of them—and the rest when they make money, cannot enjoy it. That is grand! I do not say it is bad to try to be rich. It is marvellous, wonderful. Why, what does it show? It shows that one can have the same amount of energy and struggle for freedom as one has for money. We know we have to give up money and all other things when we die, and yet, see the amount of energy we can put forth for them. But we, the same human beings, should we not put forth a thousandfold more strength and energy to acquire that which never fades, but which remains to us forever? For this is the one great friend, our own good deeds, our own spiritual excellence, that follows us beyond the grave. Everything else is left behind here with the body.

That is the one great first step—the real desire for the ideal. Everything comes easy after that. That the Indian mind found out; there, in India, men go to any length to find truth. But here, in the West, the difficulty is that everything is made so easy. It is not truth, but development, that is the great aim. The struggle is the great lesson. Mind you, the great benefit in this life is struggle. It is through that we pass. If there is any road to Heaven, it is through Hell. Through Hell to Heaven is always the way. When the soul has wrestled with circumstance and has met death, a thousand times death on the way, but nothing daunted has struggled forward again and again and yet again—then the soul comes out as a giant and laughs at the ideal he has been struggling for, because he finds how much greater is he than the ideal. I am the end, my own Self, and nothing else, for what is there to compare to my own Self? Can a bag of gold be the ideal of my Soul? Certainly not! My Soul is the highest ideal that I can have. Realising my own real nature is the one goal of my life.

There is nothing that is absolutely evil. The devil has a place here as well as God, else he would not be here. Just as I told you, it is through Hell that we pass to Heaven. Our mistakes have places here. Go on! Do not look back if you think you have done something that is not right. Now, do you believe you could be what you are today, had you not made those mistakes before? Bless your mistakes, then. They have been angels unawares. Blessed be torture! Blessed be happiness! Do not care what be your lot. Hold on to the ideal. March on! Do not look back upon little mistakes and things. In this battlefield of ours, the dust of mistakes must be raised. Those who are so thin-skinned that they cannot bear the dust, let them get out of the ranks.

So, then, this tremendous determination to struggle, a hundredfold more determination than that which you put forth to gain anything which belongs to this life, is the first great preparation.

And then along with it, there must be meditation. Meditation is the one thing. Meditate! The greatest thing is meditation. It is the nearest approach to spiritual life—the mind meditating. It is the one moment in our daily life that we are not at all material—the Soul thinking of Itself, free from all matter—this marvellous touch of the Soul!

The body is our enemy, and yet is our friend. Which of you can bear the sight of misery? And which of you cannot do so when you see it only as a painting? Because it is unreal, we do not identify ourselves with it; we know it is only a painting; it cannot bless us, it cannot hurt us. The most terrible misery painted upon a piece of canvas, we may even enjoy; we praise the technique of the artist, we wonder at his marvellous genius, even though the scene he paints is most horrible. That is the secret; that non-attachment. Be the Witness.

No breathing, no physical training of Yoga, nothing is of any use until you reach to the idea, "I am the Witness." Say, when the tyrant hand is on your neck, "I am the Witness! I am the Witness!" Say, "I am the Spirit! Nothing external can touch me." When evil thoughts arise, repeat that, give that sledge-hammer blow on their heads, "I am the Spirit! I am the Witness, the Ever-Blessed! I have no reason to do, no reason to suffer, I have finished with everything, I am the Witness. I am in my picture gallery—this universe is my museum, I am looking at these successive paintings. They are all beautiful. Whether good or evil. I see the marvellous skill, but it is all one. Infinite flames of the Great Painter!" Really speaking, there is naught—neither volition, nor desire. He is all. He—She—the Mother, is playing, and we are like dolls, Her helpers in this play. Here, She puts one now in the garb of a beggar, another moment in the garb of a king, the next moment in the garb of a saint, and again in the garb of a devil. We are putting on different garbs to help the Mother Spirit in Her play.

When the baby is at play, she will not come even if called by her mother. But when she finishes her play, she will rush to her mother, and will have no play. So there come moments in our life, when we feel our play is finished, and we want to rush to the Mother. Then all our toil here will be of no value; men, women, and children—wealth, name, and fame, joys and glories of life—punishments and successes—will be no more, and the whole life will seem like a show. We shall see only the infinite rhythm going on, endless and purposeless, going we do not know where. Only this much shall we say; our play is done.

Reincarnation

Contributed to the Metaphysical Magazine,
New York, March 1895

Both you and I have passed through many births;
You know them not, I know them all.
—*Bhagavad Gita,* Chap. IV, v. 5

Of the many riddles that have perplexed the intellect of Man in all climes and times, the most intricate is himself. Of the myriad mysteries that have called forth his energies to struggle for solution from the very dawn of history, the most mysterious is his own nature. It is at once the most insoluble enigma and the problem of all problems. As the starting-point and the repository of all we know and feel and do, there never has been, nor will be, a time when man's own nature will cease to demand his best and foremost attention.

Though through hunger after that truth, which of all others has the most intimate connection with his very existence, though through an all-absorbing desire for an inward standard by which to measure the outward universe, though through the absolute and inherent necessity of finding a fixed point in a universe of change, Man has sometimes clutched at handfuls of dust for gold, and even when urged on by a voice higher than reason or intellect, he has many times failed rightly to interpret the real meaning of the divinity within—still there never was a time since the search began, When some race, or some individuals, did not hold aloft the lamp of truth.

Taking a one-sided, cursory and prejudiced view of the surroundings and the unessential details, sometimes disgusted also with the vagueness of many schools and sects, and often, alas, driven to the opposite extreme by the violent superstitions of organised priestcraft—men have not been wanting, especially among advanced intellects, in either ancient or modern times, who not only gave up the search in despair, but declared it fruitless and useless. Philosophers might fret and sneer, and priests ply their trade even at the point of the sword, but truth comes to those alone who worship at her shrine for her sake only, without fear and without shopkeeping.

Light comes to individuals through the conscious efforts of their intellect; it comes, slowly though, to the whole race through unconscious percolations. The philosophers show the volitional struggles of great minds; history reveals the silent process of permeation through which truth is absorbed by the masses.

Of all the theories that have been held by Man about himself, that of a soul entity, separate from the body and immortal, has been the most widespread; and among those that held the belief in such a soul, the majority of the thoughtful had always believed also in its pre-existence.

At present the greater portion of the human race, having organised religion, believe in it; and many of the best thinkers in the most favoured lands, though nurtured in religions avowedly hostile to every idea of the pre-existence of the soul, have endorsed it. Hinduism and Buddhism have it for their foundation; the educated classes among the ancient Egyptians believed in it; the ancient Persians arrived at it; the Greek philosophers made it the corner-stone of their philosophy; the Pharisees among the Hebrews accepted it; and the Sufis among the Mohammedans almost universally acknowledged its truth.

There must be peculiar surroundings which generate and foster certain forms of belief among nations. It required ages for the ancient races to arrive at any idea about a part, even of the body, surviving after death; it took ages more to come to any rational idea about this something which persists and lives apart from the body. It was only when the idea was reached of an entity whose connection with the body was only for a time, and only among those nations who arrived at such a conclusion, that the unavoidable question arose: Whither? Whence?

The ancient Hebrews never disturbed their equanimity by questioning themselves about the soul. With them death ended all. Karl Heckel justly says, "Though it is true that in the Old Testament, preceding the exile, the Hebrews distinguish a life-principle, different from the body, which is sometimes called 'Nephesh', or 'Ruakh', or 'Neshama', yet all these words correspond rather to the idea of breath than to that of spirit or soul. Also in the writings of the Palestinian Jews, after the exile, there is never made mention of an individual immortal soul, but always only of a life-breath emanating from God, which, after the body is dissolved, is reabsorbed into the Divine 'Ruakh'."

The ancient Egyptians and the Chaldeans had peculiar beliefs of their own about the soul; but their ideas about this living part after death must not be confused with those of the ancient Hindu, the Persian, the Greek, or any other Aryan race. There was, from the earliest times, a broad distinction between the Aryas and the non-Sanskrit speaking Mlechchhas in the conception of the soul. Externally it was typified by their disposal of the dead—the Mlechchhas mostly trying their best to preserve the dead bodies either by careful burial or by the more elaborate processes of mummifying, and the Aryas generally burning their dead.

Herein lies the key to a great secret—the fact that no Mlechchha race, whether Egyptian, Assyrian, or Babylonian, ever attained to the idea of the soul as a separate entity which can live independent of the body, without the help of the Aryas, especially of the Hindus.

Although Herodotus States that the Egyptians were the first to conceive the idea of the immortality of the soul, and states as a doctrine of the Egyptians "that the soul after the dissolution of the body enters again and again into a creature that comes to life; then, that the soul wanders through all the animals of the land and the sea and through all the birds, and finally after three thousand years returns to a human body," yet, modern researches into Egyptology have hitherto found no trace of metempsychosis in the popular Egyptian religion. On the other hand, the most recent researches of Maspero, A. Erman, and other eminent Egyptologists tend to confirm the supposition that the doctrine of palingenesis was not at home with the Egyptians.

With the ancient Egyptians the soul was only a double, having no individuality of its own, and never able to break its connection with the body. It persists only so long as the body lasts; and if by chance the corpse is destroyed, the departed soul must suffer a second death and annihilation. The soul after death was allowed to roam freely all over the world, but always returning at night to where the corpse was, always miserable, always hungry and thirsty, always extremely desirous to enjoy life once more, and never being able to fulfil the desire. If any part of its old body was injured, the soul was also invariably injured in its corresponding part. And this idea explains the solicitude of the ancient Egyptians to preserve their dead. At first the deserts were chosen as the burial-place, because the dryness of the air did not allow the body to perish soon, thus granting to the departed soul a long lease of existence. In course of time one of the gods discovered the process of making mummies, through which the devout hoped to preserve the dead bodies of their ancestors for almost an infinite length of time, thus securing immortality to the departed ghost, however miserable it might be.

The perpetual regret for the world, in which the soul can take no further interest, never ceased to torture the deceased. "O, my brother," exclaims the departed, "withhold not thyself from drinking and eating, from drunkenness, from love, from all enjoyment, from following thy desire by night and by day; put not sorrow within thy heart, for, what are the years of Man upon earth? The West is a land of sleep and of heavy shadows, a place wherein the inhabitants, when once installed, slumber on in their mummy forms, never more waking to see their brethren; never more to recognise their fathers and mothers, with hearts forgetful of their wives and children. The living water, which earth giveth to all who dwell upon it, is for me stagnant and dead; that water floweth to all who are on earth, while for me it is but liquid putrefaction, this water that is mine. Since I came into this funeral valley I know not where nor what I am. Give me to drink of running water let me be placed by the edge of the water with my face to the North, that the breeze may caress me and my heart be refreshed from its sorrow."*

Among the Chaldeans also, although they did not speculate so much as the Egyptians as to the condition of the soul after death, the soul is still a double and is bound to its sepulchre. They also could not conceive of a state without this physical body, and expected a resurrection of the corpse again to life; and though the goddess Ishtar, after great perils and adventures, procured the resurrection of her shepherd husband, Dumuzi, the son of Ea and Damkina, "The most pious votaries pleaded in vain from temple to temple, for the resurrection of their dead friends."

---

* This text has been translated into German by Brugsch, *Die Egyptische Gräberwelt*, pp. 39, 40, and into French by Maspero, *Etudes Egyptiennes*, vol. I., pp. 181–90.

Thus we find, that the ancient Egyptians or Chaldeans never could entirely dissociate the idea of the soul from the corpse of the departed or the sepulchre. The state of earthly existence was best after all; and the departed are always longing to have a chance once more to renew it; and the living are fervently hoping to help them in prolonging the existence of the miserable double and striving the best they can to help them.

This is not the soil out of which any higher knowledge of the soul could spring. In the first place it is grossly materialistic, and even then it is one of terror and agony. Frightened by the almost innumerable powers of evil, and with hopeless, agonised efforts to avoid them, the souls of the living, like their ideas of the souls of the departed—wander all over the world though they might—could never get beyond the sepulchre and the crumbling corpse.

We must turn now for the source of the higher ideas of the soul to another race, whose God was an all-merciful, all-pervading Being manifesting Himself through various bright, benign, and helpful Devas, the first of all the human race who addressed their God as Father—"Oh, take me by the hands even as a father takes his dear son"; with whom life was a hope and not a despair; whose religion was not the intermittent groans escaping from the lips of an agonised man during the intervals of a life of mad excitement; but whose ideas come to us redolent with the aroma of the field and forest; whose songs of praise —spontaneous, free, joyful, like the songs which burst forth from the throats of the birds when they hail this beautiful world illuminated by the first rays of the lord of the day—come down to us even now through the vista of eighty centuries as fresh calls from heaven; we turn to the ancient Aryas.

"Place me in that deathless, undecaying world where is the light of heaven, and everlasting lustre shines"; "Make me immortal in that realm where dwells the King Vivasvan's son, where is the secret shrine of heaven"; "Make me immortal in that realm where they move even as they list"; "In the third sphere of inmost heaven, where worlds are full of light, make me immortal in that realm of bliss"—These are the prayers of the Aryas in their oldest record, the Rig Veda Samhita.

We find at once a whole world of difference between the Mlechchha and the Aryan ideals. To the one, this body and this world are all that are real, and all that are desirable. A little life-fluid which flies off from the body at death, to feel torture and agony at the loss of the enjoyments of the senses, can, they fondly hope, be brought back if the body is carefully preserved; and thus a corpse became more an object of care than the living man. The other found out that, that which left the body was the real man; and when separated from the body, it enjoyed a state of bliss higher than it ever enjoyed when in the body. And they hastened to annihilate the corrupted corpse by burning it.

Here we find the germ out of which a true idea of the soul could come. Here it was—where the real man was not the body, but the soul, where all ideas of an inseparable connection between the real man and the body were utterly absent—that a noble idea of the freedom of the soul could rise. And it was when the Aryas penetrated even beyond the shining cloth of the body with which the departed soul was enveloped, and found its real nature of a formless, individual, unit principle, that the question inevitably arose: Whence?

It was in India and among the Aryas that the doctrine of the pre-existence, the immortality, and the individuality of the soul first arose. Recent researches in Egypt have failed to show any trace of the doctrines of an independent and individual soul existing before and after the earthly phase of existence. Some of the mysteries were no doubt in possession of this idea, but in those it has been traced to India.

"I am convinced," says Karl Heckel, "that the deeper we enter into the study of the Egyptian religion, the clearer it is shown that the doctrine of metempsychosis was entirely foreign to the popular Egyptian religion; and that even that which single mysteries possessed of it was not inherent to the Osiris teachings, but derived from Hindu sources."

Later on, we find the Alexandrian Jews imbued with the doctrine of an individual soul, and the Pharisees of the time of Jesus, as already stated, not only had faith in an individual soul, but believed in its wandering through various bodies; and thus it is easy to find how Christ was recognised as an incarnation of an older Prophet, and Jesus himself directly asserted that John the Baptist was the Prophet Elias come back again. "If ye will receive it, this is Elias, which was for to come."(*Matt.* XI. 14.)

The ideas of a soul and of its individuality among the Hebrews, evidently came through the higher mystical teachings of the Egyptians, who in their turn derived it from India. And that it should come through Alexandria is significant, as the Buddhistic records clearly show Buddhistic missionary activity in Alexandria and Asia Minor.

Pythagoras is said to have been the first Greek who taught the doctrine of palingenesis among the Hellenes. As an Aryan race, already burning their dead and believing in the doctrine of an individual soul, it was easy for the Greeks to accept the doctrine of reincarnation through the Pythagorean teachings. According to Apuleius, Pythagoras had come to India, where he had been instructed by the Brahmins.

So far we have learnt that wherever the soul was held to be an individual, the real man, and not a vivifying part of the body only, the doctrine of its pre-existence had inevitably come, and that externally those nations that believed in the independent individuality of the soul had almost always signified it by burning the bodies of the departed. Though one of the ancient Aryan races, the Persian, developed at an early period and without any Semitic influence a peculiar method of disposing of the bodies of the dead, the very name by which they call their "Towers of Silence", comes from the root *Dah,* to burn.

In short, the races who did not pay much attention to the analysis of their own nature, never went beyond the material body as their all in all, and even when driven by higher light to penetrate beyond, they only came to the conclusion that somehow or other, at some distant period of time, this body will become incorruptible.

On the other hand, that race which spent the best part of its energies in the inquiry into the nature of Man as a thinking being—the Indo-Aryan—soon found out that beyond this body, beyond even the shining body which their forefathers longed after, is the real man, the principle, the individual who clothes himself with this body, and then throws it off when worn out. Was such a principle created? If creation means something coming out of nothing, their answer is a decisive *"No"*. This soul is without birth and without death; it is not a compound or combination but an independent individual, and as such it cannot be created or destroyed. It is only travelling through various states.

Naturally, the question arises: Where was it all this time? The Hindu philosophers say, "It was passing through different bodies in the physical sense, or, really and metaphysically speaking, passing through different mental planes."

Are there any proofs apart from the teachings of the Vedas upon which the doctrine of reincarnation has been founded by the Hindu philosophers? There are, and we hope to show later on that there are grounds as valid for it as for any other universally accepted doctrine. But first we will see what some of the greatest of modern European thinkers have thought about reincarnation.

H. Fichte, speaking about the immortality of the soul, says:

"It is true there is one analogy in nature which might be brought forth in refutation of the continuance. It is the well-known argument that everything that has a beginning in time must also perish at some period of time; hence, that the claimed past existence of the soul necessarily implies its pre-existence. This is a fair conclusion, but instead of being an objection to, it is rather an additional argument for its continuance. Indeed, one needs only to understand the full meaning of the metaphysico-physiological axiom that in reality nothing can be created or annihilated, to recognise that the soul must have existed prior to its becoming visible in a physical body."

Schopenhauer, in his book, *Die Welt als Wille und Vorstellung,* speaking about palingenesis, says: "What sleep is for the individual, death is for the 'will'. It would not endure to continue the same actions and sufferings throughout an eternity without true gain, if memory and individuality remained to it. It flings them off, and this is Lethe, and through this sleep of death it reappears fitted out with another intellect as a new being; a new day tempts to new shores. These constant new births, then, constitute the succession of the life-dreams of a will which in itself is indestructible, until instructed and improved by so much and such various successive knowledge in a constantly new form, it abolishes and abrogates itself. It must not be neglected that even empirical grounds support a palingenesis of this kind. As a matter of fact, there does exist a connection between the birth of the newly appearing beings and the death of those that are worn out. It shows itself in the great fruitfulness of the human race which appears as a consequence of devastating diseases. When in the fourteenth century the Black Death had for the most part depopulated the Old World, a quite abnormal fruitfulness appeared among the human race, and twin-births were very frequent. The circumstance was also remarkable that none of the children born at this time obtained their full number of teeth; thus nature, exerting itself to the utmost, was niggardly in details. This is related by F. Schnurrer in his *Chronik der Seuchen,* 1825. Casper, also, in his *Ueber die Wahrscheinliche Lebensdauer des Menschen,* 1835, confirms the principle that the number of births in a given population has the most decided influence upon the length of life and mortality in it, as this always keeps pace with mortality; so that always and everywhere the deaths and the births increase and decrease in like proportion, which he places beyond doubt by an accumulation of evidence collected from many lands and their various provinces. And yet it is impossible that there can be physical, causal connection between my early death and the fruitfulness of a marriage with which I have nothing to do, or conversely. Thus here the metaphysical appears undeniable, and in a stupendous manner, as the immediate ground of explanation of the physical. Every new-born being comes fresh and blithe into the new existence, and enjoys it as a free gift; but there is and can be nothing freely given. Its fresh existence is paid for by the old age and death of a worn-out existence which has perished, but which contained the indestructible seed out of which the new existence has arisen; they are one being."

The great English philosopher Hume, nihilistic though he was, says in the sceptical essay on immortality, "The metempsychosis is, therefore, the only system of this kind that philosophy can listen to." The philosopher Lessing, with a deep poetical insight, asks, "Is this hypothesis so laughable merely because it is the oldest, because the human understanding, before the sophistries of the schools had dissipated and debilitated it, lighted upon it at once? Why should not I come back as often as I am capable of acquiring fresh knowledge, fresh experience? Do I bring away so much from once that there is nothing to repay the trouble of coming back?"

The arguments for and against the doctrine of a pre-existing soul reincarnating through many lives have been many, and some of the greatest thinkers of all ages have taken up the gauntlet to defend it; and so far as we can see, if there is an individual soul, that it existed before seems inevitable. If the soul is not an individual but a combination of 'Skandhas' (notions), as the Madhyamikas among the Buddhists insist, still they find pre-existence absolutely necessary to explain their position.

The argument showing the impossibility of an infinite existence beginning in time is unanswerable, though attempts have been made to ward it off by appealing to the omnipotence of God to do anything, however contrary to reason it may be. We are sorry to find this most fallacious argument proceeding from some of the most thoughtful persons.

In the first place, God being the universal and common cause of all phenomena, the question was to find the natural causes of certain phenomena in the human soul, and the *Deus ex machina* theory is, therefore, quite irrelevant. It amounts to nothing less than confession of ignorance. We can give that answer to every question asked in every branch of human knowledge and stop all inquiry and, therefore, knowledge altogether.

Secondly, this constant appeal to the omnipotence of God is only a word puzzle. The cause, as cause, is and can only be known to us as sufficient for the effect, and nothing more. As such we have no more idea of an infinite effect than of an omnipotent cause. Moreover, all our ideas of God are only limited; even the idea of cause limits our idea of God. Thirdly, even taking the position for granted, we are not bound to allow any such absurd theories as "Something coming out of nothing", or "Infinity beginning in time", so long as we can give a better explanation.

A so-called great argument is made against the idea of pre-existence by asserting that the majority of mankind are not conscious of it. To prove the validity of this argument, the party who offers it must prove that the whole of the soul of Man is bound up in the faculty of memory. If memory be the test of existence, then all that part of our lives which is not now in it must be non-existent, and every person who in a state of coma or otherwise loses his memory must be non-existent also.

The premises from which the inference is drawn of a previous existence, and that too on the plane of conscious action, as adduced by the Hindu philosophers, are chiefly these:

First, how else to explain this world of inequalities? Here is one child born in the province of a just and merciful God, with every circumstance conducing to his becoming a good and useful member of the human race, and perhaps at the same instant and in the same city another child is born under circumstances every one of which is against his becoming good. We see children born to suffer, perhaps all their lives, and that owing to no fault of theirs. Why should it be so? What is the cause? Of whose ignorance is it the result? If not the child's, why should it suffer for its parents' actions?

It is much better to confess ignorance than to try to evade the question by the allurements of future enjoyments in proportion to the evil here, or by posing "mysteries". Not only undeserved suffering forced upon us by any agent is immoral—not to say unjust—but even the future-making-up theory has no legs to stand upon.

How many of the miserably born struggle towards a higher life, and how many more succumb to the circumstances they are placed under? Should those who grow worse and more wicked by being forced to be born under evil circumstances be rewarded in the future for the wickedness of their lives? In that case the more wicked the man is here, the better will be his deserts hereafter.

There is no other way to vindicate the glory and the liberty of the human soul and reconcile the inequalities and the horrors of this world than by placing the whole burden upon the legitimate cause—our own independent actions or Karma. Not only so, but every theory of the creation of the soul from nothing inevitably leads to fatalism and preordination, and instead of a Merciful Father, places before us a hideous, cruel, and an ever-angry God to worship. And so far as the power of religion for good or evil is concerned, this theory of a created soul, leading to its corollaries of fatalism and predestination, is responsible for the horrible idea prevailing among some Christians and Mohammedans that the heathens are the lawful victims of their swords, and all the horrors that have followed and are following it still.

But an argument which the philosophers of the Nyaya school have always advanced in favour of reincarnation, and which to us seems conclusive, is this: Our experiences cannot be annihilated. Our actions (Karma) though apparently disappearing, remain still unperceived (Adrishta), and reappear again in their effect as tendencies (Pravrittis). Even little babies come with certain tendencies—fear of death, for example.

Now if a tendency is the result of repeated actions, the tendencies with which we are born must be explained on that ground too. Evidently we could not have got them in this life; therefore, we must have to seek for their genesis in the past. Now it is also evident that some of our tendencies are the effects of the self-conscious efforts peculiar to man; and if it is true that we are born with such tendencies, it rigorously follows that their causes were conscious efforts in the past—that is, we must have been on the same mental plane which we call the human plane, before this present life.

So far as explaining the tendencies of the present life by past conscious efforts goes, the reincarnationists of India and the latest school of evolutionists are at once; the only difference is that the Hindus, as spiritualists, explain it by the conscious efforts of individual souls, and the materialistic school of evolutionists, by a hereditary physical transmission. The schools which hold to the theory of creation out of nothing are entirely out of court.

The issue has to be fought out between the reincarnationists—who hold that all experiences are stored up as tendencies in the subject of those experiences, the individual soul, and are transmitted by reincarnation of that unbroken individuality—and the materialists who hold that the brain is the subject of all actions and the theory of the transmission through cells.

It is thus that the doctrine of reincarnation assumes an infinite importance to our mind, for the fight between reincarnation and mere cellular transmission is, in reality, the fight between spiritualism and materialism. If cellular transmission is the all-sufficient explanation, materialism is inevitable, and there is no necessity for the theory of a soul. If it is not a sufficient explanation, the theory of an individual soul bringing into this life the experiences of the past is as absolutely true. There is no escape from the alternative, reincarnation or materialism. Which shall we accept?

V

Shiva And Krishna

The Dance Of Shiva

Translated from the Bengali

Lo, the God is dancing
—Shiva the All-destroyer and Lord of Creation, The Master of Yoga and the Wielder of Pinaka (trident),
His flaming locks have filled the sky,
Seven worlds play the rhythm
As the trembling earth sways almost to dissolution,
Lo, the Great God Shiva is dancing.

Shiva In Ecstasy

Translated from the Bengali

Shiva is dancing, lost in the ecstasy of Self, sounding his own cheeks.
His tabor is playing and the garland of skulls is swinging in rhythm.
The waters of the Ganga are roaring among his matted locks.
The great trident is vomiting fire, and the moon on his forehead is fiercely flaming.

To Shri Krishna

Translated from the Hindi

O Krishna, my friend, let me go to the water,
O let me go today.
Why play tricks with one who is already thy slave?
Friend, let me go today, let me go.
Have to fill my pitcher in the waters of the Jamuna.
I pray with folded hands, friend, let me go.

The Story Of The Boy Gopala

O mother! I am so afraid to go to school through the woods alone; other boys have servants or somebody to bring them to school or take them home—why cannot I have someone to bring me home?"—thus said Gopala, a little Brahmin boy, to his mother one winter afternoon when he was getting ready for school. The school hours were in the morning and afternoon. It was dark when the school closed in the afternoon, and the path lay through the woods.

Gopala's mother was a widow. His father who had lived as a Brahmin should—never caring for the goods of the world, studying and teachings worshipping and helping others to worship—died when Gopala was a baby. And the poor widow retired entirely from the concerns of the world—even from that little she ever had—her soul given entirely to God, and waiting patiently with prayers, fasting, and discipline, for the great deliverer death, to meet in another life, him who was the eternal companion of her joys and sorrows, her partner in the good and evil of the beginningless chain of lives. She lived in her little cottage. A small rice-field her husband received as sacred gift to learning brought her sufficient rice; and the piece of land that surrounded her cottage, with its clumps of bamboos, a few coconut palms, a few mangoes and lichis, with the help of the kindly village folk, brought forth sects under the English domination, in which social differences with the conquering race are more glaring than the spiritual. The Hindu sects of the century seem to have set one ideal of truth before them—the approval of their English masters. No wonder that these sects have mushroom lives to live. The vast body of the Indian people religiously hold aloof from them, and the only popular recognition they get is the jubilation of the people when they die.

But possibly, for some time yet, it cannot be otherwise.

VI

On India

Historical Evolution Of India

Om Tat Sat
Om Namo Bhagavate Ramakrishnaya

नासतः सत् जायते—Existence cannot be produced by non-existence.

Non-existence can never be the cause of what exists. Something cannot come out of nothing. That the law of causation is omnipotent and knows no time or place when it did not exist is a doctrine as old as the Aryan race, sung by its ancient poet-seers, formulated by its philosophers, and made the corner-stone upon which the Hindu man even of today builds his whole scheme of life.

There was an inquisitiveness in the race to start with, which very soon developed into bold analysis, and though, in the first attempt, the work turned out might be like the attempts with shaky hands of the future master-sculptor, it very soon gave way to strict science, bold attempts, and startling results.

Its boldness made these men search every brick of their sacrificial altars; scan, cement, and pulverise every word of their scriptures; arrange, re-arrange, doubt, deny, or explain the ceremonies. It turned their gods inside out, and assigned only a secondary place to their omnipotent, omniscient, omnipresent Creator of the universe, their ancestral Father-in-heaven; or threw Him altogether overboard as useless, and started a world-religion without Him with even now the largest following of any religion. It evolved the science of geometry from the arrangements of bricks to build various altars, and startled the world with astronomical knowledge that arose from the attempts accurately to time their worship and oblations. It made their contribution to the science of mathematics the largest of any race, ancient or modern, and to their knowledge of chemistry, of metallic compounds in medicine, their scale of musical notes, their invention of the bow-instruments—(all) of great service in the building of modern European civilisation. It led them to invent the science of building up the child-mind through shining fables, of which every child in every civilised country learns in a nursery or a school and carries an impress through life.

Behind and before this analytical keenness, covering it as in a velvet sheath, was the other great mental peculiarity of the race—poetic insight. Its religion, its philosophy, its history, its ethics, its politics were all inlaid in a flower-bed of poetic imagery—the miracle of language which was called Sanskrit or "perfected", lending itself to expressing and manipulating them better than any other tongue. The aid of melodious numbers was invoked even to express the hard facts of mathematics.

This analytical power and the boldness of poetical visions which urged it onward are the two great internal causes in the make-up of the Hindu race. They together formed, as it were, the keynote to the national character. This combination is what is always making the race press onwards beyond the senses—the secret of those speculations which are like the steel blades the artisans used to manufacture—cutting through bars of iron, yet pliable enough to be easily bent into a circle.

They wrought poetry in silver and gold; the symphony of jewels, the maze of marble wonders, the music of colours, the fine fabrics which belong more to the fairyland of dreams than to the real—have back of them thousands of years of working of this national trait.

Arts and sciences, even the realities of domestic life, are covered with a mass of poetical conceptions, which are pressed forward till the sensuous touches the supersensuous, and the real gets the rose-hue of the unreal.

The earliest glimpses we have of this race show it already in the possession of this characteristic, as an instrument of some use in its hands. Many forms of religion and society must have been left behind in the onward march, before we find the race as depicted in the scriptures, the Vedas.

An organised pantheon, elaborate ceremonials, divisions of society into hereditary classes necessitated by a variety of occupations, a great many necessaries and a good many luxuries of life are already there.

Most modern scholars are agreed that surroundings as to climate and conditions, purely Indian, were not yet working on the race.

Onwards through several centuries, we come to a multitude surrounded by the snows of Himalayas on the north and the heat of the south—vast plains, interminable forests, through which mighty rivers roll their tides. We catch a glimpse of different races—Dravidians, Tartars, and Aboriginals pouring in their quota of blood, of speech, of manners and religions. And at last a great nation emerges to our view—still keeping the type of the Aryan—stronger, broader, and more organised by the assimilation. We see the central assimilative core giving its type and character to the whole mass, clinging on with great pride to its name of "Aryan", and, though willing to give other races the benefits of its civilisation, it was by no means willing to admit them within the "Aryan" pale.

The Indian climate again gave a higher direction to the genius of the race. In a land where nature was propitious and yielded easy victories, the national mind started to grapple with and conquer the higher problems of life in the field of thought. Naturally the thinker, the priest, became the highest class in the Indian society, and not the man of the sword. The priests again, even at that dawn of history, put most of their energy in elaborating rituals; and when the nation began to find the load of ceremonies and lifeless rituals too heavy — came the first philosophical speculations, and the royal race was the first to break through the maze of killing rituals.

On the one hand, the majority of the priests impelled by economical considerations were bound to defend that form of religion which made their existence a necessity of society and assigned them the highest place in the scale of caste; on the other hand, the king-caste, whose strong right hand guarded and guided the nation and who now found itself as leading in the higher thoughts also, were loath to give up the first place to men who only knew how to conduct a ceremonial. There were then others, recruited from both the priests and king-castes, who ridiculed equally the ritualists and philosophers, declared spiritualism as fraud and priestcraft, and upheld the attainment of material comforts as the highest goal of life. The people, tired of ceremonials and wondering at the philosophers, joined in masses the materialists. This was the beginning of that caste question and that triangular fight in India between ceremonials, philosophy, and materialism which has come down unsolved to our own days.

The first solution of the difficulty attempted was by applying the eclecticism which from the earliest days had taught the people to see in differences the same truth in various garbs. The great leader of this school, Krishna—himself of royal race—and his sermon, the *Gita*, have after various vicissitudes, brought about by the upheavals of the Jains, the Buddhists, and other sects, fairly established themselves as the "Prophet" of India and the truest philosophy of life. Though the tension was toned down for the time, it did not satisfy the social wants which were among the causes—the claim of the king-race to stand first in the scale of caste and the popular intolerance of priestly privilege. Krishna had opened the gates of spiritual knowledge and attainment to all irrespective of sex or caste, but he left undisturbed the same problem on the social side. This again has come down to our own days, in spite of the gigantic struggle of the Buddhists, Vaishnavas, etc., to attain social equality for all.

Modern India admits spiritual equality of all souls—but strictly keeps the social difference.

Thus we find the struggle renewed all along the line in the seventh century before the Christian era and finally in the sixth, overwhelming the ancient order of things under Shakya Muni, the Buddha. In their reaction against the privileged priesthood, Buddhists swept off almost every bit of the old ritual of the Vedas, subordinated the gods of the Vedas to the position of servants to their own human saints, and declared the "Creator and Supreme Ruler" as an invention of priestcraft and superstition.

But the aim of Buddhism was reform of the Vedic religion by standing against ceremonials requiring offerings of animals, against hereditary caste and exclusive priesthood, and against belief in permanent souls. It never attempted to destroy that religion, or overturn the social order. It introduced a vigorous method by organising a class of Sannyasins into a strong monastic brotherhood, and the Brahmavadinis into a body of nuns—by introducing images of saints in the place of altar-fires.

It is probable that the reformers had for centuries the majority of the Indian people with them. The older forces were never entirely pacified, but they underwent a good deal of modification during the centuries of Buddhistic supremacy.

In ancient India the centres of national life were always the intellectual and spiritual and not political. Of old, as now, political and social power has been always subordinated to spiritual and intellectual. The outburst of national life was round colleges of sages and spiritual teachers. We thus find the Samitis of the Panchalas, of the Kashyas (of Varanasi), the Maithilas standing out as great centres of spiritual culture and philosophy, even in the Upanishads. Again these centres in turn became the focus of political ambition of the various divisions of the Aryans.

The great epic Mahabharata tells us of the war of the Kurus and Panchalas for supremacy over the nation, in which they destroyed each other. The spiritual supremacy veered round and centred in the East among the Magadhas and Maithilas, and after the Kuru-Panchala war a sort of supremacy was obtained by the kings of Magadha.

The Buddhist reformation and its chief field of activity were also in the same eastern region; and when the Maurya kings, forced possibly by the bar sinister on their escutcheon, patronised and led the new movement, the new priest power joined hands with the political power of the empire of Pataliputra. The popularity of Buddhism and its fresh vigour made the Maurya kings the greatest emperors that India ever had. The power of the Maurya sovereigns made Buddhism that world-wide religion that we see even today.

The exclusiveness of the old form of Vedic religions debarred it from taking ready help from outside. At the same time it kept it pure and free from many debasing elements which Buddhism in its propagandist zeal was forced to assimilate.

This extreme adaptability in the long run made Indian Buddhism lose almost all its individuality, and extreme desire to be of the people made it unfit to cope with the intellectual forces of the mother religion in a few centuries. The Vedic party in the meanwhile got rid of a good deal of its most objectionable features, as animal sacrifice, and took lessons from the rival daughter in the judicious use of images, temple processions, and other impressive performances, and stood ready to take within her fold the whole empire of Indian Buddhism, already tottering to its fall.

And the crash came with the Scythian invasions and the total destruction of the empire of Pataliputra.

The invaders, already incensed at the invasion of their central Asiatic home by the preachers of Buddhism, found in the sun-worship of the Brahmins a great sympathy with their own solar religion—and when the Brahminist party were ready to adapt and spiritualise many of the customs of the new-comers, the invaders threw themselves heart and soul into the Brahminic cause.

Then there is a veil of darkness and shifting shadows; there are tumults of war, rumors of massacres; and the next scene rises upon a new phase of things.

The empire of Magadha was gone. Most of northern India was under the rule of petty chiefs always at war with one another. Buddhism was almost extinct except in some eastern and Himalayan provinces and in the extreme south and the nation after centuries of struggle against the power of hereditary priesthood awoke to find itself in the clutches of a double priesthood of hereditary Brahmins and exclusive monks of the new regime, with all the powers of the Buddhistic organisation and without their sympathy for the people.

A renascent India, bought by the valour and blood of the heroic Rajputs, defined by the merciless intellect of a Brahmin from the same historical thought-centre of Mithila, led by a new philosophical impulse organised by Shankara and his bands of Sannyasins, and beautified by the arts and literature of the courts of Malava—arose on the ruins of the old.

The task before it was profound, problems vaster than any their ancestors had ever faced. A comparatively small and compact race of the same blood and speech and the same social and religious aspiration, trying to save its unity by unscalable walls around itself, grew huge by multiplication and addition during the Buddhistic supremacy; and (it) was divided by race, colour, speech, spiritual instinct, and social ambitions into hopelessly jarring factions. And this had to be unified and welded into one gigantic nation. This task Buddhism had also come to solve, and had taken it up when the proportions were not so vast.

So long it was a question of Aryanising the other types that were pressing for admission and thus, out of different elements, making a huge Aryan body. In spite of concessions and compromises, Buddhism was eminently successful and remained the national religion of India. But the time came when the allurements of sensual forms of worship, indiscriminately taken in along with various low races, were too dangerous for the central Aryan core, and a longer contact would certainly have destroyed the civilisation of the Aryans. Then came a natural reaction for self-preservation, and Buddhism as a separate sect ceased to live in most parts of its land of birth.

The reaction-movement, led in close succession by Kumarila in the north, and Shankara and Ramanuja in the south, has become the last embodiment of that vast accumulation of sects and doctrines and rituals called Hinduism. For the last thousand years or more, its great task has been assimilation, with now and then an outburst of reformation. This reaction first wanted to revive the rituals of the Vedas—failing which, it made the Upanishads or the philosophic portions of the Vedas its basis. It brought Vyasa's system of Mimamsa philosophy and Krishna's sermon, the *Gita*, to the forefront; and all succeeding movements have followed the same. The movement of Shankara forced its way through its high intellectuality; but it could be of little service to the masses, because of its adherence to strict caste-laws, very small scope for ordinary emotion, and making Sanskrit the only vehicle of communication. Ramanuja on the other hand, with a most practical philosophy, a great appeal to the emotions, an entire denial of birthrights before spiritual attainments, and appeals through the popular tongue completely succeeded in bringing the masses back to the Vedic religion.

The northern reaction of ritualism was followed by the fitful glory of the Malava Empire. With the destruction of that in a short time, northern India went to sleep as it were, for a long period, to be rudely awakened by the thundering onrush of Mohammedan cavalry across the passes of Afghanistan. In the south, however, the spiritual upheaval of Shankara and Ramanuja was followed by the usual Indian sequence of united races and powerful empires. It was the home of refuge of Indian religion and civilisation, when northern India from sea to sea lay bound at the feet of Central Asiatic conquerors. The Mohammedan tried for centuries to subjugate the south, but can scarcely be said to have got even a strong foothold; and when the strong and united empire of the Moguls was very near completing its conquest, the hills and plateaus of the south poured in their bands of fighting peasant horsemen, determined to die for the religion which Ramdas preached and Tuka sang; and in a short time the gigantic empire of the Moguls was only a name.

The movements in northern India during the Mohammedan period are characterised by their uniform attempt to hold the masses back from joining the religion of the conquerors—which brought in its train social and spiritual equality for all.

The friars of the orders founded by Ramananda, Kabir, Dadu, Chaitanya, or Nanak were all agreed in preaching the equality of man, however differing from each other in philosophy. Their energy was for the most part spent in checking the rapid conquest of Islam among the masses, and they had very little left to give birth to new thoughts and aspirations. Though evidently successful in their purpose of keeping the masses within the fold of the old religion, and tempering the fanaticism of the Mohammedans, they were mere apologists, struggling to obtain permission to live.

One great prophet, however, arose in the north, Govind Singh, the last Guru of the Sikhs, with creative genius; and the result of his spiritual work was followed by the well-known political organisation of the Sikhs. We have seen throughout the history of India, a spiritual upheaval is almost always succeeded by a political unity extending over more or less area of the continent, which in its turn helps to strengthen the spiritual aspiration that brings it to being. But the spiritual aspiration that preceded the rise of the Mahratta or the Sikh empire was entirely reactionary. We seek in vain to find in the court of Poona or Lahore even a ray of reflection of that intellectual glory which surrounded the courts of the Moguls, much less the brilliance of Malava or Vidyanagara. It was intellectually the darkest period of Indian history; and both these meteoric empires, representing the upheaval of mass-fanaticism and hating culture with all their hearts, lost all their motive power as soon as they had succeeded in destroying the rule of the hated Mohammedans.

Then there came again a period of confusion. Friends and foes, the Mogul empire and its destroyers, and the till then peaceful foreign traders, French and English, all joined in a melee of fight. For more than half a century there was nothing but war and pillage and destruction. And when the smoke and dust cleared, England was stalking victorious over the rest. There has been half a century of peace and law and order under the sway of Britain. Time alone will prove if it is the order of progress or not.

There have been a few religious movements amongst the Indian people during the British rule, following the same line that was taken up by northern Indian sects during the sway of the empire of Delhi. They are the voices of the dead or the dying—the feeble tones of a terrorised people, pleading for permission to live. They are ever eager to adjust their spiritual or social surroundings according to the tastes of the conquerors—if they are only left the right to live, especially the sects under the English domination, in which social differences with the conquering race are more glaring than the spiritual. The Hindu sects of the century seem to have set one ideal of truth before them—the approval of their English masters. No wonder that these sects have mushroom lives to live. The vast body of the Indian people religiously hold aloof from them, and the only popular recognition they get is the jubilation of the people when they die. But possibly, for some time yet, it cannot be otherwise.

The Story Of Jada Bharata

Delivered in California

There was a great monarch named Bharata. The land which is called India by foreigners is known to her children as Bharata Varsha. Now, it is enjoined on every Hindu when he becomes old, to give up all worldly pursuits—to leave the cares of the world, its wealth, happiness, and enjoyments to his son—and retire into the forest, there to meditate upon the Self which is the only reality in him, and thus break the bonds which bind him to life. King or priest, peasant or servant, man or woman, none is exempt from this duty; for all the duties of the householder—of the son, the brother, the husband, the father, the wife, the daughter, the-mother, the sister—are but preparations towards that one stage, when all the bonds which bind the soul to matter are severed asunder forever.

The great king Bharata in his old age gave over his throne to his son, and retired into the forest. He who had been ruler over millions and millions of subjects, who had lived in marble palaces, inlaid with gold and silver, who had drunk out of jewelled cups—this king built a little cottage with his own hands, made of reeds and grass, on the banks of a river in the Himalayan forests. There he lived on roots and wild herbs, collected by his own hands, and constantly meditated upon Him who is always present in the soul of man. Days, months,' and years passed. One day, a deer came to drink water near by where the royal sage was meditating. At the same moment, a lion roared at a little distance off. The deer was so terrified that she, without satisfying her thirst, made a big jump to cross the river. The deer was with young, and this extreme exertion and sudden fright made her give birth to a little fawn, and immediately after she fell dead. The fawn fell into the water and was being carried rapidly away by the foaming stream, when it caught the eyes of the king. The king rose from his position of meditation and rescuing the fawn from the water, took it to his cottage, made a fire, and with care and attention fondled the little thing back to life. Then the kindly sage took the fawn under his protection, bringing it up on soft grass and fruits. The fawn thrived under the paternal care of the retired monarch, and grew into a beautiful deer. Then, he whose mind had been strong enough to break away from lifelong attachment to power, position and family, became attached to the deer which he had saved from the stream. And as he became fonder and fonder of the deer, the less and less he could concentrate his mind upon the Lord. When the deer went out to graze in the forest, if it were late in returning, the mind of the royal sage would become anxious and worried. He would think, "Perhaps my little one has been attacked by some tiger—or perhaps some other danger has befallen it; otherwise, why is it late?"

Some years passed in this way, but one day death came, and the royal sage laid himself down to die. But his mind, instead of being intent upon the Self, was thinking about the deer; and with his eyes fixed upon the sad looks of his beloved deer, his soul left the body. As the result of this, in the next birth he was born as a deer. But no Karma is lost, and all the great and good deeds done by him as king and sage bore their fruit. This deer was a born Jatismara, and remembered his past birth, though he was bereft of speech and was living in an animal body. He always left his companions and was instinctively drawn to graze near hermitages where oblations were offered and the Upanishads were preached.

After the usual years of a deer's life had been spent, it died and was next born as the youngest son of a rich Brahmin. And in that life also, he remembered all his past, and even in his childhood was determined no more to get entangled in the good and evil of life. The child, as it grew up, was strong and healthy, but would not speak a word, and lived as one inert and insane, for fear of getting mixed up with worldly affairs. His thoughts were always on the Infinite, and he lived only to wear out his past Prarabdha Karma. In course of time the father died, and the sons divided the property among themselves; and thinking that the youngest was a dumb, good-for-nothing man, they seized his share. Their charity, however, extended only so far as to give him enough food to live upon. The wives of the brothers were often very harsh to him, putting him to do all the hard work; and if he was unable to do everything they wanted, they would treat him very unkindly. But he showed neither vexation nor fear, and neither did he speak a word. When they persecuted him very much, he would stroll out of the house and sit under a tree, by the hour, until their wrath was appeased, and then he would quietly go home again.

One day, when the wives of the brothers had treated him with more than usual unkindness, Bharata went out of the house, seated himself under the shadow of a tree and rested. Now it happened that the king of the country was passing by, carried in a palanquin on the shoulders of bearers. One of the bearers had unexpectedly fallen ill, and so his attendants were looking about for a man to replace him. They came upon Bharata seated under a tree; and seeing he was a strong young man, they asked him if he would take the place of the sick man in bearing the king's palanquin. But Bharata did not reply. Seeing that he was so able-bodied, the king's servants caught hold of him and placed the pole on his shoulders. Without speaking a word, Bharata went on. Very soon after this, the king remarked that the palanquin was not being evenly carried, and looking out of the palanquin addressed the new bearer, saying "Fool, rest a while; if thy shoulders pain thee, rest a while." Then Bharata laying the pole of the palanquin down, opened his lips for the first time in his life, and spoke, "Whom dost thou, O King, call a fool? Whom dost thou ask to lay down the palanquin? Who dost thou say is weary? Whom dost thou address as 'thou'? If thou meanest, O King, by the word 'thee' this mass of flesh, it is composed of the same matter as thine; it is unconscious, and it knoweth no weariness, it knoweth no pain. If it is the mind, the mind is the same as thine; it is universal. But if the word 'thee' is applied to something beyond that, then it is the Self, the Reality in me, which is the same as in thee, and it is the One in the universe. Dost thou mean, O King, that the Self can ever be weary, that It can ever be tired, that It can ever be hurt? I did not want, O King—this body did not want—to trample upon the poor worms crawling on the road, and, therefore, in trying to avoid them, the palanquin moved unevenly. But the Self was never tired; It was never weak; It never bore the pole of the palanquin: for It is omnipotent and omnipresent." And so he dwelt eloquently on the nature of the soul, and on the highest knowledge, etc. The king, who was proud of his learning, knowledge, and philosophy, alighted from the palanquin, and fell at the feet of Bharata, saying, "I ask thy pardon, O mighty one, I did not know that thou wast a sage, when I asked thee to carry me." Bharata blessed him and departed. He then resumed the even tenor of his previous life. When Bharata left the body, he was freed forever from the bondage of birth wherever and whenever they could, as for their hymn-singing and Soma-bibbing; or are we to follow the celibate Rishis who upheld Brahmacharya as the *sine qua non* of spirituality?

Then there are the usual backsliders, who ought to come in for a load of abuse—monks who could not keep up to their ideal—weak, wicked.

But if the ideal is straight and sound, a backsliding monk is head and shoulders above any householder in the land, on the principle, "It is better to have loved and lost."

Compared to the coward that never made the attempt, he is a hero.

If the searchlight of scrutiny were turned on the inner workings of our social reform conclave, angels would have to take note of the percentage of backsliders as between the monk and the householder; and the recording angel is in our own heart.

But then, what about this marvellous experience of standing alone, discarding all help, breasting the storms of life, of working without any sense of recompense, without any sense of putrid duty? Working a whole life, joyful, free—not goaded on to work like slaves by false human love or ambition?

This the monk alone can have. What about religion? Has it to remain or vanish? If it remains, it requires its experts, its soldiers. The monk is the religious expert, having made religion his one *métier* of life. He is the soldier of God. What religion dies so long as it has a band of devoted monks?

Why are Protestant England and America shaking before the onrush of the Catholic monk?

Vive Ranade and the Social Reformers! But, O India! Anglicised India! Do not forget, child, that there are in this society problems that neither you nor your Western Guru can yet grasp the meaning of—much less solve!

India's Message To The World

The following notes were discovered among Swami Vivekananda's papers. He intended to write a book and jotted down forty-two points as a syllabus for the work, but only a few points were dealt with as an introduction by him and the work was left unfinished. We give the manuscript as found.

SYLLABUS

1. Bold has been my message to the people of the West. Bolder to those at home.

2. Four years of residence in the marvellous West has made India only the better understood. The shades are deeper and the lights brighter.

3. The survey—it is not true that the Indians have degenerated.

4. The problem here has been as it has been everywhere else—the assimilation of various races, but nowhere has it been so vast as here.

5. Community of language, government and, above all, religion has been the power of fusion.

6. In other lands this has been attempted by "force", that is, the enforcement of the culture of *one* race only over the rest. The result being the production of a short-lived vigorous national life; then, dissolution.

7. In India, on the other hand, the attempts have been as gentle as the problem vast, and from the earliest times, the customs, and especially the religions, of the different elements tolerated.

8. Where it was a small problem and force was sufficient to form a unity, the effect really was the nipping in the bud of various healthy types in the germ of all the elements except the dominant one. It was only one set of brains using the vast majority for its own good, thus losing the major portion of the possible amount of development; and thus when the dominant type had spent itself, the apparently impregnable building tottered to its ruins, e.g., Greece, Rome, the Norman.

9. A common language would be a great desideratum; but the same criticism applies to it, the destruction of the vitality of the various existing ones.

10. The only solution to be reached was the finding of a great sacred language of which all the others would be considered as manifestations, and that was found in the Sanskrit.

11. The Dravidian languages may or may not have been originally Sanskritic, but for practical purposes they are so now, and every day we see them approaching the ideal more and more, yet keeping their distinctive vital peculiarities.

12. A racial background was found—the Aryas.

13. The speculation whether there was a distinct, separate race called the Aryas living in Central Asia to the Baltic.

14. The so-called types. Races were always mixed.

15. The "blonde" and the "brunette".

16. Coming to practical common sense from so-called historical imagination. The Aryas in their oldest records were in the land between Turkistan and the Punjab and N.W. Tibet.

17. This leads to the attempt at fusion between races and tribes of various degrees of culture.

18. Just as Sanskrit has been the linguistic solution, so the Arya the racial solution. So the Brahminhood is the solution

of the varying degrees of progress and culture as well as that of all social and political problems.

19. The great ideal of India—Brahminhood.

20. Property-less, selfless, subject to no laws, no king except the moral.

21. Brahminhood by descent—various races have claimed and acquired the right in the past as well as in the present.

22. No claim is made by the doer of great deeds, only by lazy worthless fools.

23. Degradation of Brahminhood and Kshatriyahood. The Puranas said there will be only non-Brahmins in the Kali Yuga, and that is true, becoming truer every day. Yet a few Brahmins remain, and in India alone.

24. Kshatriyahood—we must pass through that to become a Brahmin. Some may have passed through in the past, but the present must show that.

25. But the disclosure of the whole plan is to be found in religion.

26. The different tribes of the same race worship similar gods, under a generic name as the Baals of the Babylonians, the Molochs of the Hebrews.

27. The attempt in Babylonia of making all the Baals merge in Baal-Merodach —the attempt of the Israelites to merge all the Molochs in the Moloch Yavah or Yahu.

28. The Babylonians destroyed by the Persians; and the Hebrews who took the Babylonian mythology and adapted it to their own needs, succeeded in producing a strict monotheistic religion.

29. Monotheism like absolute monarchy is quick in executing orders, and a great centralisation of force, but it grows no farther, and its worst feature is its cruelty and persecution. All nations coming within its influence perish very soon after a flaring up of a few years.

30. In India the same problem presented itself—the solution found—एकं सद्विप्रा बहुधा वदन्ति।

This is the keynote to everything which has succeeded, and the keystone of the arch.

31. The result is that wonderful toleration of the Vedantist.

32. The great problem, therefore, is to harmonise and unify without destroying the individuality of these various elements.

33. No form of religion which depends upon persons, either of this earth or even of heaven, is able to do that.

34. Here is the glory of the Advaita system preaching a principle, not a person, yet allowing persons, both human and divine, to have their full play.

35. This has been going on all the time; in this sense we have been always progressing. The Prophets during the Mohammedan rule.

36. It was fully conscious and vigorous in old days, and less so of late; in this sense alone we have degenerated.

37. This is going to be in the future. If the manifestation of the power of one tribe utilising the labours of the rest produced wonderful results at least for a certain length of time, here is going to be the accumulation and the concentration of all the races that have been slowly and inevitably getting mixed up in blood and ideas, and in my mind's eye, I see the future giant slowly maturing. The future of India, the youngest and the most glorious of the nations of earth as well as the oldest.

38. The way—we will have to work. Social customs as barriers, some as founded upon the Smritis. But none from the Shrutis. The Smritis must change with time. This is the admitted law.

39. The principles of the Vedanta not only should be preached everywhere in India, but also outside. Our thought must enter into the make-up of the minds of every nation, not through writings, but through persons.

40. Gift is the only Karma in Kali Yuga. None attaining knowledge until purified by Karma.

41. Gift of spiritual and secular knowledge.

42. Renunciation—Renouncers—the national call.

INTRODUCTION

Bold has been my message to the people of the West, bolder is my message to you, my beloved countrymen. The message of ancient India to new Western nations I have tried my best to voice—ill done or well done the future is sure to show; but the mighty voice of the same future is already sending forward soft but distinct murmurs, gaining strength as the days go by, the message of India that is to be to India as she is at present.

Many wonderful institutions and customs, and many wonderful manifestations of strength and power it has been my good fortune to study in the midst of the various races I have seen, but the most wonderful of all was to find that beneath all these apparent variations of manners and customs, of culture and power, beats the same mighty human heart under the impulsion of the same joys and sorrows, of the same weakness and strength.

Good and evil are everywhere and the balance is wondrously even; but, above all, is the glorious soul of Man everywhere which never fails to understand any one who knows how to speak its own language. Men and women are to be found in every race whose lives are blessings to humanity, verifying the words of the divine Emperor Asoka: "In every land dwell Brahmins and Shramanas."

I am grateful to the lands of the West for the many warm hearts that received me with all the love that pure and disinterested souls alone could give; but my life's allegiance is to this my motherland; and if I had a thousand lives, every moment of the whole series would be consecrated to your service, my countrymen, my friends.

For to this land I owe whatever I possess, physical, mental, and spiritual; and if I have been successful in anything, the glory is yours, not mind. Mine alone are my weaknesses and failures, as they come through my inability of profiting by the mighty lessons with which this land surrounds one, even from his very birth.

And what a land! Whosoever stands on this sacred land, whether alien or a child of the soil, feels himself surrounded —unless his soul is degraded to the level of brute animals—by the living thoughts of the earth's best and purest sons, who have been working to raise the animal to the divine through centuries, whose beginning history fails to trace. The very air is full of the pulsations of spirituality. This land is sacred to philosophy, to ethics and spirituality, to all that tends to give a respite to Man in his incessant struggle for the preservation of the animal, to all training that makes Man throw off the garment of brutality and stand revealed as the spirit immortal, the birthless, the deathless, the ever-blessed—the land where the cup of pleasure was full, and fuller has been the cup of misery, until here, first of all, Man found out that it was all vanity; here, first of all in the prime of youth, in the lap of luxury, in the height of glory and plenitude of power, he broke through the fetters of delusion. Here, in this ocean of humanity, amidst the sharp interaction of strong currents of pleasure and pain, of strength and weakness, of wealth and poverty, of joy and sorrow, of smile and tear, of life and death, in the melting rhythm of eternal peace and calmness, arose the throne of renunciation! Here in this land, the great problems of life and death, of the thirst for life, and the vain mad struggles to preserve it only resulting in the accumulation of woes, were first grappled with and solved—solved as they never were before and never will be hereafter; for here and here alone was discovered that even life itself is an evil, the shadow only of something which alone is real. This is the land where alone religion was practical and real, and here alone men and women plunged boldly in to realise the goal, just as in other lands they madly plunge in to realise the pleasures of life by robbing their weaker brethren. Here and here alone the human heart expanded till it included not only the human, but birds, beasts, and plants; from the highest gods to grains of sand, the highest and the lowest, all find a place in the heart of man, grown great, infinite. And here alone, the human soul studied the universe as one i unbroken unity whose every pulse was his own pulse.

We all hear so much about the degradation of India. There was a time when I also believed in it. But today: standing on the vantage-ground of experience, with eyes cleared of obstructive predispositions and above all, cf the highly-coloured pictures of other countries toned down to their proper shade and light by actual contact, I confess in all humility that I was wrong. Thou blessed land of the Aryas, thou wast never degraded. Sceptres have been broken and thrown away, the ball of power has passed from hand to hand, but in India, courts and kings always touched only a few; the vast mass of the people, from the highest to the lowest, has been left to pursue its own inevitable course, the current of national life flowing at times slow and half-conscious, at others, strong and awakened. I stand in awe before the unbroken procession of scores of shining centuries, with here and there a dim link in the chain, only to flare up with added brilliance in the next, and there she is walking with her own majestic steps—my motherland—to fulfil her glorious destiny, which no power on earth or in heaven can check—the regeneration of Man the brute into Man the God.

Ay, a glorious destiny, my brethren, for as far back as the days of the Upanishads we have thrown the challenge to the world: न प्रजया धनेन त्यागेनैके अमृतत्वमानशुः—"Not by progeny, not by wealth, but by renunciation alone immortality is reached." Race after race has taken the challenge up and tried their utmost to solve the world-riddle on the plane of desires. They have all failed in the past—the old ones have become extinct under the weight of wickedness and misery, which lust for power and gold brings in its train, and the new ones are tottering to their fall. The question has yet to be decided whether peace will survive or war; whether patience will survive or non-forbearance, whether goodness will survive or wickedness; whether muscle will survive or brain; whether worldliness will survive or spirituality. We have solved our problem ages ago, and held on to it through good or evil fortune, and mean to hold on to it till the end of time. Our solution is unworldliness—renunciation.

This is the theme of Indian life-work, the burden of her eternal songs, the backbone of her existence, the foundation of her being, the *raison d'être* of her very existence—the spiritualisation of the human race. In this her life-course she has never deviated, whether the Tartar ruled or the Turk, whether the Mogul ruled or the English.

And I challenge anybody to show one single period of her national life when India was lacking in spiritual giants capable of moving the world. But her work is spiritual, and that cannot be done with blasts of war trumpets or the march of cohorts. Her influence has always fallen upon the world like that of the gentle dew, unheard and scarcely marked, yet bringing into bloom the fairest flowers of the earth. This influence, being in its nature gentle, would have to wait for a fortunate combination of circumstances, to go out of the country into other lands, though it never ceased to work within the limits of its native land. As such, every educated person knows that whenever the empire-building Tartar or Persian or Greek or Arab brought this land in contact with the outside world, a mass of spiritual influence immediately flooded the world from here. The very same circumstances have presented themselves once more before us. The English high roads over land and sea and the wonderful power manifested by the inhabitants of that little island have once more brought India in contact with the rest of the world, and the same work has already begun. Mark my words, this is but the small beginning, big things are to follow; what the result of the present work outside India will be I cannot exactly state, but this I know for certain that millions, I say deliberately, millions in every civilised land are waiting for the message that will save them from the hideous abyss of materialism into which modern money-worship is driving them headlong, and many of the leaders of the new social movements have already discovered that Vedanta in its highest form can alone spiritualise their social aspirations. I shall have to return to this towards the end. I take up therefore the other great subject, the work within the country.

The problem assumes a twofold aspect, not only spiritualisation but assimilation of the various elements of which the nation is composed. The assimilation of different races into one has been the common task in the life of every nation.

The Education That India Needs*

In reply to your questions about the methods of work, the most important thing I have to say is that the work should be started on a scale which would be commensurate with the results desired. I have heard much of your liberal mind, patriotism, and steady perseverance from my friend Miss Muller; and the proof of your erudition is evident. I look upon it as a great good fortune that you are desirous to know what little this insignificant life has been able to attempt; I shall state it to you here, as far as I can. But first I shall lay before you my mature convictions for your deliberation.

We have been slaves forever, *i.e.* it has never been given to the masses of India to express the inner light which is their inheritance. The Occident has been rapidly advancing towards freedom for the last few centuries. In India, it was the king who used to prescribe everything from Kulinism down to what one should eat and what one should not. In Western countries, the people do everything themselves.

The king now has nothing to say in any social matter; on the other hand, the Indian people have not yet even the least faith in themselves, what to say of self-reliance. The

* Written to Shrimati Sarala Ghosal, B.A., Editor, *Bharati*, from Darjeeling, 24 April 1897. Translated from the Bengali.

faith in one's own Self, which is the basis of Vedanta, has not yet been even slightly carried into practice. It is for this reason that the Western method—i.e. first of all, discussion about the wished-for end, then the carrying it out by the combination of all the forces—is of no avail even now in this country; it is for this reason that we appear so greatly conservative under foreign rule. If this be true, then it is a vain attempt to do any great work by means of public discussion. "There is no chance of a headache where there is no head"—where is the public? Besides, we are so devoid of strength that our whole energy is exhausted if we undertake to discuss anything, none is left for work. It is for this reason, I suppose, we observe in Bengal almost always—"Much cry but little wool." Secondly, as I have written before, I do not expect anything from the rich people of India. It is best to work among the youth in whom lies our hope—patiently, steadily, and without noise.

Now about work. From the day when education and culture etc., began to spread gradually from patricians to plebeians, grew the distinction between the modern civilisation as of Western countries, and the ancient civilisation as of India, Egypt, Rome, etc. I see it before my eyes, a nation is advanced in proportion as education and intelligence spread among the masses. The chief cause of India's ruin has been the monopolising of the whole education and intelligence of the land, by dint of pride and royal authority, among a handful of men. If we are to rise again, we shall have to do it in the same way, *i.e.* by spreading education among the masses. A great fuss has been made for half a century about social reform. Travelling through various places of India these last ten years, I observed the country full of social reform associations. But I did not find one association for them by sucking whose blood the people known as "gentlemen" have become and continue to be gentlemen! How many sepoys were brought by the Mussulmans? How many Englishmen are there? Where, except in India, can be had millions of men who will cut the throats of their own fathers and brothers for six rupees? Sixty millions of Mussulmans in seven hundred years of Mohammedan rule, and two millions of Christians in one hundred years of Christian rule—what makes it so? Why has originality entirely forsaken the country? Why are our deft-fingered artisans daily becoming extinct, unable to compete with the Europeans? By what power again has the German labourer succeeded in shaking the many-century-grounded firm footing of the English labourer?

Education, education, education alone! Travelling through many cities of Europe and observing in them the comforts and education of even the poor people, there was brought to my mind the state of our own poor people, and I used to shed tears. What made the difference? Education was the answer I got. Through education comes faith in one's own Self, and through faith in one's own Self the inherent Brahman is waking up in them, while the Brahman in us is gradually becoming dormant. In New York I used to observe the Irish colonists come—downtrodden, haggard-looking, destitute of all possessions at home, penniless, and wooden-headed—with their only belongings, a stick and a bundle of rags hanging at the end of it, fright in their steps, alarm in their eyes. A different spectacle in six months—the man walks upright, his attire is changed! In his eyes and steps there is no more sign of fright. What is the cause? Our Vedanta says that that Irishman was kept surrounded by contempt in his own country—the whole of nature was telling him with one voice, "Pat, you have no more hope, you are born a slave and will remain so." Having been thus told from his birth, Pat believed in it and hypnotised himself that he was very low, and the Brahman in him shrank away. While no sooner had he landed in America than he heard the shout going up on all sides, "Pat, you are a man as we are. It is Man who has done all, a man like you and me can do everything: have courage!" Pat raised his head and saw that it was so, the Brahman within woke up. Nature herself spoke, as it were, "Arise, awake, and stop not till the goal is reached." (*Katha Upanishad,* I. iii. 14.)

Likewise the education that our boys receive is very negative. The schoolboy learns nothing, but has everything of his own broken down—want of Shraddha is the result. The Shraddha which is the keynote of the Veda and the Vedanta—the Shraddha which emboldened Nachiketa to face Yama and question him, through which Shraddha this world moves—the annihilation of that Shraddha! अज्ञश्चाश्रदधानश्च संशयात्मा विनश्यति —"The ignorant the man devoid of Shraddha, the doubting self runs to ruin." Therefore, are we so near destruction. The remedy now is the spread of education. First of all, Self-knowledge. I do not mean thereby, matted hair, staff, Kamandalu, and mountain caves which the word suggests. What do I mean then? Cannot the knowledge, by which is attained even freedom from the bondage of worldly existence, bring ordinary material prosperity? Certainly it can. Freedom, dispassion, renunciation all these are the very highest ideals, but स्वल्पमप्यस्य धर्मस्य त्रायते महतो भयात्—"Even a little of this Dharma saves one from the great fear (of birth and death)." Dualist, qualified-monist, monist, Shaiva, Vaishnava, Shakta, even the Buddhist and the Jain and others—whatever sects have arisen in India—are all at one in this respect that infinite power is latent in this Jivatman (individualised soul); from the ant to the perfect man there is the same Atman in all, the difference being only in manifestation. "As a farmer breaks the obstacles (to the course of water)" (Patanjali's *Yoga Sutra,* Kaivalyapada, 3). That power manifests as soon as it gets the opportunity and the right place and time. From the highest god to the meanest grass, the same power is present in all—whether manifested or not. We shall have to call forth that power by going from door to door.

Secondly, along with this, education has to be imparted.

That is easy to say, but how to reduce it into practice? There are thousands of unselfish, kind-hearted men in our country who have renounced everything. In the same way as they travel about and give religious instructions without any remuneration, so at least half of them can be trained as teachers or bearers of such education as we need most. For that, we want first of all a centre in the capital of each Presidency, from whence to spread slowly throughout the whole of India. Two centres have recently been started in Madras and Calcutta; there is hope of more soon. Then, the greater part of the education to the poor should be given orally, time is not yet ripe for schools. Gradually in these main centres will be taught agriculture, industry, etc., and workshops will be established for the furtherance of arts. To sell the manufactures of those workshops in Europe and America, associations will be started like those already in existence. It will be necessary to start centres for women, exactly like those for men. But you are aware how difficult that is in this country. Again, "The snake which bites must take out its own poison"—and that this is going to be is my firm conviction; the money required for these works would have to come from the West. And for that reason, our religion should be preached in Europe and America. Modern science has undermined the basis of religions like Christianity. Over and above that, luxury is about to kill the religious instinct itself. Europe and America are now looking towards India with expectant eyes: this is the time for philanthropy, this is the time to occupy the hostile strongholds.

In the West, women rule; all influence and power are theirs. If bold and talented women like yourself versed in Vedanta, go to England to preach, I am sure that every year hundreds of men and women will become blessed by adopting the religion of the land of Bharata. The only woman who went over from our country was Ramabai; her knowledge of English, Western science and art was limited; still she surprised all. If anyone like you goes, England will be stirred, what to speak of America! If an Indian woman in Indian dress preach there the religion which fell from the lips of the Rishis of India—I see a prophetic vision—there will rise a great wave which will inundate the whole Western world. Will there be no woman in the land of Maitreyi, Khana, Lilavati, Savitri and Ubhayabharati, who will venture to do this? The Lord knows. England we shall conquer, England we shall possess, through the power of spirituality. नान्यः पन्था विद्यतेऽयनाय—"There is no other way of salvation." Can salvation ever come by getting up meetings and societies? Our conquerors must be made Devas by the power of our spirituality. I am a humble mendicant, an itinerant monk; I am helpless and alone. What can I do? You have the power of wealth, intellect, and education; will you forgo this opportunity? Conquest of England, Europe, and America—this should be our one supreme Mantra at present, in it lies the well-being of the country. Expansion is the sign of life, and we must spread over the world with our spiritual ideals. Alas! This frame is poor, moreover, the physique of a Bengali; even under this labour a fatal disease has attacked it, but there is the hope:

> उत्पत्स्येतऽस्ति मम कोऽपि समानधर्मा।
> कालो ह्ययं निरवधिर्विपुला च पृथ्वी।।

—"A kindred spirit is or will be born out of the limitless time and populous earth to accomplish the work" (Bhavabhuti).

About vegetarian diet I have to say this—first, my Master was a vegetarian; but if he was given meat offered to the Goddess, he used to hold it up to his head. The taking of life is undoubtedly sinful; but so long as vegetable food is not made suitable to the human system through progress in chemistry, there is no other alternative but meat-eating. So long as Man shall have to live a Rajasika (active) life under circumstances like the present, there is no other way except through meat-eating. It is true that the Emperor Asoka saved the lives of millions of animals by the threat of the sword; but is not the slavery of a thousand years more dreadful than that? Taking the life of a few goats as against the inability to protect the honour of one's own wife and daughter, and to save the morsels for one's children from robbing hands—which of these is more sinful? Rather let those belonging to the upper ten, who do not earn their livelihood by manual labour, not take meat; but the forcing of vegetarianism upon those who have to earn their bread by labouring day and night is one of the causes of the loss of our national freedom. Japan is an example of what good and nourishing food can do.

May the All-powerful Vishveshari inspire your heart!

Struggle For Expansion*

The old dilemma, whether the tree precedes the seed or the seed the tree, runs through all our forms of knowledge. Whether intelligence is first in the order of being or matter; whether the ideal is first or the external manifestation; whether freedom is our true nature or bondage of law; whether thought creates matter or matter thought; whether the incessant change in nature precedes the idea of rest or the idea of rest precedes the idea of change—all these are questions of the same insoluble nature. Like the rise and fall of a series of waves, they follow one another in an invariable succession and men take this side or that according to their tastes or education or peculiarity of temperaments.

For instance, if it be said on the one hand that, seeing the adjustment in nature of different parts, it is clear that it is the effect of intelligent work; on the other hand it may be argued that intelligence itself being created by matter and force in the course of evolution could not have been before this world. If it be said that the production of every form must be preceded by an ideal in the mind, it can be argued, with equal force, that the ideal was itself created by various

* Written by Swami Vivekananda during his first visit to America to address questions put by a Western disciple.

external experiences. On the one hand, the appeal is to our ever-present idea of freedom; on the other, to the fact that nothing in the universe being causeless, everything, both mental and physical, is rigidly bound by the law of causation. If it be affirmed that, seeing the changes of the body induced by volition, it is evident that thought is the creator of this body, it is equally clear that as change in the body induces a change in the thought, the body must have produced the mind. If it be argued that the universal change must be the outcome of a preceding rest; equally logical argument can be adduced to show that the idea of unchangeability is only an illusory relative notion, brought about by the comparative differences in motion.

Thus in the ultimate analysis all knowledge resolves itself into this vicious circle: the indeterminate interdependence of cause and effect. Judging by the laws of reasoning, such knowledge is incorrect; and the most curious fact is that this knowledge is proved to be incorrect, not by comparison with knowledge which is true, but by the very laws which depend for their basis upon the selfsame vicious circle. It is clear, therefore, that the peculiarity of all our knowledge is that it proves its own insufficiency. Again, we cannot say that it is unreal, for all the reality we know and can think of is within this knowledge. Nor can we deny that it is sufficient for all practical purposes. This state of human knowledge which embraces within its scope both the external and the internal worlds is called Maya. It is unreal because it proves its own incorrectness. It is real in the sense of being sufficient for all the needs of the animal man.

Acting in the external world Maya manifests itself as the two powers of attraction and repulsion. In the internal its manifestations are desire and non-desire (Pravritti and Nivritti). The whole universe is trying to rush outwards. Each atom is trying to fly off from its centre. In the internal world, each thought is trying to go beyond control. Again each particle in the external world is checked by another force, the centripetal, and drawn towards the centre. Similarly in the thought-world the controlling power is checking all these outgoing desires.

Desires of materialisation, that is, being dragged down more and more to the plane of mechanical action, belong to the animal man. It is only when the desire to prevent all such bondage to the senses arises that religion dawns in the heart of man. Thus we see that the whole scope of religion is to prevent Man from falling into the bondage of the senses and to help him to assert his freedom. The first effort of this power of Nivritti towards that end is called morality. The scope of all morality is to prevent this degradation and break this bondage. All morality can be divided into the positive and the negative elements; it says either, "Do this" or "Do not do this". When it says, "Do not", it is evident that it is a check to a certain desire which would make a man a slave. When it says, "Do", its scope is to show the way to freedom and to the breaking down of a certain degradation which has already seized the human heart.

Now this morality is only possible if there be a liberty to be attained by man. Apart from the question of the chances of attaining perfect liberty, it is clear that the whole universe is a case of struggle to expand, or in other words, to attain liberty. This infinite space is not sufficient for even one atom. The struggle for expansion must go on eternally until perfect liberty is attained. It cannot be said that this struggle to gain freedom is to avoid pain or to attain pleasure. The lowest grade of beings, who can have no such feeling, are also struggling for expansion; and according to many, Man himself is the expansion of these very beings.

The Problem Of Modern India And Its Solution*

The ancient history of India is full of descriptions of the gigantic energies and their multifarious workings, the boundless spirit, the combination of indomitable action and reaction of the various forces, and, above all, the profound thoughtfulness of a godly race. If the word "history" is understood to mean merely narratives of kings and emperors, and pictures of society—tyrannised over from time to time by the evil passions, haughtiness, avarice, etc., of the rulers of the time, portraying the acts resulting from their good or evil propensities, and how these reacted upon the society of that time—such a history India perhaps does not possess. But every line of that mass of the religious literature of India, her ocean of poetry, her philosophies and various scientific works reveal to us—a thousand times more clearly than the narratives of the life-incidents and genealogies of particular kings and emperors can ever do—the exact position and every step made in advance by that vast body of men who, even before the dawn of civilisation, impelled by hunger and thirst, lust and

---

* Translation of the first Bengali article written by Swami Vivekananda as an introduction to *Udbodhana*, started on 14 January 1899, as the Bengali fortnightly (later a monthly) journal of the Ramakrishna Order.

greed, etc., attracted by the charm of beauty, endowed with a great and indomitable mental power, and moved by various sentiments, arrived through various ways and means at that stage of eminence. Although the heaps of those triumphal flags which they gathered in their innumerable victories over nature with which they had been waging war for ages, have, of late, been torn and tattered by the violent winds of adverse circumstances and become worn out through age, yet they still proclaim the glory of Ancient India.

Whether this race slowly proceeded from Central Asia, Northern Europe, or the Arctic regions, and gradually came down and sanctified India by settling there at last, or whether the holy land of India was their original native place, we have no proper means of knowing now. Or whether a vast race living in or outside India, being displaced from its original abode, in conformity with natural laws, came in the course of time to colonise and settle over Europe and other places—and whether these people were white or black, blue-eyed or dark-eyed, golden-haired or black-haired—all these matters—there is no sufficient ground to prove now, with the one exception of the fact of the kinship of Sanskrit with a few European languages. Similarly, it is not easy to arrive at a final conclusion as to the modern Indians, whether they all are the pure descendants of that race, or how much of the blood of that race is flowing in their veins, or again, what races amongst them have any of that even in them.

However, we do not, in fact, lose much by this uncertainty.

But there is one fact to remember. Of that ancient Indian race, upon which the rays of civilisation first dawned, where deep thoughtfulness first revealed itself in full glory, there are still found hundreds of thousands of its children, born of its mind—the inheritors of its thoughts and sentiments—ready to claim them.

Crossing over mountains, rivers, and oceans, setting at naught, as it were, the obstacles of the distance of space and time, the blood of Indian thought has flowed, and is still flowing into the veins of other nations of the globe, whether in a distinct or in some subtle unknown way. Perhaps to us belongs the major portion of the universal ancient inheritance.

In a small country lying in the eastern comer of the Mediterranean Sea, beautiful and adorned by nature, and garlanded by well-formed and beautiful-looking islands, lived a race of men who were few in number, but of a very charming aspect, perfectly formed, and strong in muscles and sinews, light of body, yet possessing steadiness and perseverance, and who were unrivalled for the creation of all earthly beauties, as well as endowed with extraordinary practicality and intellect. The other ancient nations used to call them Yavanas, but they called themselves Greeks. This handful of a vigorous and wonderful race is a unique example in the annals of man. Wherever and in whatever nation there has been, or is, any advance made in earthly science up to the present day—such as social, martial, political, sculptural, etc.,—there the shadow of ancient Greece has fallen. Let us leave apart the consideration of ancient times, for even in this modern age, we, the Bengalis, think ourselves proud and enlightened simply by following the footmarks of these Yavana Gurus for these last fifty years, illumining our homes with what light of theirs is reaching us through the European literature.

The whole of Europe nowadays is, in every respect, the disciple of ancient Greece, and her proper inheritor; so much so that a wise man of England had said, "Whatever nature has not created, that is the creation of the Greek mind."

These two gigantic rivers (Aryans and Yavanas), issuing from far-away and different mountains (India and Greece), occasionally come in contact with each other, and whenever such confluence takes place, a tremendous intellectual or spiritual tide, rising in human societies, greatly expands the range of civilisation and confirms the bond of universal brotherhood among men.

Once in far remote antiquity, the Indian philosophy, coming in contact with Greek energy, led to the rise of the Persian, the Roman, and other great nations. After the invasion of Alexander the Great, these two great waterfalls colliding with each other, deluged nearly half of the globe with spiritual tides, such as Christianity. Again, a similar commingling, resulting in the improvement and prosperity of Arabia, laid the foundation of modern European civilisation. And perhaps, in our own day, such a time for the conjunction of these two gigantic forces has presented itself again. This time their centre is India.

The air of India pre-eminently conduces to quietness, the nature of the Yavana is the constant expression of power; profound meditation characterises the one, the indomitable spirit of dexterous activity, the other; one's motto is "renunciation", the other's "enjoyment". One's whole energy is directed inwards, the other's, outwards; one's whole learning consists in the knowledge of the Self or the Subject, the other's, in the knowledge of the not-Self or the object (perishable creation); one loves Moksha (spiritual freedom), the other loves political independence; one is unmindful of gaining prosperity in this world, the other sets his whole heart on making a heaven of this world; one, aspiring after eternal bliss, is indifferent to all the ephemeral pleasures of this life, and the other, doubting the existence of eternal bliss, or knowing it to be far away, directs his whole energy to the attainment of earthly pleasures as much as possible.

In this age, both these types of mankind are extinct, only their physical and mental children, their works and thoughts are existing.

Europe and America are the advanced children of the Yavanas, a glory to their forefathers; but the modern inhabitants of the land of Bharata are not the glory of the ancient Aryas. But, as fire remains intact under cover of ashes, so the ancestral fire still remains latent in these modern Indians. Through the grace of the Almighty Power, it is sure to manifest itself in time.

What will accrue when that ancestral fire manifests itself?

Would the sky of India again appear clouded over by waving masses of smoke springing from the Vedic sacrificial fire? Or is the glory of Rantideva again going to be revived in the blood of the sacrificed animals? Are the old customs of Gomedha, Ashvamedha, or perpetuating the lineage from a husband's brother, and other usages of a like nature to come back again? Or is the deluge of a Buddhistic propaganda again going to turn the whole of India into a big monastery? Are the laws of Manu going to be rehabilitated as of yore? Or is the discrimination of food, prescribed and forbidden, varying in accordance with geographical dimensions, as it is at the present day, alone going to have its all-powerful domination over the length and breadth of the country? Is the caste system to remain, and is it going to depend eternally upon the birth-right of a man, or is it going to be determined by his qualification? And again in that caste system, is the discrimination of food, its touchable-ness or untouchable-ness, dependent upon the purity or the impurity of the man who touches it, to be observed as it is in Bengal, or will it assume a form more strict as it does in Madras? Or, as in the Punjab, will all such restrictions be obliterated? Are the marriages of different Varnas to take place from the upper to the lower Varna in the successive order, as in Manu's days, and as it is still in vogue in Nepal? Or, as in Bengal and other places, are they to be kept restricted to a very limited number of individuals constituting one of the several communities of a certain class of the Varna? To give a conclusive answer to all these questions is extremely difficult. They become the more difficult of solution, considering the difference in the customs prevailing in different parts of the country—nay, as we find even in the same part of the country such a wide divergence of customs among different castes and families.

Then what is to be?

What we should have is what we have not, perhaps what our forefathers even had not—that which the Yavanas had; that, impelled by the life-vibration of which, is issuing forth in rapid succession from the great dynamo of Europe, the electric flow of that tremendous power vivifying the whole world. We want that. We want that energy, that love of independence, that spirit of self-reliance, that immovable fortitude, that dexterity in action, that bond of unity of purpose, that thirst for improvement. Checking a little the constant looking back to the past, we want that expansive vision infinitely projected forward; and we want—that intense spirit of activity (Rajas) which will flow through our every vein, from head to foot.

What can be a greater giver of peace than renunciation? A little ephemeral worldly good is nothing in comparison with eternal good; no doubt of that. What can bring greater strength than Sattva Guna (absolute purity of mind)? It is indeed true that all other kinds of knowledge are but non-knowledge in comparison with Self-knowledge. But I ask: How many are there in the world fortunate enough to gain that Sattva Guna? How many in this land of Bharata? How many have that noble heroism which can renounce all, shaking off the idea of "I and mine"? How many are blessed enough to possess that far-sight of wisdom which makes the earthly pleasures appear to be but vanity of vanities? Where is that broad-hearted man who is apt to forget even his own body in meditating over the beauty and glory of the Divine? Those who are such are but a handful in comparison to the population of the whole of India; and in order that these men may attain to their salvation, will the millions and millions of men and women of India have to be crushed under the wheel of the present-day society and religion?

And what good can come out of such a crushing?

Do you not see—taking up this plea of Sattva, the country has been slowly and slowly drowned in the ocean of Tamas or dark ignorance? Where the most dull want to hide their stupidity by covering it with a false desire for the highest knowledge which is beyond all activities, either physical or mental; where one, Born and bred in lifelong laziness, wants to throw the veil of renunciation over his own unfitness for work; where the most diabolical try to make their cruelty appear, under the cloak of austerity, as a part of religion; where no one has an eye upon his own incapacity, but everyone is ready to lay the whole blame on others; where knowledge consists only in getting some books by heart, genius consists in chewing the cud of others' thoughts, and the highest glory consists in taking the name of ancestors: do we require any other proof to show that that country is being day by day drowned in utter Tamas?

Therefore, Sattva or absolute purity is now far away from us. Those amongst us who are not yet fit, but who hope to be fit, to reach to that absolutely pure Paramahamsa state—for them the acquirement of Rajas or intense activity is what is most beneficial now. Unless a man passes through Rajas, can he ever attain to that perfect Sattvika state? How can one expect Yoga or union with God, unless one has previously finished with his thirst for Bhoga or enjoyment? How can renunciation come where there is no Vairagya or dispassion for all the charms of enjoyment?

On the other hand, the quality of Rajas is apt to die down as soon as it comes up, like a fire of palm leaves. The presence of Sattva and the Nitya or Eternal Reality is almost in a state of juxtaposition—Sattva is nearly Nitya. Whereas the nation in which the quality of Rajas predominates is not so long-lived, but a nation with a preponderance of Sattva is, as it were, immortal. History is a witness to this fact.

In India, the quality of Rajas is almost absent; the same is the case with Sattva in the West. It is certain, therefore, that the real life of the Western world depends upon the influx, from India, of the current of Sattva or transcendentalism; and it is also certain that unless we overpower and submerge our Tamas by the opposite tide of Rajas, we shall never gain any worldly good or welfare in this life; and it is also equally certain that we shall meet many formidable obstacles in the path of realisation of those noble aspirations and ideals connected with our after-life.

The one end and aim of the *Udbodhana* is to help the union and intermingling of these two forces, as far as it lies in its power.

True, in so doing there is a great danger—lest by this huge wave of Western spirit are washed away all our most precious jewels, earned through ages of hard labour; true, there is fear lest falling into its strong whirlpool, even the land of Bharata forgets itself so far as to be turned into a battlefield in the struggle after earthly enjoyments; ay, there is fear, too, lest going to imitate the impossible and impracticable foreign ways, rooting out as they do our national customs and ideals, we lose all that we hold dear in this life and be undone in the next!

To avoid these calamities we must always keep the wealth of our own home before our eyes, so that every one down to the masses may always know and see what his own ancestral property is. We must exert ourselves to do that; and side by side, we should be brave to open our doors to receive all available light from outside. Let rays of light come in, in sharp-driving showers from the four quarters of the earth; let the intense flood of light flow in from the West—what of that? Whatever is weak and corrupt is liable to die—what are we to do with it? If it goes, let it go, what harm does it do to us? What is strong and invigorating is immortal. Who can destroy that?

How many gushing springs and roaring cataracts, how many icy rivulets and ever-flowing streamlets, issuing from the eternal snow-capped peaks of the Himalayas, combine and flow together to form the gigantic river of the gods, the Ganga, and rush impetuously towards the ocean! So what a variety of thoughts and ideas, how many currents of forces, issuing from innumerable saintly hearts, and from brains of geniuses of various lands have already enveloped India, the land of Karma, the arena for the display of higher human activities! Look how under the dominion of the English, in these days of electricity, railroad, and steamboat, various sentiments, manners, customs, and morals are spreading all over the land with lightning speed. Nectar is coming, and along with it, also poison; good is coming, as well as evil. There has been enough of angry opposition and bloodshed; the power of stemming this tide is not in Hindu society. Everything, from water filtered by machinery and drawn from hydrants, down to sugar purified with bone-ash, is being quietly and freely taken by almost every one, in spite of much show of verbal protest. Slowly and slowly, by the strong dint of law, many of our most cherished customs are falling off day by day—we have no power to withstand that. And why is there no power? Is truth really powerless? "Truth alone conquers and not falsehood—Is this Divine Vedic saying false? Or who knows but that those very customs which are being swept away by the deluge of the power of Western sovereignty or of Western education were not real Acharas, but were Anacharas after all. This also is a matter for serious consideration.

बहुजनहिताय बहुजनसुखाय—"For the good of the many, as well as for the happiness of the many"—in an unselfish manner, with a heart filled with love and reverence, the *Udbodhana* invites all wise and large-hearted men who love their motherland to discuss these points and solve these problems; and, being devoid of the feeling of hatred or antagonism, as well as turning itself away from the infliction of abusive language directed towards any individual, or society, or any sect, it offers its whole self for the service of all classes.

To work we have the right, the result is in the hands of the Lord. We only pray: "O Thou Eternal Spirit, make us spiritual; O Thou Eternal Strength, make us strong; O Thou Mighty One, make us mighty."

VII

Man and Freedom

Nature And Man

The modern idea of nature includes only that part of the universe that is manifested on the physical plane. That which is generally understood to be mind is not considered to be nature.

Philosophers endeavouring to prove the freedom of the will have excluded the mind from nature; for as nature is bound and governed by law, strict unbending law, mind, if considered to be in nature, would be bound by law also. Such a claim would destroy the doctrine of free will; for how can that be free which is bound by law?

The philosophers of India have taken the reverse stand. They hold all physical life, manifest and unmanifest, to be bound by law. The mind as well as external nature, they claim, is bound by law, and by one and the same law. If mind is not bound by law, if the thoughts we think are not the necessary results of preceding thoughts, if one mental state is not followed by another which it produces, then mind is irrational; and who can claim free will and at the same time deny the operation of reason? And on the other hand, who can admit that the mind is governed by the law of causation and claim that the will is free?

Law itself is the operation of cause and effect. Certain things happen according to certain other things which have gone before. Every precedent has its consequent. Thus it is in nature. If this operation of law obtains in the mind, the mind is bound and is, therefore, not free. No, the will is not free. How can it be? But we all know, we all feel, that we are free. Life would have no meaning, it would not be worth living, if we were not free,

The Eastern philosophers accepted this doctrine, or rather propounded it, that the mind and the will are within time, space, and causation, the same as so-called matter; and that they are, therefore, bound by the law or causation. We think in time; our thoughts are bound by time; all that exists, exists in time and space. All is bound by the law of causation.

Now that which we call matter and mind are one and the same substance. The only difference is in the degree of vibration. Mind at a very low rate of vibration is what is known as matter. Matter at a high rate of vibration is what is known as mind. Both are the same substance; and, therefore, as matter is bound by time and space and causation, mind which is matter at a high rate of vibration is bound by the same law.

Nature is homogeneous. Differentiation is in manifestation. The Sanskrit word for nature is Prakriti, and means literally differentiation. All is one substance, but it is manifested variously.

Mind becomes matter, and matter in its turn becomes mind, it is simply a question of vibration.

Take a bar of steel and charge it with a force sufficient to cause it to vibrate, and what would happen? If this were done in a dark room, the first thing you would be aware of would be a sound, a humming sound. Increase the force, and the bar of steel would become luminous; increase it still more, and the steel would disappear altogether. It would become mind.

Take another illustration: If I do not eat for ten days, I cannot think. Only a few stray thoughts are in my mind. I am very weak and perhaps do not know my own name. Then

I eat some bread, and in a little while I begin to think; my power of mind has returned. The bread has become mind. Similarly, the mind lessens its rate of vibration and manifests itself in the body, becomes matter.

As to which is first—matter or mind, let me illustrate: A hen lays an egg; the egg brings out another hen; that hen lays another egg; that egg brings out another hen, and so on in an endless chain. Now which is first—the egg or the hen? You cannot think of an egg that was not laid by a hen, or a hen that was not hatched out of an egg. It makes no difference which is first. Nearly all our ideas run themselves into the hen and egg business.

The greatest truths have been forgotten because of their very simplicity. Great truths are simple because they are of universal application. Truth itself is always simple. Complexity is due to man's ignorance.

Man's free agency is not of the mind, for that is bound. There is no freedom there. Man is not mind, he is soul. The soul is ever free, boundless, and eternal. Herein is man's freedom, in the soul. The soul is always free, but the mind identifying itself with its own ephemeral waves, loses sight of the soul and becomes lost in the maze of time, space, and causation—Maya.

This is the cause of our bondage. We are always identifying ourselves with the mind, and the mind's phenomenal changes.

Man's free agency is established in the soul, and the soul, realising itself to be free, is always asserting the fact in spite of the mind's bondage: "I am free! I am what I am! I am what I am!" This is our freedom. The soul—ever free, boundless, eternal—through aeons and aeons is manifesting itself more and more through its instrument, the mind.

What relation then does Man bear to nature? From the lowest form of life to man, the soul is manifesting itself through nature. The highest manifestation of the soul is involved in the lowest form of manifest life and is working itself outward through the process called evolution.

The whole process of evolution is the soul's struggle to manifest itself. It is a constant struggle against nature. It is a struggle against nature, and not conformity to nature, that makes Man what he is. We hear a great deal about living in harmony with nature, of being in tune with nature. This is a mistake. This table, this pitcher, the minerals, a tree, are all in harmony with nature. Perfect harmony there, no discord. To be in harmony with nature means stagnation, death. How did Man build this house? By being in harmony with nature? No. By fighting against nature. It is the constant struggle against nature that constitutes human progress, not conformity with it.

The Reality And Shadow

That which differentiates one thing from another is time, space, and causation.

The differentiation is in the form, not in the substance. You may destroy the form and it disappears forever; but the substance remains the same. You can never destroy the substance.

Evolution is in nature, not in the soul—evolution of nature, manifestation of the soul.

Maya is not illusion as it is popularly interpreted. Maya is real, yet it is not real. It is real in that the Real is behind it and gives it its appearance of reality. That which is real in Maya is the Reality in and through Maya. Yet the Reality is never seen; and hence that which is seen is unreal, and it has no real independent existence of itself, but is dependent upon the Real for its existence.

Maya then is a paradox—real, yet not real, an illusion, yet not an illusion.

He who knows the Real sees in Maya not illusion, but reality. He who knows not the Real sees in Maya illusion and thinks it real.

The Power Of The Mind

The cause becomes the effect. The cause is not one thing and the effect something else that exists as a result. The effect is always the cause worked out. Always, the cause becomes the effect. The popular idea is that the effect is the result of the operation of a cause which is something independent and aloof from the effect. This is not so. The effect is always the cause worked out into another condition.

The universe is really homogeneous. Heterogeneity is only in appearance. There seem to be different substances, different powers, etc., throughout nature. But take two different substances, say a piece of glass and a piece of wood, grind them up together fine enough, reduce them till there is nothing more to reduce, and the substance remaining appears homogeneous. All substances in the last analysis are one. Homogeneity is the substance, the reality; heterogeneity is the appearance of many things as though they were many substances. The One is homogeneity; the appearance of the One as many is heterogeneity.

Hearing, seeing, or tasting, etc. is the mind in different states of action.

The atmosphere of a room may be hypnotised so that everybody who enters it will see all sorts of things—men and objects flying through the air.

Everybody is hypnotised already. The work of attaining freedom, of realising one's real nature, consists in de-hypnotisation.

One thing to be remembered is that we are not gaining powers at all. We have them already. The whole process of growth is de-hypnotisation.

The purer the mind, the easier it is to control. Purity of the mind must be insisted upon if you would control it. Do not think covetously about mere mental powers. Let them go. One who seeks the powers of the mind succumbs to them. Almost all who desire powers become ensnared by them.

Perfect morality is the all in all of complete control over mind. The man who is perfectly moral has nothing more to do; he is free. The man who is perfectly moral cannot possibly hurt anything or anybody. Non-injuring has to be attained by him who would be free. No one is more powerful than he who has attained perfect non-injuring. No one could fight, no one could quarrel, in his presence. Yes, his very presence, and nothing else, means peace, means love wherever he may be. Nobody could be angry or fight in his presence. Even the animals, ferocious animals, would be peaceful before him.

I once knew a Yogi, a very old man, who lived in a hole in the ground all by himself. All he had was a pan or two to cook his meals in. He ate very little, and wore scarcely anything, and spent most of his time meditating.

With him all people were alike. He had attained to non-injuring. What he saw in everything, in every person, in every animal, was the Soul, the Lord of the Universe. With him, every person and every animal was "my Lord". He never addressed any person or animal in any other way. Well, one day a thief came his way and stole one of his pans. He saw him and ran after him. The chase was a long one. At last the thief from exhaustion had to stop, and the Yogi, running up to him, fell on his knees before him and said, "My Lord, you do me a great honour to come my way. Do me the honour to accept the other pan. It is also yours." This old man is dead now. He was full of love for everything in the world. He would have died for an ant. Wild animals instinctively knew this old man to be their friend. Snakes and ferocious animals would go into his hole and sleep with him. They all loved him and never fought in his presence.

Never talk about the faults of others, no matter how bad they may be. Nothing is ever gained by that. You never help one by talking about his fault; you do him an injury, and injure yourself as well.

All regulations in eating, practising, etc., are all right so long as they are complementary to a spiritual aspiration but they are not ends in themselves; they are only helps.

Never quarrel about religion. All quarrels and disputations concerning religion simply show that spirituality is not present. Religious quarrels are always over the husks. When purity, when spirituality goes, leaving the soul dry, quarrels begin, and not before.

The Importance Of Psychology

The idea of psychology in the West is very much degraded. Psychology is the science of sciences; but in the West it is placed upon the same plane as all other sciences; that is, it is judged by the same criterion—utility.

How much practical benefit will it do to humanity? How much will it add to our rapidly growing happiness? How much will it detract from our rapidly increasing pain? Such is the criterion by which everything is judged in the West.

People seem to forget that about ninety per cent of all our knowledge cannot, in the very nature of things, be applied in a practical way to add to our material happiness or to lessen our misery. Only the smallest fraction of our scientific knowledge can have any such practical application to our daily lives. This is so because only an infinitely small percentage of our conscious mind is on the sensuous plane. We have just a little bit of sensuous consciousness and imagine that to be our entire mind and life; but, as a matter of fact, it is but a drop in the mighty ocean of subconscious mind. If all there is of us were a bundle of sense-perceptions, all the knowledge we could gain could be utilised in the gratification of our sense-pleasures. But fortunately such is not the case. As we get further and further away from the animal state, our sense-pleasures become less and less;

and our enjoyment, in a rapidly increasing consciousness of scientific and psychological knowledge, becomes more and more intense; and "knowledge for the sake of knowledge", regardless of the amount of sense-pleasures it may conduce to, becomes the supreme pleasure of the mind.

But even taking the Western idea of utility as a criterion by which to judge, psychology, by such a standard even, is the science of sciences. Why? We are all slaves to our senses, slaves to our own minds, conscious and subconscious. The reason why a criminal is a criminal is not because he desires to be one, but because he has not his mind under control and is, therefore, a slave to his own conscious and subconscious mind, and to the mind of everybody else. He must follow the dominant trend of his mind; he cannot help it; he is forced onward in spite of himself, in spite of his own better promptings, his own better nature; he is forced to obey the dominant mandate of his own mind. Poor man, he cannot help himself. We see this in our own lives constantly. We are constantly doing things against the better side of our nature, and afterwards we upbraid ourselves for so doing and wonder what we could have been thinking of, how we could do such a thing! Yet again and again we do it, and again and again we suffer for it and upbraid ourselves. At the time, perhaps, we think we desire to do it, but we only desire it because we are forced to desire it. We are forced onward, we are helpless! We are all slaves to our own and to everybody else's mind; whether we are good or bad, that makes no difference. We are led here and there because we cannot help ourselves. We say we think, we do, etc. It is not so. We think because we have to think. We act because we have to. We are slaves to ourselves and to others. Deep down in our subconscious mind are stored up all the thoughts and acts of the past, not only of this life, but of all other lives we have lived. This great boundless ocean of subjective mind is full of all the thoughts and actions of the past. Each one of these is striving to be recognised, pushing outward for expression, surging, wave after wave, out upon the objective mind, the conscious mind. These thoughts, the stored-up energy, we take for natural desires, talents, etc. It is because we do not realise their true origin. We obey them blindly, unquestioningly; and slavery, the most helpless kind of slavery, is the result; and we call ourselves free. Free! We who cannot for a moment govern our own minds, nay, cannot hold our minds on a subject, focus it on a point to the exclusion of everything else for a moment! Yet we call ourselves free. Think of it! We cannot do as we know we ought to do even for a very short space of time. Some sense-desire will crop up, and immediately we obey it. Our conscience smites us for such weakness, but again and again we do it, we are always doing it. We cannot live up to a high standard of life, try as we will. The ghosts of past thoughts, past lives hold us down. All the misery of the world is caused by this slavery to the senses. Our inability to rise above the sense-life—the striving for physical pleasures, is the cause of all the horrors and miseries in the world.

It is the science of psychology that teaches us to hold in check the wild gyrations of the mind, place it under the control of the will, and thus free ourselves from its tyrannous mandates. Psychology is, therefore, the science of sciences, without which all sciences and all other knowledge are worthless.

The mind uncontrolled and unguided will drag us down, down, forever—rend us, kill us; and the mind controlled and guided will save us, free us. So it must be controlled, and psychology teaches us how to do it.

To study and analyse any material science, sufficient data are obtained. These facts are studied and analysed, and a knowledge of the science is the result.

But in the study and analysis of the mind, there are no data, no facts acquired from without, such as are equally at the command of all. The mind is analysed by itself. The greatest science, therefore, is the science of the mind, the science of psychology.

In the West, the powers of the mind, especially unusual powers, are looked upon as bordering on witchcraft and mysticism. The study of higher psychology has been retarded by its being identified with mere alleged psychic phenomena, as is done by some mystery-mongering order of Hindu fakirs.

Physicists obtain pretty much the same results the world over. They do not differ in their general facts, nor in the results which naturally follow from such facts. This is because the data of physical science are obtainable by all and are universally recognised, and the results are logical conclusions based upon these universally recognised facts. In the realm of the mind, it is different. Here there are no data, no facts observable by the physical senses, and no universally recognised materials, therefore, from which to build a system of psychology after their being equally experimented upon by all who study the mind.

Deep, deep within, is the soul, the essential man, the Atman. Turn the mind inward and become united to that; and from that standpoint of stability, the gyrations of the mind can be watched and facts observed, which are to be found in all persons. Such facts, such data, are to be found by those who go deep enough, and only by such. Among that large class of self-styled mystics the world over, there is a great difference of opinion as to the mind, its nature, powers, etc. This is because such people do not go deep enough. They have noticed some little activity of their own and others' minds and, without knowing anything about the real character of such superficial manifestations, have published them as facts universal in their application; and every religious and mystical crank has facts, data, etc., which, he claims, are reliable criteria for investigation, but which are in fact nothing more or less than his own imaginings.

If you intend to study the mind, you must have systematic training; you must practise to bring the mind under your control, to attain to that consciousness from which you will be able to study the mind and remain unmoved by any of its wild gyrations. Otherwise the facts observed will not be reliable; they will not apply to all people and, therefore, will not be truly facts or data at all.

Among that class who have gone deeply into the study of the mind, the facts observed have been the same, no matter in what part of the world such persons may be or what religious belief they may have. The results obtained by all who go deep enough into the mind are the same.

The mind operates by perception and impulsion. For instance, the rays of the light enter by eyes, are carried by the nerves to the brain, and still I do not see the light. The brain then conveys the impulse to the mind, but yet I do not see the light; the mind then reacts, and the light flashes across the mind. The mind's reaction is impulsion, and as a result the eye perceives the object.

To control the mind you must go deep down into the subconscious mind, classify and arrange in order all the different impressions, thoughts, etc., stored up there, and control them. This is the first step. By the control of the subconscious mind you get control over the conscious.

Freedom Of The Self

As we cannot know except through effects that we have eyes, so we cannot see the Self except by Its effects. It cannot be brought down to the low plane of sense-perception. It is the condition of everything in the universe, though Itself unconditioned. When we know that we are the Self, then we are free. The Self can never change. It cannot be acted on by a cause, because It is Itself the cause. It is self-caused. If we can find in ourself something that is not acted on by any cause, then we have known the Self.

Freedom is inseparably connected with immortality. To be free one must be above the laws of nature. Law exists so long as we are ignorant. When knowledge comes, then we find that law nothing but freedom in ourselves. The will can never be free, because it is the slave of cause and effect. But the "I" behind the will is free; and this is the Self. "I am free"—that is the basis on which to build and live. And freedom means immortality.

Law And Freedom

The struggle never had meaning for the man who is free. But for us it has a meaning, because it is name-and-form that creates the world.

We have a place for struggle in the Vedanta, but not for fear. All fears will vanish when you begin to assert your own nature. If you think that you are bound, bound you will remain. If you think you are free, free you will be.

That sort of freedom which we can feel when we are yet in the phenomenal is a glimpse of the real but not yet the real.

I disagree with the idea that freedom is obedience to the laws of nature. I do not understand what it means. According to the history of human progress, it is disobedience to nature that has constituted that progress. It may be said that the conquest of lower laws was through the higher. But even there, the conquering mind was only trying to be free; and as soon as it found that the struggle was also through law, it wanted to conquer that also. So the ideal was freedom in every case. The trees never disobey law. I never saw a cow steal. An oyster never told a lie. Yet they are not greater than man. This life is a tremendous assertion of freedom; and this obedience to law, carried far enough, would make us simply matter—either in society, or in politics, or in religion. Too many laws are a sure sign of death. Wherever in any society there are too many laws, it is a sure sign that that society will soon die. If you study the characteristics of India, you will find that no nation possesses so many laws as the Hindus, and national death is the result. But the Hindus had one peculiar idea—they never made any doctrines or dogmas in religion; and the latter has had the greatest growth. Eternal law cannot be freedom, because to say that the eternal is inside law is to limit it.

There is no purpose in view with God, because if there were some purpose, He would be nothing better than a man. Why should He need any purpose? If He had any, He would be bound by it. There would be something besides Him which was greater. For instance, the carpet-weaver makes a piece of carpet. The idea was outside of him, something greater. Now where is the idea to which God would adjust Himself? Just as the greatest emperors sometimes play with dolls, so He is playing with this nature; and what we call law is this. We call it law, because we can see only little bits which run smoothly. All our ideas of law are within the little bit. It is nonsense to say that law is infinite, that throughout all time stones will fall. If all reason be based upon experience, who was there to see if stones fell five millions of years ago? So law is not constitutional in man. It is a scientific assertion as to Man that where we begin, there we end. As a matter of fact, we get gradually outside of law, until we get out altogether, but with the added experience of a whole life. In God and freedom we began, and freedom and God will be the end. These laws are in the middle state through which we have to pass. Our Vedanta is the assertion of freedom always. The very idea of law will frighten the Vedantist; and eternal law is a very dreadful thing for him, because there would be no escape. If there is to be an eternal law binding him all the time, where is the difference between him and a blade of grass? We do not believe in that abstract idea of law.

We say that it is freedom that we are to seek, and that that freedom is God. It is the same happiness as in everything else; but when Man seeks it in something which is finite, he gets only a spark of it. The thief when he steals gets the same happiness as the man who finds it in God; but the thief gets only a little spark with a mass of misery. The real happiness is God. Love is God, freedom is God; and everything that is bondage is not God.

Man has freedom already, but he will have to discover it. He has it, but every moment forgets it. That discovering, consciously or unconsciously, is the whole life of every one. But the difference between the sage and the ignorant man is that one does it consciously and the other unconsciously. Every one is struggling for freedom—from the atom to the star. The ignorant man is satisfied if he can get freedom within a certain limit—if he can get rid of the bondage of hunger or of being thirsty. But that sage feels that there is a stronger bondage which has to be thrown off. He would not consider the freedom of the Red Indian as freedom at all.

According to our philosophers, freedom is the goal. Knowledge cannot be the goal, because knowledge is a compound. It is a compound of power and freedom, and it is freedom alone that is desirable. That is what men struggle after. Simply the possession of power would not be knowledge. For instance, a scientist can send an electric shock to a distance of some miles; but nature can send it to an unlimited distance. Why do we not build statues to nature then? It is not law that we want but ability to break law. We want to be outlaws. If you are bound by laws, you will be a lump of clay. Whether you are beyond law or not is not the question; bu t the thought that we are beyond law—upon that is based the whole history of humanity. For instance, a man lives in a forest, and never has had any education or knowledge. He sees a stone falling down—a natural phenomenon happening—and he thinks it is freedom. He thinks it has a soul, and the central idea in that is freedom. But as soon as he knows that it must fall, he calls it nature—dead, mechanical action. I may or may not go into the street. In that is my glory as a man. If I am sure that I must go there, I give myself up and become a machine. Nature with its infinite power is only a machine; freedom alone constitutes sentient life.

The Vedanta says that the idea of the man in the forest is the right one; his glimpse is right, but the explanation is wrong. He holds to this nature as freedom and not as governed by law. Only after all this human experience we will come back to think the same, but in a more philosophical sense. For instance, I want to go out into the street. I get the impulse of my will, and then I stop; and in the time that intervenes between the will and going into the street, I am working uniformly. Uniformity of action is what we call law. This uniformity of my actions, I find, is broken into very short periods, and so I do not call my actions under law. I work through freedom. I walk for five minutes; but before those five minutes of walking, which are uniform, there was the action of the will, which gave the impulse to walk. Therefore, man says he is free, because all his actions can be cut up into small periods; and although there is sameness in the small periods, beyond the period there is not the same sameness. In this perception of non-uniformity is the idea of freedom. In nature we see only very large periods of uniformity; but the beginning and end must be free impulses. The impulse of freedom was given just at the beginning, and that has rolled on; but this, compared with our periods, is much longer. We find by analysis on philosophic grounds that we are not free. But there will remain this factor, this consciousness that I am free. What we have to explain is, how that comes. We will find that we have these two impulsions in us. Our reason tells us that all our actions are caused, and at the same time, with every impulse we are asserting our freedom. The solution of the Vedanta is that there is freedom inside—that the soul is really free—but that that soul's actions are percolating through body and mind, which are not free.

As soon as we react, we become slaves. A man blames me, and I immediately react in the form of anger. A little vibration which he created made me a slave. So we have to demonstrate our freedom. They alone are the sages who see in the highest, most learned man, or the lowest animal, or the worst and most wicked of mankind, neither a man nor a sage nor an animal, but the same God in all of them. Even in this life they have conquered relativity, and have taken a firm stand upon this equality. God is pure, the same to all. Therefore, such a sage would be a living God. This is the goal towards which we are going; and every form of worship, every action of mankind, is a method of attaining to it. The man who wants money is striving for freedom—to get rid of the bondage of poverty. Every action of Man is worship, because the idea is to attain to freedom, and all action, directly or indirectly, tends to that. Only, those actions that deter are to be avoided. The whole universe is worshipping, consciously or unconsciously; only it does not know that even while it is cursing, it is in another form worshipping the same God it is cursing, because those who are cursing are also struggling for freedom. They never think that in reacting from a thing they are making themselves slaves to it. It is hard to kick against the pricks.

If we could get rid of the belief in our limitations, it would be possible for us to do everything just now. It is only a question of time. If that is so, add power, and so diminish time. Remember the case of the professor who learnt the secret of the development of marble and who made marble in twelve years, while it took nature centuries.

Man The Maker Of His Destiny

There was a very powerful dynasty in Southern India. They made it a rule to take the horoscope of all the prominent men living from time to time, calculated from the time of their birth. In this way they got a record of leading facts predicted, and compared them afterwards with events as they happened. This was done for a thousand years, until they found certain agreements; these were generalised and recorded and made into a huge book. The dynasty died out, but the family of astrologers lived and had the book in their possession. It seems possible that this is how astrology came into existence. Excessive attention to the minutiae of astrology is one of the superstitions which has hurt the Hindus very much.

I think the Greeks first took astrology to India and took from the Hindus the science of astronomy and carried it back with them to Europe. Because in India you will find old altars made according to a certain geometrical plan, and certain things had to be done when the stars were in certain positions, therefore, I think the Greeks gave the Hindus astrology, and the Hindus gave them astronomy.

I have seen some astrologers who predicted wonderful things; but I have no reason to believe they predicted them only from the stars, or anything of the sort. In many cases it is simply mind-reading. Sometimes wonderful predictions are made, but in many cases it is arrant trash.

In London, a young man used to come to me and ask me, "What will become of me next year?" I asked him why he asked me so. "I have lost all my money and have become very, very poor." Money is the only God of many beings. Weak men, when they lose everything and feel themselves weak, try all sorts of uncanny methods of making money, and come to astrology and all these things. "It is the coward and the fool who says, 'This is fate'"—so says the Sanskrit proverb. But it is the strong man who stands up and says, "I will make my fate." It is people who are getting old who talk of fate. Young men generally do not come to astrology. We *may* be under planetary influence, but it should not matter much to us. Buddha says, "Those that get a living by calculation of the stars by such art and other lying tricks are to be avoided"; and he ought to know, because he was the greatest Hindu ever born. Let stars come, what harm is there? If a star disturbs my life, it would not be worth a cent. You will find that astrology and all these mystical things are generally signs of a weak mind; therefore, as soon as they are becoming prominent in our minds, we should see a physician, take good food and rest.

If you can get an explanation of a phenomenon from within its nature, it is nonsense to look for an explanation from outside. If the world explains itself, it is nonsense to go outside for an explanation. Have you found any phenomena in the life of a man that you have ever seen which cannot be explained by the power of the man himself? So what is the use of going to the stars or anything else in the world? My own Karma is sufficient explanation of my present state. So in the case of Jesus himself. We know that his father was only a carpenter. We need not go to anybody else to find an explanation of his power. He was the outcome of his own past, all of which was a preparation for that Jesus. Buddha goes back and back to animal bodies and tells how he ultimately became Buddha. So what is the use of going to stars for explanation? They may have a little influence; but it is our duty to ignore them rather than hearken to them and make ourselves nervous. This I lay down as the first essential in all I teach: anything that brings spiritual, mental, or physical weakness, touch it not with the toes of your feet. Religion is the manifestation of the natural strength that is in man. A spring of infinite power is coiled up and is inside this little body, and that spring is spreading itself. And as it goes on spreading, body after body is found insufficient; it throws them off and takes higher bodies. This is the history of man, of religion, civilisation, or progress. That giant Prometheus, who is bound, is getting himself unbound. It is always a manifestation of strength, and all these ideas such as astrology, although there may be a grain of truth in them, should be avoided.

There is an old story of an astrologer who came to a king and said, "You are going to die in six months." The king was frightened out of his wits and was almost about to die then and there from fear. But his minister was a clever man, and this man told the king that these astrologers were fools. The king would not believe him. So the minister saw no other way to make the king see that they were fools but to invite the astrologer to the palace again. There he asked him if his calculations were correct. The astrologer said that there could not be a mistake, but to satisfy him he went through the whole of the calculations again and then said that they were perfectly correct. The king's face became livid. The minister said to the astrologer, "And when do you think you will die?" "In twelve years," was the reply. The minister quickly drew his sword and separated the astrologer's head from the body and said to the king, "Do you see this liar? He is dead this moment."

If you want your nation to live, keep away from all these things. The only test of good things is that they make us strong. Good is life, evil is death. These superstitious ideas are springing like mushrooms in your country, and women wanting in logical analysis of things are ready to believe them. It is because women are striving for liberation, and women have not yet established themselves intellectually. One gets by heart a few lines of poetry from the top of a novel and says she knows the whole of Browning. Another attends a course of three lectures and then thinks she knows everything in the world. The difficulty is that they are unable to throw off the natural superstition of women. They have a lot of money and some intellectual learning, but when they have passed through this transition stage and get on firm ground, they will be all right. But they are played upon by charlatans. Do not be sorry; I do not mean to hurt any one, but I have to tell the truth. Do you not see how open you are to these things? Do you not see how sincere these women are, how that divinity latent in all never dies? It is only to know how to appeal to the Divine.

The more I live, the more I become convinced every day that every human being is divine. In no man or woman, however vile, does that divinity die. Only he or she does not know how to reach it and is waiting for the Truth. And wicked people are trying to deceive him or her with all sorts of fooleries. If one man cheats another for money, you say he is a fool and a blackguard. How much greater is the iniquity of one who wants to fool others spiritually! This is too bad. It is the one test, that truth must make you strong and put you above superstition. The duty of the philosopher is to raise you above superstition. Even this world, this body and mind are superstitions; what infinite souls you are! And to be tricked by twinkling stars! It is a shameful condition. You are divinities; the twinkling stars owe their existence to you.

I was once travelling in the Himalayas, and the long road stretched before us. We poor monks cannot get any one to carry us, so we had to make all the way on foot. There was an old man with us. The way goes up and down for hundreds of miles, and when that old monk saw what was before him, he said, "Oh Sir, how to cross it; I cannot walk any more; my chest will break." I said to him, "Look down at your feet." He did so, and I said, "The road that is under your feet is the road that you have passed over and is the same road that you see before you; it will soon be under your feet." The highest things are under your feet, because you are Divine Stars; all these things are under your feet. You can swallow the stars by the handful if you want; such is your real nature. Be strong, get beyond all superstitions, and be free.

On Doing Good To The World

We are asked: What good is your Religion to society? Society is made a test of truth. Now this is very illogical. Society is only a stage of growth through which we are passing. We might just as well judge the good or utility of a scientific discovery by its use to the baby. It is simply monstrous. If the social state were permanent, it would be the same as if the baby remained a baby. There can be no perfect man-baby; the words are a contradiction in terms, so there can be no perfect society. Man must and will grow out of such early stages. Society is good at a certain stage, but it cannot be our ideal; it is a constant flux. The present mercantile civilisation must die, with all its pretensions and humbugs—all a kind of "Lord Mayor's Show". What the world wants is thought-power through individuals. My Master used to say, "Why don't you help your own lotus flower to bloom? The bees will then come of themselves." The world needs people who are mad with the love of God. You must believe in yourself, and then you will believe in God. The history of the world is that of six men of faith, six men of deep pure character. We need to have three things; the heart to feel, the brain to conceive, the hand to work. First we must go out of the world and make ourselves fit instruments. Make yourself a dynamo. *Feel* first for the world. At a time when all men are ready to work, where is the man of *feeling?* Where is the feeling that produced an Ignatius Loyola? Test your love and humility. That man is not humble or loving who is jealous. Jealousy is a terrible, horrible sin; it enters a man so mysteriously. Ask yourself, does your mind react in hatred or jealousy? Good works are continually being undone by the tons of hatred and anger which are being poured out on the world. If you are pure, if you are strong, *you, one* man, are equal to the whole world.

The brain to conceive the next condition of doing good works is only a dry Sahara after all; it cannot do anything alone unless it has the *feeling* behind it. Take love, which has never failed; and then the brain will conceive, and the hand will work righteousness. Sages have dreamed of and have *seen* the vision of God. "The pure in heart shall see God." All the great ones claim to have *seen* God. Thousands of years ago has the vision been seen, and the unity which lies beyond has been recognised; and now the only thing we can do is to fill in these glorious outlines.

The Goal

Dualism recognises God and nature to be eternally separate: the universe and nature eternally dependent upon God.

The extreme monists make no such distinction. In the last analysis, they claim, all is God: the universe becomes lost in God; God is the eternal life of the universe.

With them infinite and finite are mere terms. The universe, nature, etc., exist by virtue of differentiation. Nature is itself differentiation.

Such questions as, "Why did God create the universe?" "Why did the All-perfect create the imperfect?" etc., can never be answered, because such questions are logical absurdities. Reason exists in nature; beyond nature it has no existence. God is omnipotent, hence to ask why He did so and so is to limit Him; for it implies that there is a purpose in His creating the universe. If He has a purpose, it must be a means to an end, and this would mean that He could not have the end without the means. The questions, why and wherefore, can only be asked of something which depends upon something else.

Work Is Worship

The highest man cannot work, for there is no binding element, no attachment, no ignorance in him. A ship is said to have passed over a mountain of magnet ore, and all the bolts and bars were drawn out, and it went to pieces. It is in ignorance that struggle remains, because we are all really atheists. Real theists cannot work. We are atheists more or less. We do not see God or believe in Him. He is G-O-D to us, and nothing more. There are moments when we think He is near, but then we fall down again. When you see Him, who struggles for whom? Help the Lord! There is a proverb in our language, "Shall we teach the Architect of the universe how to build?" So those are the highest of mankind who do not work. The next time you see these silly phrases about the world and how we must all help God and do this or that for Him, remember this. Do not think such thoughts; they are too selfish. All the work you do is subjective, is done for your own benefit. God has not fallen into a ditch for you and me to help Him out by building a hospital or something of that sort. He *allows* you to work. He allows you to exercise your muscles in this great gymnasium, not in order to help Him but that you may help yourself. Do you think even an ant will die for want of your help? Most arrant blasphemy! The world does not need you at all. The world goes on, you are like a drop in the ocean. A leaf does not move, the wind does not blow without Him. Blessed are we that we are given the privilege of working for Him, not of helping Him. Cut out this word "help" from your mind. You cannot help; it is blaspheming. You are here yourself at His pleasure. Do you mean to say, you help Him? You worship. When you give a morsel of food to the dog, you worship the dog as God. God is in that dog. He is the dog. He is all and in all. We are allowed to worship Him. Stand in that reverent attitude to the whole universe, and then will come perfect non-attachment. This should be your duty. This is the proper attitude of work. This is the secret taught by Karma Yoga.

On Charity

During his stay in Madras the Swami presided at the annual meeting of the Chennapuri Annadana Samajam, an institution of a charitable nature, and in the course of a brief address referred to a remark by a previous speaker deprecating special alms-giving to the Brahmin over and above the other castes. Swamiji pointed out that this had its good as well as its bad side. All the culture, practically, which the nation possessed, was among the Brahmins, and they also had been the thinkers of the nation. Take away the means of living which enabled them to be thinkers, and the nation as a whole would suffer. Speaking of the indiscriminate charity of India as compared with the legal charity of other nations, he said, the outcome of their system of relief was that the vagabond of India was contented to receive readily what he was given readily and lived a peaceful and contented life; while the vagabond in the West, unwilling to go to the poor-house—for Man loves liberty more than food—turned a robber, the enemy of society, and necessitated the organisation of a system of magistracy, police, jails, and other establishments. Poverty there must be, so long as the disease known as civilisation existed; and hence the need for relief. So that they had to choose between the indiscriminate charity of India, which, in the case of Sannyasins at any rate, even if they were not sincere men. at least forced them to learn some little of their scriptures

On Fanaticism

There are fanatics of various kinds. Some people are wine fanatics and cigar fanatics. Some think that if men gave up smoking cigars, the world would arrive at the millennium. Women are generally amongst these fanatics. There was a young lady here one day, in this class. She was one of a number of ladies in Chicago who have built a house where they take in the working people and give them music and gymnastics. One day this young lady was talking about the evils of the world and said she knew the remedy. I asked, "How do you know?" and she answered, "Have you seen Hull House?" In her opinion, this Hull House is the one panacea for all the evils that flesh is heir to. This will grow upon her. I am sorry for her. There are some fanatics in India who think that if a woman could marry again when her husband died, it would cure all evil. This is fanaticism.

When I was a boy I thought that fanaticism was a great element in work, but now, as I grow older, I find out that it is not.

There may be a woman who would steal and make no objection to taking someone else's bag and going away with it. But perhaps that woman does not smoke. She becomes a smoke fanatic, and as soon as she finds a man smoking, she strongly disapproves of him, because he smokes a cigar. There may be a man who goes about cheating people; there is no trusting him; no woman is safe with him. But perhaps this scoundrel does not drink wine. If so, he sees nothing good in anyone who drinks wine. All these wicked things that he himself does are of no consideration. This is only natural human selfishness and one-sidedness.

You must also remember that the world has God to govern it, and He has not left it to our charity. The Lord God is its Governor and Maintainer, and in spite of these wine fanatics and cigar fanatics, and all sorts of marriage fanatics, it would go on. If all these persons were to die, it would go on none the worse.

Do you not remember in your own history how the "Mayflower" people came out here, and began to call themselves Puritans? They were very pure and good as far as they went, until they began to persecute other people; and throughout the history of mankind it has been the same. Even those that run away from persecution indulge in persecuting others as soon as a favourable opportunity to do so occurs.

In ninety cases out of a hundred, fanatics must have bad livers, or they are dyspeptics, or are in some way diseased. By degrees even physicians will find out that fanaticism is a kind of disease. I have seen plenty of it. The Lord save me from it!

My experience comes to this, that it is rather wise to avoid all sorts of fanatical reforms. This world is slowly going on; let it go slowly. Why are you in a hurry? Sleep well and keep your nerves in good order; eat right food, and have sympathy with the world. Fanatics only make hatred. Do you mean to say that the temperate fanatic loves these poor people who become drunkards? A fanatic is a fanatic simply because he expects to get something for himself in return. As soon as the battle is over, he goes for the spoil. When you come out of the company of fanatics you may learn how really to love and sympathise. And the more you attain of love and sympathy, the less will be the city of Minneapolis. There was a cowboy on the train. He was a rough sort of a fellow and a Presbyterian of the blue nose type. He walked up and asked me where I was from. I told him India. 'What are you?' he said. 'Hindu',

I replied. 'Then you must go to hell', he remarked. I told him of this theory, and after [my] explaining it, he said he had always believed in it because he said that one day when he was chopping a log, his little sister came out in her clothes and said that she used to be a man. That is why he believed in the transmigration of souls. The whole basis of the theory is this: If a man's actions be good, he must be a higher being, and vice versa.

"There is another beauty in this theory—the moral motor [motive] it supplies. What is done is done. It says, 'Ah, that it were done better.' Do not put your finger in the fire again. Every moment is a new chance."

Vive Kananda spoke in this strain for some time, and he was frequently applauded.

Swami Vive Kananda will lecture again this afternoon at 4 o'clock at La Salette Academy on "The Manners and Customs of India."

Worldwide Unity

Speaking of the world-wide unity, before the Oak Beach Christian Unity, Swami Vivekananda said:

"All religions are, at the bottom, alike. This is so, although the Christian Church, like the Pharisee in the parable, thanks God that it alone is right and thinks that all other religions are wrong and in need of Christian light. Christianity must become tolerant before the world will be willing to unite with the Christian Church in a common charity. God has not left Himself without a witness in any heart, and men, especially men who follow Jesus Christ, should be willing to admit this. In fact, Jesus Christ was willing to admit every good man to the family of God. It is not the man who believes a certain something, but the man who does the will of the Father in heaven, who is right. On this basis—being right and doing right—the whole world can unite."

The Free Soul

Delivered in New York, 1896

The analysis of the Sankhyas stops with the duality of existence—Nature and souls. There are an infinite number of souls, which, being simple, cannot die, and must, therefore, be separate from Nature. Nature in itself changes and manifests all these phenomena; and the soul, according to the Sankhyas, is inactive. It is a simple by itself, and Nature works out all these phenomena for the liberation of the soul; and liberation consists in the soul discriminating that it is not Nature. At the same time we have seen that the Sankhyas were bound to admit that every soul was omnipresent. Being a simple, the soul cannot be limited, because all limitation comes either through time, space, or causation. The soul being entirely beyond these cannot have any limitation. To have limitation one must be in space, which means the body; and that which is body must be in Nature. If the soul had form, it would be identified with Nature; therefore, the soul is formless, and that which is formless cannot be said to exist here, there, or anywhere. It must be omnipresent. Beyond this the Sankhya philosophy does not go.

The first argument of the Vedantists against this is that this analysis is not a perfect one. If their Nature be absolute and the soul be also absolute, there will be two absolutes, and all the arguments that apply in the case of the soul to show that it is omnipresent will apply in the case of Nature, and Nature too will be beyond all time, space, and causation, and as the result there will be no change or manifestation. Then will come the difficulty of having two absolutes, which is impossible. What is the solution of the Vedantist? His solution is that, just as the Sankhyas say, it requires some sentient Being as the motive power behind, which makes the mind think and Nature work, because Nature in all its modifications, from gross matter up to Mahat (intelligence), is simply insentient. Now, says the Vedantist, this sentient Being which is behind the whole universe is what we call God, and consequently this universe is not different from Him. It is He Himself who has become this universe. He not only is the instrumental cause of this universe, but also the material cause. Cause is never different from effect, the effect is but the cause reproduced in another form. We see that every day. So this Being is the cause of Nature. All the forms and phases of Vedanta, either dualistic, or qualified-monistic, or monistic, first take this position that God is not only the instrumental, but also the material cause of this universe, that everything which exists is He. The second step in Vedanta is that these souls are also a part of God, one spark of that Infinite Fire. "As from a mass of fire millions of small particles fly, even so from this Ancient One have come all these souls." So far so good, but it does not yet satisfy. What is meant by a part of the Infinite? The Infinite is indivisible; there cannot be parts of the Infinite. The Absolute cannot be divided. What is meant, therefore, by saying that all these sparks are from Him? The Advaitist, the non-dualistic Vedantist, solves the problem by maintaining that there is really no part; that each soul is really not a part of the Infinite, but actually is the Infinite Brahman. Then how can there be so many? The sun reflected from millions of globules of water appears to be millions of suns, and in each globule is a miniature picture of the sun-form; so all these souls are but reflections and not real. They are not the real "I" which is the God of this universe, the one undivided Being of the universe. And all these little different beings, men and animals etc. are but reflections, and not real. They are simply illusory reflections upon Nature. There is but one Infinite Being in the universe, and that Being appears as you and as I; but this appearance of divisions is after all a delusion. He has not been divided, but only appears to be divided. This apparent division is caused by looking at Him through the network of time, space, and causation. When I look at God through the network of time, space, and causation, I see Him as the material world. When I look at Him from a little higher plane, yet through the same network, I see Him as an animal, a little higher as a man, a little higher as a god, but yet He is the One Infinite Being of the universe, and that Being we are. I am That, and you are That. Not parts of It, but the whole of It. "It is the Eternal Knower standing behind the whole phenomena; He Himself is the phenomena." He is both the subject and the object, He is the "I" and the "You". How is this? "How to know the Knower? The Knower cannot know Himself; I see everything but cannot see myself. The Self, the Knower, the Lord of all, the Real Being, is the cause of all the vision that is in the universe, but it is impossible for Him to see Himself or know Himself, excepting through reflection. You cannot see your own face except in a mirror, and so the Self cannot see Its own nature until It is reflected, and this whole universe, therefore, is the Self trying to realise Itself. This reflection is thrown back first from the protoplasm, then from plants and animals, and so on and on from better and better reflectors, until the best reflector, the perfect man, is reached—just as a man who, wanting to see his face, looks first in a little pool of muddy water, and sees just an outline; then he comes to clear water, and sees a better image; then to a piece of shining metal, and sees a still better image; and at last to a looking-glass, and sees himself reflected as he is. Therefore, the perfect man is the highest reflection of that Being who is both subject and object. You now find why Man instinctively worships everything, and how perfect men are instinctively worshipped as God in every country. You may talk as you like, but it is they who are bound to be worshipped. That is why men worship Incarnations, such as Christ or Buddha. They are the most perfect manifestations of the eternal Self. They are much higher than all the conceptions of God that you or I can make. A perfect man is much higher than such conceptions. In him the circle becomes complete; the subject and the object become one. In him all delusions go away and in their place comes the realisation that he has always been that perfect Being. How came this bondage then? How was it possible for this perfect Being to degenerate into the imperfect? How was it possible that the free became bound? The Advaitist says, he was never bound, but was always free. Various clouds of various colours come before the sky. They remain there a minute and then pass away. It is the same eternal blue sky stretching there for ever. The sky never changes: it is the cloud that is changing. So you are always perfect, eternally perfect. Nothing ever changes your nature, or ever will. All these ideas that I am imperfect, I am a man, or a woman, or a sinner, or I am the mind, I have thought, I will think—all are hallucinations; you never think, you never had a body; you never were imperfect. You are the blessed Lord of this universe, the one Almighty ruler of everything that is and ever will be, the one mighty ruler of these suns and stars and moons and earths and planets and all the little bits of our universe. It is through you that the sun shines and the stars shed their lustre, and the earth becomes beautiful. It is through your blessedness that they all love and are attracted to each other. You are in all, and you are all. Whom to avoid, and whom to take? You are the all in all. When this knowledge comes delusion immediately vanishes.

I was once travelling in the desert in India. I travelled for over a month and always found the most beautiful landscapes before me, beautiful lakes and all that. One day I was very thirsty and I wanted to have a drink at one of these lakes; but when I approached that lake it vanished. Immediately with a blow came into my brain the idea that this was a mirage about which I had read all my life; and then I remembered and smiled at my folly, that for the last month all the beautiful landscapes and lakes I had been seeing were this mirage, but I could not distinguish them then. The next morning I again began my march; there was the lake and the landscape, but with it immediately came the idea, "This is a mirage." Once known it had lost its power of illusion. So this illusion of the universe will break one day. The whole of this will vanish, melt away. This is realisation. Philosophy is no joke or talk. It has to be realised; this body will vanish, this earth and everything will vanish, this idea that I am the body or the mind will for some time vanish, or if the Karma is ended it will disappear, never to come back; but if one part of the Karma remains, then as a potter's wheel, after the potter has finished the pot, will sometimes go on from the past momentum, so this body, when the delusion has vanished altogether, will go on for some time. Again this world will come, men and women and animals will come, just as the mirage came the next day, but not with the same force; along with it will come the idea that I know its nature now, and it will cause no bondage, no more pain, nor grief, nor misery. Whenever anything miserable will come, the mind will be able to say, "I know you as hallucination." When a man has reached that state, he is called Jivanmukta, living-free, free even while living. The aim and end in this life for the Jnana Yogi is to become this Jivanmukta, "living-free". He is Jivanmukta who can live in this world without being attached. He is like the lotus leaves in water, which are never wetted by the water. He is the highest of human beings, nay, the highest of all beings, for he has realised his identity with the Absolute, he has realised that he is one with God. So long as you think you have the least difference from God, fear will seize you, but when you have known that you are He, that there is no difference, entirely no difference, that you are He, all of Him, and the whole of Him, all fear ceases. "There, who sees whom? Who worships whom? Who talks to whom? Who hears whom? Where one sees another, where one talks to another, where one hears another, that is little. Where none sees none, where none speaks to none, that is the highest, that is the great, that is the Brahman." Being That, you are always That. What will become of the world then? What good shall we do to the world? Such questions do not arise "What becomes of my gingerbread if I become old?" says the baby! "What becomes of my marbles if I grow? So I will not grow," says the boy! "What will become of my dolls if I grow old?" says the little child! It is the same question in connection with this world, it has no existence in the past, present, or future. If we have known the Atman as It is, if we have known that there is nothing else but this Atman, that everything else is but a dream, with no existence in reality, then this world with its poverties, its miseries, its wickedness, and its goodness will cease to disturb us. If they do not exist, for whom and for what shall we take trouble? This is what the Jnana Yogis teach. Therefore, dare to be free, dare to go as far as your thought leads, and dare to carry that out in your life. It is very hard to come to Jnana. It is for the bravest and most daring, who dare to smash all idols, not only intellectual, but in the senses. This body is not I; it must go. All sorts of curious things may come out of this. A man stands up and says, "I am not the body, therefore, my headache must be cured"; but where is the headache if not in his body? Let a thousand headaches and a thousand bodies come and go. What is that to me? I have neither birth nor death; father or mother I never had; friends and foes I have none, because they are all I. I am my own friend, and I am my own enemy. I am Existence-Knowledge-Bliss Absolute. I am He, I am He. If in a thousand bodies I am suffering from fever and other ills, in millions of bodies I am healthy. If in a thousand bodies I am starving, in other thousand bodies I am feasting. If in thousands of bodies I am suffering misery, in thousands of bodies I am happy. Who shall blame whom, who praise whom? Whom to seek, whom to avoid? I seek none, nor avoid any, for I am all the universe. I praise myself, I blame myself, I suffer for myself, I am happy at my own will, I am free. This is the Jnani, the brave and daring. Let the whole universe tumble down; he smiles and says it never existed, it was all a hallucination. He sees the universe tumble down. Where was it! Where has it gone!

Before going into the practical part, we will take up one more intellectual question. So far the logic is tremendously rigorous. If Man reasons, there is no place for him to stand until he comes to this, that there is but One Existence, that everything else is nothing. There is no other way left for rational mankind but to take this view. But how is it that what is infinite, ever perfect, ever blessed, Existence-Knowledge-Bliss Absolute, has come under these delusions? It is the same question that has been asked all the world over. In the vulgar form the question becomes, "How did sin come into this world?" This is the most vulgar and sensuous form of the question, and the other is the most philosophic form, but the answer is the same. The same question has been asked in various grades and fashions, but in its lower forms it finds no solution, because the stories of apples and serpents and women do not give the explanation. In that state, the question is childish, and so is the answer. But the question has assumed very high proportions now: "How did this illusion come?" And the answer is as fine. The answer is that we cannot expect any answer to an impossible question. The very question is impossible in terms. You have no right to ask that question. Why? What is perfection? That which is beyond time, space, and causation—that is perfect. Then you ask how the perfect became imperfect. In logical language the question may be put in this form: "How did that which is beyond causation become caused?" You contradict yourself. You first admit it is beyond causation, and then ask what causes it. This question can only be asked within the limits of causation. As far as time and space and causation extend, so far can this question be asked. But beyond that it will be nonsense to ask it, because the question is illogical. Within time, space, and causation it can never be answered, and what answer may lie beyond these limits can only be known when we have transcended them; therefore, the wise will let this question rest. When a man is ill, he devotes himself to curing his disease without insisting that he must first learn how he came to have it.

There is another form of this question, a little lower, but more practical and illustrative: What produced this delusion? Can any reality produce delusion? Certainly not. We see that one delusion produces another, and so on. It is delusion always that produces delusion. It is disease that produces disease, and not health that produces disease. The wave is the same thing as the water, the effect is the cause in another form. The effect is delusion, and, therefore, the cause must be delusion. What produced this delusion? Another delusion. And so on without beginning. The only question that remains for you to ask is: Does not this break your monism, because you get two existences in the universe, one yourself and the other the delusion? The answer is: Delusion cannot be called an existence. Thousands of dreams come into your life, but do not form any part of your life. Dreams come and go; they have no existence. To call delusion existence will be sophistry. Therefore, there is only one individual existence in the universe, ever free, and ever blessed; and that is what you are. This is the last conclusion reached by the Advaitists.

It may then be asked: What becomes of all these various forms of worship? They will remain; they are simply groping in the dark for light, and through this groping light will come. We have just seen that the Self cannot see Itself. Our knowledge is within the network of Maya (unreality), and beyond that is freedom. Within the network there is slavery, it is all under law; beyond that there is no law. So far as the universe is concerned, existence is ruled by law, and beyond that is freedom. As long as you are in the network of time, space, and causation, to say you are free is nonsense, because in that network all is under rigorous law, sequence, and consequence. Every thought that you think is caused, every feeling has been caused; to say that the will is free is sheer nonsense. It is only when the infinite existence comes, as it were, into this network of Maya that it takes the form of will. Will is a portion of that being, caught in the network of Maya, and, therefore, "free will" is a misnomer. It means nothing—sheer nonsense. So is all this talk about freedom. There is no freedom in Maya.

Every one is as much bound in thought, word, deed, and mind, as a piece of stone or this table. That I talk to you now is as rigorous in causation as that you listen to me. There is no freedom until you go beyond Maya. That is the real freedom of the soul. Men, however sharp and intellectual, however clearly they see the force of the logic that nothing here can be free, are all compelled to think they are free; they cannot help it. No work can go on until we begin to say we are free. It means that the freedom we talk about is the glimpse of the blue sky through the clouds and that the real freedom—the blue sky itself— is behind. True freedom cannot exist in the midst of this delusion, this hallucination, this nonsense of the world, this universe of the senses, body, and mind. All these dreams, without beginning or end, uncontrolled and uncontrollable, ill-adjusted, broken, inharmonious, form our idea of this universe. In a dream, when you see a giant with twenty heads chasing you, and you are flying from him, you do not think it is inharmonious; you think it is proper and right. So is this law. All that you call law is simply chance without meaning. In this dream state you call it law. Within Maya, so far as this law of time, space and causation exists, there is no freedom; and all these various forms of worship are within this Maya. The idea of God and the ideas of brute and of Man are within this Maya, and as such are equally hallucinations; all of them are dreams. But you must take care not to argue like some extraordinary men of whom we hear at the present time. They say the idea of God is a delusion, but the idea of this world is true. Both ideas stand or fall by the same logic. He alone has the right to be an atheist who denies this world, as well as the other. The same argument is for both. The same mass of delusion extends from God to the lowest animal, from a blade of grass to the Creator. They stand or fall by the same logic. The same person who sees falsity in the idea of God ought also to see it in the idea of his own body or his own mind. When God vanishes, then also vanish the body and mind; and when both vanish, that which is the Real Existence remains for ever. "There the eyes cannot go, nor the speech, nor the mind. We cannot see it, neither know it." And we now understand that so far as speech and thought and knowledge and intellect go, it is all within this Maya within bondage. Beyond that is Reality. There neither thought, nor mind, nor speech, can reach.

So far it is intellectually all right, but then comes the practice. The real work is in the practice. Are any practices necessary to realise this Oneness? Most decidedly. It is not that you become this Brahman. You are already that. It is not that you are going to become God or perfect; you are already perfect; and whenever you think you are not, it is a delusion. This delusion which says that you are Mr. So-and-so or Mrs. So-and-so can be got rid of by another delusion, and that is practice. Fire will eat fire, and you can use one delusion to conquer another delusion. One cloud will come and brush away another cloud, and then both will go away. What are these practices then? We must always bear in mind that we are not going to be free, but are free already. Every idea that we are bound is a delusion. Every idea that we are happy or unhappy is a tremendous delusion; and another delusion will come—that we have got to work and worship and struggle to be free—and this will chase out the first delusion, and then both will stop.

The fox is considered very unholy by the Mohammedans and by the Hindus. Also, if a dog touches any bit of food, it has to be thrown out, it cannot be eaten by any man. In a certain Mohammedan house a fox entered and took a little bit of food from the table, ate it up, and fled. The man was a poor man, and had prepared a very nice feast for himself, and that feast was made unholy, and he could not eat it. So he went to a Mulla, a priest, and said, "This has happened to me; a fox came and took a mouthful out of my meal. What can be done? I had prepared a feast and wanted so much to eat it, and now comes this fox and destroys the whole affair." The Mulla thought for a minute and then found only one solution and said, "The only way for you is to get a dog and make him eat a bit out of the same plate, because dogs and foxes are eternally quarrelling. The food that was left by the fox will go into your stomach, and that left by the dog will go there too, and both will be purified." We are very much in the same predicament. This is a hallucination that we are imperfect; and we take up another, that we have to practice to become perfect. Then one will chase the other, as we can use one thorn to extract another and then throw both away. There are people for whom it is sufficient knowledge to hear, "Thou art That." With a flash this universe goes away and the real nature shines, but others have to struggle hard to get rid of this idea of bondage.

The first question is: Who are fit to become Jnana Yogis? Those who are equipped with these requisites: First, renunciation of all fruits of work and of all enjoyments in this life or another life. If you are the creator of this universe, whatever you desire you will have, because you will create it for yourself. It is only a question of time. Some get it immediately; with others the past Samskaras (impressions) stand in the way of getting their desires. We give the first place to desires for enjoyment, either in this or another life. Deny that there is any life at all; because life is only another name for death. Deny that you are a living being. Who cares for life? Life is one of these hallucinations, and death is its counterpart. Joy is one part of these hallucinations, and misery the other part, and so on. What have you to do with life or death ? These are all creations of the mind. This is called giving up desires of enjoyment either in this life or another.

Then comes controlling the mind, calming it so that it will not break into waves and have all sorts of desires, holding the mind steady, not allowing it to get into waves from external or internal causes, controlling the mind perfectly, just by the power of will. The Jnana Yogi does not take any one of these physical helps or mental helps: simply philosophic reasoning, knowledge, and his own will, these are the instrumentalities he believes in. Next comes Titiksha, forbearance, bearing all miseries without murmuring, without complaining. When an injury comes, do not mind it. If a tiger comes, stand there. Who flies? There are men who practice Titiksha, and succeed in it.

There are men who sleep on the banks of the Ganga in the midsummer sun of India, and in winter float in the waters of the Ganga for a whole day; they do not care. Men sit in the snow of the Himalayas, and do not care to wear any garment. What is heat? What is cold? Let things come and go, what is that to me, I am not the body. It is hard to believe this in these Western countries, but it is better to know that it is done. Just as your people are brave to jump at the mouth of a cannon, or into the midst of the battlefield, so our people are brave to think and act out their philosophy. They give up their lives for it. "I am Existence-Knowledge-Bliss Absolute; I am He, I am He." Just as the Western ideal is to keep up luxury in practical life, so ours is to keep up the highest form of spirituality, to demonstrate that religion is riot merely frothy words, but can be carried out, every bit of it, in this life. This is Titiksha, to bear everything, not to complain of anything. I myself have seen men who say, "I am the soul; what is the universe to me? Neither pleasure nor pain, nor virtue nor vice, nor heat nor cold is anything to me." That is Titiksha; not running after the enjoyments of the body. What is religion? To pray, "Give me this and that?" Foolish ideas of religion! Those who believe them have no true idea of God and soul. My Master used to say, "The vulture rises higher and higher until he becomes a speck, but his eye is always on the piece of rotten carrion on the earth." After all, what is the result of your ideas of religion? To cleanse the streets and have more bread and clothes? Who cares for bread and clothes? Millions come and go every minute. Who cares? Why care for the joys and vicissitudes of this little world? Go beyond that if you dare; go beyond law, let the whole universe vanish, and stand alone. "I am Existence-Absolute, Knowledge-Absolute, Bliss-Absolute; I am He, I am He."

VIII

Yoga

Four Paths Of Yoga*

Our main problem is to be free. It is evident then that until we realise ourselves as the Absolute, we cannot attain to deliverance. Yet there are various ways of attaining to this realisation. These methods have the generic name of Yoga (to join, to join ourselves to our reality). These Yogas, though divided into various groups, can principally be classed into four; and as each is only a method leading indirectly to the realisation of the Absolute, they are suited to different temperaments. Now it must be remembered that it is not that the assumed man becomes the real man or Absolute. There is no becoming with the Absolute. It is ever free, ever perfect; but the ignorance that has covered Its nature for a time is to be removed. Therefore, the whole scope of all systems of Yoga (and each religion represents one) is to clear up this ignorance and allow the Atman to restore its own nature. The chief helps in this liberation are Abhyasa and Vairagya. Vairagya is non-attachment to life, because it is the will to enjoy that brings all this bondage in its train; and Abhyasa is constant practice of any one of the Yogas.

---

* Written by Swami Vivekananda during his first visit to America to address questions put by a Western disciple.

Karma Yoga is purifying the mind by means of work. Now if any work is done, good or bad, it must produce as a result a good or bad effect; no power can stay it, once the cause is present. Therefore, good action producing good Karma, and bad action, bad Karma, the soul will go on in eternal bondage without ever hoping for deliverance. Now Karma belongs only to the body or the mind, never to the Atman (Self); only it can cast a veil before the Atman. The veil cast by bad Karma is ignorance. Good Karma has the power to strengthen the moral powers. And thus it creates non-attachment; it destroys the tendency towards bad Karma and thereby purifies the mind. But if the work is done with the intention of enjoyment, it then produces only that very enjoyment and does not purify the mind or Chitta. Therefore, all work should be done without any desire to enjoy the fruits thereof. All fear and all desire to enjoy here or hereafter must be banished forever by the Karma Yogi. Moreover, this Karma without desire of return will destroy the selfishness, which is the root of all bondage. The watchword of the Karma-Yogi is "not I, but Thou", and no amount of self-sacrifice is too much for him. But he does this without any desire to go to heaven, or gain name or fame or any other benefit in this world. Although the explanation and rationale of this unselfish work is only in Jnana Yoga, yet the natural divinity of Man makes him love all sacrifice simply for the good of others, without any ulterior motive, whatever his creed or opinion. Again, with many the bondage of wealth is very great; and Karma Yoga is absolutely necessary for them as breaking the crystallisation that has gathered round their love of money.

Next is Bhakti Yoga. Bhakti or worship or love in some form or other is the easiest, pleasantest, and most natural way of man. The natural state of this universe is attraction; and that is surely followed by an ultimate disunion. Even so, love is the natural impetus of union in the human heart; and though itself a great cause of misery, properly directed towards the proper object, it brings deliverance. The object of Bhakti is God. Love cannot be without a subject and an object. The object of love again must be at first a being who can reciprocate our love. Therefore, the God of love must be in some sense a human God. He must be a God of love. Aside from the question whether such a God exists or not, it is a fact that to those who have love in their heart this Absolute appears as a God of love, as personal.

The lower forms of worship, which embody the idea of God as a judge or punisher or someone to be obeyed through fear, do not deserve to be called love, although they are forms of worship gradually expanding into higher forms. We pass on to the consideration of love itself. We will illustrate love by a triangle, of which the first angle at the base is fearlessness. So long as there is fear, it is not love. Love banishes all fear. A mother with her baby will face a tiger to save her child. The second angle is that love never asks, never begs. The third or the apex is that love loves for the sake of love itself. Even the idea of object vanishes. Love is the only form in which love is loved. This is the highest abstraction and the same as the Absolute.

Next is Raja Yoga. This Yoga fits in with every one of these Yogas. It fits inquirers of all classes with or without any belief, and it is the real instrument of religious inquiry. As each science has its particular method of investigation, so is this Raja Yoga the method of religion. This science also is variously applied according to various constitutions. The chief parts are the Pranayama, concentration, and meditation. For those who believe in God, a symbolical name, such as Om or other sacred words received from a Guru, will be very helpful. Om is the greatest, meaning the Absolute. Meditating on the meaning of these holy names while repeating them is the chief practice.

Next is Jnana Yoga. This is divided into three parts. First: hearing the truth—that the Atman is the only reality and that everything else is Maya (relativity). Second: reasoning upon this philosophy from all points of view. Third: giving up all further argumentation and realising the truth. This realisation comes from (1) being certain that Brahman is real and everything else is unreal; (2) giving up all desire for enjoyment; (3) controlling the senses and the mind; (4) intense desire to be free. Meditating on this reality always and reminding the soul of its real nature are the only ways in this Yoga. It is the highest, but most difficult. Many persons get an intellectual grasp of it, but very few attain realisation.

Karma In Its Effect On Character

The word karma is derived from the Sanskrit "Kri", to do; all action is Karma. Technically, this word also means the effects of actions. In connection with metaphysics, it sometimes means the effects, of which our past actions were the causes. But in Karma Yoga we have simply to do with the word "Karma" as meaning work. The goal of mankind is knowledge. That is the one ideal placed before us by Eastern philosophy. Pleasure is not the goal of man, but knowledge. Pleasure and happiness come to an end. It is a mistake to suppose that pleasure is the goal. The cause of all the miseries we have in the world is that men foolishly think pleasure to be the ideal to strive for. After a time Man finds that it is not happiness, but knowledge, towards which he is going, and that both pleasure and pain are great teachers, and that he learns as much from evil as from good. As pleasure and pain pass before his soul they have upon it different pictures, and the result of these combined impressions is what is called man's "character". If you take the character of any man, it really is but the aggregate of tendencies, the sum total of the bent of his mind; you will find that misery and happiness are equal factors in the formation of that character. Good and evil have an equal share in moulding character, and in some instances misery is a greater teacher than happiness. In studying the great characters the world has produced,

I dare say, in the vast majority of cases, it would be found that it was misery that taught more than happiness, it was poverty that taught more than wealth, it was blows that brought out their inner fire more than praise.

Now this knowledge, again, is inherent in man. No knowledge comes from outside; it is all inside. What we say a man "knows", should, in strict psychological language, be what he "discovers" or "unveils"; what a man "learns" is really what he "discovers", by taking the cover off his own soul, which is a mine of infinite knowledge.

We say Newton discovered gravitation. Was it sitting anywhere in a corner waiting for him? It was in his own mind; the time came and he found it out. All knowledge that the world has ever received comes from the mind; the infinite library of the universe is in your own mind. The external world is simply the suggestion, the occasion, which sets you to study your own mind, but the object of your study is always your own mind. The falling of an apple gave the suggestion to Newton, and he studied his own mind. He rearranged all the previous links of thought in his mind and discovered a new link among them, which we call the law of gravitation. It was not in the apple nor in anything in the centre of the earth.

All knowledge, therefore, secular or spiritual, is in the human mind. In many cases it is not discovered, but remains covered, and when the covering is being slowly taken off, we say, "We are learning," and the advance of knowledge is made by the advance of this process of uncovering. The man from whom this veil is being lifted is the more knowing man, the man upon whom it lies thick is ignorant, and the man from whom it has entirely gone is all-knowing, omniscient. There have been omniscient men, and, I believe, there will be yet; and that there will be myriads of them in the cycles to come.

Like fire in a piece of flint, knowledge exists in the mind; suggestion is the friction which brings it out. So with all our feelings and actions—our tears and our smiles, our joys and our griefs, our weeping and our laughter, our curses and our blessings, our praises and our blames—every one of these we may find, if we calmly study our own selves, to have been brought out from within ourselves by so many blows. The result is what we are. All these blows taken together are called Karma—work, action. Every mental and physical blow that is given to the soul, by which, as it were, fire is struck from it, and by which its own power and knowledge are discovered, is Karma, this word being used in its widest sense. Thus we are all doing Karma all the time. I am talking to you: that is Karma. You are listening: that is Karma. We breathe: that is Karma. We walk: Karma. Everything we do, physical or mental, is Karma, and it leaves its marks on us.

There are certain works which are, as it were, the aggregate, the sum total, of a large number of smaller works. If we stand near the seashore and hear the waves dashing against the shingle, we think it is such a great noise, and yet we know that one wave is really composed of millions and millions of minute waves. Each one of these is making a noise, and yet we do not catch it; it is only when they become the big aggregate that we hear. Similarly, every pulsation of the heart is work. Certain kinds of work we feel and they become tangible to us; they are, at the same time, the aggregate of a number of small works. If you really want to judge of the character of a man, look not at his great performances. Every fool may become a hero at one time or another. Watch a man do his most common actions; those are indeed the things which will tell you the real character of a great man. Great occasions rouse even the lowest of human beings to some kind of greatness, but he alone is the really great man whose character is great always, the same wherever he be.

Karma in its effect on character is the most tremendous power that Man has to deal with. Man is, as it were, a centre, and is attracting all the powers of the universe towards himself, and in this centre is fusing them all and again sending them off in a big current. Such a centre is the *real* man—the almighty, the omniscient—and he draws the whole universe towards him. Good and bad, misery and happiness, all are running towards him and clinging round him; and out of them he fashions the mighty stream of tendency called character and throws it outwards. As he has the power of drawing in anything, so has he the power of throwing it out.

All the actions that we see in the world, all the movements in human society, all the works that we have around us, are simply the display of thought, the manifestation of the will of man. Machines or instruments, cities, ships, or men-of-war, all these are simply the manifestation of the will of man; and this will is caused by character, and character is manufactured by Karma. As is Karma, so is the manifestation of the will. The men of mighty will the world has produced have all been tremendous workers—gigantic souls, with wills powerful enough to overturn worlds, wills they got by persistent work, through ages, and ages. Such a gigantic will as that of a Buddha or a Jesus could not be obtained in one life, for we know who their fathers were. It is not known that their fathers ever spoke a word for the good of mankind. Millions and millions of carpenters like Joseph had gone; millions are still living. Millions and millions of petty kings like Buddha's father had been in the world. If it was only a case of hereditary transmission, how do you account for this petty prince, who was not, perhaps, obeyed by his own servants, producing this son, whom half a world worships? How do you explain the gulf between the carpenter and his son, whom millions of human beings worship as God? It cannot be solved by the theory of heredity. The gigantic will which Buddha and Jesus threw over the world, whence did it come? Whence came this accumulation of power? It must have been there through ages and ages, continually growing bigger and bigger, until it burst on society in a Buddha or a Jesus, even rolling down to the present day.

All this is determined by Karma, work. No one can get anything unless he earns it. This is an eternal law. We may sometimes think it is not so, but in the long run we become convinced of it. A man may struggle all his life for riches; he may cheat thousands, but he finds at last that he did not deserve to become rich, and his life becomes a trouble and a nuisance to him. We may go on accumulating things for our physical enjoyment, but only what we earn is really ours. A fool may buy all the books in the world, and they will be in his library; but he will be able to read only those that he deserves to; and this deserving is produced by Karma. Our Karma determines what we deserve and what we can assimilate. We are responsible for what we are; and whatever we wish ourselves to be, we have the power to make ourselves. If what we are now has been the result of our own past actions, it certainly follows that whatever we wish to be in future can be produced by our present actions; so we have to know how to act. You will say, "What is the use of learning how to work? Everyone works in some way or other in this world." But there is such a-thing as frittering away our energies. With regard to Karma Yoga, the *Gita* says that it is doing work with cleverness and as a science; by knowing how to work, one can obtain the greatest results. You must remember that all work is simply to bring out the power of the mind which is already there, to wake up the soul. The power is inside every man, so is knowing; the different works are like blows to bring them out, to cause these giants to wake up.

Man works with various motives. There cannot be work without motive. Some people want to get fame, and they work for fame. Others want money, and they work for money. Others want to have power, and they work for power. Others want to get to heaven, and they work for the same. Others want to leave a name when they die, as they do in China, where no man gets a title until he is dead; and that is a better way, after all, than with us. When a man does something very good there, they give a title of nobility to his father, who is dead, or to his grandfather. Some people work for that. Some of the followers of certain Mohammedan sects work all their lives to have a big tomb built for them when they die. I know sects among whom, as soon as a child is born, a tomb is prepared for it; that is among them the most important work a man has to do, and the bigger and the finer the tomb, the better off the man is supposed to be. Others work as a penance; do all sorts of wicked things, then erect a temple, or give something to the priests to buy them off and obtain from them a passport to heaven. They think that this kind of beneficence will clear them and they will go scot-free in spite of their sinfulness. Such are some of the various motives for work.

Work for work's sake. There are some who are really the salt of the earth in every country and who work for work's sake, who do not care for name, or fame, or even to go to heaven. They work just because good will come of it. There are others who do good to the poor and help mankind from still higher motives, because they believe in doing good and love good. The motive for name and fame seldom brings immediate results, as a rule; they come to us when we are old and have almost done with life. If a man works without any selfish motive in view, does he not gain anything? Yes, he gains the highest. Unselfishness is more paying, only people have not the patience to practise it. It is more paying from the point of view of health also. Love, truth, and unselfishness are not merely moral figures of speech, but they form our highest ideal, because in them lies such a manifestation of power. In the first place, a man who can work for five days, or even for five minutes, without any selfish motive whatever, without thinking of future, of heaven, of punishment, or anything of the kind, has in him the capacity to become a powerful moral giant. It is hard to do it, but in the heart of our hearts we know its value, and the good it brings. It is the greatest manifestation of power—this tremendous restraint; self-restraint is a manifestation of greater power than all outgoing action. A carriage with four horses may rush down a hill unrestrained, or the coachman may curb the horses. Which is the greater manifestation of power, to let them go or to hold them? A cannon-ball flying through the air goes a long distance and falls. Another is cut short in its flight by striking against a wall, and the impact generates intense heat. All outgoing energy following a selfish motive is frittered away; it will not 'cause power to return to you; but if restrained, it will result in development of power. This self-control will tend to produce a mighty will, a character which makes a Christ or a Buddha. Foolish men do not know this secret; they nevertheless want to rule mankind. Even a fool may rule the whole world if he works and waits. Let him wait a few years, restrain that foolish idea of governing; and when that idea is wholly gone, he will be a power in the world. The majority of us cannot see beyond a few years, just as some animals cannot see beyond a few steps. Just a little narrow circle—that is our world. We have not the patience to look beyond, and thus become immoral and wicked. This is our weakness, our powerlessness.

Even the lowest forms of work are not to be despised. Let the man, who knows no better, work for selfish ends, for name and fame; but everyone should always try to get towards higher and higher motives and to understand them. "To work we have the right, but not to the fruits thereof:" Leave the fruits alone. Why care for results? If you wish to help a man, never think what that man's attitude should be towards you. If you want to do a great or a good work, do not trouble to think what the result will be.

There arises a difficult question in this ideal of work. Intense activity is necessary; we must always work. We cannot live a minute without work. What then becomes of rest?

Here is one side of the life-struggle—work, in which we are whirled rapidly round. And here is the other—that of calm, retiring renunciation: everything is peaceful around, there is very little of noise and show, only nature with her animals and flowers and mountains. Neither of them is a perfect picture. A man used to solitude, if brought in contact with the surging whirlpool of the world, will be crushed by it; just as the fish that lives in the deep sea water, as soon as it is brought to the surface, breaks into pieces, deprived of the weight of water on it that had kept it together. Can a man who has been used to the turmoil and the rush of life live at ease if he comes to a quiet place? He suffers and perchance may lose his mind. The ideal man is he who, in the midst of the greatest silence and solitude, finds the intensest activity, and in the midst of the intensest activity finds the silence and solitude of the desert. He has learnt the secret of restraint, he has controlled himself. He goes through the streets of a big city with all its traffic, and his mind is as calm as if he were in a cave, where not a sound could reach him; and he is intensely working all the time. That is the ideal of Karma Yoga, and if you have attained to that you have really learnt the secret of work.

But we have to begin from the beginning, to take up the works as they come to us and slowly make ourselves more unselfish every day. We must do the work and find out the motive power that prompts us; and, almost without exception, in the first years, we shall find that our motives are always selfish; but gradually this selfishness will melt by persistence, till at last will come the time when we shall be able to do really unselfish work. We may all hope that some day or other, as we struggle through the paths of life, there will come a time when we shall become perfectly unselfish; and the moment we attain to that, all our powers will be concentrated, and the knowledge which is ours will be manifest.

The Ideal Of Karma Yoga

The grandest idea in the religion of the Vedanta is that we may reach the same goal by different paths; and these paths I have generalised into four, *viz* those of work, love, psychology, and knowledge. But you must, at the same time, remember that these divisions are not very marked and quite exclusive of each other. Each blends into the other. But according to the type which prevails, we name the divisions. It is not that you can find men who have no other faculty than that of work, nor that you can find men who are no more than devoted worshippers only, nor that there are men who have no more than mere knowledge. These divisions are made in accordance with the type or the tendency that may be seen to prevail in a man. We have found that, in the end, all these four paths converge and become one. All religions and all methods of work and worship lead us to one and the same goal.

I have already tried to point out that goal. It is freedom as I understand it. Everything that we perceive around us is struggling towards freedom, from the atom to the man, from the insentient, lifeless particle of matter to the highest existence on earth, the human soul. The whole universe is in fact the result of this struggle for freedom. In all combinations every particle is trying to go on its own way, to fly from the other particles; but the others are holding it in check. Our earth is trying to fly away from the sun, and the moon from the earth. Everything has a tendency to infinite dispersion. All that we see in the universe has for its basis this one struggle towards freedom; it is under the impulse of this tendency that the saint prays and the robber robs. When the line of action taken is not a proper one, we call it evil; and when the manifestation of it is proper and high, we call it good. But the impulse is the same, the struggle towards freedom. The saint is oppressed with the knowledge of his condition of bondage, and he wants to get rid of it; so he worships God. The thief is oppressed with the idea that he does not possess certain things, and he tries to get rid of that want, to obtain freedom from it; so he steals. Freedom is the one goal of all nature, sentient or insentient; and consciously or unconsciously, everything is struggling towards that goal. The freedom which the saint seeks is very different from that which the robber seeks; the freedom loved by the saint leads him to the enjoyment of infinite, unspeakable bliss, while that on which the robber has set his heart only forges other bonds for his soul.

There is to be found in every religion the manifestation of this struggle towards freedom. It is the groundwork of all morality, of unselfishness, which means getting rid of the idea that men are the same as their little body. When we see a man doing good work, helping others, it means that he cannot be confined within the limited circle of "me and mine". There is no limit to this getting out of selfishness. All the great systems of ethics preach absolute unselfishness as the goal. Supposing this absolute unselfishness can be reached by a man, what becomes of him? He is no more the little Mr. So-and-so; he has acquired infinite expansion The little personality which he had before is now lost to him forever; he has become infinite, and the attainment of this infinite expansion is indeed the goal of all religions and of all moral and philosophical teachings. The personalist, when he hears this idea philosophically put, gets frightened. At the same time, if he preaches morality, he after all teaches the very same idea himself. He puts no limit to the unselfishness of man. Suppose a man becomes perfectly unselfish under the personalistic system, how are we to distinguish him from the perfected ones in other systems? He has become one with the universe and to become that is the goal of all; only the poor personalist has not the courage to follow out his own reasoning to its right conclusion. Karma Yoga is the attaining through unselfish work of that freedom which is the goal of all human nature. Every selfish action, therefore, retards our reaching the goal, and every unselfish action takes us towards the goal; that is why the only definition that can be given of morality is this: *That which is selfish is immoral, and that which is unselfish is moral.*

But, if you come to details, the matter will not be seen to be quite so simple. For instance, environment often makes the details different as I have already mentioned. The same action under one set of circumstances may be unselfish, and under another set quite selfish. So we can give only a general definition, and leave the details to be worked out by taking into consideration the differences in time, place, and circumstances. In one country one kind of conduct is considered moral, and in another the very same is immoral, because the circumstances differ. The goal of all nature is freedom, and freedom is to be attained only by perfect unselfishness; every thought, word, or deed that is unselfish takes us towards the goal, and, as such, is called moral. That definition, you will find, holds good in every religion and every system of ethics. In some systems of thought morality is derived from a Superior Being—God. If you ask why a man ought to do this and not that, their answer is: "Because such is the command of God." But whatever be the source from which it is derived, their code of ethics also has the same central idea—not to think of self but to give up self. And yet some persons, in spite of this high ethical idea, are frightened at the thought of having to give up their little personalities. We may ask the man who clings to the idea of little personalities to consider the case of a person who has become perfectly unselfish, who has no thought for himself, who does no deed for himself, who speaks no word for himself, and then say where his "himself" is. That "himself" is known to him only so long as he thinks, acts, or speaks for himself. If he is only conscious of others, of the universe, and of the all, where is his "himself"? It is gone forever.

Karma Yoga, therefore, is a system of ethics and religion intended to attain freedom through unselfishness, and by good works. The Karma-Yogi need not believe in any doctrine whatever. He may not believe even in God, may not ask what his soul is, nor think of any metaphysical speculation. He has got his own special aim of realising selflessness; and he has to work it out himself. Every moment of his life must be realisation, because he has to solve by mere work, without the help of doctrine or theory, the very same problem to which the Jnani applies his reason and inspiration and the Bhakta his love.

Now comes the next question: What is this work? What is this doing good to the world? Can we do good to the world? In an absolute sense, no; in a relative sense, yes. No permanent or everlasting good can be done to the world; if it could be done, the world would not be this world. We may satisfy the hunger of a man for five minutes, but he will be hungry again. Every pleasure with which we supply a man may be seen to be momentary. No one can permanently cure this ever-recurring fever of pleasure and pain. Can any permanent happiness be given to the world? In the ocean we cannot raise a wave without causing a hollow somewhere else. The sum total of the good things in the world has been the same throughout in its relation to man's need and greed. It cannot be increased or decreased. Take the history of the human race as we know it today. Do we not find the same miseries and the same happiness, the same pleasures and pains, the same differences in position? Are not some rich, some poor, some high, some low, some healthy, some unhealthy? All this was just the same with the Egyptians, the Greeks, and the Romans in ancient times as it is with the Americans today. So far as history is known, it has always been the same; yet at the same time we find that, running along with all these incurable differences of pleasure and pain, there has ever been the struggle to alleviate them. Every period of history has given birth to thousands of men and women who have worked hard to smooth the passage of life for others. And how far have they succeeded? We can only play at driving the ball from one place to another. We take away pain from the physical plane, and it goes to the mental one. It is like that picture in Dante's hell where the misers were given a mass of gold to roll up a hill. Every time they rolled it up a little, it again rolled down. All our talks about the millennium are very nice as school-boys' stories, but they are no better than that. All nations that dream of the millennium also think that, of all peoples in the world, they will have the best of it then for themselves. This is the wonderfully unselfish idea of the millennium!

We cannot add happiness to this world; similarly, we cannot add pain to it either. The sum total of the energies of pleasure and pain displayed here on earth will be the same throughout. We just push it from this side to the other side, and from that side to this, but it will remain the same, because to remain so is its very nature. This ebb and flow, this rising and falling, is in the world's very nature; it would be as logical to hold otherwise as to say that we may have life without death. This is complete nonsense, because the very idea of life implies death and the very idea of pleasure implies pain. The lamp is constantly burning out, and that is its life. If you want to have life, you have to die every moment for it. Life and death are only different expressions of the same thing looked at from different standpoints; they are the falling and the rising of the same wave, and the two form one whole. One looks at the "fall" side and becomes a pessimist, another looks at the "rise" side and becomes an optimist. When a boy is going to school and his father and mother are taking care of him, everything seems blessed to him; his wants are simple, he is a great optimist. But the old man, with his varied experience, becomes calmer, and is sure to have his warmth considerably cooled down. So, old nations, with signs of decay all around them, are apt to be less hopeful than new nations. There is a proverb in India: "A thousand years a city, and a thousand years a forest." This change of city into forest and vice versa is going on everywhere, and it makes people optimists or pessimists according to the side they see of it.

The next idea we take up is the idea of equality. These millennium ideas have been great motive powers to work. Many religions preach this an element in them—that God is coming to rule the universe, and that then there will be no difference at all in conditions. The people who preach this doctrine are mere fanatics, and fanatics are indeed the sincerest of mankind. Christianity was preached just on the basis of the fascination of this fanaticism, and that is what made it so attractive to the Greek and the Roman slaves. They believed that under the millennial religion there would be no more slavery, that there would be plenty to eat and drink; and, therefore, they flocked round the Christian standard. Those who preached the idea first were of course ignorant fanatics, but very sincere. In modern times this millennial aspiration takes the form of equality—of liberty, equality, and fraternity. This is also fanaticism. True equality has never been and never can be on earth. How can we all be equal here? This impossible kind of equality implies total death. What makes this world what it is? Lost balance. In the primal state, which is called chaos, there is perfect balance. How do all the formative forces of the universe come then? By struggling, competition, conflict. Suppose that all the particles of matter were held in equilibrium, would there be then any process of creation? We know from science that it is impossible. Disturb a sheet of water, and there you find every particle of the water trying to become calm again, one rushing against the other; and in the same way all the phenomena which we call the universe—all things therein—are struggling to get back to the state of perfect balance. Again a disturbance comes, and again we have combination and creation. Inequality is the very basis of creation. At the same time the forces struggling to obtain equality are as much a necessity of creation as those which destroy it.

Absolute equality, that which means a perfect balance of all the struggling forces in all the planes, can never be in this world. Before you attain that state, the world will have become quite unfit for any kind of life, and no one will be there. We find, therefore, that all these ideas of the millennium and of absolute equality are not only impossible but also that, if we try to carry them out, they will lead us surely enough to the day of destruction. What makes the difference between Man and Man? It is largely the difference in the brain. Nowadays no one but a lunatic will say that we are all born with the same brain power. We come into the world with unequal endowments; we come as greater men or as lesser men, and there is no getting away from that prenatally determined condition. The American Indians were in this country for thousands of years, and a few handfuls of your ancestors came to their land. What difference they have caused in the appearance of the country! Why did not the Indians make improvements and build cities, if all were equal? With your ancestors a different sort of brain power came into the land, different bundles of past impressions came, and they worked out and manifested themselves. Absolute non-differentiation is death. So long as this world lasts, differentiation there will and must be, and the millennium of perfect equality will come only when a cycle of creation comes to its end. Before that, equality cannot be. Yet this idea of realising the millennium is a great motive power. Just as inequality is necessary for creation itself, so the struggle to limit it is also necessary. If there were no struggle to become free and get back to God, there would be no creation either. It is the difference between these two forces that determines the nature of the motives of men. There will always be these motives to work, some tending towards bondage and others towards freedom.

This world's wheel within wheel is a terrible mechanism; if we put our hands in it, as soon as we are caught we are gone. We all think that when we have done a certain duty, we shall be at rest; but before we have done a part of that duty, another is already in waiting. We are all being dragged along by this mighty, complex world-machine. There are only two ways out of it; one is to give up all concerns with the machine, to let it go and stand aside, to give up our desires. That is very easy to say, but is almost impossible to do. I do not know whether in twenty millions of men one can do that. The other way is to plunge into the world and learn the secret of work, and that is the way of Karma Yoga. Do not fly away from the wheels of the world-machine, but stand inside it and learn the secret of work. Through proper work done inside, it is also possible to come out. Through this machinery itself is the way out.

We have now seen what work is. It is a part of nature's foundation, and goes on always. Those that believe in God understand this better, because they know that God is not such an incapable being as will need our help. Although this universe will go on always, our goal is freedom, our goal is unselfishness; and according to Karma Yoga, that goal is to be reached through work. All ideas of making the world perfectly happy may be good as motive powers for fanatics;

but we must know that fanaticism brings forth as much evil as good. The Karma Yogi asks why you require any motive to work other than the inborn love of freedom. Be beyond the common worldly motives. "To work you have the right, but not to the fruits thereof." Man can train himself to know and to practise that, says the Karma Yogi. When the idea of doing good becomes a part of his very being, then he will not seek for any motive outside. Let us do good because it is good to do good; he who does good work even in order to get to heaven binds himself down, says the Karma Yogi. Any work that is done with any the least selfish motive, instead of making us free, forges one more chain for our feet.

So the only way is to give up all the fruits of work, to be unattached to them. Know that this world is not we, nor are we this world; that we are really not the body; that we really do not work. We are the Self, eternally at rest and at peace. Why should we be bound by anything? It is very good to say that we should be perfectly non-attached, but what is the way to do it? Every good work we do without any ulterior motive, instead of forging a new chain, will break one of the links in the existing chains. Every good thought that we send to the world without thinking of any return, will be stored up there and break one link in the chain, and make us purer and purer, until we become the purest of mortals. Yet all this may seem to be rather quixotic and too philosophical, more theoretical than practical. I have read many arguments against the *Bhagavad Gita*, and many have said that without motives you cannot work. They have never seen unselfish work except under the influence of fanaticism, and, therefore, they speak in that way.

Let me tell you in conclusion a few words about one man who actually carried this teaching of Karma Yoga into practice. That man is Buddha. He is the one man who ever carried this into perfect practice. All the prophets of the world, except Buddha, had external motives to move them to unselfish action. The prophets of the world, with this single exception, may be divided into two sets, one set holding that they are incarnations of God come down on earth, and the other holding that they are only messengers from God; and both draw their impetus for work from outside, expect reward from outside, however highly spiritual may be the language they use. But Buddha is the only prophet who said, "I do not care to know your various theories about God. What is the use of discussing all the subtle doctrines about the soul? Do good and be good. And this will take you to freedom and to whatever truth there is." He was, in the conduct of his life, absolutely without personal motives; and what man worked more than he? Show me in history one character who has soared so high above all. The whole human race has produced but one such character, such high philosophy, such wide sympathy. This great philosopher, preaching the highest philosophy, yet had the deepest sympathy for the lowest of animals, and never put forth any claims for himself. He is the ideal Karma Yogi, acting entirely without motive, and the history of humanity shows him to have been the greatest man ever born; beyond compare the greatest combination of heart and brain that ever existed, the greatest soul-power that has ever been manifested. He is the first great reformer the world has seen. He was the first who dared to say, "Believe not because some old manuscripts are produced, believe not because it is your national belief, because you have been made to believe it from your childhood; but reason it all out, and after you have analysed it, then, if you find that it will do good to one and all, believe it, live up to it, and help others to live up to it." He works best who works without any motive, neither for money, nor for fame, nor for anything else; and when a man can do that, he will be a Buddha, and out of him will come the power to work in such a manner as will transform the world. This man represents the very highest ideal of Karma Yoga.

Bhakti Yoga

PRAYER

स तन्मयो ह्यमृत ईशसंस्थो ज्ञः सर्वगो भुवनस्यास्य गोप्ता।
य ईशेऽस्य जगतो नित्यमेव नान्यो हेतुर्विद्यत ईशनाय।।
यो ब्रह्माणं विदधाति पूर्वं यो वै वेदांश्च प्रहिणोति तस्मै।
तं ह देवमात्मबुद्धिप्रकाशं मुमुक्षुर्वै शरणमहं प्रपद्ये।।

"He is the Soul of the Universe; He is Immortal; His is the Rulership; He is the All-knowing, the All-pervading, the Protector of the Universe, the Eternal Ruler. None else is there efficient to govern the world eternally. He who at the beginning of creation projected Brahma (i.e. the universal consciousness), and who delivered the Vedas unto him—seeking liberation I go for refuge unto that Effulgent One, whose light turns the understanding towards the Atman."

Shvetashvatara Upanishad, VI. 17-18.

DEFINITION OF BHAKTI

Bhakti Yoga is a real, genuine search after the Lord, a search beginning, continuing and ending in love. One single moment of the madness of extreme love to God brings us eternal freedom. "Bhakti," says Narada in his explanation of the

Bhakti aphorisms, "is intense love to God"; "When a man gets it, he loves all, hates none; he becomes satisfied forever"; "This love cannot be reduced to any earthly benefit", because so long as worldly desires last, that kind of love does not come; "Bhakti is greater than Karma, greater than Yoga, because these are intended for an object in view, while Bhakti is its own fruition, its own means and its own end."

Bhakti has been the one constant theme of our sages. Apart from the special writers on Bhakti, such as Shandilya or Narada, the great commentators on the *Vyasa Sutras,* evidently advocates of knowledge (Jnana), have also something very suggestive to say about love. Even when the commentator is anxious to explain many, if not all, of the texts so as to make them import a sort of dry knowledge, the *Sutras,* in the chapter on worship especially, do not lend themselves to be easily manipulated in that fashion.

There is not really so much difference between knowledge (Jnana) and love (Bhakti) as people sometimes imagine. We shall see, as we go on, that in the end they converge and meet at the same point. So also is it with Raja Yoga, which when pursued as a means to attain liberation, and not (as unfortunately it frequently becomes in the hands of charlatans and mystery-mongers) as an instrument to hoodwink the unwary, leads us also to the same goal.

The one great advantage of Bhakti is that it is the easiest and most natural way to reach the great divine end in view; its great disadvantage is that in its lower forms it oftentimes degenerates into hideous fanaticism. The fanatical crew in Hinduism, or Mohammedanism, or Christianity, have always been almost exclusively recruited from these worshippers on the lower planes of Bhakti. That singleness of attachment (Nishtha) to a loved object, without which no genuine love can grow, is very often also the cause of the denunciation of everything else. All the weak and undeveloped minds in every religion or country have only one way of loving their own ideal, *i.e.* by hating every other ideal. Herein is the explanation of why the same man who is so lovingly attached to his own ideal of God, so devoted to his own ideal of religion, becomes a howling fanatic as soon as he sees or hears anything of any other ideal. This kind of love is somewhat like the canine instinct of guarding the master's property from intrusion; only, the instinct of the dog is better than the reason of man, for the dog never mistakes its master for an enemy in whatever dress he may come before it. Again, the fanatic loses all power of judgment. Personal considerations are in his case of such absorbing interest that to him it is no question at all what a man says—whether it is right or wrong; but the one thing he is always particularly careful to know is who says it. The same man who is kind, good, honest, and loving to people of his own opinion, will not hesitate to do the vilest deeds when they are directed against persons beyond the pale of his own religious brotherhood.

But this danger exists only in that stage of Bhakti which is called the preparatory (Gauni). When Bhakti has become ripe and has passed into that form which is called the supreme (Para), no more is there any fear of these hideous manifestations of fanaticism; that soul which is overpowered by this higher form of Bhakti is too near the God of Love to become an instrument for the diffusion of hatred.

It is not given to all of us to be harmonious in the building up of our characters in this life: yet we know that that character is of the noblest type in which all these three—knowledge and love and Yoga—are harmoniously fused. Three things are necessary for a bird to fly—the two wings and the tail as a rudder for steering. Jnana (knowledge) is the one wing, Bhakti (love) is the other, and Yoga is the tail that keeps up the balance. For those who cannot pursue all these three forms of worship together in harmony and take up, therefore, Bhakti alone as their way, it is necessary always to remember that forms and ceremonials, though absolutely necessary for the progressive soul, have no other value than taking us on to that state in which we feel the most intense love to God.

There is a little difference in opinion between the teachers of knowledge and those of love, though both admit the power of Bhakti. The Jnanis hold Bhakti to be an instrument of liberation, the Bhaktas look upon it both as the instrument and the thing to be attained. To my mind this is a distinction without much difference. In fact, Bhakti, when used as an instrument, really means a lower form of worship, and the higher form becomes inseparable from the lower form of realisation at a later stage. Each seems to lay a great stress upon his own peculiar method of worship, forgetting that with perfect love true knowledge is bound to come even unsought, and that from perfect knowledge true love is inseparable.

Bearing this in mind let us try to understand what the great Vedantic commentators have to say on the subject. In explaining the Sutra Avrittirasakridupadeshat*, Bhagvan Shankara says, "Thus people say, 'He is devoted to the king, he is devoted to the Guru'; they say this of him who follows his Guru, and does so, having that following as the one end in view. Similarly they say, 'The loving wife meditates on her loving husband'; here also a kind of eager and continuous remembrance is meant." This is devotion according to Shankara.

"Meditation again is a constant remembrance (of the thing meditated upon) flowing like an unbroken stream of oil poured out from one vessel to another. When this kind of remembering has been attained (in relation to God) all bondages break. Thus it is spoken of in the scriptures regarding constant remembering as a means to liberation. This remembering again is of the same form as seeing, because it is of the same meaning as in the passage, 'When He who is far and near is seen, the bonds of the heart are

* Meditation is necessary, that having been often enjoined.

broken, all doubts vanish, and all effects of work disappear.' He who is near can be seen, but he who is far can only be remembered. Nevertheless the scripture says that we have to see Him who is near as well as Him who is far, thereby indicating to us that the above kind of *remembering* is as good as *seeing*. This remembrance when exalted assumes the same form as seeing. Worship is constant remembering as may be seen from the essential texts of scriptures. Knowing, which is the same as repeated worship, has been described as constant remembering. Thus the memory, which has attained to the height of what is as good as direct perception, is spoken of in the Shruti as a means of liberation. 'This Atman is not to be reached through various sciences, nor by intellect, nor by much study of the Vedas. Whomsoever this Atman desires, by him is the Atman attained, unto him this Atman discovers Himself.' Here, after saying that mere hearing, thinking and meditating are not the means of attaining this Atman, it is said, 'Whom this Atman desires, by him the Atman is attained.' The extremely beloved is desired; by whomsoever this Atman is extremely beloved, he becomes the most beloved of the Atman. So that this beloved may attain the Atman, the Lord Himself helps. For it has been said by the Lord: 'Those who are constantly attached to Me and worship Me with love—I give that direction to their will by which they come to Me.' Therefore, it is said that, to whomsoever this remembering, which is of the same form as direct perception, is very dear, because it is dear to the Object of such memory perception, he is desired by the Supreme Atman, by him the Supreme Atman is attained. This constant remembrance is denoted by the word 'Bhakti'." So says Bhagvan Ramanuja in his commentary on the Sutra Athato Brahma Jijnasa.*

* Hence follows a dissertation on Brahman.

In commenting on the *Sutra* of Patanjali, Ishvara Pranidhanadva, *i.e.* "Or by the worship of the Supreme Lord"—Bhoja says, "Pranidhana is that sort of Bhakti in which, without seeking results, such as sense-enjoyments etc., all works are dedicated to that Teacher of teachers." Bhagvan Vyasa also, when commenting on the same, defines Pranidhana as "the form of Bhakti by which the mercy of the Supreme Lord comes to the Yogi, and blesses him by granting him his desires." According to Shandilya, "Bhakti is intense love to God." The best definition is, however, that given by the king of Bhaktas, Prahlada: या प्रीतिरविवेकानां विषयेष्वनपायिनी। त्वामनुस्मरतः सा मे हृदयान्मापसर्पतु।। "That deathless love which the ignorant have for the fleeting objects of the senses—as I keep meditating on Thee—may not that love slip away from the heart!" *Love!* For whom? For the Supreme Lord Ishvara. Love for any other being, however great cannot be Bhakti; for, as Ramanuja says in his *Shri Bhashya,* quoting an ancient Acharya, *i.e.* a great teacher: आब्रह्मस्तम्बपर्यन्ताः जगदन्तर्व्यवस्थिताः। प्राणिनः कर्मजनितसंसार-वशवर्तिनः।। यतस्ततो न ते ध्याने ध्यानिनामुपकारकाः। अविद्यान्तर्गतास्सर्वे ते हि संसारगोचराः।। "From Brahma to a clump of grass, all things that live in the world are slaves of birth and death caused by Karma; therefore, they cannot be helpful as objects of meditation, because they are all in ignorance and subject to change." In commenting on the word "Anurakti" used by Shandilya, the commentator Svapneshvara says that it means Anu, after, and Rakti, attachment; *i.e.* the attachment which comes after the knowledge of the nature and glory of God; else a blind attachment to any one, e.g. to wife or children, would be Bhakti. We plainly see, therefore, that Bhakti is a series or succession of mental efforts at religious realisation beginning with ordinary worship and ending in a supreme intensity of love for Ishvara, of even the worship of Adityas etc. Brahman Himself bestows, because He is the Ruler of all." Says Shankara in his *Brahma Sutra Bhashya*—ईदृशं चात्र ब्रह्मण उपास्यत्वं यतः प्रतीकेषु तत्दृष्टयाध्यारोपणं प्रतिमादिषु इव विष्णवादीनाम्।

"Here in this way does Brahman become the object of worship, because He, as Brahman, is superimposed on the Pratikas, just as Vishnu etc., are superimposed upon images etc."

The same ideas apply to the worship of the Pratimas as to that of the Pratikas; that is to say, if the image stands for a god or a saint, the worship is not the result of Bhakti, and does not lead to liberation; but if it stands for the one God, the worship thereof will bring both Bhakti and Mukti. Of the principal religions of the world we see Vedantism, Buddhism, and certain forms of Christianity freely using images; only two religions, Mohammedanism and Protestantism, refuse such help. Yet the Mohammedans use the grave of their saints and martyrs almost in the place of images; and the Protestants, in rejecting all concrete helps to religion, are drifting away every year farther and farther from spirituality till at present there is scarcely any difference between the advanced Protestants and the followers of August Comte, or agnostics who preach ethics alone Again, in Christianity and Mohammedanism whatever exists of image worship is made to fall under that category in which the Pratika or the Pratima is worshipped in itself, but not as a "help to the vision" (Drishtisaukaryam) of God; therefore, it is at best only of the nature of ritualistic Karmas and cannot produce either Bhakti or Mukti. In this form of image-worship, the allegiance of the soul is given to other things than Ishvara, and, therefore, such use of images, or graves, or temples, or tombs, is real idolatry; it is in itself neither sinful nor wicked—it is a rite—a Karma, and worshippers must and will get the fruit thereof.

The Chosen Ideal

The next thing to be considered is what we know as Ishta Nishtha. One who aspires to be a Bhakta must know that "so many opinions are so many ways". He must know that all the various sects of the various religions are the various manifestations of the glory of the same Lord. "They call You by so many names; they divide You, as it were, by different names, yet in each one of these is to be found Your omnipotence. You reach the worshipper through all of these, neither is there any special time so long as the soul has intense love for You. You are so easy of approach; it is my misfortune that I cannot love You." Not only this, the Bhakta must take care not to hate, nor even to criticise those radiant sons of light who are the founders of various sects; he must not even hear them spoken ill of. Very few indeed are those who are at once the possessors of an extensive sympathy and power of appreciation, as well as an intensity of love. We find, as a rule, that liberal and sympathetic sects lose the intensity of religious feeling, and in their hands, religion is apt to degenerate into a kind of politico-social club life. On the other hand, intensely narrow sectaries, whilst displaying a very commendable love of their own ideals, are seen to have acquired every particle of that love by hating every one who is not of exactly the same opinions as themselves. Would to God that this world was full of men who were as intense in their love as worldwide in their sympathies! But such are only few and far between. Yet we know that it is practicable to educate large numbers of human beings into the ideal of a wonderful blending of both the width and the intensity of love; and the way to do that is by this path of the Ishta Nishtha or "steadfast devotion, to the chosen ideal". Every sect of every religion presents only one ideal of its own to mankind, but the eternal Vedantic religion opens to mankind an infinite number of doors for ingress into the inner shrine of divinity, and places before humanity an almost inexhaustible array of ideals, there being in each of them a manifestation of the Eternal One. With the kindest solicitude, the Vedanta points out to aspiring men and women the numerous roads, hewn out of the solid rock of the realities of human life, by the glorious sons, or human manifestations, of God, in the past and in the present, and stands with outstretched arms to welcome all—to welcome even those that are yet to be—to that Home of Truth and that Ocean of Bliss, wherein the human soul, liberated from the net of Maya, may transport itself with perfect freedom and with eternal joy.

Bhakti Yoga, therefore, lays on us the imperative command not to hate or deny any one of the various paths that lead to salvation. Yet the growing plant must be hedged round to protect it until it has grown into a tree. The tender plant of spirituality will die if exposed too early to the action of a constant change of ideas and ideals. Many people, in the name of what may be called religious liberalism, may be seen feeding their idle curiosity with a continuous succession of different ideals. With them, hearing new things grows into a kind of disease, a sort of religious drink-mania. They want to hear new things just by way of getting a temporary nervous excitement, and when one such exciting influence has had its effect on them, they are ready for another. Religion is with these people a sort of intellectual opium-eating, and there it ends. "There is another sort of man," says Bhagvan

Ramakrishna, "who is like the pearl-oyster of the story. The pearl-oyster leaves its bed at the bottom of the sea, and comes up to the surface to catch the rain-water when the star Svati is in the ascendant. It floats about on the surface of the sea with its shell wide open, until it has succeeded in catching a drop of the rain-water, and then it dives deep down to its seabed, and there rests until it has succeeded in fashioning a beautiful pearl out of that raindrop."

This is indeed the most poetical and forcible way in which the theory of Ishta Nishtha has ever been put. This Eka Nishtha or devotion to one ideal is absolutely necessary for the beginner in the practice of religious devotion. He must say with Hanuman in the Ramayana, "Though I know that the Lord of Shri and the Lord of Janaki are both manifestations of the same supreme Being, yet my all in all is the lotus-eyed Rama." Or, as was said by the sage Tulasidasa, he must say, "Take the sweetness of all, sit with all, take the name of all, say yea, yea, but keep your seat firm." Then, if the devotional aspirant is sincere, out of this little seed will come a gigantic tree like the Indian banyan, sending out branch after branch and root after root to all sides, till it covers the entire field of religion. Thus will the true devotee realise that He who was his own ideal in life is worshipped in all ideals by all sects, under all names, and through all forms.

The Method And The Means

In regard to the method and the means of Bhakti Yoga we read in the commentary of Bhagvan Ramanuja on the *Vedanta Sutras*: "The attaining of That comes through discrimination, controlling the passions, practice, sacrificial work, purity, strength, and suppression of excessive joy." Viveka or discrimination is, according to Ramanuja, discriminating, among other things, the pure food from the impure. According to him, food becomes impure from three causes: (1) by the nature of the food itself, as in the case of garlic etc.; (2) owing to its coming from wicked and accursed persons; and (3) from physical impurities, such as dirt, or hair, etc. The Shrutis say, "When the food is pure, the Sattva element gets purified, and the memory becomes unwavering," and Ramanuja quotes this from the *Chhandogya Upanishad*.

The question of food has always been one of the most vital with the Bhaktas. Apart from the extravagance into which some of the Bhakti sects have run, there is a great truth underlying this question of food. We must remember that, according to the Sankhya philosophy, the Sattva, Rajas, and Tamas, which in the state of homogeneous equilibrium form the Prakriti, and in the heterogeneous disturbed condition form the universe—are both the substance and the quality of Prakriti. As such they are the materials out of which every human form has been manufactured, and the predominance of the Sattva material is what is absolutely necessary for spiritual development. The materials which we receive through our food into our body-structure go a great way to determine our mental constitution; therefore, the food we eat has to be particularly taken care of. However, in this matter, as in others, the fanaticism into which the disciples invariably fall is not to be laid at the door of the masters.

And this discrimination of food is, after all, of secondary importance. The very same passage quoted above is explained by Shankara in his *Bhashya* on the Upanishads in a different way by giving an entirely different meaning to the word "Ahara", translated generally as food. According to him, "That which is gathered in is Ahara. The knowledge of the sensations, such as sound etc., is gathered in for the enjoyment of the enjoyer (self); the purification of the knowledge which gathers in the perception of the senses is the purifying of the food (Ahara). The word 'purification-of-food' means the acquiring of the knowledge of sensations untouched by the defects of attachment, aversion, and delusion; such is the meaning. Therefore, such knowledge or Ahara being purified, the Sattva material of the possessor of it—the internal organ—will become purified, and the Sattva being purified, an unbroken memory of the Infinite One, who has been known in His real nature from scriptures, will result."

These two explanations are apparently conflicting, yet both true and necessary. The manipulating and controlling of what may be called the finer body, *viz* the mind, are no doubt higher functions than the controlling of the grosser body of flesh. But the control of the grosser is absolutely necessary to enable one to arrive at the control of the finer. The beginner, therefore, must pay particular attention to all such dietetic rules as have come down from the line of his accredited teachers; but the extravagant, meaningless fanaticism, which has driven religion entirely to the kitchen, as may be noticed in the case of many of our sects, without any hope of the noble truth of that religion ever coming out to the sunlight of spirituality, is a peculiar sort of pure and simple materialism. It is neither Jnana, nor Bhakti, nor Karma; it is a special kind of lunacy, and those who pin their souls to it are more likely to go to lunatic asylums than to Brahmaloka. So it stands to reason that discrimination in the choice of food is necessary for the attainment of this higher state of mental composition which cannot be easily obtained otherwise.

Controlling the passions is the next thing to be attended to. To restrain the Indriyas (organs) from going towards the objects of the senses, to control them and bring them under the guidance of the will, is the very central virtue in religious culture. Then comes the practice of self-restraint and self-denial. All the immense possibilities of divine realisation in the soul cannot get actualised without struggle and without such practice on the part of the aspiring devotee. "The mind must always think of the Lord." It is very hard at first to compel the mind to think of the Lord always, but with every new effort the power to do so grows stronger in us. "By practice, O son of Kunti, and by non-attachment is it attained," says Shri Krishna in the *Gita*. And then as to sacrificial work, it is understood that the five great sacrifices* (Panchamahayajna) have to be performed as usual.

Purity is absolutely the basic work, the bed-rock upon which the whole Bhakti-building rests. Cleansing the external body and discriminating the food are both easy, but without internal cleanliness and purity, these external observances are of no value whatsoever. In the list of qualities conducive to purity, as given by Ramanuja, there are enumerated, Satya, truthfulness; Arjava, sincerity; Daya, doing good to others without any gain to one's self; Ahimsa, not injuring others by thought, word, or deed; Anabhidhya, not coveting others'

* To gods, sages, manes, guests, and all creatures.

goods, not thinking vain thoughts, and not brooding over injuries received from another. In this list, this one idea that deserves special notice is Ahimsa, non-injury to others. This duty of non-injury is, so to speak, obligatory on us in relation to all beings. As with some, it does not simply mean the non-injuring of human beings and mercilessness towards the lower animals; nor, as with some others, does it mean the protecting of cats and dogs and feeding of ants with sugar—with liberty to injure brother-man in every horrible way! It is remarkable that almost every good idea in this world can be carried to a disgusting extreme. A good practice carried to an extreme and worked in accordance with the letter of the law becomes a positive evil. The stinking monks of certain religious sects, who do not bathe lest the vermin on their bodies should be killed, never think of the discomfort and disease they bring to their fellow human beings. They do not, however, belong to the religion of the Vedas!

The test of Ahimsa is absence of jealousy. Any man may do a good deed or make a good gift on the spur of the moment or under the pressure of some superstition or priestcraft; but the real lover of mankind is he who is jealous of none. The so-called great men of the world may all be seen to become jealous of each other for a small name, for a little fame, and for a few bits of gold. So long as this jealousy exists in a heart, it is far away from the perfection of Ahimsa. The cow does not eat meat, nor does the sheep. Are they great Yogis, great non-injurers (Ahimsakas)? Any fool may abstain from eating this or that; surely that gives him no more distinction than to herbivorous animals. The man who will mercilessly cheat widows and orphans and do the vilest deed for money is worse than any brute even if he lives entirely on grass. The man whose heart never cherishes even the thought of injury to any one, who rejoices at the prosperity of even his greatest enemy, that man is the Bhakta, he is the Yogi, he is the Guru of all, even though he lives every day of his life on the flesh of swine. Therefore, we must always remember that external practices have value only as helps to develop internal purity. It is better to have internal purity alone when minute attention to external observances is not practicable. But woe unto the man and woe unto the nation that forgets the real, internal, spiritual essentials of religion and mechanically clutches with death-like grasp at all external forms and never lets them go. The forms have value only so far as they are expressions of the life within. If they have ceased to express life, crush them out without mercy.

The next means to the attainment of Bhakti Yoga is strength (Anavasada). "This Atman is not to be attained by the weak," says the Shruti. Both physical weakness and mental weakness are meant here. "The strong, the hardy" are the only fit students. What can puny, little, decrepit things do? They will break to pieces whenever the mysterious forces of the body and mind are even slightly awakened by the practice of any of the Yogas. It is "the young, the healthy, the strong" that can score success. Physical strength, therefore, is absolutely necessary. It is the strong body alone that can bear the shock of reaction resulting from the attempt to control the organs. He who wants to become a Bhakta must be strong, must be healthy. When the miserably weak attempt any of the Yogas, they are likely to get some incurable malady, or they weaken their minds. Voluntarily weakening the body is really no prescription for spiritual enlightenment.

The mentally weak also cannot succeed in attaining the Atman. The person who aspires to be a Bhakta must be cheerful. In the Western world the idea of a religious man is that he never smiles, that a dark cloud must always' hang over his face, which, again, must be long-drawn with the jaws almost collapsed. People with emaciated bodies and long faces are fit subjects for the physician, they are not Yogis. It is the cheerful mind that is persevering. It is the strong mind that hews its way through a thousand difficulties. And this, the hardest task of all, the cutting of our way out of the net of Maya, is the work reserved only for giant wills.

Yet at the same time excessive mirth should be avoided (Anuddharsha). Excessive mirth makes us unfit for serious thought. It also fritters away the energies of the mind in vain. The stronger the will, the less the yielding to the sway of the emotions. Excessive hilarity is quite as objectionable as too much of sad seriousness, and all religious realisation is possible only when the mind is in a steady, peaceful condition of harmonious equilibrium.

It is thus that one may begin to learn how to love the Lord.

The Mantra: Om: Word And Wisdom

But we are now considering not these Maha Purushas, the great Incarnations, but only the Siddha Gurus (teachers who have attained the goal); they, as a rule, have to convey the germs of spiritual wisdom to the disciple by means of words (Mantras) to be meditated upon. What are these Mantras? The whole of this universe has, according to Indian philosophy, both name and form (Nama Rupa) as its conditions of manifestation. In the human microcosm, there cannot be a single wave in the mind-stuff (Chitta Vritti) unconditioned by name and form. If it be true that nature is built throughout on the same plan, this kind of conditioning by name and form must also be the plan of the building of the whole, of the cosmos, यथा एकेन मृत्पिण्डेन सर्वं मृन्मयं विज्ञातं स्यात्—"As one lump of clay being known, all things of day are known," so the knowledge of the microcosm must lead to the knowledge of the macrocosm. Now form is the outer crust, of which the name or the idea is the inner essence or kernel. The body is the form, and the mind or the Antahkarana is the name, and sound-symbols are universally associated with Nama (name) in all beings having the power of speech. In the individual man the thought-waves rising in the limited Mahat or Chitta (mind-stuff), must manifest themselves, first as words, and then as the more concrete forms.

In the universe, Brahma or Hiranyagarbha or the cosmic Mahat first manifested himself as name, and then as form, *i.e.* as this universe. All this expressed sensible universe is the form, behind which stands the eternal inexpressible Sphota, the manifester as Logos or Word. This eternal Sphota, the essential eternal material of all ideas or names, is the power through which the Lord creates the universe; nay, the Lord first becomes conditioned as the Sphota, and then evolves Himself out as the yet more concrete sensible universe. This Sphota has one word as its only possible symbol, and this is the ओं (Om). And as by no possible means of analysis can we separate the word from the idea, this Om and the eternal Sphota are inseparable; and, therefore, it is out of this holiest of all holy words, the mother of all names and forms, the eternal Om, that the whole universe may be supposed to have been created. But it may be said that, although thought and word are inseparable, yet as there may be various word-symbols for the same thought, it is not necessary that this particular word Om should be the word representative of the thought, out of which the universe has become manifested. To this objection we reply that this Om is the only possible symbol which covers the whole ground, and there is none other like it. The Sphota is the material of all the words, yet it is not any definite word in its fully formed state. That is to say, if all the peculiarities which distinguish one word from another be removed, then what remains will be the Sphota; therefore, this Sphota is called the Nada Brahma, the Sound Brahman.

Now, as every word-symbol, intended to express the inexpressible Sphota, will so particularise it that it will no longer be the Sphota, that symbol which particularises it the least and at the same time most approximately expresses its nature, will be the truest symbol thereof; and this is the Om, and the Om only; because the three letters अ उ म

(A.U.M.), pronounced in combination as Om, may well be the generalised symbol of all possible sounds. The letter A is the least differentiated of all sounds, therefore, Krishna says in the *Gita* अक्षराणामकाराऽस्मि—"I am A among the letters." Again, all articulate sounds are produced in the space within the mouth beginning with the root of the tongue and ending in the lips—the throat sound is A, and M is the last lip sound, and the U exactly represents the rolling forward of the impulse which begins at the root of the tongue till it ends in the lips. If properly pronounced, this Om will represent the whole phenomenon of sound production, and no other word can do this; and this, therefore, is the fittest symbol of the Sphota, which is the real meaning of the Om. And as the symbol can never be separated from the thing signified, the Om and the Sphota are one. And as the Sphota, being the finer side of the manifested universe, is nearer to God, and is indeed that first manifestation of divine wisdom, this Om is truly symbolic of God. Again, just as the "One only" Brahman, the Akhanda Sachchidananda, the undivided Existence-Knowledge-Bliss, can be conceived by imperfect human souls only from particular standpoints and associated with particular qualities, so this universe, His body, has also to be thought of along the line of the thinker's mind.

This direction of the worshipper's mind is guided by its prevailing elements or Tattvas. The result is that the same God will be seen in various manifestations as the possessor of various predominant qualities, and the same universe will appear as full of manifold forms. Even as in the case of the least differentiated and the most universal symbol Om, thought and sound-symbol are seen to be inseparably associated with each other, so also this law of their inseparable association applies to the many differentiated views of God and the universe: each of them, therefore, must have a particular word-symbol to express it. These word-symbols, evolved out of the deepest spiritual perception of sages, symbolise and express, as nearly as possible, the particular view of God and the universe they stand for. And as the Om represents the Akhanda, the undifferentiated Brahman, the others represent the Khanda or the differentiated views of the same Beings; and they are all helpful to divine meditation and the acquisition of true knowledge.

Worship Of Substitutes And Images

The next points to be considered are the worship of Pratikas or of things more or less satisfactory as substitutes for God, and the worship of Pratimas or images. What is the worship of God through a Pratika? It is अब्रह्मणि ब्रह्मदृष्ट्याऽनुसन्धानम् —"Joining the mind with devotion to that which is not Brahman, taking it to be Brahman"—says Bhagvan Ramanuja. "Worship the mind as Brahman, this is internal; and the Akasha as Brahman, this is with regard to the Devas," says Shankara. The mind is an internal Pratika, the Akasha is an external one; and both have to be worshipped as substitutes of God. He continues, "Similarly—'the Sun is Brahman, this is the command', 'He who worships Name as Brahman'—in all such passages the doubt arises as to the worship of Pratikas." The word "Pratika" means going towards; and worshipping a Pratika is worshipping something as a substitute which is, in some one or more respects, like Brahman more and more, but is not Brahman. Along with the Pratikas mentioned in the Shrutis there are various others to be found in the Puranas and the Tantras. In this kind of Pratika-worship may be included all the various forms of Pitri-worship and Deva-worship.

Now worshipping Ishvara and Him alone is Bhakti; the worship of anything else—Deva, or Pitri, or any other being—cannot be Bhakti. The various kinds of worship of the various Devas are all to be included in ritualistic Karma, which gives to the worshipper only a particular result in the form of some celestial enjoyment, but can neither give rise to Bhakti nor lead to Mukti. One thing, therefore, has to be carefully borne in mind. If, as it may happen in some cases, the highly philosophical ideal, the supreme Brahman, is dragged down by Pratika-worship to the level of the Pratika, and the Pratika itself is taken to be the Atman of the worshipper or his Antaryamin (inner ruler), the worshipper gets entirely misled, as no Pratika can really be the Atman of the worshipper.

But where Brahman Himself is the object of worship, and the Pratika stands only as a substitute or a suggestion thereof, that is to say, where, through the Pratika the omnipresent Brahman is worshipped—the Pratika itself being idealised into the cause of all, Brahman—the worship is positively beneficial; nay, it is absolutely necessary for all mankind until they have all got beyond the primary or preparatory state of the mind in regard to worship. When, therefore, any gods or other beings are worshipped in and for themselves, such worship is only a ritualistic Karma; and as a Vidya (Science) it gives us only the fruit belonging to that particular Vidya; but when the Devas or any other beings are looked upon as Brahman and worshipped, the result obtained is the same as by the worshipping of Ishvara. This explains how, in many cases, both in the Shrutis and the Smritis, a god, or a sage, or some other extraordinary being is taken up and lifted, as it were, out of his own nature and idealised into Brahman, and is then worshipped. Says the Advaitin, "Is not everything Brahman when the name and the form have been removed from it?" "Is not He, the Lord, the innermost Self of every one?" says the Vishishtadvaitin. फलम् आदित्याद्युपासनेषु ब्रह्मैव दास्यति सर्वाध्यक्षत्वात्।—"The fruition of even the worship of Adityas etc., Brahman Himself bestows, because He is the Ruler of all." Says Shankara in his Brahma-Sutra-Bhâsya—ईदृशं चात्र ब्रह्मण उपास्यत्वं यतः प्रतीकेषु तत्दृष्ट्याध्यारोपणं प्रतिमादिषु इव विष्ण

वादीनाम्। "Here in this way does Brahman become the object of worship, because He, as Brahman, is superimposed on the Pratikas, just as Vishnu etc., are superimposed upon images etc."

The same ideas apply to the worship of the Pratimas as to that of the Pratikas; that is to say, if the image stands for a god or a saint, the worship is not the result of Bhakti, and does not lead lo liberation; but if it stands for the one God, the worship thereof will bring both Bhakti and Mukti. Of the principal religions of the world, we see Vedantism, Buddhism, and certain forms of Christianity freely using images; only two religions, Mohammedanism and Protestantism, refuse such help. Yet the Mohammedans use the grave of their saints and martyrs almost in the place of images; and the Protestants, in rejecting all concrete helps to religion, are drifting away every year farther and farther from spirituality till at present there is scarcely any difference between the advanced Protestants and the followers of August Comte, or agnostics who preach ethics alone.

Again, in Christianity and Mohammedanism whatever exists of image-worship is made to fall under that category in which the Pratika or the Pratima is worshipped in itself, but not as a "help to the vision" (Drishtisaukaryam) of God; therefore, it is at best only of the nature of ritualistic Karmas and cannot produce either Bhakti or Mukti. In this form of image-worship, the allegiance of the soul is given to other things than Ishvara, and, therefore, such use of images, or graves, or temples, or tombs, is real idolatry; it is in itself neither sinful nor wicked—it is a rite—a Karma, and worshippers must and will get the fruit thereof.

Preface To Raja Yoga

Since the dawn of history, various extraordinary phenomena have been recorded as happening amongst human beings. Witnesses are not wanting in modern times to attest to the fact of such events, even in societies living under the full blaze of modern science. The vast mass of such evidence is unreliable, as coming from ignorant, superstitious, or fraudulent persons. In many instances the so-called miracles are imitations. But what do they imitate? It is not the sign of a candid and scientific mind to throw overboard anything without proper investigation. Surface scientists, unable to explain the various extraordinary mental phenomena, strive to ignore their very existence. They are, therefore, more culpable than those who think that their prayers are answered by a being, or beings, above the clouds, or than those who believe that their petitions will make such beings change the course of the universe. The latter have the excuse of ignorance, or at least of a defective system of education, which has taught them dependence upon such beings, a dependence which has become a part of their degenerate nature. The former have no such excuse.

For thousands of years such phenomena have been studied, investigated, and generalised, the whole ground of the religious faculties of Man has been analysed, and the practical result is the science of Raja Yoga. Raja Yoga does not, after the unpardonable manner of some modern scientists, deny the existence of facts which are difficult to explain; on the other hand, it gently yet in no uncertain terms tells the superstitious that miracles, and answers to prayers, and powers of faith, though true as facts, are not rendered comprehensible through the superstitious explanation of attributing them to the agency of a being, or beings, above the clouds. It declares that each man is only a conduit for the infinite ocean of knowledge and power that lies behind mankind. It teaches that desires and wants are in man, that the power of supply is also in man; and that wherever and whenever a desire, a want, a prayer has been fulfilled, it was out of this infinite magazine that the supply came, and not from any supernatural being. The idea of supernatural beings may rouse to a certain extent the power of action in man, but it also brings spiritual decay. It brings dependence; it brings fear; it brings superstition. It degenerates into a horrible belief in the natural weakness of man. There is no supernatural, says the Yogi, but there are in nature gross manifestations and subtle manifestations. The subtle are the causes, the gross the effects. The gross can be easily perceived by the senses; not so the subtle. The practice of Raja Yoga will lead to the acquisition of the more subtle perceptions.

All the orthodox systems of Indian philosophy have one goal in view, the liberation of the soul through perfection. The method is by Yoga. The word "Yoga" covers an immense ground, but both the Sankhya and the Vedanta Schools point to Yoga in some form or other.

The subject of the present book is that form of Yoga known as Raja Yoga. The aphorisms of Patanjali are the highest authority on Raja Yoga, and form its textbook. The other philosophers, though occasionally differing from Patanjali in some philosophical points, have, as a rule, acceded to his method of practice a decided consent. The first part of this book comprises several lectures to classes delivered by the present writer in New York. The second part is a rather free translation of the aphorisms (sutras) of Patanjali, with a running commentary. Effort has been made to avoid technicalities as far as possible, and to keep to the free and easy style of conversation. In the first part some simple and specific directions are given for the student who wants to practise, but all such are especially and earnestly reminded that, with few exceptions, Yoga can only be safely learnt by direct contact with a teacher. If these conversations succeed in awakening a desire for further information on the subject, the teacher will not be wanting.

The system of Patanjali is based upon the system of the Sankhyas, the points of difference being very few. The two most important differences are, first, that Patanjali admits a Personal God in the form of a first teacher, while the only God the Sankhyas admit is a nearly perfected being, temporarily in charge of a cycle of creation. Second, the Yogis hold the mind to be equally all-pervading with the soul, or Purusha, and the Sankhyas do not.

Each soul is potentially divine.

The goal is to manifest this Divinity within by controlling nature, external and internal

Do this either by work, or worship, or psychic control, or philosophy—by one, or more, or all of these—and be free.

This is the whole of religion. Doctrines, or dogmas, or rituals, or books, or temples, or forms, are but secondary details.

Prana

Pranayama is not, as many think, something about breath; breath indeed has very little to do with it, if anything. Breathing is only one of the many exercises through which we get to the real Pranayama. Pranayama means the control of Prana. According to the philosophers of India, the whole universe is composed of two materials, one of which they call Akasha. It is the omnipresent, all-penetrating existence. Everything that has form, everything that is the result of combination, is evolved out of this Akasha. It is the Akasha that becomes the air, that becomes the liquids, that becomes the solids; it is the Akasha that becomes the sun, the earth, the moon, the stars, the comets; it is the Akasha that becomes the human body, the animal body, the plants, every form that we see, everything that can be sensed, everything that exists. It cannot be perceived; it is so subtle that it is beyond all ordinary perception; it can only be seen when it has become gross, has taken form. At the beginning of creation there is only this Akasha. At the end of the cycle the solids, the liquids, and the gases all melt into the Akasha again, and the next creation similarly proceeds out of this Akasha.

By what power is this Akasha manufactured into this universe? By the power of Prana. Just as Akasha is the infinite omnipresent material of this universe, so is this Prana the infinite, omnipresent manifesting power of this universe. At the beginning and at the end of a cycle everything becomes Akasha, and all the forces that are in the universe resolve back into the Prana; in the next cycle, out of this Prana is evolved everything that we call energy, everything that we call force. It is the Prana that is manifesting as motion; it is the Prana that is manifesting as gravitation, as magnetism. It is the Prana that is manifesting as the actions of the body, as the nerve currents, as thought force. From thought down to the lowest force, everything is but the manifestation of Prana. The sum total of all forces in the universe, mental or physical, when resolved back to their original state, is called Prana. "When there was neither aught nor naught, when darkness was covering darkness, what existed then? That Akasha existed without motion." The physical motion of the Prana was stopped, but it existed all the same.

At the end of a cycle the energies now displayed in the universe quiet down and become potential. At the beginning of the next cycle they start up, strike upon the Akasha, and out of the Akasha evolve these various forms, and as the Akasha changes, this Prana changes also into all these manifestations of energy. The knowledge and control of this Prana is really what is meant by Pranayama.

This opens to us the door to almost unlimited power. Suppose, for instance, a man understood the Prana perfectly, and could control it, what power on earth would not be his? He would be able to move the sun and stars out of their places, to control everything in the universe, from the atoms to the biggest suns, because he would control the Prana. This is the end and aim of Pranayama. When the Yogi becomes perfect, there will be nothing in nature not under his control. If he orders the gods or the souls of the departed to come, they will come at his bidding. All the forces of nature will obey him as slaves. When the ignorant see these powers of the Yogi, they call them the miracles. One peculiarity of the Hindu mind is that it always inquires for the last possible generalisation, leaving the details to be worked out afterwards. The question is raised in the Vedas, "What is that, knowing which, we shall know everything?" Thus, all books, and all philosophies that have been written, have been only to prove that by knowing which everything is known. If a man wants to know this universe bit by bit he must know every individual grain of sand, which means infinite time; he cannot know all of them. Then how can knowledge be? How is it possible for a man to be all-knowing through particulars? The Yogis say that behind this particular manifestation there is a generalisation. Behind all particular ideas stands a generalised, an abstract principle; grasp it, and you have grasped everything. Just as this whole universe has been generalised in the Vedas into that One Absolute Existence, and he who has grasped that Existence has grasped the whole universe, so all forces have been generalised into this Prana, and he who has grasped the Prana has grasped all the forces of the universe, mental or physical. He who has controlled the Prana has controlled his own mind, and all the minds that exist. He who has controlled the Prana has controlled his body, and all the bodies that exist, because the Prana is the generalised manifestation of force.

How to control the Prana is the one idea of Pranayama. All the trainings and exercises in this regard are for that one end. Each man must begin where he stands, must learn how to control the things that are nearest to him. This body is very near to us, nearer than anything in the external universe, and this mind is the nearest of all. The Prana which is working this mind and body is the nearest to us of all the Prana in this universe. This little wave of the Prana which represents our own energies, mental and physical, is the nearest to us of all the waves of the infinite ocean of Prana. If we can succeed in controlling that little wave, then alone we can hope to control the whole of Prana. The Yogi who has done this gains perfection; no longer is he under any power.

He becomes almost almighty, almost all-knowing. We see sects in every country who have attempted this control of Prana. In this country there are mind-healers, faith-healers, spiritualists, Christian scientists, hypnotists, etc., and if we examine these different bodies, we shall find at the back of each this control of the Prana, whether they know it or not. If you boil all their theories down, the residuum will be that. It is the one and the same force they are manipulating, only unknowingly. They have stumbled on the discovery of a force and are using it unconsciously without knowing its nature, but it is the same as the Yogi uses, and which comes from Prana.

The Prana is the vital force in every being. Thought is the finest and highest action of Prana. Thought, again, as we see, is not all. There is also what we call instinct or unconscious thought, the lowest plane of action. If a mosquito stings us, our hand will strike it automatically, instinctively. This is one expression of thought. All reflex actions of the body belong to this plane of thought. There is again the other plane of thought, the conscious. I reason, I judge, I think, I see the pros and cons of certain things, yet that is not all. We know that reason is limited. Reason can go only to a certain extent, beyond that it cannot reach. The circle within which it runs is very limited indeed. Yet at the same time, we find facts rush into this circle. Like the coming of comets certain things come into this circle; it is certain they come from outside the limit, although our reason cannot go beyond. The causes of the phenomena intruding themselves in this small limit are outside of this limit. The mind can exist on a still higher plane, the superconscious. When the mind has attained to that state, which is called Samadhi—perfect concentration, superconsciousness—it goes beyond the limits of reason, and comes face to face with facts which no instinct or reason can ever know. All manipulations of the subtle forces of the body, the different manifestations of Prana, if trained, give a push to the mind, help it to go up higher, and become superconscious, from where it acts.

In this universe there is one continuous substance on every plane of existence. Physically this universe is one: there is no difference between the sun and you. The scientist will tell you it is only a fiction to say the contrary. There is no real difference between the table and me; the table is one point in the mass of matter, and I another point. Each form represents, as it were, one whirlpool in the infinite ocean of matter, of which not one is constant. Just as in a rushing stream there may be millions of whirlpools, the water in each of which is different every moment, turning round and round for a few seconds, and then passing out, replaced by a fresh quantity, so the whole universe is one constantly changing mass of matter, in which all forms of existence are so many whirlpools. A mass of matter enters into one whirlpool, say a human body, stays there for a period, becomes changed, and goes out into another, say an animal body this time, from which again after a few years, it enters into another whirlpool, called a lump of mineral. It is a constant change. Not one body is constant. There is no such thing as my body, or your body, except in words. Of the one huge mass of matter, one point is called a moon, another a sun, another a man, another the earth, another a plant, another a mineral. Not one is constant, but everything is changing, matter eternally concreting and disintegrating. So it is with the mind. Matter is represented by the ether; when the action of Prana is most subtle, this very ether, in the finer state of vibration, will represent the mind, and there it will be still one unbroken mass. If you can simply get to that subtle vibration, you will see and feel that the whole universe is composed of subtle vibrations. Sometimes certain drugs have the power to take us, while as yet in the senses, to that condition. Many of you may remember the celebrated experiment of Sir Humphrey Davy, when the laughing gas overpowered him—how, during the lecture, he remained motionless, stupefied and, after that, he said that the whole universe was made up of ideas. For the time being, as it were, the gross vibrations had ceased, and only the subtle vibrations which he called ideas, were present to him. He could only see the subtle vibrations round him; everything had become thought; the whole universe was an ocean of thought, he and everyone else had become little thought whirlpools.

Thus, even in the universe of thought we find unity, and at last, when we get to the Self, we know that that Self can only be One. Beyond the vibrations of matter in its gross and subtle aspects, beyond motion there is but One. Even in manifested motion there is only unity. These facts can no more be denied. Modern Physics also has demonstrated that the sum total of the energies in the universe is the same throughout. It has also been proved that this sum total of energy exists in two forms. It becomes potential, toned down, and calmed, and next it comes out manifested as all these various forces; again it goes back to the quiet state, and again it manifests. Thus it goes on evolving and involving through eternity. The control of this Prana, as before stated, is what is called Pranayama.

The most obvious manifestation of this Prana in the human body is the motion of the lungs. If that stops, as a rule all the other manifestations of force in the body will immediately stop. But there are persons who can train themselves in such a manner that the body will live on, even when this motion has stopped. There are some persons who can bury themselves for days, and yet live without breathing. To reach the subtle we must take the help of the grosser, and so, slowly, travel towards the most subtle until we gain our point. Pranayama really means controlling this motion of the lungs, and this motion is associated with the breath. Not that breath is producing it; on the contrary *it* is producing breath. This motion draws in the air by pump action. The Prana is moving the lungs, the movement of the lungs draws in the air. So Pranayama is not breathing, but controlling that muscular power which moves the lungs. That muscular power which goes out through the nerves to the muscles and from them to the lungs, making them move in a certain manner, is the Prana, which we have to control in the practice of Pranayama. When the Prana has become controlled then we shall immediately find that all the other actions of the Prana in the body will slowly come under control. I myself have seen men who have controlled almost every muscle of the body; and why not? If I have control over certain muscles, why not over every muscle and nerve of the body? What impossibility is there? At present the control is lost, and the motion has become automatic. We cannot move our ears at will, but we know that animals can. We have not that power because we do not exercise it. This is what is called atavism.

Again, we know that motion which has become latent can be brought back to manifestation. By hard work and practice certain motions of the body which are most dormant can be brought back under perfect control. Reasoning thus we find there is no impossibility, but, on the other hand, every probability that each part of the body can be brought under perfect control. This the Yogi does through Pranayama. Perhaps some of you have read that in Pranayama, when drawing in the breath, you must fill your whole body with Prana. In the English translations Prana is given as breath, and you are inclined to ask how that is to be done. The fault is with the translator. Every part of the body can be filled with Prana, this vital force, and when you are able to do that, you can control the whole body. All the sickness and misery felt in the body will be perfectly controlled; not only so, you will be able to control another's body. Everything is infectious in this world, good or bad. If your body be in a certain state of tension, it will have a tendency to produce the same tension in others. If you are strong and healthy, those that live near you will also have the tendency to become strong and healthy, but if you are sick and weak, those around you will have the tendency to become the same. In the case of one man trying to heal another, the first idea is simply transferring his own health to the other. This is the primitive sort of healing. Consciously or unconsciously, health can be transmitted. A very strong man, living with a weak man, will make him a little stronger, whether he knows it or not. When consciously done, it becomes quicker and better in its action. Next come those cases in which a man may not be very healthy himself, yet we know that he can bring health to another. The first man, in such a case, has a little more control over the Prana, and can rouse, for the time being, his Prana, as it were, to a certain state of vibration, and transmit it to another person.

There have been cases where this process has been carried on at a distance, but in reality there is no distance in the sense of a break. Where is the distance that has a break? Is there any break between you and the sun? It is a continuous mass of matter, the sun being one part, and you another. Is there a break between one part of a river and another? Then why cannot any force travel? There is no reason against it. Cases of healing from a distance are perfectly true. The Prana can be transmitted to a very great distance; but to one genuine case, there are hundreds of frauds. This process of healing is not so easy as it is thought to be. In the most ordinary cases of such healing you will find that the healers simply take advantage of the naturally healthy state of the human body. An allopath comes and treats cholera patients, and gives them his medicines. The homoeopath comes and gives his medicines, and cures perhaps more than the allopath does, because the homoeopath does not disturb his patients, but allows nature to deal with them. The Faith-healer cures more still, because he brings the strength of his mind to bear, and rouses, through faith, the dormant Prana of the patient.

There is a mistake constantly made by faith-healers: they think that faith directly heals a man. But faith alone does not cover all the ground. There are diseases where the worst symptoms are that the patient never thinks that he has that disease. That tremendous faith of the patient is itself one symptom of the disease, and usually indicates that he will die quickly. In such cases the principle that faith cures does not apply. If it were faith alone that cured, these patients also would be cured. It is by the Prana that real curing comes. The pure man, who has controlled the Prana, has the power of bringing it into a certain state of vibration, which can be conveyed to others, arousing in them a similar vibration. You see that in everyday actions. I am talking to you. What am I trying to do? I am, so to say, bringing my mind to a certain state of vibration, and the more I succeed in bringing it to that state, the more you will be affected by what I say. All of you know that the day I am more enthusiastic, the more you enjoy the lecture; and when I am less enthusiastic, you feel lack of interest.

The gigantic will-powers of the world, the world-movers, can bring their Prana into a high state of vibration, and it is so great and powerful that it catches others in a moment, and thousands are drawn towards them, and half the world think as they do. Great prophets of the world had the most wonderful control of the Prana, which gave them tremendous will-power; they had brought their Prana to the highest state of motion, and this is what gave them power to sway the world. All manifestations of power arise from this control. Men may not know the secret, but this is the one explanation. Sometimes in your own body the supply of Prana gravitates more or less to one part; the balance is disturbed, and when the balance of Prana is disturbed, what we call disease is produced. To take away the superfluous Prana, or to supply the Prana that is wanting, will be curing the disease. That again is Pranayama—to learn when there is more or less Prana in one part of the body than there should be. The feelings will become so subtle that the mind will feel that there is less Prana in the toe or the finger than there should be, and will possess the power to supply it. These are among the various functions of Pranayama. They have to be learned slowly and gradually, and as you see, the whole scope of Raja Yoga is really to teach the control and direction in different planes of the Prana. When a man has concentrated his energies, he masters the Prana that is in his body. When a man is meditating, he is also concentrating the Prana.

In an ocean there are huge waves, like mountains, then smaller waves, and still smaller, down to little bubbles, but back of all these is the infinite ocean. The bubble is connected with the infinite ocean at one end, and the huge wave at the other end. So, one may be a gigantic man, and another a little bubble, but each is connected with that infinite ocean of energy, which is the common birthright of every animal that exists. Wherever there is life, the storehouse of infinite energy is behind it. Starting as some fungus, some very minute, microscopic bubble, and all the time drawing from that infinite storehouse of energy, a form is changed slowly and steadily until in course of time it becomes a plant, then an animal, then man, ultimately God. This is attained through millions of aeons, but what is time? An increase of speed, an increase of struggle, is able to bridge the gulf of time. That which naturally takes a long time to accomplish can be shortened by the intensity of the action, says the Yogi. A man may go on slowly drawing in this energy from the infinite mass that exists in the universe, and, perhaps, he will require a hundred thousand years to become a Deva, and then, perhaps, five hundred thousand years to become still higher, and, perhaps, five millions of years to become perfect. Given rapid growth, the time will be lessened. Why is it not possible, with sufficient effort, to reach this very perfection in six months or six years? There is no limit.

Reason shows that. If an engine, with a certain amount of coal, runs two miles an hour, it will run the distance in less time with a greater supply of coal. Similarly, why shall not the soul, by intensifying its action, attain perfection in this very life? All beings will at last attain to that goal, we know. But who cares to wait all these millions of aeons? Why not reach it immediately, in this body even, in this human form? Why shall I not get that infinite knowledge, infinite power, now?

The ideal of the Yogi, the whole science of Yoga, is directed to the end of teaching men how, by intensifying the power of assimilation, to shorten the time for reaching perfection, instead of slowly advancing from point to point and waiting until the whole human race has become perfect. All the great prophets, saints, and seers of the world—what did they do? In one span of life they lived the whole life of humanity, traversed the whole length of time that it takes ordinary humanity to come to perfection. In one life they perfect themselves; they have no thought for anything else, never live a moment for any other idea, and thus the way is shortened for them. This is what is meant by concentration, intensifying the power of assimilation, thus shortening the time. Raja Yoga is the science which teaches us how to gain the power of concentration.

What has Pranayama to do with spiritualism? Spiritualism is also a manifestation of Pranayama. If it be true that the departed spirits exist, only we cannot see them, it is quite probable that there may be hundreds and millions of them about us we can neither see, feel, nor touch. We may be continually passing and repassing through their bodies, and they do not see or feel us. It is a circle within a circle, universe within universe. We have five senses, and we represent Prana in a certain state of vibration. All beings in the same state of vibration will see one another, but if there are beings who represent Prana in a higher state of vibration, they will not be seen. We may increase the intensity of a light until we cannot see it at all, but there may be beings with eyes so powerful that they can see such light. Again, if its vibrations are very low, we do not see a light, but there are animals that may see it, as cats and owls. Our range of vision is only one plane of the vibrations of this Prana. Take this atmosphere, for instance; it is piled up layer on layer, but the layers nearer to the earth are denser than those above, and as you go higher the atmosphere become finer and finer. Or take the case of the ocean; as you go deeper and deeper the pressure of the water increases, and animals which live at the bottom of the sea can never come up, or they will be broken into pieces.

Think of the universe as an ocean of ether, consisting of layer after layer of varying degrees of vibration under the action of Prana; away from the centre the vibrations are less, nearer to it they become quicker and quicker; one order of vibration makes one plane. Then suppose these ranges of vibrations are cut into planes, so many millions of miles one set of vibration, and then so many millions of miles another still higher set of vibration, and so on. It is, therefore, probable, that those who live on the plane of a certain state of vibration will have the power of recognising one another, but will not recognise those above them. Yet, just as by the telescope and the microscope we can increase the scope of our vision, similarly we can by Yoga bring ourselves to the state of vibration of another plane, and thus enable ourselves to see what is going on there. Suppose this room is full of beings whom we do not see. They represent Prana in a certain state of vibration while we represent another. Suppose they represent a quick one, and we the opposite. Prana is the material of which they are composed, as well as we. All are parts of the same ocean of Prana, they differ only in their rate of vibration. If I can bring myself to the quick vibration, this plane will immediately change for me: I shall not see you any more; you vanish and they appear. Some of you, perhaps, know this to be true. All this bringing of the mind into a higher state of vibration is included in one word in Yoga—Samadhi. All these states of higher vibration, superconscious vibrations of the mind, are grouped in that one word, Samadhi, and the lower states of Samadhi give us visions of these beings. The highest grade of Samadhi is when we see the real thing, when we see the material out of which the whole of these grades of beings are composed, and that one lump of clay being known, we know all the clay in the universe.

Thus we see that Pranayama includes all that is true of spiritualism even. Similarly, you will find that wherever any sect or body of people is trying to search out anything occult and mystical, or hidden, what they are doing is really this Yoga, this attempt to control the Prana. You will find that wherever there is any extraordinary display of power, it is the manifestation of this Prana. Even the physical sciences can be included in Pranayama. What moves the steam engine? Prana, acting through the steam. What are all these phenomena of electricity and so forth but Prana? What is physical science? The science of Pranayama, by external means. Prana, manifesting itself as mental power, can only be controlled by mental means. That part of Pranayama which attempts to control the physical manifestations of the Prana by physical means is called physical science, and that part which tries to control the manifestations of the Prana as mental force by mental means is called Raja Yoga.

The Psychic Prana

According to the yogis, there are two nerve currents in the spinal column, called Pingala and Ida, and a hollow canal called Sushumna running through the spinal cord. At the lower end of the hollow canal is what the Yogis call the "Lotus of the Kundalini". They describe it as triangular in form in which, in the symbolical language of the Yogis, there is a power called the Kundalini, coiled up. When that Kundalini awakes, it tries to force a passage through this hollow canal, and as it rises step by step, as it were, layer after layer of the mind becomes open and all the different visions and wonderful powers come to the Yogi. When it reaches the brain, the Yogi is perfectly detached from the body and mind; the soul finds itself free. We know that the spinal cord is composed in a peculiar manner. If we take the figure eight horizontally (∞) there are two parts which are connected in the middle. Suppose you add eight after eight, piled one on top of the other, that will represent the spinal cord. The left is the Ida, the right Pingala, and that hollow canal which runs through the centre of the spinal cord is the Sushumna. Where the spinal cord ends in some of the lumbar vertebrae, a fine fibre issues downwards, and the canal runs up even within that fibre, only much finer. The canal is closed at the lower end, which is situated near what is called the sacral plexus, which, according to modern physiology, is triangular in form, The different plexuses that have their centres in the spinal canal can very well stand for the different "lotuses" of the Yogi.

The Yogi conceives of several centres, beginning with the Muladhara, the basic, and ending with the Sahasrara, the thousand-petalled lotus in the brain. So, if we take these different plexuses as representing these lotuses, the idea of the Yogi can be understood very easily in the language of modern physiology. We know there are two sorts of actions in these nerve currents, one afferent, the other efferent; one sensory and the other motor; one centripetal, and the other centrifugal. One carries the sensations to the brain, and the other from the brain to the outer body. These vibrations are all connected with the brain in the long run. Several other facts we have to remember, in order to clear the way for the explanation which is to come. This spinal cord, at the brain, ends in a sort of bulb, in the medulla, which is not attached to the brain, but floats in a fluid in the brain, so that if there be a blow on the head the force of that blow will be dissipated in the fluid, and will not hurt the bulb. This is an important fact to remember. Secondly, we have also to know that, of all the centres, we have particularly to remember three, the Muladhara (the basic), the Sahasrara (the thousand-petalled lotus of the brain) and the Manipura (the lotus of the navel).

Next we shall take one fact from Physics. We all hear of electricity and various other forces connected with it. What electricity is no one knows, but so far as it is known, it is a sort of motion. There are various other motions in the universe; what is the difference between them and electricity? Suppose this table moves—that the molecules which compose this table are moving in different directions; if they are all made to move in the same direction, it will be through electricity. Electric motion makes the molecules of a body move in the same direction. If all the air molecules in a room are made to move in the same direction, it will make a gigantic battery of electricity of the room. Another point from physiology we must remember, that the centre which regulates the respiratory system, the breathing system, has a sort of controlling action over the system of nerve currents.

Now we shall see why breathing is practised. In the first place, from rhythmical breathing comes a tendency of all the molecules in the body to move in the same direction. When mind changes into will, the nerve currents change into a motion similar to electricity, because the nerves have been proved to show polarity under the action of electric currents. This shows that when the will is transformed into the nerve currents, it is changed into something like electricity. When all the motions of the body have become perfectly rhythmical, the body has, as it were, become a gigantic battery of will. This tremendous will is exactly what the Yogi wants. This is, therefore, a physiological explanation of the breathing exercise. It tends to bring a rhythmic action in the body, and helps us, through the respiratory centre, to control the other centres. The aim of Pranayama here is to rouse the coiled-up power in the Muladhara, called the Kundalini.

Everything that we see, or imagine, or dream, we have to perceive in space. This is the ordinary space, called the Mahakasha, or elemental space. When a Yogi reads the thoughts of other men, or perceives supersensuous objects, he sees them in another sort of space called the Chittakasha, the mental space. When perception has become objectless, and the soul shines in its own nature, it is called the Chidakasha, or knowledge space. When the Kundalini is aroused, and enters the canal of the Sushumna, all the perceptions are in the mental space. When it has reached that end of the canal which opens out into the brain, the objectless perception is in the knowledge space. Taking the analogy of electricity, we find that Man can send a current only along a wire,* but

---

* Said before the discovery of wireless telegraphy.

nature requires no wires to send her tremendous currents. This proves that the wire is not really necessary, but that only our inability to dispense with it compels us to use it.

Similarly, all the sensations and motions of the body are being sent into the brain, and sent out of it, through these wires of nerve fibres. The columns of sensory and motor fibres in the spinal cord are the Ida and Pingala of the Yogis. They are the main channels through which the afferent and efferent currents travel. But why should not the mind send news without any wire, or react without any wire? We see this is done in nature. The Yogi says, if you can do that, you have got rid of the bondage of matter. How to do it? If you can make the current pass through the Sushumna, the canal in the middle of the spinal column, you have solved the problem. The mind has made this network of the nervous system, and has to break it, so that no wires will be required to work through. Then alone will all knowledge come to us—no more bondage of body; that is why it is so important that we should get control of that Sushumna. If we can send the mental current through that hollow canal without any nerve fibres to act as wires, the Yogi says, the problem is solved, and he also says it can be done.

This Sushumna is in ordinary persons closed up at the lower extremity; no action comes through it. The Yogi proposes a practice by which it can be opened, and the nerve currents made to travel through. When a sensation is carried to a centre, the centre reacts. This reaction, in the case of automatic centres, is followed by motion; in the case of conscious centres it is followed first by perception, and secondly by motion. All perception is the reaction to action from outside. How, then, do perceptions in dreams arise? There is then no action from outside. The sensory motions, therefore, are coiled up somewhere. For instance, I see a city; the perception of that city is from the reaction to the sensations brought from outside objects comprising that city.

That is to say, a certain motion in the brain molecules has been set up by the motion in the in carrying nerves, which again are set in motion by external objects in the city. Now, even after a long time I can remember the city. This memory is exactly the same phenomenon, only it is in a milder form. But whence is the action that sets up even the milder form of similar vibrations in the brain? Not certainly from the primary sensations. Therefore, it must be that the sensations are coiled up somewhere, and they, by their acting, bring out the mild reaction which we call dream perception.

Now the centre where all these residual sensations are, as it were, stored up, is called the Muladhara, the root receptacle, and the coiled-up energy of action is Kundalini, "the coiled up". It is very probable that the residual motor energy is also stored up in the same centre, as, after deep study or meditation on external objects, the part of the body where the Muladhara centre is situated (probably the sacral plexus) gets heated. Now, if this coiled-up energy be roused and made active, and then consciously made to travel up the Sushumna canal, as it acts upon centre after centre, a tremendous reaction will set in. When a minute portion of energy travels along a nerve fibre and causes reaction from centres, the perception is either dream or imagination. But when by the power of long internal meditation the vast mass of energy stored up travels along the Sushumna, and strikes the centres, the reaction is tremendous, immensely superior to the reaction of dream or imagination, immensely more intense than the reaction of sense-perception. It is supersensuous perception. And when it reaches the metropolis of all sensations, the brain, the whole brain, as it were, reacts, and the result is the full blaze of illumination, the perception of the Self. As this Kundalini force travels from centre to centre, layer after layer of the mind, as it were, opens up, and this universe is perceived by the Yogi in its fine, or causal form. Then alone the causes of this universe, both as sensation and reaction, are known as they are, and hence comes all knowledge.

The causes being known, the knowledge of the effects is sure to follow.

Thus the rousing of the Kundalini is the one and only way to attaining Divine Wisdom, superconscious perception, realisation of the spirit. The rousing may come in various ways, through love for God, through the mercy of perfected sages, or through the power of the analytic will of the philosopher. Wherever there was any manifestation of what is ordinarily called supernatural power or wisdom, there a little current of Kundalini must have found its way into the Sushumna. Only, in the vast majority of such cases, people had ignorantly stumbled on some practice which set free a minute portion of the coiled up Kundalini. All worship, consciously or unconsciously, leads to this end. The man who thinks that he is receiving response to his prayers does not know that the fulfilment comes from his own nature, that he has succeeded by the mental attitude of prayer in waking up a bit of this infinite power which is coiled up within himself. What, thus, men ignorantly worship under various names, through fear and tribulation, the Yogi declares to the world to be the real power coiled up in every being, the mother of eternal happiness, if we but know how to approach her. And Raja Yoga is the science of religion, the rationale of all worship, all prayers, forms, ceremonies, and miracles.

Pratyahara And Dharana

The next step is called Pratyahara. What is this? You know how perceptions come. First of all there are the external instruments, then the internal organs acting in the body through the brain centres, and there is the mind. When these come together and attach themselves to some external object, then we perceive it. At the same time it is a very difficult thing to concentrate the mind and attach it to one organ only; the mind is a slave.

We hear "Be good", and "Be good", and "Be good", taught all over the world. There is hardly a child, born in any country in the world, who has not been told, "Do not steal," "Do not tell a lie," but nobody tells the child how he can help doing them. Talking will not help him. Why should he not become a thief? We do not teach him how not to steal; we simply tell him, "Do not steal." Only when we teach him to control his mind do we really help him. All actions, internal and external, occur when the mind joins itself to certain centres, called the organs. Willingly or unwillingly it is drawn to join itself to the centres, and that is why people do foolish deeds and feel miserable, which, if the mind were under control, they would not do. What would be the result of controlling the mind? It then would not join itself to the centres of perception, and, naturally, feeling and willing would be under control. It is clear so far. Is it possible? It is perfectly possible. You see it in modern times; the faith-healers teach people to deny misery and pain and evil. Their philosophy is rather roundabout, but it is a part of Yoga upon which they have somehow stumbled. Where they succeed in making a person throw off suffering by denying it, they really use a part of Pratyahara, as they make the mind of the person strong enough to ignore the senses. The hypnotists in a similar manner, by their suggestion, excite in the patient a sort of morbid Pratyahara for the time being. The so-called hypnotic suggestion can only act upon a weak mind. And until the operator, by means of fixed gaze or otherwise, has succeeded in putting the mind of the subject in a sort of passive, morbid condition, his suggestions never work.

Now the control of the centres which is established in a hypnotic patient or the patient of faith-healing, by the operator, for a time, is reprehensible, because it leads to ultimate ruin. It is not really controlling the brain centres by the power of one's own will, but is, as it were, stunning the patient's mind for a time by sudden blows which another's will delivers to it. It is not checking by means of reins and muscular strength the mad carrier of a fiery team, but rather by asking another to deliver heavy blows on the heads of the horses, to stun them for a time into gentleness. At each one of these processes the man operated upon loses a part of his mental energies, till at last, the mind, instead of gaining the power of perfect control, becomes a shapeless, powerless mass, and the only goal of the patient is the lunatic asylum.

Every attempt at control which is not voluntary, not with the controller's own mind, is not only disastrous, but it defeats the end. The goal of each soul is freedom, mastery—freedom from the slavery of matter and thought, mastery of external and internal nature. Instead of leading towards that, every will-current from another, in whatever form it comes, either as direct control of organs, or as forcing to control them while under a morbid condition, only rivets one link more to the already existing heavy chain of bondage of past thoughts, past superstitions. Therefore, beware how you allow yourselves to be acted upon by others. Beware how you unknowingly bring another to ruin. True, some succeed in doing good to many for a time, by giving a new trend to their propensities, but at the same time, they bring ruin to millions by the unconscious suggestions they throw around, rousing in men and women that morbid, passive, hypnotic condition which makes them almost soulless at last. Whosoever, therefore, asks any one to believe blindly, or drags people behind him by the controlling power of his superior will, does an injury to humanity, though he may not intend it.

Therefore, use your own minds, control body and mind yourselves, remember that until you are a diseased person, no extraneous will can work upon you; avoid everyone, however great and good he may be, who asks you to believe blindly. All over the world there have been dancing and jumping and howling sects, who spread like infection when they begin to sing and dance and preach; they also are a sort of hypnotists. They exercise a singular control for the time being over sensitive persons, alas! Often, in the long run, to degenerate whole races. Ay, it is healthier for the individual or the race to remain wicked than be made apparently good by such morbid extraneous control. One's heart sinks to think of the amount of injury done to humanity by such irresponsible yet well-meaning religious fanatics. They little know that the minds which attain to sudden spiritual upheaval under their suggestions, with music and prayers, are simply making themselves passive, morbid, and powerless, and opening themselves to any other suggestion, be it ever so evil. Little do these ignorant, deluded persons dream that whilst they are congratulating themselves upon their miraculous power to transform human hearts, which power they think was poured upon them by some Being above the clouds, they are sowing the seeds of future decay, of crime, of lunacy, and of death. Therefore, beware of everything that takes away your freedom. Know that it is dangerous, and avoid it by all the means in your power.

He who has succeeded in attaching or detaching his mind to or from the centres at will has succeeded in Pratyahara, which means, "gathering towards," checking the outgoing powers of the mind, freeing it from the thraldom of the senses. When we can do this, we shall really possess character; then alone we shall have taken a long step towards freedom; before that we are mere machines.

How hard it is to control the mind! Well has it been compared to the maddened monkey. There was a monkey, restless by his own nature, as all monkeys are. As if that were not enough some one made him drink freely of wine, so that he became still more restless. Then a scorpion stung him. When a man is stung by a scorpion, he jumps about for a whole day; so the poor monkey found his condition worse than ever. To complete his misery a demon entered into him. What language can describe the uncontrollable restlessness of that monkey? The human mind is like that monkey, incessantly active by its own nature; then it becomes drunk with the wine of desire, thus increasing its turbulence. After desire takes possession comes the sting of the scorpion of jealousy at the success of others, and last of all the demon of pride enters the mind, making it think itself of all importance. How hard to control such a mind!

The first lesson, then, is to sit for some time and let the mind run on. The mind is bubbling up all the time. It is like that monkey jumping about. Let the monkey jump as much as he can; you simply wait and watch. Knowledge is power, says the proverb, and that is true. Until you know what the mind is doing you cannot control it. Give it the rein; many hideous thoughts may come into it; you will be astonished that it was possible for you to think such thoughts. But you will find that each day the mind's vagaries are becoming less and less violent, that each day it is becoming calmer. In the first few months you will find that the mind will have a great many thoughts, later you will find that they have somewhat decreased, and in a few more months they will be fewer and fewer, until at last the mind will be under perfect control; but we must patiently practise every day. As soon as the steam is turned on, the engine must run; as soon as things are before us we must perceive; so a man, to prove that he is not a machine, must demonstrate that he is under the control of nothing. This controlling of the mind, and not allowing it to join itself to the centres, is Pratyahara. How is this practised? It is a tremendous work, not to be done in a day. Only after a patient, continuous struggle for years can we succeed.

After you have practised Pratyahara for a time, take the next step, the Dharana, holding the mind to certain points. What is meant by holding the mind to certain points? Forcing the mind to feel certain parts of the body to the exclusion of others. For instance, try to feel only the hand, to the exclusion of other parts of the body. When the Chitta, or mind-stuff, is confined and limited to a certain place it is Dharana. This Dharana is of various sorts, and along with it, it is better to have a little play of the imagination. For instance, the mind should be made to think of one point in the heart. That is very difficult; an easier way is to imagine a lotus there. That lotus is full of light, effulgent light. Put the mind there. Or think of the lotus in the brain as full of light, or of the different centres in the Sushumna mentioned before.

The Yogi must always practise. He should try to live alone; the companionship of different sorts of people distracts the mind; he should not speak much, because to speak distracts the mind; not work much, because too much work distracts the mind; the mind cannot be controlled after a whole day's hard work. One observing the above rules becomes a Yogi. Such is the power of Yoga that even the least of it will bring a great amount of benefit. It will not hurt anyone, but will benefit everyone. First of all, it will tone down nervous excitement, bring calmness, enable us to see things more clearly. The temperament will be better, and the health will be better. Sound health will be one of the first signs, and a beautiful voice. Defects in the voice will be changed. This will be among the first of the many effects that will come. Those who practise hard will get many other signs. Sometimes there will be sounds, as a peal of bells heard at a distance, commingling, and falling on the ear as one continuous sound. Sometimes things will be seen, little specks of light floating and becoming bigger and bigger; and when these things come, know that you are progressing fast.

Those who want to be Yogis, and practise hard, must take care of their diet at first. But for those who want only a little practice for everyday business sort of life, let them not eat too much; otherwise they may eat whatever they please. For those who want to make rapid progress, and to practise hard, a strict diet is absolutely necessary. They will find it advantageous to live only on milk and cereals for some months. As the organisation becomes finer and finer, it will be found in the beginning that the least irregularity throws one out of balance. One bit of food more or less will disturb the whole system, until one gets perfect control, and then one will be able to eat whatever one likes.

When one begins to concentrate, the dropping of a pin will seem like a thunderbolt going through the brain. As the organs get finer, the perceptions get finer. These are the stages through which we have to pass, and all those who persevere will succeed. Give up all argumentation and other distractions. Is there anything in dry intellectual jargon? It only throws the mind off its balance and disturbs it. Things of subtler planes have to be realised. Will talking do that? So give up all vain talk. Read only those books which have been written by persons who have had realisation.

Be like the pearl oyster. There is a pretty Indian fable to the effect that if it rains when the star Svati is in the ascendant, and a drop of rain falls into an oyster, that drop becomes a pearl. The oysters know this, so they come to the surface when that star shines, and wait to catch the precious raindrop. When a drop falls into them, quickly the oysters close their shells and dive down to the bottom of the sea, there to patiently develop the drop into the pearl. We should be like that. First hear, then understand, and then, leaving all distractions, shut your minds to outside influences, and devote yourselves to developing the truth within you. There is the danger of frittering away your energies by taking up an idea only for its novelty, and then giving it up for another that is newer. Take one thing up and do it, and see the end of it, and before you have seen the end, do not give it up. He who can become mad with an idea, he alone sees light. Those that only take a nibble here and a nibble there will never attain anything. They may titillate their nerves for a moment, but there it will end. They will be slaves in the hands of nature, and will never get beyond the senses.

Those who really want to be Yogis must give up, once for all, this nibbling at things. Take up one idea. Make that one idea your life—think of it, dream of it, live on that idea. Let the brain, muscles, nerves, every part of your body, be full of that idea, and just leave every other idea alone. This is the way to success, and this is the way great spiritual giants are produced. Others are mere talking machines. If we really want to be blessed, and make others blessed, we must go deeper. The first step is not to disturb the mind, not to associate with persons whose ideas are disturbing. All of you know that certain persons, certain places, certain foods, repel you. Avoid them; and those who want to go to the highest, must avoid all company, good or bad. Practise hard; whether you live or die does not matter. You have to plunge in and work, without thinking of the result. If you are brave enough, in six months you will be a perfect Yogi. But those who take up just a bit of it and a little of everything else make no progress. It is of no use simply to take a course of lessons. To those who are full of Tamas, ignorant and dull—those whose minds never get fixed on any idea, who only crave for something to amuse them—religion and philosophy are simply objects of entertainment. These are the unpersevering. They hear a talk, think it very nice, and then go home and forget all about it. To succeed, you must have tremendous perseverance, tremendous will. "I will drink the ocean," says the persevering soul, "at my will mountains will crumble up." Have that sort of energy, that sort of will, work hard, and you will reach the goal.

Dhyana And Samadhi

We have taken a cursory view of the different steps in Raja Yoga, except the finer ones, the training in concentration, which is the goal, to which Raja Yoga will lead us. We see, as human beings, that all our knowledge which is called rational is referred to consciousness. My consciousness of this table, and of your presence, makes me know that the table and you are here. At the same time, there is a very great part of my existence of which I am not conscious. All the different organs inside the body, the different parts of the brain—nobody is conscious of these.

When I eat food, I do it consciously; when I assimilate it, I do it unconsciously. When the food is manufactured into blood, it is done unconsciously. When out of the blood all the different parts of my body are strengthened, it is done unconsciously. And yet it is I who am doing all this; there cannot be twenty people in this one body. How do I know that I do it, and nobody else? It may be urged that my business is only in eating and assimilating the food, and that strengthening the body by the food is done for me by somebody else. That cannot be, because it can be demonstrated that almost every action of which we are now unconscious can be brought up to the plane of consciousness. The heart is beating apparently without our control. None of us here can control the heart;

it goes on its own way. But by practice men can bring even the heart under control, until it will just beat at will, slowly, or quickly, or almost stop. Nearly every part of the body can be brought under control. What does this show? That the functions which are beneath consciousness are also performed by us, only we are doing it unconsciously. We have, then, two planes in which the human mind works. First is the conscious plane, in which all work is always accompanied with the feeling of egoism. Next comes the unconscious plane, where all work is unaccompanied by the feeling of egoism. That part of mind-work which is unaccompanied with the feeling of egoism is unconscious work, and that part which is accompanied with the feeling of egoism is conscious work. In the lower animals this unconscious work is called instinct. In higher animals, and in the highest of all animals, man, what is called conscious work prevails.

But it does not end here. There is a still higher plane upon which the mind can work. It can go beyond consciousness. Just as unconscious work is beneath consciousness, so there is another work which is above consciousness, and which also is not accompanied with the feeling of egoism. The feeling of egoism is only on the middle plane. When the mind is above or below that line, there is no feeling of "I", and yet the mind works. When the mind goes beyond this line of self-consciousness, it is called Samadhi or superconsciousness. How, for instance, do we know that a man in Samadhi has not gone below consciousness, has not degenerated instead of going higher? In both cases the works are unaccompanied with egoism. The answer is, by the effects, by the results of the work, we know that which is below, and that which is above. When a man goes into deep sleep, he enters a plane beneath consciousness. He works the body all the time, he breathes, he moves the body, perhaps, in his sleep, without any accompanying feeling of ego; he is unconscious, and when he returns from his sleep, he is the same man who went into it. The sum total of the knowledge which he had before he went into the sleep remains the same; it does not increase at all. No enlightenment comes. But when a man goes into Samadhi, if he goes into it a fool, he comes out a sage.

What makes the difference? From one state a man comes out the very same man that he went in, and from another state the man comes out enlightened, a sage, a prophet, a saint, his whole character changed, his life changed, illumined. These are the two effects. Now the effects being different, the causes must be different. As this illumination with which a man comes back from Samadhi is much higher than can be got from unconsciousness, or much higher than can be got by reasoning in a conscious state, it must, therefore, be superconsciousness, and Samadhi is called the superconscious state.

This, in short, is the idea of Samadhi. What is its application? The application is here. The field of reason, or of the conscious workings of the mind, is narrow and limited. There is a little circle within which human reason must move. It cannot go beyond. Every attempt to go beyond is impossible, yet it is beyond this circle of reason that there lies all that humanity holds most dear. All these questions, whether there is an immortal soul, whether there is a God, whether there is any supreme intelligence guiding this universe or not, are beyond the field of reason. Reason can never answer these questions. What does reason say? It says, "I am agnostic; I do not know either yea or nay," Yet these questions are so important to us. Without a proper answer to them, human life will be purposeless. All our ethical theories, all our moral attitudes, all that is good and great in human nature, have been moulded upon answers that have come from beyond the circle. It is very important, therefore, that we should have answers to these questions. If life is only a short play, if the universe is only a "fortuitous combination of atoms," then why should I do good to another? Why should there be mercy justice, or fellow-feeling? The best thing for this world would be to make hay while the sun shines, each man for himself. If there is no hope, why should I love my brother, and not cut his throat? If there is nothing beyond, if there is no freedom, but only rigorous dead laws, I should only try to make myself happy here. You will find people saying nowadays that they have utilitarian grounds as the basis of morality. What is this basis? Procuring the greatest amount of happiness to the greatest number. Why should I do this? Why should I not produce the greatest unhappiness to the greatest number, if that serves my purpose? How will utilitarians answer this question? How do you know what is right, or what is wrong? I am impelled by my desire for happiness, and I fulfil it, and it is in my nature; I know nothing beyond. I have these desires, and must fulfil them; why should you complain? Whence come all these truths about human life, about morality, about the immortal soul, about God, about love and sympathy, about being good, and, above all, about being unselfish?

All ethics, all human action and all human thought, hang upon this one idea of unselfishness. The whole idea of human life can be put into that one word, unselfishness. Why should we be unselfish? Where is the necessity, the force, the power, of my being unselfish? You call yourself a rational man, a utilitarian; but if you do not show me a reason for utility, I say you are irrational. Show me the reason why I should not be selfish. To ask one to be unselfish may be good as poetry, but poetry is not reason. Show me a reason. Why shall I be unselfish, and why be good? Because Mr. and Mrs. So-and-so say so does not weigh with me. Where is the utility of my being unselfish? My utility is to be selfish if utility means the greatest amount of happiness. What is the answer? The utilitarian can never give it. The answer is that this world is only one drop in an infinite ocean, one link in an infinite chain.

Where did those that preached unselfishness, and taught it to the human race, get this idea? We know it is not instinctive;

the animals, which have instinct, do not know it. Neither is it reason; reason does not know anything about these ideas. Whence then did they come?

We find, in studying history, one fact held in common by all the great teachers of religion the world ever had. They all claim to have got their truths from beyond, only many of them did not know where they got them from. For instance, one would say that an angel came down in the form of a human being, with wings, and said to him, "Hear, O man, this is the message." Another says that a Deva, a bright being, appeared to him. A third says he dreamed that his ancestor came and told him certain things. He did not know anything beyond that. But this is common that all claim that this knowledge has come to them from beyond, not through their reasoning power. What does the science of Yoga teach? It teaches that they were right in claiming that all this knowledge came to them from beyond reasoning, but that it came from within themselves.

The Yogi teaches that the mind itself has a higher state of existence, beyond reason, a superconscious state, and when the mind gets to that higher state, then this knowledge, beyond reasoning, comes to man. Metaphysical and transcendental knowledge comes to that man. This state of going beyond reason, transcending ordinary human nature, may sometimes come by chance to a man who does not understand its science; he, as it were, stumbles upon it. When he stumbles upon it, he generally interprets it as coming from outside. So this explains why an inspiration, or transcendental knowledge, may be the same in different countries, but in one country it will seem to come through an angel, and in another through a Deva, and in a third through God. What does it mean? It means that the mind brought the knowledge by its own nature, and that the finding of the knowledge was interpreted according to the belief and education of the person through whom it came. The real fact is that these various men, as it were, stumbled upon this superconscious state.

The Yogi says there is a great danger in stumbling upon this state. In a good many cases there is the danger of the brain being deranged, and, as a rule, you will find that all those men, however great they were, who had stumbled upon this superconscious state without understanding it, groped in the dark, and generally had, along with their knowledge, some quaint superstition. They opened themselves to hallucinations. Mohammed claimed that the Angel Gabriel came to him in a cave one day and took him on the heavenly horse, Harak, and he visited the heavens. But with all that, Mohammed spoke some wonderful truths. If you read the Koran, you find the most wonderful truths mixed with superstitions. How will you explain it? That man was inspired, no doubt, but that inspiration was, as it were, stumbled upon. He was not a trained Yogi, and did not know the reason of what he was doing. Think of the good Mohammed did to the world, and think of the great evil that has been done through his fanaticism! Think of the millions massacred through his teachings, mothers bereft of their children, children made orphans, whole countries destroyed, millions upon millions of people killed!

So we see this danger by studying the lives of great teachers like Mohammed and others. Yet we find, at the same time, that they were all inspired. Whenever a prophet got into the superconscious state by heightening his emotional nature, he brought away from it not only some truths, but some fanaticism also, some superstition which injured the world as much as the greatness of the teaching helped. To get any reason out of the mass incongruity we call human life, we have to transcend our reason, but we must do it scientifically, slowly, by regular practice, and we must cast off all superstition. We must take up the study of the super conscious state just as any other science. On reason we must have to lay our foundation, we must follow reason as far as it leads, and when reason fails, reason itself will show us the way to the highest plane. When you hear a man say, "I am inspired," and then talk irrationally, reject it. Why? Because these three states—instinct, reason, and superconsciousness, or the unconscious, conscious, and super conscious states—belong to one and the same mind. There are not three minds in one man, but one state of it develops into the others. Instinct develops into reason, and reason into the transcendental consciousness; therefore, not one of the states contradicts the others. Real inspiration never contradicts reason, but fulfils it. Just as you find the great prophets saying, "I come not to destroy but to fulfil," so inspiration always comes to fulfil reason, and is in harmony with it.

All the different steps in Yoga are intended to bring us scientifically to the superconscious state, or Samadhi. Furthermore, this is a most vital point to understand, that inspiration is as much in every man's-nature as it was in that of the ancient prophets. These prophets were not unique; they were men as you or I. They were great Yogis. They had gained this superconsciousness, and you and I can get the same. They were not peculiar people. The very fact that one man ever reached that state, proves that it is possible for every man to do so. Not only is it possible, but every man must, eventually, get to that state, and that is religion. Experience is the only teacher we have. We may talk and reason all our lives, but we shall not understand a word of truth, until we experience it ourselves. You cannot hope to make a man a surgeon by simply giving him a few books. You cannot satisfy my curiosity to see a country by showing me a map; I must have actual experience. Maps can only create curiosity in us to get more perfect knowledge. Beyond that, they have no value whatever. Clinging to books only degenerates the human mind. Was there ever a more horrible blasphemy than the statement that all the knowledge of God is confined to this or that book? How dare men call God infinite, and yet try to compress Him within the covers of a little book! Millions of people have been killed because they did not believe what the books said, because they would not see all the knowledge of God within the covers of a book. Of course this killing and murdering has gone by, but the world is still tremendously bound up in a belief in books.

In order to reach the superconscious state in a scientific manner it is necessary to pass through the various steps of Raja Yoga I have been teaching. After Pratyahara and Dharana, we come to Dhyana, meditation. When the mind has been trained to remain fixed on a certain internal or external location, there comes to it the power of flowing in an unbroken current, as it were, towards that point. This state is called Dhyana. When one has so intensified the power of Dhyana as to be able to reject the external part of perception and remain meditating only on the internal part, the meaning, that state is called Samadhi. The three—Dharana, Dhyana, and Samadhi—together, are called Samyama. That is, if the mind can first concentrate upon an object, and then is able to continue in that concentration for a length of time, and then, by continued concentration, to dwell only on the internal part of the perception of which the object was the effect, everything comes under the control of such a mind.

This meditative state is the highest state of existence. So long as there is desire, no real happiness can come. It is only the contemplative, witness-like study of objects that brings to us real enjoyment and happiness. The animal has its happiness in the senses, the man in his intellect, and the god in spiritual contemplation. It is only to the soul that has attained to this contemplative state that the world really becomes beautiful. To him who desires nothing, and does not mix himself up with them, the manifold changes of nature are one panorama of beauty and sublimity.

These ideas have to be understood in Dhyana, or meditation. We hear a sound. First, there is the external vibration; second, the nerve motion that carries it to the mind; third, the reaction from the mind, along with which flashes the knowledge of the object which was the external cause of these different changes from the ethereal vibrations to the mental reactions. These three are called in Yoga, Shabda (sound), Artha (meaning), and Jnana (knowledge). In the language of physics and physiology they are called the ethereal vibration, the motion in the nerve and brain, and the mental reaction. Now these, though distinct processes, have become mixed up in such a fashion as to become quite indistinct. In fact, we cannot now perceive any of these, we only perceive their combined effect, what we call the external object. Every act of perception includes these three, and there is no reason why we should not be able to distinguish them.

When, by the previous preparations, it becomes strong and controlled, and has the power of finer perception, the mind should be employed in meditation. This meditation must begin with gross objects and slowly rise to finer and finer, until it becomes objectless. The mind should first be employed in perceiving the external causes of sensations, then the internal motions, and then its own reaction. When it has succeeded in perceiving the external causes of sensations by themselves, the mind will acquire the power of perceiving all fine material existences, all fine bodies and forms. When it can succeed in perceiving the motions inside by themselves, it will gain the control of all mental waves, in itself or in others, even before they have translated themselves into physical energy; and when he will be able to perceive the mental reaction by itself, the Yogi will acquire the knowledge of everything, as every sensible object, and every thought is the result of this reaction. Then will he have seen the very foundations of his mind, and it will be under his perfect control. Different powers will come to the Yogi, and if he yields to the temptations of any one of these, the road to his further progress will be barred. Such is the evil of running after enjoyments. But if he is strong enough to reject even these miraculous powers, he will attain to the goal of Yoga, the complete suppression of the waves in the ocean of the mind. Then the glory of the soul, undisturbed by the distractions of the mind, or motions of the body, will shine in its full effulgence; and the Yogi will find himself as he is and as he always was, the essence of knowledge, the immortal, the all-pervading.

Samadhi is the property of every human being—nay, every animal. From the lowest animal to the highest angel, some time or other, each one will have to come to that state, and then, and then alone, will real religion begin for him. Until then we only struggle towards that stage. There is no difference now between us and those who have no religion, because we have no experience. What is concentration good for, save to bring us to this experience? Each one of the steps to attain Samadhi has been reasoned out, properly adjusted, scientifically organised, and, when faithfully practised, will surely lead us to the desired end. Then will all sorrows cease, all miseries vanish; the seeds for actions will be burnt, and the soul will be free forever.

Introduction To Jnana Yoga

This is the rational and philosophic side of Yoga and very difficult, but I will take you slowly through it. Yoga means the method of joining Man and God. When you understand this, you can go on with your own definitions of Man and God, and you will find the term Yoga fits in with every definition. Remember always, there are different Yogas for different minds, and that if one does not suit you, another may. All religions are divided into theory and practice. The Western mind has given itself up to the theory and only sees the practical part of religion as good works. Yoga is the practical part of religion and shows that religion is a practical power apart from good works.

At the beginning of the nineteenth century Man tried to find God through reason, and Deism was the result. What little was left of God by this process was destroyed by Darwinism and Millism. Men were then thrown back upon historical and comparative religion. They thought, religion was derived from element worship (ref: Max Muller on the sun myths etc.); others thought that religion was derived from ancestor worship (ref: Herbert Spencer). But taken as a whole, these methods have proved a failure. Man cannot get at Truth by external methods.

"If I know one lump of clay, I know the whole mass of clay." The universe is all built on the same plan. The individual is only a part, like the lump of clay. If we know the human soul—which is one atom—its beginning and general history, we know the whole of nature. Birth, growth, development, decay, death—this is the sequence in all nature and is the same in the plant and the man. The difference is only in time. The whole cycle may be completed in one case in a day, in the other in three score years and ten; the methods are the same. The only way to reach a sure analysis of the universe is by the analysis of our own minds. A proper psychology is essential to the understanding of religion. To reach Truth by reason alone is impossible, because imperfect reason cannot study its own fundamental basis. Therefore, the only way to study the mind is to get at facts, and then intellect will arrange them and deduce the principles. The intellect has to build the house; but it cannot do so without bricks, and *it* cannot make bricks. Jnana Yoga is the surest way of arriving at facts.

First we have the physiology of mind. We have organs of the senses, which are divided into organs of action and organs of perception. By organs I do not mean the external sense-instruments. The ophthalmic centre in the brain is the organ of sight, not the eye alone. So with every organ, the function is internal. Only when the mind reacts, is the object truly perceived. The sensory and motor nerves are necessary to perception.

Then there is the mind itself. It is like a smooth lake which when struck, say by a stone, vibrates. The vibrations gather together and react on the stone, and all through the lake they will spread and be felt. The mind is like the lake; it is constantly being set in vibrations, which leave an impression on the mind; and the idea of the Ego, or personal self, the "I", is the result of these impressions. This "I", therefore, is only the very rapid transmission of force and is in itself no reality.

The mind-stuff is a very fine material instrument used for taking up the Prana. When a man dies, the body dies; but a little bit of the mind, the seed, is left when all else is shattered; and this is the seed of the new body called by St. Paul "the spiritual body". This theory of the materiality of the mind accords with all modern theories. The idiot is lacking in intelligence because his mind-stuff is injured. Intelligence cannot be in matter nor can it be produced by any combinations of matter. Where then is intelligence? It is behind matter; it is the Jiva, the real Self, working through the instrument of matter. Transmission of force is not possible without matter, and as the Jiva cannot travel alone, some part of mind is left as a transmitting medium when all else is shattered by death.

How are perceptions made? The wall opposite sends an impression to me, but I do not see the wall until my mind reacts, that is to say, the mind cannot know the wall by mere sight. The reaction that enables the mind to get a perception of the wall is an intellectual process. In this way the whole universe is seen through our eyes plus mind (or perceptive faculty); it is necessarily coloured by our own individual tendencies. The *real* wall, or the *real* universe, is outside the mind, and is unknown and unknowable. Call this universe X, and our statement is that the seen universe is X plus mind.

What is true of the external must also apply to the internal world. Mind also wants to know itself, but this Self can only be known through the medium of the mind and is, like the wall, unknown. This self we may call Y, and the statement would then be, Y plus mind is the inner self. Kant was the first to arrive at this analysis of mind, but it was long ago stated in the Vedas. We have thus, as it were, mind standing between X and Y and reacting on both.

If X is unknown, then any qualities we give to it are only derived from our own mind. Time, space, and causation are the three conditions through which mind perceives. Time is the condition for the transmission of thought, and space for the vibration of grosser matter. Causation is the sequence in which vibrations come. Mind can only cognise through these. Anything, therefore, beyond mind must be beyond time, space, and causation.

To the blind man the world is perceived by touch and sound. To us with five senses it is another world. If any of us developed an electric sense and the faculty of seeing electric waves, the world would appear different. Yet the world, as the X to all of these, is still the same. As each one brings his own mind, he sees his own world. There is X plus one sense; X plus two senses, up to five, as we know humanity. The result is constantly varied, yet X remains always unchanged. Y is also beyond our minds and beyond time, space, and causation.

But, you may ask, "How do we know there are two things (X and Y) beyond time, space, and causation?" Quite true, time makes differentiation, so that, as both are really beyond time, they must be really one. When mind sees this *one,* it calls it variously—X, when it is the outside world, and Y, when it is the inside world. This unit exists and is looked at through the lens of minds.

The Being of perfect nature, universally appearing to us, is God, is Absolute. The undifferentiated is the perfect condition; all others must be lower and not permanent.

What makes the undifferentiated appear differentiated to mind? This is the same kind of question as what is the origin of evil and free will? The question itself is contradictory and impossible, because the question takes for granted cause and effect. There is no cause and effect in the undifferentiated; the question assumes that the undifferentiated is in the same condition as the differentiated. "Whys" and "wherefores" are in mind only. The Self is beyond causation, and It alone is free. Its light it is which percolates through every form of mind. With every action I assert I am free, and yet every action proves that I am bound. The real Self is free, yet when mixed with mind and body, It is not free. The will is the first manifestation of the real Self; the first limitation, therefore, of this real Self is the will. Will is a compound of Self and mind. Now, no compound can be permanent, so that when we will to live, we must die. Immortal life is a contradiction in terms, for life, being a compound, cannot be immortal. True Being is undifferentiated and *eternal.* How does this Perfect Being become mixed up with will, mind, thought—all defective things? It never has become mixed. You are the real you (the Y of our former statement); you never were will; you never have changed; you as a person never existed; It is illusion. Then on what, you will say, do the phenomena of illusion rest? This is a bad question. Illusion never rests on Truth, but only on illusion. Everything struggles to go back to what was before these illusions, to be free in fact. What then is the value of life? It is to give us experience. Does this view do away with evolution? On the contrary, it explains it. It is really the process of refinement of matter allowing the real Self to manifest Itself. It is as if a screen or a veil were between us and some other object. The object becomes clear as the screen is gradually withdrawn. The question is simply one of manifestation of the higher Self.

Maya And Illusion

Delivered in London

Almost all of you have heard of the word "Maya". Generally it is used, though incorrectly, to denote illusion, or delusion, or some such thing. But the theory of Maya forms one of the pillars upon which the Vedanta rests; it is, therefore, necessary that it should be properly understood. I ask a little patience of you, for there is a great danger of its being misunderstood. The oldest idea of Maya that we find in Vedic literature is the sense of delusion; but then the real theory had not been reached. We find such passages as, "Indra through his Maya assumed various forms." Here it is true the word "Maya" means something like magic, and we find various other passages, always taking the same meaning. The word "Maya" then dropped out of sight altogether. But in the meantime the idea was developing. Later, the question was raised: "Why can't we know this secret of the universe?" And the answer given was very significant: "Because we talk in vain, and because we are satisfied with the things of the senses, and because we are running after desires; therefore, we, as it were, cover the Reality with a mist." Here the word "Maya" is not used at all, but we get the idea that the cause of our ignorance is a kind of mist that has come between us and the Truth. Much later on, in one of the latest Upanishads, we find the word "Maya" reappearing, but this time, a transformation has taken place in it, and a mass of new meaning has attached itself to the word. Theories had been propounded and repeated, others had been taken up, until at last the idea of Maya became fixed. We read in the *Shvetashvatara Upanishad*, "Know nature to be Maya and the Ruler of this Maya is the Lord Himself." Coming to our philosophers, we find that this word Maya has been manipulated in various fashions, until we come to the great Shankaracharya. The theory of Maya was manipulated a little by the Buddhists too, but in the hands of the Buddhists it became very much like what is called Idealism, and that is the meaning that is now generally given to the word "Maya". When the Hindu says the world is Maya, at once people get the idea that the world is an illusion. This interpretation has some basis, as coming through the Buddhistic philosophers, because there was one section of philosophers who did not believe in the external world at all. But the Maya of the Vedanta, in its last developed form, is neither Idealism nor Realism, nor is it a theory. It is a simple statement of facts—what we are and what we see around us.

As I have told you before, the minds of the people from whom the Vedas came were intent upon following principles, discovering principles. They had no time to work upon details or to wait for them; they wanted to go deep into the heart of things. Something beyond was calling them, as it were, and they could not wait. Scattered through the Upanishads, we find that the details of subjects which we now call modern sciences are often very erroneous, but, at the same time, their principles are correct. For instance, the idea of ether, which is one of the latest theories of modern science, is to be found in our ancient literature in forms much more developed than is the modern scientific theory of ether today, but it was in principle. When they tried to demonstrate the workings of that principle, they made many mistakes. The theory of the all-pervading life principle, of which all life in this universe is but a differing manifestation, was understood in Vedic times; it is found in the Brahmanas. There is a long hymn in the Samhitas in praise of Prana of which all life is but a manifestation. By the by, it may interest some of you to know that there are theories in the Vedic philosophy about the origin of life on this earth very similar to those which have been advanced by some modern European scientists. You, of course, all know that there is a theory that life came from other planets. It is a settled doctrine with some Vedic philosophers that life comes in this way from the moon.

Coming to the principles, we find these Vedic thinkers very courageous and wonderfully bold in propounding large and generalised theories. Their solution of the mystery of the universe, from the external world, was as satisfactory as it could be. The detailed workings of modern science do not bring the question one step nearer to solution, because the principles have failed. If the theory of ether failed in ancient times to give a solution of the mystery of the universe, working out the details of that ether theory would not bring us much nearer to the truth. If the theory of all-pervading life failed as a theory of this universe, it would not mean anything more if worked out in detail, for the details do not change the principle of the universe. What I mean is that in their inquiry into the principle, the Hindu thinkers were as bold, and in some cases, much bolder than the moderns. They made some of the grandest generalisations that have yet been reached, and some still remain as theories, which modern science has yet to get even as theories. For instance, they not only arrived at the ether theory, but went beyond and classified mind also as a still more rarefied ether. Beyond that again, they found a still more rarefied ether. Yet that was no solution, it did not solve the problem. No amount of knowledge of the external world could solve the problem. "But," says the scientists, "we are just beginning to know a little: wait a few thousand years and we shall get the solution." "No," says the

Vedantist, for he has proved beyond all doubt that the mind is limited, that it cannot go beyond certain limits—beyond time, space, and causation. As no man can jump out of his own self, so no man can go beyond the limits that have been put upon him by the laws of time and space. Every attempt to solve the laws of causation, time, and space would be futile, because the very attempt would have to be made by taking for granted the existence of these three. What does the statement of the existence of the world mean, then? "This world has no existence." What is meant by that? It means that it has no absolute existence. It exists only in relation to my mind, to your mind, and to the mind of everyone else. We see this world with the five senses but if we had another sense, we would see in it something more. If we had yet another sense, it would appear as something still different. It has, therefore, no real existence; it has no unchangeable, immovable, infinite existence. Nor can it be called non-existence, seeing that it exists, and we have to work in and through it. It is a mixture of existence and non-existence.

Coming from abstractions to the common, everyday details of our lives, we find that our whole life is a contradiction, a mixture of existence and non-existence. There is this contradiction in knowledge. It seems that man can know everything, if he only wants to know; but before he has gone a few steps, he finds an adamantine wall which he cannot pass. All his work is in a circle, and he cannot go beyond that circle. The problems which are nearest and dearest to him are impelling him on and calling, day and night, for a solution, but he cannot solve them, because he cannot go beyond his intellect. And yet that desire is implanted strongly in him. Still we know that the only good is to be obtained by controlling and checking it. With every breath, every impulse of our heart asks us to be selfish. At the same time, there is some power beyond us which says that it is unselfishness alone which is good. Every child is a born optimist; he dreams golden dreams. In youth he becomes still more optimistic. It is hard for a young man to believe that there is such a thing as death, such a thing as defeat or degradation. Old age comes, and life is a mass of ruins. Dreams have vanished into the air, and the man becomes a pessimist. Thus we go from one extreme to another, buffeted by nature, without knowing where we are going. It reminds me of a celebrated song in the *Lalita Vistara,* the biography of Buddha. Buddha was born, says the book, as the saviour of mankind, but he forgot himself in the luxuries of his palace. Some angels came and sang a song to rouse him. And the burden of the whole song is that we are floating down the river of life which is continually changing with no stop and no rest. So are our lives, going on and on without knowing any rest. What are we to do? The man who has enough to eat and drink is an optimist, and he avoids all mention of misery, for it frightens him. Tell not to him of the sorrows and the sufferings of the world; go to him and tell that it is all good. "Yes, I am safe," says he. "Look at me! I have a nice house to live in. I do not fear cold and hunger; therefore, do not bring these horrible pictures before me." But, on the other hand, there are others dying of cold and hunger. If you go and teach *them* that it is all good, they will not hear you. How can they wish others to be happy when they are miserable? Thus we are oscillating between optimism and pessimism.

Then, there is the tremendous fact of death. The whole world is going towards death; everything dies. All our progress, our vanities, our reforms, our luxuries, our wealth, our knowledge, have that one end—death. That is all that is certain. Cities come and go, empires rise and fall, planets break into pieces and crumble into dust, to be blown about by the atmospheres of other planets. Thus it has been going on from time without beginning. Death is the end of everything. Death is the end of life, of beauty, of wealth, of power, of virtue too. Saints die and sinners die, kings die and beggars die. They are all going to death, and yet this tremendous clinging on to life exists. Somehow, we do not know why, we cling to life; we cannot give it up. And this is Maya.

The mother is nursing a child with great care; all her soul, her life, is in that child. The child grows, becomes a man, and perchance becomes a blackguard and a brute, kicks her and beats her every day; and yet the mother clings to the child; and when her reason awakes, she covers it up with the idea of love. She little thinks that it is not love, that it is something which has got hold of her nerves, which she cannot shake off; however she may try, she cannot shake off the bondage she is in. And this is Maya.

We are all after the Golden Fleece. Every one of us thinks that this will be his. Every reasonable man sees that his chance is, perhaps, one in twenty millions, yet everyone struggles for it. And this is Maya.

Death is stalking day and night over this earth of ours, but at the same time we think we shall live eternally. A question was once asked of King Yudhisthira, "What is the most wonderful thing on this earth?" And the king replied, "Every day people are dying around us, and yet men think they will never die." And this is Maya.

These tremendous contradictions in our intellect, in our knowledge, yea, in all the facts of our life face us on all sides. A reformer arises and wants to remedy the evils that are existing in a certain nation; and before they have been remedied, a thousand other evils arise in another place. It is like an old house that is falling; you patch it up in one place and the ruin extends to another. In India, our reformers cry and preach against the evils of enforced widowhood. In the West, non-marriage is the great evil. Help the unmarried on one side; they are suffering. Help the widows on the other; they are suffering. It is like chronic rheumatism: you drive it from the head, and it goes to the body; you drive it from there, and it goes to the feet. Reformers arise and preach that learning, wealth, and culture should not be in the hands of a select few; and they do their best to make them accessible to all. These may bring more happiness to some, but, perhaps as culture comes, physical happiness lessens. The knowledge of happiness brings the knowledge of unhappiness. Which way then shall we go? The least amount of material prosperity that we enjoy is causing the same amount of misery elsewhere. This is the law. The young, perhaps, do not see it clearly, but those who have lived long enough and those who have struggled enough will understand it. And this is Maya. These things are going on, day and night, and to find a solution of this problem is impossible. Why should it be so? It is impossible to answer this, because the question cannot be logically formulated. There is neither *how* nor *why* in fact; we only know that it *is* and that we cannot help it. Even to grasp it, to draw an exact image of it in our own mind, is beyond our power. How can we solve it then?

Maya is a statement of the fact of this universe, of how it is going on. People generally get frightened when these things are told to them. But bold we must be. Hiding facts is not the way to find a remedy. As you all know, a hare hunted by dogs puts its head down and thinks itself safe; so, when we run into optimism, we do just like the hare, but that is no remedy. There are objections against this, but you may remark that they are generally from people who possess many of the good things of life. In this country (England) it is very difficult to become a pessimist. Everyone tells me how wonderfully the world is going on, how progressive; but what he himself is, is his own world. Old questions arise: Christianity must be the only true religion of the world, because Christian nations are prosperous! But that assertion contradicts itself, because the prosperity of the Christian nation depends on the misfortune of non-Christian nations. There must be some to prey on. Suppose the whole world were to become Christian, then the Christian nations would become poor, because there would be no non-Christian nations for them to prey upon. Thus the argument kills itself. Animals are living upon plants, men upon animals and, worst of all, upon one another, the strong upon the weak. This is going on everywhere. And this is Maya. What solution do you find for this? We hear every day many explanations, and are told that in the long run all will be good. Taking it for granted that this is possible, why should there be this diabolical way of doing good? Why cannot good be done through good, instead of through these diabolical methods? The descendants of the human beings of today will be happy; but why must there be all this suffering now? There is no solution. This is Maya.

Again, we often hear that it is one of the features of evolution that it eliminates evil, and this evil being continually eliminated from the world, at last only good will remain. That is very nice to hear, and it panders to the vanity of those who have enough of this world's goods, who have not a hard struggle to face every day and are not being crushed under the wheel of this so-called evolution. It is very good and comforting indeed to such fortunate ones. The common herd may suffer, but they do not care; let them die, they are of no consequence. Very good, yet this argument is fallacious from beginning to end. It takes for granted, in the first place, that manifested good and evil in this world are two absolute realities. In the second place, it makes a still worse assumption that the amount of good is an increasing quantity and the amount of evil is a decreasing quantity. So, if evil is being eliminated in this way by what they call evolution, there will come a time when all this evil will be eliminated and what remains will be all good. Very easy to say, but can it be proved that evil is a lessening quantity? Take, for instance, the man who lives in a forest, who does not know how to cultivate the mind, cannot read a book, has not heard of such a thing as writing. If he is severely wounded, he is soon all right again; while we die if we get a scratch. Machines are making things cheap, making for progress and evolution, but millions are crushed, that one may become rich; while one becomes rich, thousands at the same time become poorer and poorer, and whole masses of human beings are made slaves. That way it is going on. The animal man lives in the senses. If he does not get enough to eat, he is miserable; or if something happens to his body, he is miserable. In the senses both his misery and his happiness begin and end. As soon as this man progresses, as soon as his horizon of happiness increases, his horizon of unhappiness increases proportionately. The man in the forest does not know what it is to be jealous, to be in the law courts, to pay taxes, to be blamed by society, to be ruled over day and night by the most tremendous tyranny that human diabolism ever invented, which pries into the secrets of every human heart. He does not know how Man becomes a thousand times more diabolical than any other animal, with all his vain knowledge and with all his pride. Thus it is that, as we emerge out of the senses, we develop higher powers of enjoyment, and at the same time we have to develop higher powers of suffering too. The nerves become finer and capable of more suffering. In every society, we often find that the ignorant, common man, when abused, does not feel much, but he feels a good thrashing. But the gentleman cannot bear a single word of abuse; he has become so finely nerved. Misery has increased with his susceptibility to happiness. This does not go much to prove the evolutionist's case. As we increase our power to be happy, we also increase our power to suffer, and sometimes I am inclined to think that if we increase our power to become happy in arithmetical progression, we shall increase, on the other hand, our power to become miserable in geometrical progression. We who are progressing know that the more we progress, the more avenues are opened to pain as well as to pleasure. And this is Maya.

Thus we find that Maya is not a theory for the explanation of the world; it is simply a statement of facts as they exist, that the very basis of our being is contradiction, that everywhere we have to move through this tremendous contradiction, that wherever there is good, there must also be evil, and wherever there is evil, there must be some good, wherever there is life, death must follow as its shadow, and everyone who smiles will have to weep, and vice versa. Nor can this state of things be remedied. We may verily imagine that there will be a place where there will be only good and no evil, where we shall only smile and never weep. This is impossible in the very nature of things; for the conditions will remain the same. Wherever there is the power of producing a smile in us, there lurks the power of producing tears. Wherever there is the power of producing happiness, there lurks somewhere the power of making us miserable.

Thus the Vedanta philosophy is neither optimistic nor pessimistic. It voices both these views and takes things as they are. It admits that this world is a mixture of good and evil, happiness and misery, and that to increase the one, one must of necessity increase the other. There will never be a perfectly good or bad world, because the very idea is a contradiction in terms. The great secret revealed by this analysis is that good and bad are not two cut-and-dried, separate existences. There is not one thing in this world of ours which you can label as good and good alone, and there is not one thing in the universe which you can label as bad and bad alone. The very same phenomenon which is appearing to be good now, may appear to be bad tomorrow. The same thing which is producing misery in one, may produce happiness in another. The fire that burns the child, may cook a good meal for a starving man. The same nerves that carry the sensations of misery carry also the sensations of happiness. The only way to stop evil, therefore, is to stop good also; there is no other way. To stop death, we shall have to stop life also. Life without death and happiness without misery are contradictions, and neither can be found alone, because each of them is but a different manifestation of the same thing. What I thought to be good yesterday, I do not think to be good now. When I look back upon my life and see what were my ideals at different times, I find this to be so. At one time my ideal was to drive a strong pair of horses; at another time I thought, if I could make a certain kind of sweetmeat, I should be perfectly happy later I imagined that I should be entirely satisfied if I had a wife and children and plenty of money. Today I laugh at all these ideals as mere childish nonsense.

The Vedanta says, there must come a time when we shall look back and laugh at the ideals which make us afraid of giving up our individuality. Each one of us wants to keep this body for an indefinite time, thinking we shall be very happy, but there will come a time when we shall laugh at this idea. Now, if such be the truth, we are in a state of hopeless contradiction—neither existence no non-existence, neither misery nor happiness, but a mixture of them. What, then, is the use of Vedanta and all other philosophies and religions? And, above all, what is the use of doing good work? This is a question that comes to the mind. If it is true that you cannot do good without doing evil, and whenever you try to create happiness there will always be misery, people will ask you, "What is the use of doing good?" The answer is in the first place, that we must work for lessening misery, for that is the only way to make ourselves happy. Every one of us finds it out sooner or later in our lives. The bright ones find it out a little earlier and the dull ones a little later. The dull ones pay very dearly for the discovery and the bright ones less dearly. In the second place, we must do our part, because that is the only way of getting out of this life of contradiction. Both the forces of good and evil will keep this universe alive for us, until we awake from our dreams and give up this building of mud pies. That lesson we shall have to learn, and it will take a long, long time to learn it.

Attempts have been made in Germany to build a system of philosophy on the basis that the Infinite has become the finite. Such attempts are also made in England. And the analysis of the position of these philosophers is this, that the Infinite is trying to express itself in this universe, and that there will come a time when the Infinite will succeed in doing so. It is all very well, and we have used the words "Infinite" and "manifestation" and "expression", and so on, but philosophers naturally ask for a logical fundamental basis for the statement that the finite can fully express the Infinite. The Absolute and the Infinite can become this universe only by limitation. Everything must be limited that comes through the senses, or through the mind, or through the intellect; and for the limited to be the unlimited is simply absurd, and can never be. The Vedanta, on the other hand, says that it is true that the Absolute or the Infinite is trying to express itself in the finite, but there will come a time when it will find that it is impossible, and it will then have to beat a retreat, and this beating a retreat means renunciation which is the real beginning of religion. Nowadays it is very hard even to talk of renunciation. It was said of me in America that I was a man who came out of a land that had been dead and buried for five thousand years, and talked of renunciation. So says, perhaps, the English philosopher. Yet it is true that that is the only path to religion. Renounce and give up. What did Christ say? "He that loseth his life for my sake shall find it." Again and again did he preach renunciation as the only way to perfection. There comes a time when the mind awakes from this long and dreary dream—the child gives up its play and wants to go back to its mother. It finds the truth of the statement, "Desire is never satisfied by the enjoyment of desires, it only increases the more, as fire, when butter is poured upon it."

This is true of all sense-enjoyments, of all intellectual enjoyments, and of all the enjoyments of which the human mind is capable. They are nothing, they are within Maya, within this network beyond which we cannot go. We may run therein through infinite time and find no end, and whenever we struggle to get a little enjoyment, a mass of misery falls upon us. How awful is this! And when I think of it, I cannot but consider that this theory of Maya, this statement that it is all Maya, is the best and only explanation. What an amount of misery there is in this world; and if you travel among various nations you will find that one nation attempts to cure its evils by one means, and another by another. The very same evil has been taken up by various races, and attempts have been made in various ways to check it, yet no nation has succeeded. If it has been minimised at one point, a mass of evil has been crowded at another point. Thus it goes. The Hindus, to keep up a high standard of chastity in the race, have sanctioned child-marriage, which in the long run has degraded the race. At the same time, I cannot deny that this child-marriage makes the race more chaste. What would you have? If you want the nation to be more chaste, you weaken men and women physically by child-marriage. On the other hand, are you in England any better off? No, because chastity is the life of a nation. Do you not find in history that the first death-sign of a nation has been unchastity? When that has entered, the end of the race is in sight. Where shall we get a solution of these miseries then? If parents select husbands and wives for their children, then this evil is minimised. The daughters of India are more practical than sentimental. But very little of poetry remains in their lives. Again, if people select their own husbands and wives, that does not seem to bring much happiness. The Indian woman is generally very happy; there are not many cases of quarrelling between husband and wife. On the other hand in the United States, where the greatest liberty obtains, the number of unhappy homes and marriages is large. Unhappiness is here, there, and everywhere. What does it show? That, after all, not much happiness has been gained by all these ideals. We all struggle for happiness and as soon as we get a little happiness on one side, on the other side there comes unhappiness.

Shall we not work to do good then? Yes, with more zest than ever, but what this knowledge will do for us is to break down our fanaticism. The Englishman will no more be a fanatic and curse the Hindu. He will learn to respect the customs of different nations. There will be less of fanaticism and more of real work. Fanatics cannot work, they waste three-fourths of their energy. It is the level-headed, calm, practical man who works. So, the power to work will increase from this idea. Knowing that this is the state of things, there will be more patience. The sight of misery or of evil will not be able to throw us off our balance and make us run after shadows. Therefore, patience will come to us, knowing that the world will have to go on in its own way. If, for instance, all men have become good, the animals will have in the meantime evolved into men, and will have to pass through the same state, and so with the plants. But only one thing is certain; the mighty river is rushing towards the ocean, and all the drops that constitute the stream will in time be drawn into that boundless ocean. So, in this life, with all its miseries and sorrows, its joys and smiles and tears, one thing is certain, that all things are rushing towards their goal, and it is only a question of time when you and I, and plants and animals, and every particle of life that exists must reach the Infinite Ocean of Perfection, must attain to Freedom, to God.

Let me repeat, once more, that the Vedantic position is neither pessimism nor optimism. It does not say that this world is all evil or all good. It says that our evil is of no less value than our good, and our good of no more value than our evil. They are bound together. This is the world, and knowing this, you work with patience. What for? Why should we work? If this is the state of things, what shall we do? Why not become agnostics? The modern agnostics also know there is no solution of this problem, no getting out of this evil of Maya, as we say in our language; therefore, they tell us to be satisfied and enjoy life. Here, again, is a mistake, a tremendous mistake, a most illogical mistake. And it is this. What do you mean by life? Do you mean only the life of the senses? In this, every one of us differs only slightly from the brutes. I am sure that no one is present here whose life is only in the senses. Then, this present life means something more than that. Our feelings, thoughts, and aspirations are all part and parcel of our life; and is not the struggle towards the great ideal, towards perfection, one of the most important components of what we call life? According to the agnostics, we must enjoy life as it is. But this life means, above all, this search after the ideal; the essence of life is going towards perfection. We must have that, and, therefore, we cannot be agnostics or take the world as it appears. The agnostic position takes this life, minus the ideal component, to be all that exists. And this, the agnostic claims, cannot be reached, therefore, he must give up the search. This is what is called Maya—this nature, this universe.

All religions are more or less attempts to get beyond nature—the crudest or the most developed, expressed through mythology or symbology, stories of gods, angels or demons, or through stories of saints or seers, great men or prophets, or through the abstractions of philosophy—all have that one object, all are trying to get beyond these limitations. In one word, they are all struggling towards freedom. Man feels, consciously or unconsciously, that he is bound; he is not what he wants to be. It was taught to him at the very moment he began to look around. That very instant he learnt that he was bound, and he also found that there was something in him which wanted to fly beyond, where the body could not follow, but which was as yet chained down by this limitation. Even in the lowest of religious ideas, where departed ancestors and other spirits—mostly violent and cruel, lurking about the houses of their friends, fond of bloodshed and strong drink—are worshipped, even there we find that one common factor, that of freedom, The man who wants to worship the gods sees in them, above all things, greater freedom than in himself. If a door is closed, he thinks the gods can get through it, and that walls have no limitations for them. This idea of freedom increases until it comes to the ideal of a Personal God, of which the central concept is that He is a Being beyond the limitation of nature, of Maya. I see before me, as it were, that in some of those forest retreats this question is being discussed by those ancient sages of India; and in one of them, where even the oldest and the holiest fail to reach the solution, a young man stands up in the midst of them, and declares, "Hear, ye children of immortality, hear, ye who live in the highest places, I have found the way. By knowing Him who is beyond darkness we can go beyond death."

This Maya is everywhere. It is terrible. Yet we have to work through it. The man who says that he will work when the world has become all good and then he will enjoy bliss is as likely to succeed as the man who sits beside the Ganga and says, "I will ford the river when all the water has run into the ocean." The way is not with Maya, but against it. This is another fact to learn. We are not born as helpers of nature, but competitors with nature. We are its bond-masters, but we bind ourselves down. Why is this house here? Nature did not build it. Nature says, go and live in the forest. Man says, I will build a house and fight with nature, and he does so. The whole history of humanity is a continuous fight against the so-called laws of nature, and Man gains in the end. Coming to the internal world, there too the same fight is going on, this fight between the animal man and the spiritual man, between light and darkness; and here too Man becomes victorious. He, as it were, cuts his way out of nature to freedom.

We see, then, that beyond this Maya the Vedantic philosophers find something which is not bound by Maya; and if we can get there, we shall not be bound by Maya. This idea is in some form or other the common property of all religions. But, with the Vedanta, it is only the beginning of religion and not the end. The idea of a Personal God, the Ruler and Creator of this universe, as He has been styled, the Ruler of Maya, or nature, is not the end of these Vedantic ideas; it is only the beginning. The idea grows and grows until the Vedantist finds that He who, he thought, was standing outside, is he himself and is in reality within. He is the one who is free, but who through limitation thought he was bound.

The Cosmos

The Macrocosm

Delivered in New York, 19 January 1896

The flowers that we see all around us are beautiful, beautiful is the rising of the morning sun, beautiful are the variegated hues of nature. The whole universe is beautiful, and Man has been enjoying it since his appearance on earth. Sublime and awe-inspiring are the mountains; the gigantic rushing rivers rolling towards the sea, the trackless deserts, the infinite ocean, the starry heavens—all these are awe-inspiring, sublime, and beautiful indeed. The whole mass of existence which we call nature has been acting on the human mind since time immemorial. It has been acting on the thought of man, and as its reaction has come out the question: What are these, whence are they? As far back as the time of the oldest portion of that most ancient human composition, the Vedas, we find the same question asked: "Whence is this? When there was neither aught nor naught, and darkness was hidden in darkness, who projected this universe? How? Who knows the secret?" And the question has come down to us at the present time. Millions of attempts have been made to answer it, yet millions of times it will have to be answered again. It is not that each answer was a failure; every answer to this question contained a part of truth, and this truth gathers strength as time rolls on. I will try to present before you the outline of the answer that I have gathered from the ancient philosophers of India, in harmony with modern knowledge.

We find that in this oldest of questions a few points had been already solved. The first is that there was a time when there was "neither aught nor naught", when this world did not exist; our mother earth with the seas and oceans, the rivers, and mountains, cities and villages, human races, animals, plants, birds, and planets and luminaries, all this infinite variety of creation, had no existence. Are we sure of that? We will try to trace how this conclusion is arrived at. What does Man see around him? Take a little plant. He puts a seed in the ground, and later, he finds a plant peep out, lift itself slowly above the ground, and grow and grow, till it becomes a gigantic tree. Then it dies, leaving only the seed. It completes a circle—it comes out of the seed, becomes a tree, and ends in the seed again. Look at a bird, how from the egg it springs, lives its life, and then dies, leaving other eggs, seeds of future birds. So with the animals, so with man. Everything in nature begins, as it were, from certain seeds, certain rudiments, certain fine forms, and becomes grosser and grosser, and develops, going on that way for a certain time, and then again goes back to that fine form, and subsides. The raindrop in which the beautiful sunbeam is playing was drawn in the form of vapour from the ocean, went far away into the air, and reached a region where it changed into water, and dropped down in its present form—to be converted into vapour again. So with everything in nature by which we are surrounded. We know that the huge mountains are being worked upon by glaciers and rivers, which are slowly but surely pounding them and pulverising them into sand, that drifts away into the ocean where it settles down on its bed, layer after layer, becoming hard as rocks, once more to be heaped up into mountains of a future generation. Again they will be pounded and pulverised, and thus the course goes on. From sand rise these mountains; unto sand they go.

If it be true that nature is uniform throughout, if it be true, and so far no human experience has contradicted it, that the same method under which a small grain of sand is created, works in creating the gigantic suns and stars and all this universe, if it be true that the whole of this universe is built on exactly the same plan as the atom, if it be true that the same law prevails throughout the universe, then, as it has been said in the Vedas, "Knowing one lump of clay we know the nature of all the clay that is in the universe." Take up a little plant and study its life, and we know the universe as it is. If we know one grain of sand, we understand the secret of the whole universe. Applying this course of reasoning to phenomena, we find, in the first place, that everything is almost similar at the beginning and the end. The mountain comes from the sand, and goes back to the sand; the river comes out of vapour, and goes back to vapour; plant life comes from the seed, and goes back to the seed; human life comes out of human germs, and goes back to human germs. The universe with its stars and planets has come out of a nebulous state and must go back to it. What do we learn from this? That the manifested or the grosser state is the effect, and the finer state the cause. Thousands of years ago, it was demonstrated by Kapila, the great father of all philosophy, that destruction means going back to the cause. If this table here is destroyed, it will go back to its cause, to those fine forms and particles which, combined, made this form which we call a table. If a man dies, he will go back to the elements which gave him his body; if this earth dies, it will go back to the elements which gave it form. This is what is called destruction, going back to the cause. Therefore, we learn that the effect is the same as the cause, not different. It is only in another form. This glass is an effect, and it had its cause, and this cause is present in this form. A certain amount of the material called glass plus the force in the hands of the manufacturer, are the causes, the instrumental and the material, which, combined, produced this form called a glass. The force which was in the hands of the manufacturer is present in the glass as the power of adhesion, without which the particles would fall apart; and the glass material is also present. The glass is only a manifestation of these fine causes in a new shape, and if it be broken into pieces, the force which was present in the form of adhesion will go back and join its own element, and the particles of glass will remain the same until they take new forms.

Thus we find that the effect is never different from the cause. It is only that this effect is a reproduction of the cause in a grosser form. Next, we learn that all these particular forms which we call plants, animals, or men are being repeated *ad infinitum,* rising and falling. The seed produces the tree. The tree produces the seed, which again comes up as another tree, and so on and on; there is no end to it. Water-drops roll down the mountains into the ocean, and rise again as vapour, go back to the mountains and again come down to the ocean. So, rising and falling, the cycle goes on. So with all lives, so with all existence that we can see, feel, hear, or imagine. Everything that is within the bounds of our knowledge is proceeding in the same way, like breathing in and breathing out in the human body. Everything in creation goes on in this form, one wave rising, another falling, rising again, falling again. Each wave has its hollow, each hollow has its wave. The same law must apply to the universe taken as a whole, because of its uniformity. This universe must be resolved into its causes; the sun, moon, stars, and earth, the body and mind, and everything in this universe must return to their finer causes, disappear, be destroyed as it were. But they will live in the causes as fine forms. Out of these fine forms they will emerge again as new earths, suns, moons, and stars.

There is one fact more to learn about this rising and falling. The seed comes out of the tree; it does not immediately become a tree but has a period of inactivity, or rather, a period of very fine unmanifested action. The seed has to work for some time beneath the soil. It breaks into pieces, degenerates as it were, and regeneration comes out of that degeneration. In the beginning, the whole of this universe has to work likewise for a period in that minute form, unseen and unmanifested, which is called chaos, and out of that comes a new projection. The whole period of one manifestation of the universe—its going down into the finer form, remaining there for some time, and coming out again—is, in Sanskrit, called a Kalpa or Cycle. Next comes a very important question especially for modern times. We see that the finer forms develop slowly and slowly, and gradually become grosser and grosser. We have seen that the cause is the same as the effect, and the effect is only the cause in another form. Therefore, this whole universe cannot be produced out of nothing. Nothing comes without a cause, and the cause is the effect in another form.

Out of what has this universe been produced then? From a preceding fine universe. Out of what has Man been produced? The preceding fine form. Out of what has the tree been produced? Out of the seed; the whole of the tree was there in the seed. It comes out and becomes manifest. So, the whole of this universe has been created out of this very universe existing in a minute form. It has been made manifest now. It will go back to that minute form, and again will be made manifest. Now we find that the fine forms slowly come out and become grosser and grosser until they reach their limit, and when they reach their limit they go back further and further, becoming finer and finer again. This coming out of the fine and becoming gross, simply changing the arrangements of its parts, as it were, is what in modern times is called evolution. This is very true, perfectly true; we see it in our lives. No rational man can possibly quarrel with these evolutionists. But we have to learn one thing more. We have to go one step further, and what is that? That every evolution is preceded by an involution. The seed is the father of the tree, but another tree was itself the father of the seed. The seed is the fine form out of which the big tree comes, and another big tree was the form which is involved in that seed. The whole of this universe was present in the cosmic fine universe. The little cell, which becomes afterwards the man, was simply the involved man and becomes evolved as a man. If this is clear, we have no quarrel with the evolutionists, for we see that if they admit this step, instead of their destroying religion, they will be the greatest supporters of it.

We see then, that nothing can be created out of nothing. Everything exists through eternity, and will exist through eternity. Only the movement is in succeeding waves and hollows, going back to fine forms, and coming out into gross manifestations. This involution and evolution is going on throughout the whole of nature. The whole series of evolution beginning with the lowest manifestation of life and reaching up to the highest, the most perfect man, must have been the involution of something else. The question is: The involution of what? What was involved? God. The evolutionist will tell you that your idea that it was God is wrong. Why? Because you see God is intelligent, but we find that intelligence develops much later on in the course of evolution. It is in Man and the higher animals that we find intelligence, but millions of years have passed in this world before this intelligence came. This objection of the evolutionists does not hold water, as we shall see by applying our theory. The tree comes out of the seed, goes back to the seed; the beginning and the end are the same. The earth comes out of its cause and returns to it. We know that if we can find the beginning we can find the end. *E converso,* if we find the end we can find the beginning. If that is so, take this whole evolutionary series, from the protoplasm at the one end to the perfect man at the other, and this whole series is one life. In the end we find the perfect man, so in the beginning it must have been the same. Therefore, the protoplasm was the involution of the highest intelligence. You may not see it but that involved intelligence is what is uncoiling itself until it becomes manifested in the most perfect man. That can be mathematically demonstrated. If the law of conservation of energy is true, you cannot get anything out of a machine unless you put it in there first. The amount of work that you get out of an engine is exactly the same as you have put into it in the form of water and coal, neither more nor less. The work I am doing now is just what I put into me, in the shape of air, food, and other things. It is only a question of change and manifestation. There cannot be added in the economy of this universe one particle of matter or one foot-pound of force, nor can one particle of matter or one foot-pound of force be taken out. If that be the case, what is this intelligence? If it was not present in the protoplasm, it must have come all of a sudden, something coming out of nothing, which is absurd. It, therefore, follows absolutely that the perfect man, the free man, the God-man, who has gone beyond the laws of nature, and transcended everything, who has no more to go through this process of evolution, through birth and death, that man called the "Christ-man" by the Christians, and the "Buddha-man" by the Buddhists, and the "Free" by the Yogis—that perfect man who is at one end of the chain of evolution was involved in the cell of the protoplasm, which is at the other end of the same chain.

Applying the same reason to the whole of the universe, we see that intelligence must be the Lord of creation, the cause. What is the most evolved notion that Man has of this universe? It is intelligence, the adjustment of part to part, the display of intelligence, of which the ancient design theory was an attempt at expression. The beginning was, therefore, intelligence. At the beginning that intelligence becomes involved, and in the end that intelligence gets evolved. The sum total of the intelligence displayed in the universe must, therefore, be the involved universal intelligence unfolding itself. This universal intelligence is what we call God. Call it by any other name, it is absolutely certain that in the beginning there is that Infinite cosmic intelligence. This cosmic intelligence gets involved, and it manifests, evolves itself, until it becomes the perfect man, the "Christ-man," the "Buddha-man." Then it goes back to its own source. That is why all the scriptures say, "In Him we live and move and have our being." That is why all the scriptures preach that we come from God and go back to God. Do not be frightened by theological terms; if terms frighten you, you are not fit to be philosophers. This cosmic intelligence is what the theologians call God.

I have been asked many times, "Why do you use that old word, God?" Because it is the best word for our purpose; you cannot find a better word than that, because all the hopes, aspirations, and happiness of humanity have been centred in that word. It is impossible now to change the word. Words like these were first coined by great saints who realised their import and understood their meaning. But as they become current in society, ignorant people take these words, and the result is that they lose their spirit and glory. The word "God" has been used from time immemorial, and the idea of this cosmic intelligence, and all that is great and holy, is associated with it. Do you mean to say that because some fool says it is not all right, we should throw it away? Another man may come and say, "Take *my* word," and another again, "Take *my* word." So there will be no end to foolish words. Use the old word, only use it in the true spirit, cleanse it of superstition, and realise fully what this great ancient word means. If you understand the power of the laws of association, you will know that these words are associated with innumerable majestic and powerful ideas; they have been used and worshipped by millions of human souls and associated by them with all that is highest and best, all that is rational, all that is lovable, and all that is great and grand in human nature. And they come as suggestions of these associations, and cannot be given up. If I tried to express all these by only telling you that God created the universe, it would have conveyed no meaning to you. Yet, after all this struggle, we have come back to Him, the Ancient and Supreme One.

We now see that all the various forms of cosmic energy, such as matter, thought, force, intelligence and so forth, are simply the manifestations of that cosmic intelligence, or, as we shall call it henceforth, the Supreme Lord. Everything that you see, feel, or hear, the whole universe, is His creation, or to be a little more accurate, is His projection; or to be still more accurate, is the Lord Himself. It is He who is shining as the sun and the stars, He is the mother earth. He is the ocean Himself. He comes as gentle showers, He is the gentle air that we breathe in, and He it is who is working as force in the body. He is the speech that is uttered, He is the man who is talking. He is the audience that is here. He is the platform on which I stand, He is the light that enables me to see your faces. It is all He. He Himself is both the material and the efficient cause of this universe, and He it is that gets involved in the minute cell, and evolves at the other end and becomes God again. He it is that comes down and becomes the lowest atom, and slowly unfolding His nature, rejoins Himself. This is the mystery of the universe. "Thou art the man, Thou art the woman, Thou art the strong man walking in the pride of youth, Thou art the old man tottering on crutches, Thou art in everything. Thou art everything, O Lord." This is the only solution of the Cosmos that satisfies the human intellect. In one word, we are born of Him, we live in Him, and unto Him we return.

Immortality

Delivered in America

What question has been asked a greater number of times, what idea has led men more to search the universe for an answer, what question is nearer and dearer to the human heart, what question is more inseparably connected with our existence, than this one, the immortality of the human soul? It has been the theme of poets and sages, of priests and prophets; kings on the throne have discussed it, beggars in the street have dreamt of it. The best of humanity have approached it, and the worst of men have not hoped for it. The interest in the theme has not died, yet, nor will it die so long as human nature exists. Various answers have been presented to the world by various minds. Thousands, again, in every period of history have given up the discussion, and yet the question remains fresh as ever. Often in the turmoil and struggle of our lives we seem to forget it, but suddenly some one dies—one, perhaps, whom we loved, one near and dear to our hearts, is snatched away from us—and the struggle, the din and turmoil of the world around us, cease for a moment, and the soul asks the old question, "What after this?" "What becomes of the soul?"

All human knowledge proceeds out of experience; we cannot know anything except by experience. All our reasoning is based upon generalised experience, all our knowledge is but harmonised experience. Looking around us, what do we find? A continuous change. The plant comes out of the seed, grows into the tree, completes the circle, and comes back to the seed. The animal comes, lives a certain time, dies, and completes the circle. So does man. The mountains slowly but surely crumble away, the rivers slowly but surely dry up, rains come out of the sea, and go back to the sea. Everywhere circles are being completed, birth, growth, development, and decay following each other with mathematical precision. This is our everyday experience. Inside of it all, behind all this vast mass of what we call life, of millions of forms and shapes, millions upon millions of varieties, beginning from the lowest atom to the highest spiritualised man, we find existing a certain unity. Every day we find that the wall that was thought to be dividing one thing and another is being broken down, and all matter is coming to be recognised by modern science as one substance, manifesting in different ways and in various forms; the one life that runs through all like a continuous chain, of which all these various forms represent the links, link after link, extending almost infinitely, but of the same one chain. This is what is called evolution. It is an old, old idea, as old as human society, only it is getting fresher and fresher as human knowledge is progressing. There is one thing more, which the ancients perceived, but which in modern times is not yet so clearly perceived, and that is involution. The seed is becoming the plant; a grain of sand never becomes a plant. It is the father that becomes a child; a lump of clay never becomes the child. From what does this evolution come, is the question. What was the seed? It was the same as the tree. All the possibilities of a future tree are in that seed; all the possibilities of a future man are in the little baby; all the possibilities of any future life are in the germ. What is this? The ancient philosophers of India called it involution. We find then, that every evolution presupposes an involution.

Nothing can be evolved which is not already there. Here, again, modern science comes to our help. You know by mathematical reasoning that the sum total of the energy that is displayed in the universe is the same throughout. You cannot take away one atom of matter or one foot-pound of force. You cannot add to the universe one atom of matter or one foot-pound of force. As such, evolution does not come out of zero; then, where does it come from? From previous involution. The child is the man involved, and the man is the child evolved. The seed is the tree involved, and the tree is the seed evolved. All the possibilities of life are in the germ. The problem becomes a little clearer. Add to it the first idea of continuation of life. From the lowest protoplasm to the most perfect human being there is really but one life. Just as in one life we have so many various phases of expression, the protoplasm developing into the baby, the child, the young man, the old man, so, from that protoplasm up to the most perfect man we get one continuous life, one chain. This is evolution, but we have seen that each evolution presupposes an involution. The whole of this life which slowly manifests itself evolves itself from the protoplasm to the perfected human being—the Incarnation of God on earth—the whole of this series is but one life, and the whole of this manifestation must have been involved in that very protoplasm. This whole life, this very God on earth, was involved in it and slowly came out, manifesting itself slowly, slowly, slowly. The highest expression must have been there in the germ state in minute form; therefore, this one force, this whole chain, is the involution of that cosmic life which is everywhere. It is this one mass of intelligence which, from the protoplasm up to the most perfected man, is slowly and slowly uncoiling itself. Not that it grows. Take off all ideas of growth from your mind. With the idea of growth is associated something coming from outside, something extraneous, which would give the lie to the truth that the Infinite which lies latent in every life is independent of all external conditions. It can never grow; It was always there, and only manifests Itself.

The effect is the cause manifested. There is no essential difference between the effect and the cause. Take this glass, for instance. There was the material, and that material plus the will of the manufacturer made the glass; and these two were its causes and are present in it. In what form is the will present? As adhesion. If the force were not here, each particle would fall away. What is the effect then? It is the same as the cause, only taking a different form, a different composition. When the cause is changed and limited for a time, it becomes the effect. We must remember this. Applying it to our idea of life, the whole of the manifestation of this one series, from the protoplasm up to the most perfect man, must be the very same thing as cosmic life. First it got involved and became finer; and out of that fine something, which was the cause, it has gone on evolving, manifesting itself, and becoming grosser.

But the question of immortality is not yet settled. We have seen that everything in this universe is indestructible. There is nothing new; there will be nothing new. The same series of manifestations are presenting themselves alternately like a wheel, coming up and going down. All motion in this universe is in the form of waves, successively rising and falling. Systems after systems are coming out of fine forms, evolving themselves, and taking grosser forms, again melting down, as it were, and going back to the fine forms. Again they rise out of that, evolving for a certain period and slowly going back to the cause. So with all life. Each manifestation of life is coming up and then going back again. What goes down? The form. The form breaks to pieces, but it comes up again. In one sense bodies and forms even are eternal. How? Suppose we take a number of dice and throw them, and they fall in this ratio—6:5:3:4. We take the dice up and throw them again and again; there must be a time when the same numbers will come again; the same combination must come. Now each particle, each atom, that is in this universe, I take for such a die, and these are being thrown out and combined again and again. All these forms before you are one combination. Here are the forms of a glass, a table, a pitcher of water, and so forth. This is one combination; in time, it will all break. But there must come a time when exactly the same combination comes again, when you will be here, and this form will be here, this subject will be talked, and this pitcher will be here. An infinite number of times this has been, and an infinite number of times this will be repeated. Thus far with the physical forms. What do we find? That even the combination of physical forms is eternally repeated.

A most interesting conclusion that follows from this theory is the explanation of facts such as these: Some of you, perhaps, have seen a man who can read the past life of others and foretell the future. How is it possible for any one to see what the future will be, unless there is a regulated future? Effects of the past will recur in the future, and we see that it is so. You have seen the big Ferris Wheel in Chicago. The wheel revolves, and the little rooms in the wheel are regularly coming one after another; one set of persons gets into these, and after they have gone round the circle, they get out, and a fresh batch of people gets in. Each one of these batches is like one of these manifestations, from the lowest animals to the highest man. Nature is like the chain of the Ferris Wheel, endless and infinite, and these little carriages are the bodies or forms in which fresh batches of souls are riding, going up higher and higher until they become perfect and come out of the wheel. But the wheel goes on. And so long as the bodies are in the wheel, it can be absolutely and mathematically foretold where they will go, but not so of the souls. Thus it is possible to read the past and the future of nature with precision. We see, then, that there is recurrence of the same material phenomena at certain periods, and that the same combinations have been taking place through eternity. But that is not the immortality of the soul. No force can die, no matter can be annihilated. What becomes of it? It goes on changing, backwards and forwards, until it returns to the source from which it came. There is no motion in a straight line. Everything moves in a circle; a straight line, infinitely produced, becomes a circle. If that is the case, there cannot be eternal degeneration for any soul. It cannot be. Everything must complete the circle, and come back to its source. What are you and I and all these souls? In our discussion of evolution and involution, we have seen that you and I must be part of the cosmic consciousness, cosmic life, cosmic mind, which got involved and we must complete the circle and go back to this cosmic intelligence which is God. This cosmic intelligence is what people call Lord, or God, or Christ, or Buddha, or Brahman, what the materialists perceive as force, and the agnostics as that infinite, inexpressible beyond; and we are all part of that.

This is the second idea, yet this is not sufficient; there will be still more doubts. It is very good to say that there is no destruction for any force. But all the forces and forms that we see are combinations. This form before us is a composition of several component parts, and so every force that we see is similarly composite. If you take the scientific idea of force, and call it the sum total, the resultant of several forces, what becomes of your individuality? Everything that is a compound must sooner or later go back to its component parts. Whatever in this universe is the result of the combination of matter or force must sooner or later go back to its components. Whatever is the result of certain causes must die, must be destroyed.

It gets broken up, dispersed, and resolved back into its components. Soul is not a force; neither is it thought. It is the manufacturer of thought, but not thought itself; it is the manufacturer of the body, but not the body. Why so? We see that the body cannot be the soul. Why not? Because it is not intelligent. A corpse is not intelligent, nor a piece of meat in a butcher's shop. What do we mean by intelligence? Reactive power. We want to go a little more deeply into this. Here is a pitcher; I see it. How? Rays of light from the pitcher enter my eyes, and make a picture in my retina, which is carried to the brain. Yet there is no vision. What the physiologists call the sensory nerves carry this impression inwards. But up to this there is no reaction. The nerve centre in the brain carries the impression to the mind, and the mind reacts, and as soon as this reaction comes, the pitcher flashes before it. Take a more commonplace example. Suppose you are listening to me intently and a mosquito is sitting on the tip of your nose and giving you that pleasant sensation which mosquitoes can give; but you are so intent on hearing me that you do not feel the mosquito at all. What has happened? The mosquito has bitten a certain part of your skin, and certain nerves are there. They have carried a certain sensation to the brain, and the impression is there, but the mind, being otherwise occupied, does not react, so you are not aware of the presence of the mosquito. When a new impression comes, if the mind does not react, we shall not be conscious of it, but when the reaction comes we feel, we see, we hear, and so forth. With this reaction comes illumination, as the Sankhya philosophers call it. We see that the body cannot illuminate, because in the absence of attention no sensation is possible. Cases have been known where, under peculiar conditions, a man who had never learnt a particular language was found able to speak it. Subsequent inquiries proved that the man had, when a child, lived among people who spoke that language and the impressions were left in his brain. These impressions remained stored up there, until through some cause the mind reacted, and illumination came, and then the man was able to speak the language. This shows that the mind alone is not sufficient, that the mind itself is an instrument in the hands of someone. In the case of that boy the mind contained that language, yet he did not know it, but later there came a time when he did. It shows that there is someone besides the mind; and when the boy was a baby, that someone did not use the power; but when the boy grew up, he took advantage of it, and used it. First, here is the body, second, the mind, or instrument of thought, and third behind this mind is the Self of man. The Sanskrit word is Atman. As modern philosophers have identified thought with molecular changes in the brain, they do not know how to explain such a case, and they generally deny it. The mind is intimately connected with the brain which dies every time the body changes. The Self is the illuminator, and the mind is the instrument in Its hands, and through that instrument It gets hold of the external instrument, and thus comes perception. The external instruments get hold of the impressions and carry them to the organs, for you must remember always, that the eyes and ears are only receivers—it is the internal organs, the brain centres, which act. In Sanskrit these centres are called Indriyas, and they carry sensations to the mind, and the mind presents them further back to another state of the mind, which in Sanskrit is called Chitta, and there they are organised into will, and all these present them to the King of kings inside, the Ruler on His throne, the Self of man. He then sees and gives His orders. Then the mind immediately acts on the organs, and the organs on the external body. The real Perceiver, the real Ruler, the Governor, the Creator, the Manipulator of all this, is the Self of man.

We see, then, that the Self of Man is not the body, neither is It thought. It cannot be a compound. Why not? Because everything that is a compound can be seen or imagined. That which we cannot imagine or perceive, which we cannot bind together, is not force or matter, cause or effect, and cannot be a compound. The domain of compounds is only so far as our mental universe, our thought universe extends. Beyond this it does not hold good; it is as far as law reigns, and if there is anything beyond law, it cannot be a compound at all.

The Self of Man being beyond the law of causation, is not a compound. It is ever free and is the Ruler of everything that is within law.

It will never die, because death means going back to the component parts, and that which was never a compound can never die. It is sheer nonsense to say It dies.

We are now treading on finer and finer ground, and some of you, perhaps, will be frightened. We have seen that this Self, being beyond the little universe of matter and force and thought, is a simple; and as a simple It cannot die. That which does not die cannot live. For life and death are the obverse and reverse of the same coin. Life is another name for death, and death for life. One particular mode of manifestation is what we call life; another particular mode of manifestation of the same thing is what we call death. When the wave rises on the top it is life; and when it falls into the hollow it is death. If anything is beyond death, we naturally see it must also be beyond life. I must remind you of the first conclusion that the soul of Man is part of the cosmic energy that exists, which is God. We now find that it is beyond life and death. You were never born, and you will never die. What is this birth and death that we see around us? This belongs to the body only, because the soul is omnipresent. "How can that be?" you may ask. "So many people are sitting here, and you say the soul is omnipresent?" What is there, I ask, to limit anything that is beyond law, beyond causation? This glass is limited; it is not omnipresent, because the surrounding matter forces it to take that form, does not allow it to expand. It is conditioned by everything around it, and is, therefore, limited. But that which is beyond law, where there is nothing to act upon it, how can that be limited? It must be omnipresent. You are everywhere in the universe. How is it then that I am born and I am going to die, and all that? That is the talk of ignorance, hallucination of the brain. You were neither born, nor will you die. You have had neither birth, nor will have rebirth, nor life, nor incarnation, nor anything. What do you mean by coming and going? All shallow nonsense. You are everywhere. Then what is this coming and going? It is the hallucination produced by the change of this fine body which you call the mind. That is going on. Just a little speck of cloud passing before the sky. As it moves on and on, it may create the delusion that the sky moves. Sometimes you see a cloud moving before the moon, and you think that the moon is moving. When you are in a train you think the land is flying, or when you are in a boat, you think the water moves. In reality you are neither going nor coming, you are not being born, nor going to be reborn; you are infinite, ever-present, beyond all causation, and ever-free. Such a question is out of place, it is arrant nonsense. How could there be mortality when there was no birth?

One step more we will have to take to come to a logical conclusion. There is no half-way house. You are metaphysicians, and there is no crying quarter. If then we are beyond all law, we must be omniscient, ever-blessed; all knowledge must be in us and all power and blessedness. Certainly. You are the omniscient, omnipresent being of the universe. But of such beings can there be many? Can there be a hundred thousand millions of omnipresent beings? Certainly not. Then, what becomes of us all? You are only one; there is only one such Self, and that One Self is you. Standing behind this little nature is what we call the Soul. There is only One Being, One Existence, the ever-blessed, the omnipresent, the omniscient, the birthless, the deathless. "Through His control the sky expands, through His control the air breathes, through His control the sun shines, and through His control all live. He is the Reality in nature, He is the Soul of your soul, nay, more, you are He, you are one with Him." Wherever there are two, there is fear, there is danger, there is conflict, there is strife. When it is all One, who is there to hate, who is there to struggle with? When it is all He, with whom can you fight?

This explains the true nature of life; this explains the true nature of being. This is perfection, and this is God. As long as you see the many, you are under delusion. "In this world of many he who sees the One, in this ever-changing world he who sees Him who never changes, as the Soul of his own soul, as his own Self, he is free, he is blessed, he has reached the goal." Therefore, know that thou art He; thou art the God of this universe, "Tat Tvam Asi" (That thou art). All these various ideas that I am a man or a woman, or sick or healthy, or strong or weak, or that I hate or I love, or have a little power, are but hallucinations. Away with them! What makes you weak? What makes you fear? You are the One Being in the universe. What frightens you? Stand up then and be free. Know that every thought and word that weakens you in this world is the only evil that exists. Whatever makes men weak and fear is the only evil that should be shunned. What can frighten you? If the suns come down, and the moons crumble into dust, and systems after systems are hurled into annihilation, what is that to you? Stand as a rock; you are indestructible. You are the Self, the God of the universe. Say—"I am Existence Absolute, Bliss Absolute, Knowledge Absolute, I am He," and like a lion breaking its cage, break your chain and be free forever. What frightens you, what holds you down? Only ignorance and delusion; nothing else can bind you. You are the Pure One, the Ever-blessed.

Silly fools tell you that you are sinners, and you sit down in a comer and weep. It is foolishness, wickedness, downright rascality to say that you are sinners! You are all God. See you not God and call Him man? Therefore, if you dare, stand on that—mould your whole life on that. If a man cuts your throat, do not say no, for you are cutting your own throat. When you help a poor man, do not feel the least pride. That is worship for you, and not the cause of pride. Is not the whole universe you? Where is there any one that is not you? You are the Soul of this universe. You are the sun, moon, and stars, it is you that are shining everywhere. The whole universe is you. Whom are you going to hate or to fight? Know, then, that thou art He, and model your whole life accordingly; and he who knows this and models his life accordingly will no more grovel in darkness.

IX

Cities and Places

The Advaita Ashrama, Himalayas*

In Whom is the Universe, Who is in the Universe, Who is the Universe; in Whom is the Soul, Who is in the Soul, Who is the Soul of Man; knowing Him—and, therefore, the Universe—as our Self, alone extinguishes all fear, brings an end to misery and leads to Infinite Freedom. Wherever there has been expansion in love or progress in well-being, of individuals or numbers, it has been through the perception, realisation, and the practicalisation of the Eternal Truth—the oneness of all beings. "Dependence is misery. Independence is happiness." The Advaita is the only system which gives unto Man complete possession of himself, takes off all dependence and its associated superstitions, thus making us brave to suffer, brave to do, and in the long run attain to Absolute Freedom.

Hitherto it has not been possible to preach this Noble Truth entirely free from the settings of dualistic weakness; this alone, we are convinced, explains why it has not been more operative and useful to mankind at large.

To give this one truth a freer and fuller scope in elevating the lives of individuals and leavening the mass of mankind,

* Swamiji sent these lines in a letter in March 1899, to be included in the prospectus of the Advaita Ashrama, Mayavati, Almora, Himalayas.

we start this Advaita Ashrama on the Himalayan heights, the land of its first expiration.

Here it is hoped to keep Advaita free from all superstitions and weakening contaminations. Here will be taught and practised nothing but the Doctrine of Unity, pure and simple; and though in entire sympathy with all other systems, this Ashrama is dedicated to Advaita and Advaita alone.

The Shrine Of Amarnath

Place: Kashmir
Time: 29 July to 8 August 1898

29 July

From this time we saw very little of the Swami. He was full of enthusiasm about the pilgrimage and lived mostly on one meal a day, seeking no company much, save that of Sadhus. Sometimes he would come to a camping-ground, beads in hand. Tonight two of the party went roaming about Bawan, which was like a village fair, all modified by a religious tendency centering in the sacred springs. Afterwards with Dhira Mata it was possible to go and listen at the tent door to the crowd of Hindi-speaking Sadhus who were plying the Swami with questions.

On Thursday we reached Pahalgam and camped down at the lower end of the valley. We found that the Swami had to encounter high opposition over the question of our admission at all. He was supported by the Naked Swamis, one of whom said, "It is true you have this strength, Swamiji, but you ought not to manifest it!" He yielded at the word. That afternoon, however, he took his daughter round the camp to be blessed, which really meant to distribute alms—and whether because he was looked upon as rich or because he was recognised as strong, the next day our tents were moved up to a lovely knoll at the head of the camp.

30 July

How beautiful was the route to the next halt, Chandanwari! There we camped on the edge of a ravine. It rained all afternoon, and I was visited by the Swami only for a five-minute chat. But I received endless touching little kindnesses from the servants and other pilgrims.

Close to Chandanwari the Swami insisted on my doing my first glacier on foot and took care to point out every detail of interest. A tremendous climb of some thousands of feet was the next experience. Then a long walk along a narrow path that twisted round mountain after mountain, and finally another steep climb. At the top of the first mountain, the ground was simply carpeted with edelweiss. Then the road passed five hundred feet above Sheshnag with its sulky water, and at last we camped in a cold damp place amongst the snow-peaks, 18,000 feet high. The firs were far below, and all afternoon and evening the coolies had to forage for juniper in all directions. The Tahsildar's, Swami's and my own tents were all close together, and in the evening a large fire was lighted in front. But it did not burn well, and many feet below lay the glacier. I did not see the Swami after we camped.

Panchatarani—the place of the five streams—was not nearly such a long march. Moreover, it was lower than Sheshnag, and the cold was dry and exhilarating. In front of the camp was a dry riverbed, all gravel, and through this ran five streams, in all of which it was the duty of the pilgrim to bathe, walking from one to the other in wet garments. Contriving to elude observation completely, Swamiji nevertheless fulfilled the law to the last letter in this respect.

At these heights we often found ourselves in great circles of snow-peaks, those mute giants that have suggested to the Hindu mind the idea of the ashen-covered God.

2 August

On Tuesday, August the 2nd, the great day of Amarnath, the first batch of pilgrims must have left the camp at two! We left by the light of the full moon. The sun rose as we went down the narrow valley. It was not too safe at this part of the journey. But when we left our Dandies and began to climb, the real danger began. Then, having at last reached the bottom of the farther slope, we had to toil along the glacier mile after mile to the cave.

The Swami, exhausted, had by this time fallen behind. He came at last and with a word sent me on; he was going to bathe. Half an hour later he entered the cave. With a smile he knelt first at one end of the semicircle, then at the other. The place was vast, large enough to hold a cathedral; and the great ice-Shiva, in a niche of deepest shadow, seemed as if throned on its own base. A few minutes passed, and then he turned to leave the cave.

To him, the heavens had opened. He had touched the feet of Shiva. He had had to hold himself tight, he said afterwards, lest he "should swoon away." But so great was his physical exhaustion that a doctor said afterwards that his heart ought to have stopped beating, but had undergone a permanent enlargement instead. How strangely near fulfilment had been those words of his Master, "When he realises who and what he is, he will give up this body!"

"I have enjoyed it so much!" he said half an hour afterwards, as he sat on a rock above the stream-side, eating lunch with the kind Naked Swami and me. "I thought the ice Linga was Shiva Himself. And there were no thievish Brahmins, no trade, nothing wrong. It was all worship. I never enjoyed any religious place so much!"

Afterwards he would often tell of the overwhelming vision that had seemed to draw him almost into its vertex.

He would talk of the poetry of the white ice-pillar; and it was he who suggested that the first discovery of the place had been by a party of shepherds, who had wandered far in search of their flocks one summer day and had entered the cave to find themselves before the unmelting ice, in the presence of the Lord Himself. He always said too that the grace of Amarnath had been granted to him there, not to die till he himself should give consent. And to me he said, "You do not now understand. But you have made the pilgrimage, and it will go on working. Causes must bring their effects. You will understand better afterwards. The effects will come"

How beautiful was the road by which we returned next morning to Pahalgam! We struck tents that night immediately on our return to them and camped later for the night in a snowy pass a whole stage further on. We paid a coolie a few annas here to push on with a letter; but when we actually arrived next afternoon we found that this had been quite unnecessary, for all morning long relays of pilgrims had been passing the tents and dropping in, in the most friendly manner, to give the others news of us and our impending arrival. In the morning we were up and on the way long before dawn. As the sun rose before us, while the moon went down behind, we passed above the Lake of Death, into which about forty pilgrims had been buried one year by an avalanche which their hymns had started. After this we came to the tiny goat-path down the face of a steep cliff by which we were able to shorten the return journey so much. This was little better than a scramble, and everyone had perforce to do it on foot. At the bottom the villagers had something like breakfast ready. Fires were burning, Chapattis baking, and tea was ready to be served out. From this time on parties of pilgrims would leave the main body at each parting of the ways, and the feeling of solidarity that had grown up amongst us all throughout the journey became gradually less and less.

That evening on the knoll above Pahalgam, where a great fire of pine-logs was lighted and dhurries spread, we all sat and talked. Our friend the Naked Swami joined us and we had plenty of fun and nonsense, but presently, when all had gone save our own little party, we sat on with the great moon overhead and the towering snows and rushing rivers and the mountain-pines. And the Swami talked of Shiva and the cave and the great verge of vision.

8 August

We started for Islamabad next day, and on Monday morning as we sat at breakfast, we were towed safely into Srinagar.

The Vale Of Kashmir

Persons: The Swami Vivekananda and a party of Europeans and disciples, amongst whom were Dhira Mata, the "Steady Mother"; one whose name was Jaya; and Nivedita
Place: The River Jhelum—Baramulla to Srinagar
Time: 20-22 June

"It is said that the Lord Himself is the weight on the side of the fortunate!" cried the Swami in high glee, returning to our room at the Dak bungalow and sitting down with his umbrella on his knees. As he had brought no companion, he had himself to perform all the ordinary little masculine offices, and he had gone out to hire dungas (houseboats) and do what was necessary. But he had immediately fallen in with a man who, on hearing his name, had undertaken the whole business and sent him back free of responsibility.

So we enjoyed the day. We drank Kashmiri tea out of a Samovar and ate the jam of the country, and at about four o'clock we entered into possession of a flotilla of dungas, three in number, on which presently we set forth for Srinagar. The first evening, however, we were moored by the garden of the Swami's friend.

We found ourselves next day in the midst of a beautiful valley ringed round with snow mountains. This is known as the Vale of Kashmir, but it might be more accurately described, perhaps, as the Vale of Srinagar.

That first morning, taking a long walk across the fields, we came upon an immense chinar tree standing in the midst of a wide pasture. It really looked as if the passage through it might shelter the proverbial twenty cows! The Swami fell to architectural visions of how it might be fitted up as a dwelling-place for a hermit. A small cottage might in fact have been built in the hollow of this living tree. And then he talked of meditation, in a way to consecrate every chinar we should ever see.

We turned with him into the neighbouring farmyard. There we found, seated under a tree, a singularly handsome elderly woman. She wore the crimson coronet and white veil of the Kashmiri wife and sat spinning wool, while round her, helping her, were her two daughters-in-law and their children. The Swami had called at this farm once before in the previous autumn and had often spoken since of the faith and pride of this very woman. He had begged for water, which she had at once given him. Then, before going, he had asked her quietly, "And what, Mother, is your religion?" "I thank God, Sir!" had rung out the old voice in pride and triumph. "By the mercy of the Lord, I am a Mussulman!" The whole family received him now as an old friend and were ready to show every courtesy to the friends he had brought.

The journey to Srinagar took two to three days, and one evening, as we walked in the fields before supper, one who had seen the Kalighat complained to the Master of the abandonment of feeling there, which had jarred on her. "*Why* do they kiss the ground before the image?" she exclaimed. The Swami had been pointing to the crop of Til—which he thought to have been the original of the English dill—and calling it "the oldest oil-bearing seed of the Aryans." But at this question he dropped the little blue flower from his hands, and a great hush came over his voice as he stood still and said, "Is it not the same thing to kiss the ground before that image as to kiss the ground before these mountains?"

Our master had promised that before the end of the summer he would take us into retreat and teach us to meditate. It was decïded that we should first see the country and afterwards make the retreat.

The first evening in Srinagar we dined out with some Bengali officials, and in the course of conversation one of the Western guests maintained that the history of every nation illustrated and evolved certain ideals to which the people of that nation should hold themselves true. It was very curious to see how the Hindus present objected to this. To them it was clearly a bondage to which the mind of Man could not permanently submit itself. Indeed, in their revolt against the fetters of the doctrine, they appeared to be unable to do justice to the idea itself. At last the Swami intervened. "I think you must admit," he said, "that the ultimate unit is psychological. This is much more permanent than the geographical." And then he spoke of cases known to us all, of one of whom he always thought as the most typical "Christian" he had ever seen, yet she was a Bengali woman, and of another, born in the West, who was "a better Hindu than himself". And was not this, after all, the ideal state of things, that each should be born in the other's country to spread the given ideal as far as it could be carried?

At Nainital And Almora

Persons: The Swami Vivekananda, Gurubhais, and a party of Europeans and disciples, amongst whom were Dhira Mata, the "Steady Mother"; one whose name was Jaya; and Nivedita
Place: The Himalayas
Time: 11-25 May 1898

We were a large party, or, indeed, two parties, that left Howrah station on Wednesday evening and on Friday morning came in sight of the Himalayas.

Naini Tal was made beautiful by three things—the Master's pleasure in introducing to us his disciple the Raja of Khetri; the dancing girls who met us and asked us where to find him, and were received by him in spite of the remonstrances of others; and by the Mohammedan gentleman who said, "Swamiji, if in after-times any claim you as an Avatara, an especial incarnation of the Deity—remember that I, a Mohammedan, am the first!"

It was here too that we heard a long talk on Ram Mohan Roy in which he pointed out three things as the dominant notes of this teacher's message—his acceptance of the Vedanta, his preaching of patriotism, and the love that embraced the Mussulman equally with the Hindu. In all these things he claimed himself to have taken up the task that the breadth and foresight of Ram Mohan Roy had mapped out.

The incident of the dancing girls occurred in consequence of our visit to the two temples at the head of the tarn. Here, offering worship, we found two nautch-women. When they had finished, they came up to us, and we, in broken language, entered into conversation with them. We took them for respectable ladies of the town and were much astonished later at the storm which had evidently passed over the Swami's audience at his refusal to have them turned away. Am I mistaken in thinking that it was in connection with these dancing-women of Naini Tal that he first told us the story, many times repeated, of the nautch-girl of Khetri? He had been angry at the invitation to see her, but being prevailed upon to come, she sang:

> O Lord, look not upon my evil qualities!
> Thy name, O Lord, is Same-Sightedness.
> Make us both the same Brahman!
> One piece of iron is the knife in the hand of the butcher,
> And another piece of iron is the image in the temple.
> But when they touch the philosopher's stone,
> Both alike turn to gold!
> One drop of water is in the sacred Jamuna,
> And one is foul in a ditch by the roadside.
> But when they fall into the Ganges,
> Both alike become holy!
> So, Lord, look not upon my evil qualities!
> Thy name, O Lord, is Same-Sightedness.
> Make us both the same Brahman!

And then, said the Master of himself, the scales fell from his eyes, and seeing that all are indeed one, he condemned no more.

It was late in the afternoon when we left Naini Tal for Almora, and night overtook us while still travelling through the forest till we reached a quaintly placed Dak bungalow, on the mountain side in the midst of trees. There after some time Swamiji arrived with his party, full of fun and keen in his appreciation of everything that concerned the comfort of his guests.

From the day that we arrived at Almora the Swami renewed his habit of coming over to us at our early breakfast and spending some hours in talk. Then and always he was an exceedingly light sleeper, and I imagine that his visit to us, early as the hour might be, was often paid during the course of his return with his monks from a still earlier walk. Sometimes, but rarely, we saw him again in the evening, either meeting him when out for a walk or going ourselves to Captain Sevier's, where he and his party were staying, and seeing him there. And once he came at that time to call on us.

Into these morning talks at Almora a strange new element, painful but salutary to remember, had crept. There appeared to be on the one side a curious bitterness and distrust, and on the other, irritation and defiance. The youngest of the Swami's disciples at this time, it must be remembered, was an English woman, and of how much this fact meant intellectually—what a strong bias it implied, and always does imply, in the reading of India, what an idealism of the English race and all their deeds and history—the Swami himself had had no conception till the day after her initiation at the monastery. Then he had asked her some exultant question, as to which nation she now belonged, and had been startled to find with what a passion of loyalty and worship she regarded the English flag, giving to it much of the feeling that an Indian woman would give to her Thakur. His surprise and disappointment at the moment were scarcely perceptible. A startled look, no more. Nor did his discovery of the superficial way in which this disciple had joined herself with his people in any degree affect his confidence and courtesy during the remaining weeks spent in the plains.

But with Almora it seemed as if a going-to-school had commenced. It was never more than this; never the dictating of opinion or creed; never more than emancipation from partiality. Even at the end of the terrible experience when this method, as regarded race and country, was renounced, never to be taken up systematically again, the Swami did not call for any confession of faith, any declaration of new opinion. He dropped the whole question. His listener went free. But he had revealed a different standpoint in thought and feeling, so completely and so strongly as to make it impossible for her to rest, until later, by her own labours, she had arrived at a view in which both these partial presentments stood rationalised and accounted for.

"Really, patriotism like yours is sin!" he exclaimed once, many weeks later, when the process of obtaining an uncoloured judgement on some incident had been more than commonly exasperating. "All that I want you to see is that most people's actions are the expression of self-interest, and you constantly oppose to this the idea that a certain race are all angels. Ignorance so determined is wickedness!"

These morning talks at Almora, then, took the form of assaults upon deep-rooted preconceptions—social, literary and artistic—or of long comparisons of Indian and European history and sentiments, often containing extended observations of very great value. One characteristic of the Swami was the habit of attacking the abuses of a country or society openly and vigorously when he was in its midst, whereas after he had left it, it would often seem as if nothing but its virtues were remembered by him. He was always testing his disciples, and the manner of these particular discourses was probably adopted in order to put to the proof the courage and sincerity of one who was both woman and European.

The House On The Ganga

Place: A cottage at Belur, beside the Ganga
Time: March to May, 1898

Of the home by the Ganga the Master had said to one, "You will find that little house of Dhira Mata like heaven, for it is all love, from beginning to end."

It was so indeed. Within, an unbroken harmony, and without, everything alike beautiful—the green stretch of grass, the tall coconut palms, the little brown villages in the jungle, and the Nilkantha that built her nest in a tree-top beside us, on purpose to bring us the blessings of Shiva. In the morning the shadows lay behind the house, but in the afternoons we could sit in front worshipping the Ganga herself—great leonine mother!—and in sight of Dakshineswar.

There came one and another with traditions of the past, and we learnt of the Master's eight years' wanderings; of the name changed from village to village; of the Nirvikalpa Samadhi; and of that sacred sorrow, too deep for words or for common sight, that one who loved had alone seen. And there too came the Master himself, with his stories of Uma and Shiva, of Radha and Krishna, and his fragments of song and poetry.

It seemed as if he knew that the first material of a new consciousness must be a succession of vivid but isolated experiences, poured out without proper sequence so as to provoke the mind of the learner to work for its own conception of order and relation. For the most part it was the Indian religions that he portrayed for us—today dealing with one and tomorrow with another—his choice guided, seemingly, by the whim of the moment. But it was not religion only that he poured out upon us. Sometimes it would be history. Again, it would be folklore. On still another occasion it would be the manifold anomalies and inconsistencies of race, caste and custom. In fact India herself became, as heard in him, as the last and noblest of the Puranas, uttering itself through his lips.

Another point in which he had caught a great psychological secret was that of never trying to soften for us that which would at first sight be difficult or repellent. In matters Indian he would rather put forward, in its extreme form at the beginning of our experience, all that might seem impossible for European minds to enjoy. Thus he would quote, for instance, some verses about Gauri and Shankar in a single form:

> On one side grows the hair in long black curls,
> And on the other, corded like rope.
> On one side are seen the beautiful garlands,
> On the other, bone earrings and snake-like coils.
> One side is white with ashes, like the snow mountains,
> The other, golden as the light of dawn.
> For He, the Lord, took a form,
> And that was a divided form,
> Half-woman and half-man.

Whatever might be the subject of the conversation, it ended always on the note of the infinite. He might appear to take up any subject—literary, ethnological or scientific—but he always made us feel it as an illustration of the Ultimate

Vision. There was for him nothing secular. He had a loathing for bondage and a horror of those who "cover chains with flowers", but he never failed to make the true critic's distinction between this and the highest forms of art.

One day we were receiving European guests and he entered into a long talk about Persian poetry. Then suddenly, finding himself quoting the poem that says, "For one mole on the face of my Beloved, I would give all the wealth of Samarkand!" he turned and said energetically, "I would not give a straw, you know, for the man who was incapable of appreciating a love song!" His talk too teemed with epigrams.

It was that same afternoon, in the course of a long political argument, that he said, "In order to become a nation, it appears that *we need a common hate* as well as a common love."

Several months later he remarked that before one who had a mission he never talked of any of the gods save Uma and Shiva. For Shiva and the Mother made the great workers. Yet I have sometimes wondered if he knew at this time how the end of every theme was Bhakti. Much as he dreaded the luxury of spiritual emotion for those who might be enervated by it, he could not help giving glimpses of what it meant to be consumed with the intoxication of God. And so he would chant for us such poems as:

They have made Radha queen, in the beautiful groves of Vrindaban.
At her gate stands Krishna, on guard.
His flute is singing all the time:
"Radha is about to distribute infinite wealth of love.
Though I am guard, all the world may enter.
Come all ye who thirst! Say only 'Glory unto Radha!'
Enter the region of love!"

Or he would give us the great antiphonal Chorus of the Cowherds, written by his friend:*

* The Bengali dramatist Girish Chandra Ghosh.

Men: Thou art the Soul of souls,
Thou yellow-garbed,
With thy blue eyes.
Women: Thou dark One! Thou Shepherd of Vrindaban!
Kneeling at the feet of the Shepherdesses.
Men: My soul sings the praise of the
glory of the Lord,
Who took the human form.
Women: Thy beauty for us, the Gopis.
Men: Thou Lord of Sacrifice.
Saviour of the weak.
Women: Who lovest Radha and thy body floats on its own tears.

25 March

At this time the Swami kept the custom of coming to the cottage early and spending the morning hours there, and again returning in the late afternoon. On the second morning of this visit, however—Friday, the Christian feast of the Annunciation—he took us all three back to the Math, and there in the worship-room was held a little service of initiation where one was made a Brahmacharini. That was the happiest of mornings.

After the service we were taken upstairs. The Swami put on the ashes and bone-earrings and matted locks of a Shiva-Yogi and sang and played to us—Indian music on Indian instruments—for an hour.

And in the evening in our boat on the Ganga, he opened his heart to us and told us much of his questions and anxieties regarding the trust that he held from his own Master.

Another week and he was gone to Darjeeling; and till the day that the plague declaration brought him back, we saw him again no more.

3 May

Then two of us met him in the house of our Holy Mother. The political sky was black. It seemed as if a storm were about to burst. Plague, panic and riot were doing their fell work. And the Master turned to the two and said, "There are some who scoff at the existence of Kali. Yet today She is out there amongst the people. They are frantic with fear, and the soldiery have been called to deal out death. Who can say that God does not manifest Himself as evil as well as good? But only the Hindu dares to worship Him in the evil."

He had come back and the old life was resumed once more, as far as could be, seeing that an epidemic was in prospect and that measures were on hand to give the people confidence. As long as this possibility darkened the horizon, he would not leave Calcutta. But it passed away, and those happy days with it, and the time came that we should go.

Walks And Talks Beside The Jhelum

Persons: The Swami Vivekananda and a party of Europeans and disciples, amongst whom were Dhira Mata, the "Steady Mother"; one whose name was Jaya; and Nivedita
Place: Kashmir
Time: 20-29 July 20 1898

20 July

That morning the river was broad and shallow and clear, and two of us walked with the Swami across the fields and along the banks about three miles. He began by talking of the sense of sin, how it was Egyptian, Semitic and Aryan. It appears in the Vedas, but quickly passes out. The devil is recognised there as the Lord of Anger. Then, with the Buddhists he became Mara, the Lord of Lust, and one of the most loved of the Lord Buddha's titles was "Conqueror of Mara". *(Vide* the Sanskrit lexicon Amarkosha that Swami learnt to patter as a child of four!) But while Satan is the Hamlet of the Bible, in the Hindu scriptures the Lord of Anger never divides creation. He always represents defilement, never duality.

Zoroaster was a reformer of some old religion. Even Ormuzd and Ahriman with him were not supreme; they were only manifestations of the Supreme. That older religion must have been Vedantic. So the Egyptians and Semites cling to the theory of sin while the Aryans, as Indians and Greeks, quickly lose it. In India righteousness and sin become Vidya and Avidya—both to be transcended. Amongst the Aryans, Persians and Europeans become Semitised by religious ideas; hence the sense of sin.*

And then the talk drifted, as it was always so apt to do, to questions of the country and the future. What idea must be urged on a people to give them strength? The line of their own development runs in one way, A.

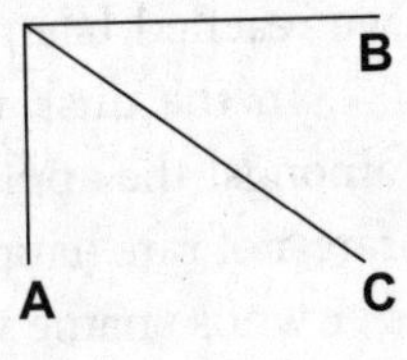

Must the new accession of force be a compensating one, B? This would produce a development midway between the two, C—a geometrical alteration merely. But it was not so.

National life was a question of organic forces. We must reinforce the current of that life itself, and leave it to do the rest. Buddha preached renunciation, and India heard. Yet within a thousand years she had reached her highest point of national prosperity. The national life in India has renunciation as its source. Its highest ideals are service and Mukti. The Hindu mother eats last. Marriage is not for individual happiness, but for the welfare of the nation and the caste. Certain individuals of the modern reform, having embarked on an experiment which could not solve the problem, "are the sacrifices over which the race has to walk".

And then the trend of conversation changed again and became all fun and merriment, jokes and stories. And as we laughed and listened, the boats came up and talk was over for the day.

---

* One of those who listened to this talk had a wonderful opportunity later of appreciating the accuracy and the breadth of the Swami's knowledge, when she saw two Parsis glad to sit at his feet and learn from him the history of their own religious ideas.

The whole of that afternoon and night the Swami lay in his boat, ill. But next day, when we landed at the temple of Bijbehara—already thronged with Amarnath pilgrims—he was able to join us for a little while. "Quickly up and quickly down," as he said of himself, was always his characteristic. After that he was with us most of the day, and in the afternoon we reached Islamabad.

In the dusk that evening one came into the little group amongst the apple trees and found the Master engaged in the rarest of rare happenings, a personal talk with Dhira Mata and her whose name was Jaya. He had taken two pebbles into his hand and was saying how, when he was well, his mind might direct itself to this and that, or his will might seem less firm; but let the least touch of pain or illness come, let him look death in the face for a while, and "I am as hard as that (knocking the stones together), for I *have* touched the feet of God."

And one remembered, apropos of this coolness, the story of a walk across the fields in England, where he and an Englishman and woman had been pursued by an angry bull. The Englishman frankly ran and reached the other side of the hill in safety. The woman ran as far as she could and then sank to the ground, incapable of further effort. Seeing this, and unable to aid her, the Swami—thinking "So *this* is the end, after all"—took up his stand in front of her, with folded arms. He told afterwards how his mind was occupied with a mathematical calculation as to how far the bull would be able to throw. But the animal suddenly stopped a few paces off and then, raising his head, retreated sullenly.

A like courage—though he himself was far from thinking of these incidents—had shown itself in his early youth when he quietly stepped up to a runaway horse and caught it in the streets of Calcutta, thus saving the life of the woman who occupied the carriage behind.

The talk drifted on, as we sat on the grass beneath the trees, and became, for an hour or two, half grave, half gay.

We heard much of the tricks the monkeys could play in Vrindaban. And we elicited stories of two separate occasions in his wandering life when he had had clear previsions of help which had been fulfilled. One of these I remember. It may possibly have occurred at the time when he was under the vow to ask for nothing, and he had been several days (perhaps five) without food. Suddenly, as he lay almost dying of exhaustion in a railway station, it flashed into his mind that he must rise up and go out along a certain road and that there he would meet a man bringing him help. He obeyed and met one carrying a tray of food. "Are you he to whom I was sent?" said this man, coming up to him and looking at him closely.

Then a child was brought to us, with its hand badly cut, and the Swami applied an old wives' cure. He bathed the wound with water and then laid on it, to stop the bleeding, the ashes of a piece of calico. The villagers were soothed and consoled, and our gossip was over for the evening.

23 July

The next morning a motley gathering of coolies assembled beneath the apple-trees and waited some hours to take us to the ruins of Marttanda. It had been a wonderful old building—evidently more abbey than temple—in a wonderful position; and its great interest lay in the obvious agglomeration of styles and periods in which it had grown up. Its presence is a perpetual reminder that the East was the original home of monasticism. The Swami was hard at work in an instant on observations and theories, pointing out the cornice that ran along the nave from the entrance to the sanctuary, to the west, surmounted by the high trefoils of the two arches and also by a frieze; or showing us the panels containing cherubs; and before we had done, had picked up a couple of coins. The ride back through the sunset light was charming. From all these hours, the day before and the day after, fragments of talk come back to me.

"No nation, not Greek or another, has ever carried patriotism so far as the Japanese. They don't talk, they act—give up all for country. There are noblemen now living in Japan as peasants, having given up their princedoms without a word to create the unity of the empire.* And not one traitor could be found in the Japanese war. Think of that!"

Again, talking of the inability of some to express feeling, "Shy and reserved people, I have noticed, are always the most brutal when roused."

Again, evidently talking of the ascetic life and giving the rules of Brahmacharya—"The Sannyasin who thinks of gold, to desire it, commits suicide", and so on.

24 July

The darkness of night and the forest, a great pine fire under the trees, two or three tents standing out white in the blackness, the forms and voices of many servants at their fires in the distance, and the Master with three disciples, such is the next picture. Suddenly the Master turned to one member of the party and said, "You never mention your school now. Do you sometimes forget it? You see", he went on, "I have much to think of. One day I turn to Madras and think of the work there. Another day I give all my attention to America or England or Ceylon or Calcutta. Now I am thinking about yours."

At that moment the Master was called away to dine, and not till he came back could the confidence he had invited be given.

He listened to it all, the deliberate wish for a tentative plan, for smallness of beginnings, and the final inclination to turn away from the idea of inclusiveness and breadth and to base the whole of an educational effort on the religious life and on the worship of Sri Ramakrishna.

* The Japanese samurais renounced their political privileges, not their estates.

"Because you must be sectarian to get that enthusiasm, must you not?" he said. "You will make a sect in order to rise above all sects. Yes I understand."

There would be obvious difficulties. The thing sounded on this scale almost impossible for many reasons. But for the moment the only care need be to will rightly; and if the plan was sound, ways and means would be found to hand, that was sure.

He waited a little when he had heard it all, and then he said, "You ask me to criticise, but that I cannot do. For I regard you as inspired, quite as much inspired as I am. You know that's the difference between other religions and us. Other people believe their founder was inspired, and so do we. But so am I also, just as much so as he, and you as I; and after you, your girls and their disciples will be. So I shall help you to do what you think best."

Then he turned to Dhira Mata and to Jaya and spoke of the greatness of the trust that he would leave in the hands of that disciple who should represent the interests of women when he should go West, of how it Would exceed the responsibility of work for men. And he added, turning to the worker of the party, Yes, you have faith, but you have not that burning enthusiasm that you need. You want to be consumed with energy. Shiva! Shiva!" And so, invoking blessing of Mahadeva, he said goodnight and left us, and we presently went to bed.

25 July

The next morning we breakfasted early in one of the tents and went on to Achhabal. One of us had had a dream of old jewels lost and restored, all bright and new. But the Swami, smiling, stopped the tale, saying, "Never talk of a dream as good as that!"

At Achhabal we found more gardens of Jehangir. Was it here or at Verinag that had been his favourite resting-place?

We roamed about the gardens and bathed in a still pool opposite the Pathan Khan's Zenana, and then we lunched in the first garden and rode down in the afternoon to Islamabad.

As we sat at lunch, the Swami invited his daughter to go to the cave of Amarnath with him and be dedicated to Shiva. Dhira Mata smiled permission, and the next half-hour was given to pleasure and congratulations. It had already been arranged that we were all to go to Pahalgam and wait there for the Swami's return from the pilgrimage. So we reached the boats that evening, packed and wrote letters, and next day in the afternoon started for Bawan.

The Belur Math: An Appeal

The success which attended the labours of the disciples of Sri Ramakrishna Paramahamsa in diffusing the principles of Hindu religion and obtaining some respect for our much abused faith in the West, gave rise to the hope of training a number of young Sannyasins to carry on the propaganda, both in and out of India. And an attempt is being made to educate a number of young men according to the Vedic principle of students living in touch with the Guru.

A Math has already been started on the Ganga near Calcutta, through the kindness of some European and American friends.

The work, to produce any visible results in a short time, requires funds and hence this appeal to those who are in sympathy with our efforts.

It is intended to extend the operation of the Math, by educating in the Math as many young men as the funds can afford, in both Western science and Indian spirituality, so that in addition to the advantages of a University education, they will acquire a manly discipline by living in contact with their teachers.

The central Math near Calcutta will gradually start branches in other parts of the country as men become ready and the means are forthcoming.

It is a work which will take time to bring forth any permanent result and requires a great deal of sacrifice on the part of our young men and on those who have the means of helping this work.

We believe the men are ready, and our appeal, therefore, is to those who really love their religion and their country and have the means to show their sympathy practically by helping the cause.

Swami Vivekananda On Education At Belur*

The Indian Mirror, *15 February 1901*

A correspondent writes: "The following is an epitome of Swami Vivekananda's speech made in Belur M.E. School on the prize-distribution day held on the 22nd instant, Sunday, when the Swami was invited to preside. The audience was composed chiefly of the boys of the school and some elderly gentlemen of Belur."

The modern student is not practical. He is quite helpless. What our students want is not so much muscularity of body as hardihood. They are wanting in self-help. They are not accustomed to use their eyes and hands. No handicraft is taught. The present system of English education is entirely literary. The student must be made to think for himself and work for himself. Suppose there is a fire. He is the first to come forward and put on [out] the fire who is accustomed to use his eyes and hands. There is much truth in the criticism of Europeans touching the laziness of the Bengali, the slipshod way of his doing things. This can be soon remedied if the students be made to learn some handicraft apart from its utilitarian aspect, it is an education in itself.

---

* *Vivekananda in Indian Newspapers*, p. 215.

Secondly, how many thousands of students I know who live upon the worst food possible, and live amidst the most horrible surroundings, what wonder that there are so many idiots, imbeciles and cowards among them. They die like flies. The education that is given is one-sided, weakening, it is killing by inches. The children are made to cram too much of useless matter, and are incarcerated in school rooms fifty or seventy in each, five hours together. They are given bad food. It is forgotten that the future health of the man is in the child. It is forgotten that nature can never be cheated and things cannot be pushed too early. In giving education to a child the law of growth has to be obeyed. And we must learn to wait. Nothing is more important than that the child must have a strong and healthy body. The body is the first thing to attain to virtue. I know we are the poorest nation in the world, and we cannot afford to do much. We can only work on the lines of least resistance. We should see at least that our children are well fed. The machine of the child's body should never be exhausted. In Europe and America a man with crores of rupees sends his son if sickly, to the farmers, to till the ground. After three years he returns to the father healthy, rosy and strong. Then he is fit to be sent to school. We ought not for these reasons push the present system of education any further.

Thirdly, our character has disappeared. Our English education has destroyed everything and left nothing in its place. Our children have lost their politeness. To talk nicely is degrading. To be reverential to one's elders is degrading. Irreverence has been the sign of liberty. It is high time that we go back to our old politeness. The reformers have nothing to give in place of what they have taken away. Yet in spite of the most adverse surrounding of climate, etc., we have been able to do much, we have to do much more. I am proud of my race, I do not despair, I am seeing daily a glorious and wonderful future in my menial mental visions. Take greatest care of these young ones on whom our future depends.

The Ramakrishna Home Of Service, Varanasi: An Appeal*

Dear—

We beg your acceptance of the past year's Report of the Ramakrishna Home of Service, Varanasi, embodying a short statement of our humble efforts towards the amelioration, however little, of the miserable state into which a good many of our fellow-beings, generally old men and women, are cast in this city.

In these days of intellectual awakening and steadily asserting public opinion, the holy places of the Hindus, their condition, and method of work have not escaped the keen eye of criticism; and this city, being the holy of holies to all Hindus, has not failed to attract its full share of censure.

In other sacred places people go to purify themselves from sin, and their connection with these places is casual, and of a few day's duration. In this, the most ancient and living centre of Aryan religious activity, there come men and women, and as a rule, old and decrepit, waiting to pass unto Eternal Freedom, through the greatest of all

* Letter written by Swami Vivekananda to accompany the First Report of the Ramakrishna Home of Service, Varanasi, February 1902.

sanctifications, death under the shadow of the temple of the Lord of the universe.

And then there are those who have renounced everything for the good of the world and have for ever lost the helping hands of their own flesh and blood and childhood's associations.

They too are overtaken by the common lot of humanity, physical evil in the form of disease.

It may be true that some blame attaches to the management of the place. It may be true that the priests deserve a good part of the sweeping criticism generally heaped upon them; yet we must not forget the great truth—like people, like priests. If the people stand be with folded hands and watch the swift current of misery rushing past their doors, dragging men, women and children, the Sannyâsin and the householder into one common whirlpool of helpless suffering, and make not the least effort to save any from the current, only waxing eloquent at the misdoings of the priests of the holy places not one particle of suffering can ever be lessened, not one ever be helped.

Do we want to keep up the faith of our forefathers in the efficacy of the Eternal City of Shiva towards salvation?

If we do, we ought to be glad to see the number of those increase from year to year who come here to die.

And blessed be the name of the Lord that the poor have this eager desire for salvation, the same as ever.

The poor who come here to die have voluntarily cut themselves off from any help they could have received in the places of their birth, and when disease overtakes them, their condition we leave to your imagination and to your conscience as a Hindu to feel and to rectify.

Brother, does it not make you pause and think of the marvellous attraction of this wonderful place of preparation for final rest? Does it not strike you with a mysterious sense of awe—this age-old and never-ending stream of pilgrims marching to salvation through death?

If it does—come and lend us a helping hand.

Never mind if your contribution is only a mite, your help only a little; blades of grass united into a rope will hold in confinement the maddest of elephants — says the old proverb.

Ever yours in the Lord of the universe,

VIVEKANANDA.

The Temple Of Pandrenthan

Persons: The Swami Vivekananda and a party of Europeans and disciples, amongst whom were Dhira Mata, the "Steady Mother"; one whose name was Jaya; and Nivedita
Place: Kashmir
Time: 16-19 July 1898

16 July

It fell to the lot of one of the Swami's disciples next day to go down the river with him in a small boat. As it went, he chanted one song after another of Ramprasad, and now and again he would translate a verse:

> I call upon thee, Mother.
> For though his mother strikes him,
> The child cries, "Mother! Oh, Mother!"
> Though I cannot see Thee,
> I am not a lost child!
> I still cry, "Mother! Mother!"

And then with the haughty dignity of an offended child, something that ended, "I am not the son to call any other woman 'Mother'!"

17 July

It must have been next day that he came into Dhira Mata's Dunga and talked of Bhakti. First it was that curious Hindu thought of Shiva and Uma in one. It is easy to give the words, but without the voice how comparatively dead they seem! And then there were the wonderful surroundings—picturesque Srinagar, tall Lombardy poplars and distant snows. There in that river valley, some space from the foot of the great mountains, he chanted to us how "the Lord took a form and that was a divided form, half woman and half man. On one side, beautiful garlands; on the other, bone earrings and coils of snakes. On one side, the hair black, beautiful and in curls; on the other, twisted like rope." And then passing immediately into the other form of the same thought, he quoted:

> God became Krishna and Radha—
> Love flows in thousands of coils.
> Whoso wants, takes it.
>
> Love flows in thousands of coils—
> The tide of love and loving past,
> And fills the soul with bliss and joy!

So absorbed was he that his breakfast stood unheeded long after it was ready, and when at last he went reluctantly—saying, "When one has all this Bhakti what does one want with food?"—it was only to come back again quickly and resume the subject.

But either now or at some other time he said that he did not talk of Radha and Krishna where he looked for deeds. It was Shiva who made stern and earnest workers, and to Him the labourer must be dedicated.

The next day he gave us a quaint saying of Sri Ramakrishna, comparing the critics of others to bees or flies, according as they chose honey or wounds.

And then we were off to Islamabad, and really, as it proved, to Amarnath.

19 July

The first afternoon, in a wood by the side of the Jhelum, we discovered the long-sought temple of Pandrenthan (Pandresthan, place of the Pandavas?).

It was sunk in a pond, and this was thickly covered with scum out of which it rose, a tiny cathedral of the long ago, built of heavy grey limestone. The temple consisted of a small cell with four doorways opening to the cardinal points. Externally it was a tapering pyramid—with its top truncated, to give foot-hold to a bush—supported on a four-pierced pedestal. In its architecture, trefoil and triangular arches were combined in an unusual fashion with each other and with the straight-lined lintel. It was built with marvellous solidity, and the necessary lines were somewhat obscured by heavy ornament.

For all but the Swami himself, this was our first peep at Indian archaeology. So when he had been through it, he taught us how to observe the interior.

In the centre of the ceiling was a large sun-medallion, set in a square whose points were the points of the compass. This left four equal triangles at the corners of the ceiling, which were filled with sculpture in low relief, male and female figures intertwined with serpents, beautifully done. On the wall were empty spaces, where seemed to have been a band of topes.

Outside, carvings were similarly distributed. In one of the trefoil arches—over, I think, the eastern door—was a fine image of the Teaching Buddha, standing, with his hand uplifted. Running round the buttresses was a much-defaced frieze of a seated woman with a tree—evidently Maya Devi, the mother of Buddha. The three other door niches were empty, but a slab by the pond-side seemed to have fallen from one, and this contained a bad figure of a king, said by the country-people to represent the sun.

The masonry of this little temple was superb and probably accounted for its long preservation. A single block of stone would be so cut as to correspond not to one brick in a wall, but to a section of the architect's plan. It would turn a corner and form part of two distinct walls, or sometimes even of three. This fact made one take the building as very, very old, possibly even earlier than Marttanda. The theory of the workmen seemed so much more that of carpentering than of building! The water about it was probably an overflow into the temple-court from the sacred spring that the chapel itself may have been placed, as the Swami thought, to enshrine.

To him, the place was delightfully suggestive. It was a direct memorial of Buddhism, representing one of the four religious periods into which he had already divided the history of Kashmir: (1) tree and snake worship, from which dated all the names of the springs ending in Nag, as Verinag, and so on; (2) Buddhism; (3) Hinduism, in the form of sun worship; and (4) Mohammedanism.

Sculpture, he told us, was the characteristic art of Buddhism, and the sun-medallion, or lotus, one of its commonest ornaments. The figures with the serpents referred to pre-Buddhism. But sculpture had greatly deteriorated under sun worship, hence the crudity of the Surya figure.

It was the time of sunset—such a sunset! The mountains in the west were all a shimmering purple. Further north they were blue with snow and cloud. The sky was green and yellow and touched with red—bright flame and daffodil colours, against a blue and opal background. We stood and looked, and then the Master, catching sight of the throne of Solomon—that little Takt which we already loved—exclaimed, "What genius the Hindu shows in placing his temples! He always chooses a grand scenic effect! See! The Takt commands the whole of Kashmir. The rock of Hari Parbat rises red out of blue water, like a lion couchant, crowned. And the temple of Marttanda has the valley at its feet!"

Our boats were moored near the edge of the wood, and we could see that the presence of the silent chapel, of the Buddha, which we had just explored, moved the Swami deeply. That evening we all fore-gathered in Dhira Mata's houseboat, and a little of the conversation has been noted down.

Our master had been talking of Christian ritual as derived from Buddhist, but one of the party would have none of the theory.

"Where did Buddhist ritual itself come from?" she asked.

"From Vedic," answered the Swami briefly.

"Or as it was present also in southern Europe, is it not better to suppose a common origin for it and the Christian and the Vedic rituals?"

"No! No!" he replied. "You forget that Buddhism was entirely within Hinduism! Even caste was not attacked—it was not yet crystallised, of course!—and Buddha merely tried to restore the ideal. *He who attains to God in this life,* says Manu, *is the Brahmin.* Buddha would have had it so, if he could."

"But how are Vedic and Christian rituals connected?" persisted his opponent. "How could they be the same? You have nothing even corresponding to the central rite of our worship!"

"Why, yes!" said the Swami. "Vedic ritual has its Mass, the offering of food to God; your Blessed Sacrament, our Prasadam. Only it is offered sitting, not kneeling, as is common in hot countries. They kneel in Tibet. Then too Vedic ritual has its lights, incense, music."

"But," was the somewhat ungracious argument, "has it any common prayer?" Objections urged in this way always elicited some bold paradox which contained a new and unthought-of generalisation.

He flashed down on the question. "No! And neither has Christianity! That is pure Protestantism and Protestantism took it from the Mohammedans, perhaps through Moorish influence!

"Mohammedanism is the only religion that has completely broken down the idea of the priest. The leader of prayer stands with his back to the people, and only the reading of the Koran may take place from the pulpit. Protestantism is an approach to this.

"Even the tonsure existed in India, in the shaven head. I have seen a picture of Justinian receiving the Law from two monks, in which the monks' heads are entirely shaven. The monk and nun both existed in pre-Buddhistic Hinduism. Europe gets her orders from the Thebaid."

"At that rate, then, you accept Catholic ritual as Aryan!"

"Yes, almost all Christianity is Aryan, I believe. I am inclined to think Christ never existed. I have doubted that ever since I had my dream—that dream off Crete!*

---

* Travelling from Naples to Port Said, on his way back to India, in January 1897, the Swami dreamt of an old bearded man who appeared before him, saying, "This is the island of Crete", and showed him a place in the island that he might afterwards identify. The vision then said that Christianity had originated in the island of Crete and in connection with this gave him two European words—one was Therapeutae—which it declared were derived from Sanskrit. Therapeutae meant "sons" (from the Sanskrit Putra) of the Theras, or Buddhist monks. The Swami was to understand that Christianity had originated in a Buddhist mission. The vision added, "The proofs are all here", pointing to the ground. "Dig and you will see!"

As he awoke, feeling that this was no common dream, the Swami rose and tumbled out on the deck. Here he met an officer turning in from his watch. "What o'clock is it?" said the Swami. "Midnight!" was the answer. "Where are we?" he then asked,. To his astonishment the answer was: "Fifty miles off Crete!"

The Swami used to laugh at himself for the impression that this dream had made on him. But he could never shake it off. That the second of the two etymologies has been lost is deeply to be regretted. The Swami said that before he had this dream, it had never occurred to him to doubt that the personality of Christ was strictly historic. However, according to Hindu philosophy, the completeness of an idea is important, and not the question of its historical authenticity. When he was a boy, the Swami once asked Sri Ramakrishna about this very matter. "Don't you think," answered his Guru, "that those who could invent such things were themselves that?"

Indian and Egyptian ideas met at Alexandria and went forth to the world, tinctured with Judaism and Hellenism, as Christianity.

"The Acts and Epistles, you know, are older than the Gospels, and S. John is spurious. The only figure we can be sure of is S. Paul, and he was not an eye-witness, and according to his own showing was capable of Jesuitry—'by all means save souls'—isn't it?

"No! Buddha and Mohammed, alone amongst religious teachers, stand out with historic distinctness—having been fortunate enough to have, while they were living, enemies as well as friends. Krishna—I doubt; a Yogi, a shepherd, and a great king have all been amalgamated in one beautiful figure, holding the *Gita* in his hand.

"Renan's life of Jesus is mere froth. It does not touch Strauss, the real antiquarian. Two things stand out as personal living touches in the life of Christ—the woman taken in adultery, the most beautiful story in literature, and the woman at the well. How strangely true is this last to Indian life! A woman coming to draw water finds, seated at the well-side, a yellow-clad monk. He asks her for water. Then he teaches her and does a little mind-reading and so on. Only in an Indian story, when she went to call the villagers to look and listen, the monk would have taken his chance and fled to the forest!

"On the whole, I think old Rabbi Hillel is responsible for the teachings of Jesus, and an obscure Jewish sect of Nazarenes—a sect of great antiquity—suddenly galvanised by S. Paul, furnished the mythic personality as a centre of worship.

"The resurrection, of course, is simply spring-cremation. Only the rich Greeks and Romans had had cremation anyway, and the new sun-myth would only stop it amongst the few.

"But Buddha! Buddha! Surely he was the greatest."

He never drew a breath for himself. Above all, he never claimed worship. He said, 'Buddha is not a man, but a state. I have found the door. Enter, all of you!'

"He went to the feast of Ambapali, 'the sinner'. He dined with the pariah, though he knew it would kill him, and sent a message to his host on his death-bed, thanking him for the great deliverance. Full of love and pity for a little goat, even before he had attained the truth! You remember how he offered his own head, that of prince and monk, if only the king would spare the kid that he was about to sacrifice, and how the king was so struck by his compassion that he saved its life? Such a mixture of rationalism and feeling was never seen! Surely, surely, there was none like him!"

On The Way To Kathgodam

11 June

On Saturday morning we left Almora. It took us two days and a half to reach Kathgodam.

Somewhere en route near a curious old water-mill and deserted forge, the Swami told Dhira Mata of a legend that spoke of this hill-side as haunted by a race of centaur-like phantoms, and of an experience known to him by which one had first seen forms there and only afterwards heard the folk tale.

The roses were gone by this time, but a flower was in bloom that crumbled at a touch, and he pointed this out because of its wealth of associations in Indian poetry.

June 12

On Sunday afternoon we rested near the plains in what we took to be an out-of-the-way hotel above a lake and fall, and there he translated for us the Rudra prayer:

> From the unreal lead us to the Real.
> From darkness lead us unto light.
> From death lead us to immortality.
> Reach us through and through our self.

And evermore protect us—O Thou Terrible! —
From ignorance, by Thy sweet, compassionate face.

He hesitated a long time over the fourth line, thinking of rendering it, "Embrace us in the heart of our heart." But at last he put his perplexity to us, saying shyly, "The real meaning is, Reach us through and through our self." He had evidently feared that this sentence, with its extraordinary intensity, might not make good sense in English. I have understood that a more literal rendering would be, "O Thou who art manifest only unto Thyself, manifest Thyself also unto us!" I now regard his translation as a rapid and direct transcript of the experience of Samadhi itself. It tears the living heart out of the Sanskrit, as it were, and renders it again in an English form.

It was indeed an afternoon of translations, and he gave us fragments of the great benediction after mourning, which is one of the most beautiful of the Hindu sacraments:

The blissful winds are sweet to us.
The seas are showering bliss on us.
May the corn in our fields bring bliss to us.
May the plants and herbs bring bliss to us.
May the cattle give us bliss.
O Father in Heaven, be Thou blissful unto us!
Thy very dust of the earth is full of bliss.
And then, the voice dying down into meditation:
It is all bliss—all bliss—all bliss.

And again we had Suradasa's song, which the Swam heard from the nautch-girl at Khetri:

O Lord, look not upon my evil qualities!
Thy name, O Lord, is Same-Sightedness.
Make of us both the same Brahman!

Was it that same day or some other that he told us of the old Sannyasin in Benares who saw him annoyed by troops of monkeys and, afraid that he might turn and run, shouted, "Always face the brute!?"

Those journeys were delightful. We were always sorry to reach a destination. At this time it took us a whole afternoon to cross the Terai by rail—that strip of malarial country on which, as he reminded us, Buddha had been born.

As we had come down the mountain roads, we had met parties of country-folk fleeing to the upper hills with their families and all their goods, to escape the fever which would be upon them with the rains. And now in the train there was the gradual change of vegetation to watch and the Master's pleasure, greater than that of any proprietor, in showing us the wild peacocks, or here and there an elephant or a train of camels.

X

Hymns

The Hymn Of Creation

Rendered from the Bengali

One Mass, devoid of form, name, and colour,
Timeless, devoid of time past and future,
Spaceless, voiceless, boundless, devoid of all—
Where rests hushed even speech of negation.*

From thence, down floweth the river causal,
Wearing the form of desire radiant,
Its heaving waters angrily roaring
The constant roar, "I am", "I am".

In that ocean of desire limitless,
Appear shining waves, countless, infinite,
Oh, of what power manifold they are,
Of what forms myriad, of what repose,
Of what movements varied, who can reckon?

Millions of moons, millions of suns,
Taking their birth in that very ocean,
Rushing headlong with din tumultuous,
Overspread the whole firmament, drowning

---

* *"Neti, Neti"*, "Not this, not this." Brahman cannot be described in any positive way.

The points of heaven in light effulgent.
In it arise and reside what beings,
Quick with life, dull, and lifeless—unnumbered,
And pleasure and pain, disease, birth, and death!
Verily, the Sun is He, His the ray,
Nay, the Sun is He, and He is the ray.

To The Awakened India*

Once more awake!
For sleep it was, not death, to bring thee life
Anew, and rest to lotus-eyes for visions
Daring yet. The world in need awaits, O Truth!
No death for thee!

Resume thy march,
With gentle feet that would not break the
Peaceful rest even of the roadside dust
That lies so low. Yet strong and steady,
Blissful, bold, and free. Awakener, ever
Forward! Speak thy stirring words.

Thy home is gone,
Where loving hearts had brought thee up and
Watched with joy thy growth. But Fate is strong—
This is the law—all things come back to the source
They sprung, their strength to renew.

Then start afresh
From the land of thy birth, where vast cloud-belted
Snows do bless and put their strength in thee,

* Written to *Prabhuddha Bharata* or *Awakened India*, in August 1898, when the journal passed from Madras to Almora Himalayas, into the hands of the Brotherhood founded by Swami Vivekananda.

For working wonders new. The heavenly
River tune thy voice to her own immortal song;
Deodar shades give thee eternal peace.

And all above,
Himala's daughter Uma, gentle, pure,
The Mother that resides in all as Power
And Life, who works all works and
Makes of One the world, whose mercy
Opens the gate to Truth and shows
The One in All, give thee untiring
Strength, which is Infinite Love.

They bless thee all,
The seers great, whom age nor clime
Can claim their own, the fathers of the
Race, who felt the heart of Truth the same,
And bravely taught to Man ill-voiced or
Well. Their servant, thou hast got
The secret—'tis but One.

Then speak, O Love!
Before thy gentle voice serene, behold how
Visions melt and fold on fold of dreams
Departs to void, till Truth and Truth alone
In all its glory shines —

And tell the world—
Awake, arise, and dream no more!
This is the land of dreams, where Karma
Weaves unthreaded garlands with our thoughts
Of flowers sweet or noxious, and none
Has root or stem, being born in naught, which
The softest breath of Truth drives back to
Primal nothingness. Be bold, and face
The Truth! Be one with it! Let visions cease,
Or, if you cannot, dream but truer dreams,
Which are Eternal Love and Service Free.

Peace

Composed at Ridgely Manor, New York, 1899

Behold, it comes in might,
The power that is not power,
The light that is in darkness,
The shade in dazzling light.

It is joy that never spoke,
And grief unfelt, profound,
Immortal life unlived,
Eternal death unmourned.

It is not joy nor sorrow,
But that which is between,
It is not night nor morrow,
But that which joins them in.

It is sweet rest in music;
And pause in sacred art;
The silence between speaking;
Between two fits of passion—
It is the calm of heart.

It is beauty never seen,
And love that stands alone,

It is song that lives unsung,
And knowledge never known.

It is death between two lives,
And lull between two storms,
The void whence rose creation,
And that where it returns.
To it the tear-drop goes, To spread the smiling form
It is the Goal of Life,
And Peace—its only home!

Requiescat In Pace

Written in memoriam to J.J. Goodwin, August 1898

Speed forth, O Soul upon thy star-strewn path;
Speed, blissful one where thought is ever free,
Where time and space no longer mist the view,
Eternal peace and blessings be with thee!

Thy service true, complete thy sacrifice,
Thy home the heart of love transcendent find;
Remembrance sweet, that kills all space and time,
Like altar roses fill thy place behind!

Thy bonds are broke, thy quest in bliss is found,
And one with That which comes as Death and Life;
Thou helpful one unselfish e'er on earth,
Ahead still help with love this world of strife!

Let one put garlands on, another kick
This frame; say naught. No praise or blame can be
Where praiser praised, and blamer blamed are one.
Thus be thou calm, Sannyasin bold! Say—

"Om Tat Sat, Om!"

Truth never comes where lust and fame and greed
Of gain reside. No man who thinks of woman

As his wife can ever perfect be;
Nor he who owns the least of things, nor he
Whom anger chains, can ever pass thro' Maya's gates.
So, give these up, Sannyasin bold! Say—

"Om Tat Sat, Om!"

Have thou no home. What home can hold thee, friend?
The sky thy roof, the grass thy bed; and food
What chance may bring, well cooked or ill, judge not.
No food or drink can taint that noble Self
Which knows Itself. Like rolling river free
Thou ever be, Sannyasin bold! Say—

"Om Tat Sat, Om!"

Few only know the truth. The rest will hate
And laugh at thee, great one; but pay no heed.
Go thou, the free, from place to place, and help
Them out of darkness, Maya's veil. Without
The fear of pain or search for pleasure, go
Beyond them both, Sannyasin bold! Say—

"Om Tat Sat, Om!"

Thus, day by day, till Karma's powers spent
Release the soul forever. No more is birth,
Nor I, nor thou, nor God, nor man. The "I"
Has All become, the All is "I" and Bliss.
Know thou art That, Sannyasin bold! Say—

"Om Tat Sat, Om!"

A Hymn To The Divinity Of Sri Ramakrishna

Rendered from the Bengali

We salute Thee!
Lord! Adored of the world,
Samsara's bondage breaker, taintless Thou,
Embodiment of blessed qualities,
Thou transcendest all Gunas; human form
Thus bearest.
Thee we salute and adore!

Refuge of mind and speech, Thou, art beyond
The reach of either. Radiance art Thou
In all radiance that is. The heart's cave
Is by Thy visitance resplendent made.
Verily Thou art that which dispelleth
The densest darkness of Tamas in man.

Lo! In variety of melody
Forth-breaking in fine harmony most sweet,
Hymns of Thy devotees, accompanied
By Mridanga* playing with music's grace,
Fill the air, in evening worship to Thee.

---

* A kind of drum.

One glancing vision at Thine eyes divine
Cleared by the collyrium of Jnana
Defies delusion. O thou blotter-out
Of all the taints of sin, Intelligence
Pure, unmingled is Thy form. Of the world
Thou art embellisher. Self-luminous
Art Thou. O Ocean of feeling sublime,
And of Love Divine, O God-maddened One,
Devotees win Thy blessed feet and cross
Safely the swelling sea of Samsara.

O Lord of the world, though Thy Yoga power
Thou shinest as the Incarnation clear
Of this our time. O thou of strict restraint,
Only through Thine unstinted grace we see
The mind in Samadhi completely merged;
Mercy Incarnate! Austere are Thy deeds.

Thou dealest to the evil of Misery
Destruction. Kali's* binding cords
Are cut by Thee asunder. Thine own life
Thou gavest freely, O sweet Sacrifice,
O best of men! O Saviour of the world!

Devoid wert Thou of the idea of sex,
Thought of possession charmed Thee not. To Thee
Obnoxious was all pleasure. Give to us,
O greatest among Tyagis,** love intense
Unto Thy sacred feet; give, we implore!

Fearless art Thou, and past all gloom of doubt;
Thy mind is wrapt in its own firm resolve;
Thy lovers, whose devotion mounts above
The realm of reason, who renounce the pride

* Of the Iron Age.

** Renouncers.

Of caste and parentage, of name and fame —
Their safe refuge art Thou alone, O Lord!

My one true treasure is Thy blessed feet,
Reaching which the whole universe itself
Seems like a puddle in the hollow made
By hoof of passing cow.
O offering

To Love! O Seer of equality
In all! O verily, in Thee the pain
And evil of this mortal world escapes,
And vanishes, O cherished One.

A Hymn To Shiva

निखिलभुवनजन्मस्थेमभङ्गप्ररोहाः
अकलितमहिमानः कल्पिता यत्र तस्मिन्।
सुविमलगगनाभे ईशसंस्थेऽप्यनीशे
मम भवतु भवेऽस्मिन् भासुरो भावबन्धः।।

Salutation to Shiva whose glory
Is immeasurable, who resembles sky
In clearness, to whom are attributed
The phenomena of all creation,
The preservation and dissolution
Of the universe! May the devotion,
The burning devotion of this my life
Attach itself to Him, to Shiva, who,
While being Lord of all, transcends Himself.

निहतनिखिलमोहेऽधीशता यत्र रूढा
प्रकटितपरप्रेम्णा यो महादेवसंज्ञः।
अशिथिलपरिरंभः प्रेमरूपस्य यस्य
प्रणयति हृदि विश्वं व्याजमात्रं विभुत्वम्

In whom Lordship is ever established,
Who causes annihilation of delusion,
Whose most surpassing love, made manifest,

Has crowned Him with a name above all names,
The name of "Mahadeva", the Great God!
Whose warm, embrace, of Love personified,
Displays, within man's heart, that all power
Is but a semblance and a passing show.

वहित विपुलवातः पूर्वसंस्काररूपः
प्रमथति बलवृन्दं घूर्णितवोर्मिमाला।
प्रचलति खलु युग्मं युष्मदस्मत्प्रतीतं
अतविकलितरूपं नौमि चित्तं शिवस्थम्।।

In which the tempest of the whole past blows,
Past Samskaras,* stirring the energies
With violence, like water lashed to waves;
In which the dual consciousness of "I" and "Thou"
Plays on: I salute that mind unstable,
Centred in Shiva, the abode of calm!

जनकजनितभावो वृत्तयः संस्कृताश्च
अगणनबहुरूपो यत्र एको यथार्थः।
शमितविकृतिवाते यत्र नान्तर्बहिश्च
तमहह हरमीडे चित्तवृत्तेर्निरोधम्।।

Where the ideas of parent and produced,
Purified thoughts and endless varied forms,
Merge in the Real one; where the existence ends
Of such conceptions as "within", "without" —
The wind of modification being stilled —
That Hara I worship, the suppression
Of movements of the mind. Shiva I hail!

गलिततिमिरमालः शुभ्रतेजः प्रकाशः
धवलकमलशोभः ज्ञानपुञ्जाटहासः।।

* The accumulated effects of past desires and actions.

यमिजनहृदिदगम्यः निष्कलं ध्यायमानः
प्रणतमवतु मां स मानसो राजहंसः ।।

From whom all gloom and darkness have dispersed;
That radiant Light, white, beautiful
As bloom of lotus white is beautiful;
Whose laughter loud sheds knowledge luminous;
Who, by undivided meditation,
Is realised in the self-controlled heart:
May that Lordly Swan of the limpid lake
Of my mind, guard me, prostrate before Him!

दुरितदलनदक्षं दक्षजादत्तदोषं
कलितकलिकलङ्कं कम्रकह्लारकान्तं ।
परहितकरणाय प्राणविच्छेदसूत्कं
नतनयननियुक्तं नीलकण्ठं नमामः ।।

Him, the Master-remover of evil,
Who wipes the dark stain of this Iron Age;
Whom Daksha's Daughter gave Her coveted hand;
Who, like the charming water-lily white,
Is beautiful; who is ready ever
To part with life for others' good, whose gaze
Is on the humble fixed; whose neck is blue*
With the poison** swallowed:
Him, we salute!

* Nilakantha, a name of Shiva.
** The all-destructive evil.

And Let Shyama Dance There

Rendered from the Bengali

Beaut'ous blossoms ravishing with perfume,
Swarms of maddened bees buzzing all around;
The silver moon—a shower of sweet smile,
Which all the dwellers of heaven above
Shed lavishly upon the homes of earth;
The soft Malaya* breeze, whose magic touch
Opens to view distant memory's folds;
Murmuring rivers and brooks, rippling lakes
With restless Bhramaras** wheeling over
Gently waving lotuses unnumbered;
Foaming flow cascades—a streaming music—
To which echo mountain caves in return;
Warblers, full of sweet-flowing melody,
Hidden in leaves, pour hearts out—love discourse;
The rising orb of day, the painter divine,
With his golden brush but lightly touches
The canvas earth and a wealth of colours
Floods at once o'er the bosom of nature,
—Truly a museum of lovely hues—

---

* A fabulous sandalwood mountain in the South. Hence, Malaya breeze means a fragrant breeze from the South.

** A beetle somewhat like a bumble-bee, which lives solely on honey.

Waking up a whole sea of sentiments.
The roll of thunder, the crashing of clouds,
War of elements spreading earth and sky;
Darkness vomiting forth blinding darkness,
The Pralaya* wind angrily roaring;
In quick bursts of dazzling splendour flashes Blood-red
terrific lightning, dealing death;
Monster waves roaring like thunder, foaming,
Rush impetuous to leap mountain peaks;
The earth booms furious, reels and totters,
Sinks down to its ruin, hurled from its place;
Piercing the ground, stream forth tremendous flames,
Mighty ranges blow up into atoms.

A lovely villa, on a lake of blue—
Festooned with clusters of water-lilies;
The heart-blood of ripe grapes capped with white foam
Whispering softly tells tale of passion;
The melody of the harp floods the ears,
And by its air, time, and harmony rich,
Enhances desire in the breast of man;
What stirring of emotions! How many
Hot sighs of Love! And warm tears coursing down!
The Bimba**-red lips of the youthful fair,
The two blue eyes—two oceans of feelings;
The two hands eager to advance—love's cage—
In which the heart, like a bird, lies captive.
The martial music bursts, the trumpets blow,
The ground shakes under the warriors' tread;
The roar of cannon, the rattle of guns,
Volumes of smoke, the gruesome battlefield,
The thundering artillery vomits fire
In thousand directions; shells burst and strike

---

* The time of cosmic destruction.
** A kind of fruit rich red in colour.

Vital parts of the body; elephants
And horses mounted are blown up in space;
The earth trembles under this infernal dance;
A million heroes mounted on steeds
Charge and capture the enemy's ordnance,
Piercing through the smoke and shower of shells
And rain of bullets; forward goes the flag,
The emblem of victory, of heroism
With the blood, yet hot, streaming down the staff,
Followed by the rifles, drunk with war-spirit;
Lo! The ensign falls, but the flag proceeds
Onwards on the shoulder of another;
Under his feet swell heaps of warriors
Perished in battle; but he falters not.
The flesh hankers for contacts of pleasure,
The senses for enchanting strains of song,
The mind hungers for peals of laughter sweet,
The heart pants to reach realms beyond sorrow;
Say, who cares exchange the soothing moonlight
For the burning rays of the noontide sun?
The wretch whose heart is like the scorching sun,
—Even he fondly loves the balmy moon;
Indeed, all thirst for joy. Breathes there the wretch
Who hugs pain and sorrow to his bosom?
Misery in his cup of happiness,
Deadly venom in his drink of nectar,
Poison in his throat—yet he clings to hope!
Lo! How all are scared by the Terrific,
None seek Elokeshi* whose form is Death.
The deadly frightful sword, reeking with blood,
They take from Her hand, and put a lute instead!
Thou dreaded Kali, the All-destroyer,
Thou alone art true; Thy shadow's shadow

* She with untied hair, a name of Kali, the Divine Mother of the Universe.

Is indeed the pleasant Vanamali.*
O Terrible Mother, cut quick the core,
Illusion dispel—the dream of happiness,
Rend asunder the fondness for the flesh.

True, they garland Thee with skulls, but shrink back
In fright and call Thee, "O All-merciful!"
At Thy thunder peal of awful laughter,
At Thy nudeness—for space is thy garment—
Their hearts sink down with terror, but they say,
"It is the demons that the Mother kills!"
They only pretend they wish to see Thee,
But when the time comes, at Thy sight they flee.
Thou art Death! To each and all in the world
Thou distributest the plague and disease
—Vessels of venom filled by Thine own hands.
O thou insane! Thou but cheatest thyself,
Thou dost not turn thy head lest thou behold,
Ay, the form terrible of the Mother.
Thou courtest hardship hoping happiness,
Thou wearest cloak of Bhakti and worship,
With mind full of achieving selfish ends.
The blood from the severed head of a kid
Fills thee with fear—thy heart throbs at the sight—
Verily a coward! Compassionate?
Bless my soul! A strange state of things indeed!
To whom shall I tell the truth?—Who will see?
Free thyself from the mighty attraction—
The maddening wine of love, the charm of sex.
Break the harp! Forward, with the ocean's cry!
Drink tears, pledge even life—let the body fall.
Awake, O hero! Shake off thy vain dreams,
Death stands at thy head —does fear become thee?

---

* Literally, he who is garlanded with wild flowers. The Shepherd Krishna in His aspect of youthful sport.

A load of misery, true though it is—
This Becoming*—know this to be thy God!
His temple—the Shmashan** among corpses
And funeral pyres; unending battle—
That verily is His sacred worship;
Constant defeat—let that not unnerve thee;
Shattered be little self, hope, name, and fame;
Set up a pyre of them and make thy heart
A burning-ground.
And let Shyama*** dance there.

---

* The wheel of constant birth and death, hence the world.
** The cremation-ground.
*** The Dark One, Kali.

The Hymn Of Samadhi

Rendered from the Bengali

Lo! The sun is not, nor the comely moon,
All light extinct; in the great void of space
Floats shadow-like the image-universe.

In the void of mind involute, there floats
The fleeting universe, rises and floats,
Sinks again, ceaseless, in the current "I".

Slowly, slowly, the shadow-multitude
Entered the primal womb, and flowed ceaseless,
The only current, the "I am", "I am".

Lo! 'Tis stopped, ev'n that current flows no more,
Void merged into Void—beyond speech and mind!
Whose heart understands, he verily does.

XI

Foreign Press

Religious Harmony

Saginaw Evening News, *22 March 1894*

Swami Vive Kananda, the much talked of Hindoo monk, spoke to a small but deeply interested audience last evening at the academy of music on "The Harmony of Religions". He was dressed in oriental costume and received an extremely cordial reception. Hon. Rowland Connor gracefully introduced the speaker, who devoted the first portion of his lecture to an explanation of the different religions of India and of the theory of transmigration of souls. The first invaders of India, the Aryans, did not try to exterminate the population of India as the Christians have done when they went into a new land, but the endeavour was made to elevate persons of brutish habits. The Hindoo is disgusted with those people of his own country who do not bathe and who eat dead animals. The Northern people of India have not tried to force their customs on the southerns, but the latter gradually adopted many ways of the former class. In southernmost portions of India there are a few persons who are Christians and who have been so for thousands [?] of years. The Spaniards came to Ceylon with Christianity. The Spaniards thought that their God commanded them to kill and murder and to tear down heathen temples.

If there were not different religions no one religion would survive. The Christian needs his selfish religion.

The Hindoo needs his own creed. Those which were founded on a book still stand. Why could not the Christian convert the Jew? Why could they not make the Persians Christians? Why not so with the Mohammedans? Why cannot any impression be made upon China or Japan? The Buddhists, the first missionary religion, have double the number of converts of any other religion and they did not use the sword. The Mohammedans used the most force, and they number the least of the three great missionary religions. The Mohammedans have had their day. Every day you read of Christian nations acquiring land by bloodshed. What missionaries preach against this? Why should the most bloodthirsty nations exalt a religion which is not the religion of Christ? The Jews and the Arabs were the fathers of Christianity, and how have they been persecuted by the Christians! The Christians have been weighed in the balance in India and found wanting.

The speaker did not wish to be unkind, but he wanted to show Christians how they looked in other eyes. The Missionaries who preach the burning pit are regarded with horror. The Mohammedans rolled wave after wave over India, waving the sword, and today where are they? The farthest that all religions can see is the existence of a spiritual entity. So no religion can teach beyond this point. In every religion there is the essential truth and non-essential casket in which this jewel lies. The believing in the Jewish book or the Hindoo book is non-essential. Circumstances change, the receptacle is different; but the central truth remains. The essentials being the same, the educated people of every community retain the essentials. The shell of the oyster is not attractive, but the pearls are within. Before a small fraction of the world is converted Christianity will be divided into many creeds. That is the law of nature. Why take a single instrument from the great religious orchestras of the earth? Let the grand symphony go on. Be pure, urged the speaker, give up superstition and see the wonderful harmony of nature. Superstition gets the better of religion. All the religions are good since the essentials are the same. Each man should have the perfect exercise of his individuality but these individualities form a perfect whole. This marvellous condition is already in existence. Each creed has had something to add to the wonderful structure.

The speaker sought throughout to vindicate the religions of his country and said that it had been proven that the entire system of the Roman Catholic Church had been taken from the books of Buddhism. He dilated at some length on the high code of morality and purity of life that the ethics of Buddha taught but allowed that as far as the belief in the personality of God was concerned, agnosticism prevailed, the main thing being to follow out Buddha's precepts which were, "Be good, be moral, be perfect."

Vedantism, And What It Is And What It Is Not*

Lecture of Swami Vivekananda on the Religion of the Hindoos

Oakland Tribune, *26 February 1900*

It is the Only Creed, He Says, that Can Be Taught Without Lies and Without Compromise

The claims of the Brahmin religion, or Vedantism, on the modern world were presented tonight at the Congress of Religions in the First Unitarian Church by Swami Vivekananda,** a remarkably eloquent expounder of that faith.

To his auditors tonight he explained Vedantism as the religion of the Vedas, or ancient Hindoo books, which, he asserted, is "the mother of religion."

"It may seem ridiculous how a book can be without beginning or end," he said, but by the Vedas no books are meant. They signify the accumulated treasury of spiritual laws discovered by different persons in different times. The Hindoo believes he is a spirit. Him the sword cannot pierce, him the fire cannot burn, him the water cannot melt, him the air cannot dry. He believes every soul is a circle whose

---

* *New Discoveries*, Vol. 5, pp. 329-31.

** The lecture was entitled "The Claims of Vedanta on the Modern World". No verbatim transcript is available.

circumference is nowhere, but whose center is located in a body. Death means the change of this center from body to body. We are the children of God. Matter is our servant.

Vedantism is a sort of rebellion against the mockery of the past. Some men are so practical that if they know that by chopping off their heads they could get salvation, there are many who would do so. That is all outward; you must turn your eyes inward to learn what is in your soul. Soul is spirit omnipresent. Where does the soul go after death? Where could the earth fall to? Where can the soul go? Where is it not already? The great cornerstone of Vedantism is the recognition of Self. Man, have faith in yourself. The soul is the same in every one. It is all purity and perfection and the more pure and perfect we [you] are the more purity and perfection you will see.

A man or preaching jack who cries, "Oh Lord, I'm only a crawling worm!" should be still and crawl into his hole. His cries only add more misery to the world. I was amused to read in one of your papers, "How would Christ edit a paper!" How foolish. How would Christ cook a meal? Yet you are the advanced people of the West. If Christ came here, you would shut up shop and go into the street with him to help the poor and downtrodden. Vedantism is the only religion that can be taught without lies, without stretching the texts, without compromise.

On The Brahmo Samaj

Iowa State Register, *1 December 1893*

Before he left the city [Des Moines, Iowa], Vive Kananda took occasion to say a warm word of praise for the Bramo-Somaj [sic], the work it is doing in India, especially for the women, and of its representative in this country. The visit of Vive Kananda, stirring as it did the intellectual centers of the city to their depths and starting a lively religious discussion, prepared the way for the present visitor [Nagarkar] from the Orient and heightened public interest in whatever he might have to say.

Child Widows Of India

Daily Eagle, *27 February 1895*

Swami Vivekananda, the Hindu monk, lectured in Historical hall Monday night under the auspices of the Brooklyn Ethical association, on "India's Gift to the World". There were about two hundred and fifty people in the hall when the Swami stepped on the platform. Much interest was manifested on account of the denial by Mrs. James McKeen, president of the Brooklyn Ramabai circle, which is interested in Christian work in India, of the statement attributed to the lecture that the child widows of India were not protected [ill-treated]. In no part of his lecture was reference made to this denial, but after he had concluded, one of the audience asked the lecturer what explanation he had to make to the statement. Swami Vivekananda said that it was untrue that child widows were abused or ill treated in any way. He added:

"It is a fact that some Hindus marry very young. Others marry when they have attained a fair age and some do not marry at all. My grandfather was married when quite a child. My father when he was 14 years old and I am 30 years old and am not yet married. When a husband dies all his possessions go to his widow. If a widow is poor she is the same as poor widows in any other country. Old men sometimes marry children, but if the husband was wealthy it was all the better for the widow the sooner he died. I have travelled all over India, but failed to see a case of the ill treatment mentioned. At one time there were religious fanatics, widows, who threw themselves into a fire and were consumed by the flames at the death of their husbands. The Hindus did not believe in this, but did not prevent it, and it was not until the British obtained control of India that it was finally prohibited. These women were considered saints and in many instances monuments were erected to their memory."

The Women Of India

Detroit Free Press, *25 March 1894*

Kananda lectured last night at the Unitarian church on "The Women of India". The speaker reverted to the women of ancient India, showing in what high regard they are held in the holy books, where women were prophetesses. Their spirituality then was admirable. It is unfair to judge women in the east by the western standard. In the west woman is the wife; in the east she is the mother. The Hindoos worship the idea of mother, and even the monks are required to touch the earth with their foreheads before their mothers. Chastity is much esteemed.

The lecture was one of the most interesting Kananda has delivered and he was warmly received.

~

Detroit Evening News, *25 March 1894*

Swami Vive Kananda lectured at the Unitarian Church last night on "The Women of India, Past, Medieval and the Present". He stated that in India the woman was the visible manifestation of God and that her whole life was given up to the thought that she was a mother, and to be a perfect mother she must be chaste. No mother in India ever abandoned her offspring, he said, and defied any one to prove the contrary. The girls of India would die if they, like American girls, were obliged to expose half their bodies to the vulgar gaze of young men. He desired that India be judged from the standard of that country and not from this.

~

Tribune, *1 April 1894*

While Swami Kananda was in Detroit he had a number of conversations, in which he answered questions regarding the women of India. It was the information he thus imparted that suggested a public lecture from him on this subject. But as he speaks without notes, some of the points he made in private conversation did not appear in his public address. Then his friends were in a measure disappointed. But one of his lady listeners has put on paper some of the things he told in his afternoon talks, and it is now for the first time given to the press:

To the great tablelands of the high Himalaya mountains first came the Aryans, and there to this day abides the pure type of Brahman, a people which we westerners can but dream of. Pure in thought, deed and action, so honest that a bag of gold left in a public place would be found unharmed twenty years after; so beautiful that, to use Kananda's own phrase, "to see a girl in the fields is to pause and marvel that God could make anything so exquisite". Their features are regular, their eyes and hair dark, and their skin the color which would be produced by the drops which fell from a pricked finger into a glass of milk. These are the Hindus in their pure type, untainted and untrammeled.

As to their property laws, the wife's dowry belongs to her exclusively, never becoming the property of the husband. She can sell or give away without his consent. The gifts from any one to herself, including those of the husband, are hers alone, to do with as she pleases.

Woman walks abroad without fear; she is as free as perfect trust in those about her can render her. There is no zenana in the Himalayas, and there is a part of India which the missionaries never reach. These villages are most difficult of access. These people, untouched by Mahometan influence, can but be reached by wearisome and toilsome climbing, and are unknown to Mahometan and Christian alike.

INDIA'S FIRST INHABITANTS

In the forest of India are found races of wild people—very wild, even to cannibalism. These are the original Indians and never were Aryan or Hindu.

As the Hindus settled in the country proper and spread over its vast area, corruptions of many kinds found home among them. The sun was scorching and the men exposed to it were dark in colour.

Five generations are but needed to change the transparent glow of the white complexion of the dwellers of the Himalaya Mountains to the bronzed hue of the Hindu of India.

Kananda has one brother very fair and one darker than himself. His father and mother are fair. The women are apt to be, the cruel etiquette of the Zenana established for protection from the Mohammedans keeping them within doors, fairer. Kananda is thirty-one years old.

A CLIP AT AMERICAN MEN

Kananda asserts with an amused twinkle in his eye that American men amuse him. They profess to worship woman, but in his opinion they simply worship youth and beauty. They never fall in love with wrinkles and gray hair. In fact he is under a strong impression that American men once had a trick—inherited, to be sure—of burning up their old women. Modern history calls this the burning of witches. It was men who accused and condemned witches, and it was usually the old age of the victim that led her to the stake. So it is seen that burning women alive is not exclusively a Hindu custom. He thought that if it were remembered that the Christian church burned old women at the stake, there would be less horror expressed regarding the burning of Hindu widows.

BURNINGS COMPARED

The Hindu widow went to her death agony amid feasting and song, arrayed in her costliest garments and believing for the most part that such an act meant the glories of Paradise for herself and family. She was worshipped as a martyr and her name was enshrined among the family records.

However horrible the rite appears to us, it is a bright picture compared to the burning of the Christian witch who, considered a guilty thing from the first, was thrown in a stifling dungeon, tortured cruelly to extort confession, subjected to an infamous trial, dragged amid jeering to the stake and consoled amid her sufferings by the bystander's comfort that the burning of her body was but the symbol for hell's everlasting fires, in which her soul would suffer even greater torment.

MOTHERS ARE SACRED

Kananda says the Hindu is taught to worship the principle of motherhood. The mother outranks the wife. The mother is holy. The motherhood of God is more in his mind than the fatherhood.

All women, whatever the caste, are exempt from corporal punishment. Should a woman murder, her head is spared. She may be placed astride a donkey facing his tail. Thus riding through the streets a drummer shouts her crime, after which she is free, her humiliation being deemed sufficient punishment to serve as a preventive for further crime.

Should she care to repent, there are religious houses open to her, where she can become purified or she can at her own option at once enter the class of monks and so become a holy woman.

The question was put to Mr. Kananda whether the freedom thus allowed in the joining the monks without a superior over them did not tend to hypocrisy among the order, as he claims, of the purest of Hindu philosophers. Kananda assented, but explained that there is no one between the people and the monk. The monk has broken down all caste. A Brahmin will not touch the low-caste Hindu but let him or her become a monk and the mightiest will prostrate himself before the low-caste monk.

The people are obliged to take care of the monk, but only as long as they believe in his sincerity. Once condemned for hypocrisy he is called a liar and falls to the depths of mendicancy—a mere wandering beggar—inspiring no respect.

OTHER THOUGHTS

A woman has the right of way with even a prince. When the studious Greeks visited Hindustan to learn of the Hindu, all doors were open to them, but when the Mohammedan with his sword and the Englishman with his bullets came their doors were closed. Such guests were not welcomed. As Kananda deliciously words it: "When the tiger comes we close our doors until he has passed by."

The United States, says Kananda, has inspired him with hopes for great possibilities in the future, but our destiny, as that of the world, rests not in the lawmakers of today, but in the women. Mr. Kananda's words: "The salvation of your country depends upon its women."

Hindu Widows

The Indian Social Reformer, *16 June 1901*

A question having arisen in America as to the Swami Vivekananda's attitude towards social questions, a lady writes to an American paper as follows: "In one of his lectures at the Pouch Mansion,* he spoke of the Hindu widows, declaring it unjust to state that they were generally subjected to cruelty or oppression in the Indians [sic] homes. He admitted that the prejudice against remarriage, and the custom which makes the widow a member of the husband's family instead of that of her own parents inflicted some hardships upon widows in India, and favoured wise efforts for their education which would render them self-supporting and in this way alleviate their condition. He emphasised his desire for the education and elevation of the women of his country, including the widows, by volunteering to give the entire proceeds of one of his lectures in support of the school of Babu Sasipada Banerjee, at Baranagar, near Calcutta, the institution of which preceded that of the Pandita Ramabai, at Poona, and where, if I am not mistaken, the Pandita herself obtained the first inspiration of her work. This lecture was given, and the proceeds were forwarded to Babu Sasipada Banerjee, and duly acknowledged."

* Probably "India's Gift to the World", delivered on 25 February 1895.

Philosophy Of Freedom*

Boston Evening Transcript, *21 March 1896*
Swami Vivekananda Compares Teachings of Hindu Wisdom and Western Religions

The Swami Vivekananda, who will be remembered as the Hindu delegate to the World's Parliament of Religions, is in the city as the March class lecturer at the Procopeia, 45 St. Botolph street.** The Swami has been doing some most valuable and successful work in systematic class lecturing in New York, with constantly increasing audiences, during the past two winters, and comes to Boston at a most opportune time.

The Swami gives the following description of his work. In explanation of the term "sannyasin", he said [*Vide* "The Sannyasin", *Complete Works,* Volume V].

In giving some idea of his work and its methods, the Swami says he left the world because he had a deep interest in religion and philosophy from his childhood, and Indian books teach renunciation as the highest ideal to which a man can aspire.

The Swami's teaching, as he expresses it, is my own interpretation of our ancient books in the light which my

* *New Discoveries,* Vol. 4, pp. 56–58.

** No verbatim transcripts of these classes are available.

master (a celebrated Hindu sage) shed upon them. I claim no supernatural authority.

Whatever in my teachings may appeal to the highest intelligence and be accepted by thinking men, the adoption of that will be my reward. All religions have for their object the teaching of devotion, or knowledge, or activity, in a concrete form. Now, the philosophy of Vedanta is the abstract science which embraces all these methods, and this is what I teach, leaving each one to apply it to his own concrete form. I refer each individual to his own experience, and where reference is made to books, the latter are procurable, and may be studied for each one by himself.

The Swami teaches no authority from hidden beings, through visible objects, any more than he claims learning from hidden books or MSS. He believes no good can come from secret societies.

Truth stands on its own authority, and truth can bear the light of day.

He teaches only the Self, hidden in the heart of every individual, and common to all. A handful of strong men, knowing that Self, and living in its light, would revolutionize the world, even today, as has been the case of single strong men before, each in his day.

His attitude towards Western religions is briefly this. He propounds a philosophy which can serve as a basis to every possible religious system in the world, and his attitude towards all of them is one of extreme sympathy. His teaching is antagonistic to none. He directs his attention to the individual, to make him strong, to teach him that he himself is divine, and he calls upon men to make themselves conscious of divinity within. His hope is to imbue individuals with the teachings to which he has referred, and to encourage them to express these to others in their own way; let them modify them as they will; he does not teach them as dogmas; truth, at length, must inevitably prevail.

India's Gift To The World

Brooklyn Standard Union, *27 February 1895*

Swami Vivekananda, the Hindoo monk, delivered a lecture Monday night under the auspices of the Brooklyn Ethical Association before a fairly large audience at the hall of the Long Island Historical Society, corner Pierrepont and Clinton streets. His subject was "India's Gift to the World".

He spoke of the wondrous beauties of his native land, "where stood the earliest cradle of ethics, arts, sciences, and literature, and the integrity of whose sons and the virtue of whose daughters have been sung by all travelers." Then the lecturer showed in rapid details, what India has given to the world.

"In religion," he said, "she has exerted a great influence on Christianity, as the very teachings of Christ would [could] be traced back to those of Buddha." He showed by quotations from the works of European and American scientists the many points of similarity between Buddha and Christ. The latter's birth, his seclusion from the world, the number of his apostles, and the very ethics of his teachings are the same as those of Buddha, living many hundred years before him.

"Is it mere chance," the lecturer asked, "or was Buddha's religion but the foreshadowing of that of Christ? The majority of your thinkers seem to be satisfied in the latter explanation, but there are some bold enough to say that Christianity is the direct offspring of Buddhism just as the earliest heresy in the Christian religion—the Monecian [Manichaean] heresy—is now universally regarded as the teaching of a sect of Buddhists. But there is more evidence that Christianity is founded in Buddhism. We find it in recently discovered inscriptions from the reign of Emperor Oshoka [Asoka] of India, about 300 BC, who made treaties with all the Grecian kings, and whose missionaries discriminated [disseminated?] in those very parts, where, centuries after, Christianity flourished, the principles of the Buddhistic religion. Thus it is explained, why you have our doctrine of trinity, of incarnation of God, and of our ethics, and why the service in our temples is so much alike to that in your present Catholic churches, from the mass to the chant and benediction. Buddhism had all these long before you. Now use your own judgment on these premise—we Hindoos stand ready to be convinced that yours is the earlier religion, although we had ours some three hundred years before yours was even thought of.

"The same holds good with respect to sciences. India has given to antiquity the earliest scientific physicians, and, according to Sir William Hunter, she has even contributed to modern medical science by the discovery of various chemicals and by teaching you how to reform misshapen ears and noses. Even more it has done in mathematics, for algebra, geometry, astronomy, and the triumph of modern science—mixed mathematics—were all invented in India, just so much as the ten numerals, the very cornerstone of all present civilization, were discovered in India, and are in reality, Sanskrit words.

"In philosophy we are even now head and shoulders above any other nation, as Schopenhauer, the great German philosopher, has confessed. In music India gave to the world her system of notation, with the seven cardinal notes and the diatonic scale, all of which we enjoyed as early as 350 BC, while it came to Europe only in the eleventh century. In philology, our Sanskrit language is now universally acknowledged to be the foundation of all European languages, which, in fact, are nothing but jargonized Sanskrit.

"In literature, our epics and poems and dramas rank as high as those of any language; our Shakuntala was summarized by Germany's greatest poet, as 'heaven and earth united'. India has given to the world the fables of Aesop, which were copied by Aesop from an old Sanskrit book; it has given the Arabian Nights, yes, even the story of Cinderella and the Bean Stalks. In manufacture, India was the first to make cotton and purple dye, it was proficient in all works of jewelry, and the very word 'sugar', as well as the article itself, is the product of India. Lastly she has invented the game of chess and the cards and the dice. So great, in fact, was the superiority of India in every respect, that it drew to her borders the hungry cohorts of Europe, and thereby indirectly brought about the discovery of America.

"And now, what has the world given to India in return for all that? Nothing but vilification and curse and contempt. The world waded in her children's life-blood, it reduced India to poverty and her sons and daughters to slavery, and now it adds insult to injury by preaching to her a religion which can only thrive on the destruction of every other religion. But India is not afraid. It does not beg for mercy at the hands of any nation. Our only fault is that we cannot: fight to conquer; but we trust in the eternity of truth. India's message to the world is first of all, her blessing; she is returning good for the evil which is done her, and thus she puts into execution this noble idea, which had its origin in India. Lastly, India's message is, that calm goodness, patience and gentleness will ultimately triumph. For where are the Greeks, the onetime masters of the earth? They are gone. Where are the Romans, at the tramp of whose cohorts the world trembled? Passed away. Where are the Arabs, who in fifty years had carried their banners from the Atlantic to the Pacific? And where are the Spaniards, the cruel murderers of millions of men? Both races are nearly extinct; but thanks to the morality of her children, the kinder race will never perish, and she will yet see the hour of her triumph."

At the close of the lecture, which was warmly applauded, Swami Vivekananda answered a number of questions in regard to the customs of India. He denied positively the truth of the statement published in yesterday's [February 25] *Standard Union,* to the effect that widows are ill-treated in India. The law guarantees her not only her own property before marriage, but also all she received from her husband, at whose death, if there be no direct heirs, the property goes to her. Widows seldom marry in India, because of the scarcity of men. He also stated that the self-sacrifices of wives at the death of their husbands as well as the fanatical self-destruction under the wheels of the Juggernaut, have wholly stopped, and referred his hearers for proof to Sir William Hunter's *The History of the Indian Empire.*

Swami Vivekananda On Love

Maidenhead Adviser, *23 October 1895*

On Thursday Swami Vivekananda delivered a lecture at the Town Hall, *Maidenhead,* taking as his subject "The Eastern Doctrine of Love." Owing to other attractions in the town the attendance was not large. Many of the public also associated the lecturer with the Theosophical Society, with which, however, he has, we are informed, nothing whatever to do, nor with any other society, neither does he propose forming any society himself. He believes in expounding his views to whoever will listen to them and leaving those individuals to advocate them as a whole, or with whatever modifications they may deem fitting, or to reject them altogether, believing that out of the strife of all opinions truth at length prevails.

The chair was taken at 8 p.m. by Mr. E. Gardner, J.P., C.C., and he very briefly introduced the lecturer, who was clad in his native costume. The Swami then proceeded to express his view upon devotion to deity, or, as more commonly expressed in the East—love (Bhakti), to the following effect: religion may be divided into two forms, the first almost entirely superstitious and the second merely metaphysical, but if either of these is to have any force it must be accompanied by love. Work alone without this element did not satisfy. The land might be covered with hospitals, penetrated by good roads; there might be great social institutions well conducted, and good sanitation, but these were all external physical processes and by themselves brought Man no nearer to Divinity. Both the realist and the idealist were necessary and complementary, one of the other. The idealist brought the bold aspiration down to earth, the realist caused it to take form through work. Love cannot be defined in positive terms, only negatively. Its nature is of the form of renunciation. In its more general sense it might be divided threefold: (1) That love which is for one's own pleasure, irrespective of pleasure or pain to others—the purely selfish, the lowest. (2) That love which exchanges—"I will love you if you love me. We will make each other mutually happy"—the partially selfish, the middle path trodden by the great majority of mankind. (3) That love which gives all and asks for nothing, without premeditation and which never regrets, unconquerable by any evil thing done to him from whom it emanates. It is the highest, the divine. Only with this last kind are we concerned here. The first is the path of the sensualist and the animal, the second the path of struggling humanity on its way to better things, the third the real path of love, trodden by those who renounce the world and set out upon that road which leads to Eternal Peace. In that love there is no fear. Love kills fear. A lion might stand over a babe and threaten its life; the mother knows no fear, she does not fly, but she opposes. At that moment love destroys terror; at other times the same woman would run from a small dog. A fierce Mahomedan [sic] warrior went to a garden to pray. In the same garden a girl had appointed to meet her lover. The warrior lay prostrate on his face according to the prescribed form of his religion. At that moment the girl espied her lover, and with joy rushing to meet him, trod upon the prostrate form. He jumped up and laying hand upon his sword would have slain the girl. "How dare you?" cried he, "vile wench, disturb my worship, my devotion to

God, with your base feet." "Worship! devotion!" cried the girl. "You do not know what they are. You had no devotion, lying there, no spirit of worship. If I, a timid girl, could so forget the presence of an object of dread like you, in my worship and devotion to my earthly lover as to tread upon you and not even know it, how much more should you, if your heart had been absorbed in love and devotion to God, have been ignorant that I touched you?" The warrior was humbled and appeased and went away. Our highest ideal of love is the image which we form for ourselves of deity. A barbarous people have a tyrannical and cruel God. A wise and noble people see God in ever and ever widening potencies. God is always God, but the views which men and nations may take of Him vary. No higher view is known than that of love. The man who bears in his heart an unrelaxing love to every creature, whether he recognise that that creature is a manifestation of God, in which he is actually present, or whether he look upon it merely as fashioned by Deity, that man is on the path to Deity, on the great path of devotion and renunciation. He cannot injure the creature of God, however repulsive to his narrower view of what should or should not be. He gives in love, not in pride; in loving Deity he loves its manifestations, works with them and abides by them.

An Indian Ascetic

Standard, *23 October 1895*

Since the days of Ramahoun [Ram Mohan] Roy, says the *Standard,* with the single exception of Keshub Chunder [Keshab Chandra] Sen, there has not appeared on an English platform a more interesting Indian figure than the Brahman who lectured in Princes' [Prince's] Hall last night....

The lecture was a most fearless and eloquent exposition of the pantheistic philosophy of the Vedanta school, and the Swami seems to have incorporated into his system a good deal also of the moral element of the Yoga school, as the closing passage of his lecture presented in a modified form not the advocacy of mortification, which is the leading feature of the latter school, but the renunciation of all so-called material comforts and blessings, as the only means of entering into perfect union with the supreme and absolute Self. The opening passages of the lecture were a review of the rise of the grosser form of Materialism in the beginning of the present century, and the later development of the various forms of metaphysical thought, which for a time swept Materialism away. From this he passed on to discuss the origin and nature of knowledge. In some respects his views on this point were almost a statement of pure Fichteism, but they were expressed in language, and they embodied illustrations, and made admissions which no German transcendentalist would have used. He admitted there was a gross material world outside, but he confessed he did not know what matter was. He asserted that mind was a finer matter, and that behind was the soul of man, which was immovable, fixed, before which outward objects passed, as it were, in a procession, which was without beginning or end—in other words, which was eternal, and finally which was God. He worked out this pantheistic conception of the personal identity of Man and God with great comprehensiveness and an ample wealth of illustration, and in passage after passage of great beauty, solemnity, and earnestness. "There is only one Soul in the Universe," he said.

There is no "you" or "me"; all variety is merged into the absolute unity, the one infinite existence—God.

From this, of course, followed the immortality of the soul, and something like the transmigration of souls towards higher manifestations of perfection. As already stated, his peroration of twenty minutes was a statement of the doctrine of renunciation. In the course of it, he made some remorselessly disparaging criticism on the work that factories, engines and other inventions, and books were doing for man, compared with half a dozen words spoken by Buddha or Jesus. The lecture was evidently quite extemporaneous, and was delivered in a pleasing voice, free from any kind of hesitation.